Faulkner and the Native South
FAULKNER AND YOKNAPATAWPHA

2016

Faulkner and the Native South

FAULKNER AND YOKNAPATAWPHA, 2016

EDITED BY
JAY WATSON,
ANNETTE TREFZER,
AND
JAMES G. THOMAS, JR.

UNIVERSITY PRESS OF MISSISSIPPI
JACKSON

The University Press of Mississippi is the scholarly publishing agency of the Mississippi Institutions of Higher Learning: Alcorn State University, Delta State University, Jackson State University, Mississippi State University, Mississippi University for Women, Mississippi Valley State University, University of Mississippi, and University of Southern Mississippi.

www.upress.state.ms.us
The University Press of Mississippi is a member
of the Association of University Presses.

Copyright © 2019 by University Press of Mississippi
All rights reserved
Manufactured in the United States of America

First printing 2019
∞

Library of Congress Cataloging-in-Publication Data

Names: Watson, Jay, editor. | Trefzer, Annette, 1960– editor. | Thomas, James
G., Jr., editor.
Title: Faulkner and the Native South / edited by Jay Watson, Annette Trefzer,
and James G. Thomas, Jr.
Description: Jackson: University Press of Mississippi, [2019] | Series:
Faulkner and Yoknapatawpha (Series) | "First printing 2019." | "Faulkner
and Yoknapatawpha, 2016." | Includes bibliographical references and index.
|Identifiers: LCCN 2018035638 (print) | LCCN 2018051147 (ebook) | ISBN
9781496818102 (epub single) | ISBN 9781496818119 (epub institutional) |
ISBN 9781496818126 (pdf single) | ISBN 9781496818133 (pdf institutional)
| ISBN 9781496818096 (cloth)
Subjects: LCSH: Faulkner, William, 1897–1962. | Faulkner, William,
1897–1962—Criticism and interpretation. | American fiction—History and
criticism—20th century.
Classification: LCC PS3511.A86 (ebook) | LCC PS3511.A86 Z783211167 2019
(print) | DDC 813/.52—dc23
LC record available at https://lccn.loc.gov/2018035638

British Library Cataloging-in-Publication Data available

Contents

Introduction VII
ANNETTE TREFZER AND JAY WATSON

Note on the Conference XLIII

Faulkner Didn't Invent Yoknapatawpha, *Everybody Knows That.* So What Other Stories Do Chickasaws and Choctaws Know about Our Homelands? 3
LEANNE HOWE

Souths as Prologues: Indigeneity, Race, and the Temporalities of Land; or, Why I Can't Read William Faulkner 15
JODI A. BYRD

Doom and Deliverance: Faulkner's Dialectical Indians 33
MELANIE BENSON TAYLOR

"Land! Hold On! Just Hold On!": Flood Waters, Hard Times, and Sacred Land in "Old Man" and *My Louisiana Love* 50
GINA CAISON

Dressing the Part: Evolution of Indian Dress in Faulkner 66
PATRICIA GALLOWAY

"A Valid Signature": Native American Sovereignty in *Requiem for a Nun* 93
ANNETTE TREFZER

"Brother: Is This Truth?": History, Fiction, and Colonialism in Faulkner's Mississippi 116
KATHERINE M. B. OSBURN

CONTENTS

The Wild and the Tame: Sam Fathers as Ecological Indian   135
  ROBBIE ETHRIDGE

Native Southern Transformations, or, *Light in August*
and Werewolves   148
  ERIC GARY ANDERSON

From the Mausoleum to a Spider Web: William Faulkner's
and Louise Erdrich's Takes on Hybridity   167
  MELANIE R. ANDERSON

Red Laughter: Humor in Faulkner's Native Narratives   181
  JOHN WHARTON LOWE

Contributors   198

Index   201

Introduction

ANNETTE TREFZER AND JAY WATSON

What Is the Native South?

In order to locate William Faulkner meaningfully within the Native South, and to locate the Native South within and around him, some background material on this historical and cultural formation is in order. After all, just two decades ago, the "Native South" was neither a term nor a concept that appeared in southern—or for that matter, American—literary scholarship. The term is a complex construction because it yokes together two concepts that are not necessarily compatible, each pulling in different theoretical and disciplinary directions. Insofar as the "Native South" was methodologically visible at all, it was primarily so for scholars in academic fields adjacent to literary studies, disciplines like anthropology, archaeology, and history.

In 1976, for example, anthropologist Charles Hudson took stock of his field by noting that "all people have blind spots in their memory of the past, but the Southeastern Indians are victims of a virtual amnesia in our historical consciousness."[1] His scholarly response to this amnesia was the book *The Southeastern Indians*, which laid the foundation for understanding southeastern US Indians as a "socially diverse, but culturally similar people" (5). Hudson identified a southeastern "culture area" that comprises the current-day states of Georgia, Florida, South Carolina, western North Carolina, Alabama, Mississippi, Louisiana, southern and eastern Arkansas, Tennessee, and portions of adjoining states (5). For information on many of the shared cultural traits of Native people living in this area, he relied on a variety of historical sources, including the journals of the de Soto expedition (1539–43) and documents by European travelers, colonists, surveyors, naturalists, military men, and government officials such as the Chickasaw agent James Adair and the Creek agent Benjamin Hawkins. In addition, Hudson examined archaeological artifacts as well as records by previous anthropologists, including

VIII   INTRODUCTION

James Mooney (1861–1921) and John Swanton (1873–1958), to establish the cultural coherence of what came to be termed the Native South.

To many historians, by contrast, the Native South is a concept based on the shared experience of forced relocation following the Removal Act of 1830. Grant Foreman's 1932 *Indian Removal: The Emigration of the Five Civilized Tribes of Indians* is an early example, followed by historical work on individual southeastern tribes such Angie Debo's *The Rise and Fall of the Choctaw Republic* (1934), David Corkran's *The Creek Frontier, 1540–1783* (1967), Arthur H. DeRosier Jr.'s *The Removal of the Choctaw Indians* (1970), and Arrell Gibson's *The Chickasaws* (1971).[2] The commonalities of the modern historical experience of Native Americans from the South eventually resulted in scholarship that combined history and ethnography in the field of ethnohistory. According to Greg O'Brien, two scholars stand out in shaping this field: Theda Perdue and Michael D. Green. In the introduction to *The Native South: Histories and Legacies*, O'Brien writes, "As two of the very few historians writing about Native southerners in the 1980s, Green and Perdue formed a working relationship that sought to legitimize their shared academic field and create a market for new studies of the Native South."[3] Green's work on Creek Indians and Perdue's work on the Cherokee advanced a regional historical perspective.[4] Both scholars were instrumental in starting a book series on Indians of the Southeast with the University of Nebraska Press that directed historians' focus towards this geographical area. More than twenty-five years later, in 2008, this press established the journal *Native South*, further consolidating the discipline and issuing a challenge to scholars of southern history to "expand their conception of the field to include more than the black and white post-colonial South that colors much of the historical literature of the region" and to investigate "Southeastern Indian history with the goals of encouraging further study and exposing the influences of Indian people on the wider South."[5]

Writing from the Native American studies point of view, historian Clara Sue Kidwell (White Earth Chippewa and Choctaw) argues that interdisciplinarity was and is crucial to current intellectual inquiry and debate within the field.[6] She highlights two conferences, at the University of Oklahoma in 2007 and at the University of Georgia in 2008, as the crucible for the formation of the Native American and Indigenous Studies Association (NAISA), as attendants from the disciplines of English, anthropology, history, religious studies, and Native American studies met and formed a new organization.[7] Such interdisciplinarity has generated new research agendas: "With recognizable intellectual premises, research methodologies, theories, journals, and an association, the field certainly has all the trappings of a discipline. Key terms—*survivance*, *communitism, intellectual sovereignty*, and *agency*—are readily recognizable in the scholarly journals, constituting a precise language of scholarship (but, heaven forbid, not a jargon)."[8] Joint scholarly conferences and journals welcoming interdisciplinarity continue to be crucial to the success of Native southern studies.

It was around this time that literary scholars in southern studies began to question prevalent constructions of a biracial South. In the 2002 collection of essays *South to a New Place*, Eric Anderson argued that "non-Native writers and other custodians of southern literature and history often downplay the long-standing Indigenous presence in, as it were, their own backyard."[9] Noting the continuing predominance of a bicultural black-and-white version of the South in a 2006 special issue of *American Literature* on the topic of new southern studies, Anderson again addressed the "relative absence of Indians in Southern literature classrooms" as a "gap in the field" and a challenge to "would-be practitioners of Native Southern Studies."[10] There it is: quite possibly one of the first uses of the "Native South" within the context of southern literary studies.[11]

And here is a crucial shift from longstanding acknowledgments of the Indian presence in the South by non-Native writers to the inclusion of Native American literature in studies of the US South. Depictions of Southeastern Indians are ubiquitous in American literature, from contact narratives by John Smith and others, to eighteenth-century narratives by William Byrd and William Bartram, to nineteenth-century fantasies of Noble Savages in novels by James Fenimore Cooper, William Gilmore Simms, and Helen Hunt Jackson, to twentieth-century depictions of Indians in southern literature by Andrew Lytle, Caroline Gordon, Eudora Welty, Alice Walker, and many others, including, of course, William Faulkner. Although scholarship on individual authors occasionally highlighted the Native American presence as character or trope in southern literature, such studies did not, however, include Native American texts or authors in the canon of southern literature and its scholarly explorations.

If southern literary studies did not typically include Native American texts, neither did Native American literature scholars especially take note of Indigenous southern authors and contexts. Anderson highlights the disconnect between Native and southern studies in work by Native American scholars, including Craig Womack, Robert Warrior, and Daniel Heath Justice, whose work on literature produced by members of the South's Indian nations does not provide "an explicit regional perspective" on those works.[12] In *Red on Red* (1999), Womack's study of the Creek literary tradition, he proposes a tribally specific framework

INTRODUCTION

emphasizing "Native American literary separatism." Womack mentions the important role of a "geographically specific Creek landscape and the language and stories that are born out of that landscape" across which Creek people mapped their migrations from their original home in Alabama.[13] But he does not posit any rootedness in or significance of the South as a literary shaping force and instead suggests a "concept of multiple homes" and continued migrations.[14] Like Womack, who seeks to explore a tribally specific epistemology, Daniel Heath Justice establishes a unique Cherokee critical paradigm in the cultural concept of the Beloved Path.[15] Though he later qualifies his "initial supposition that there was a single unitary idea of 'Cherokeeness'" as "both naïve and, ultimately, impossible, especially given the long and tangled realities of Cherokee social history," he insists on the importance of sovereign tribal literary traditions.[16] Both Craig Womack and Daniel Heath Justice continue the work of Robert Warrior, who urged Native American scholars to "recover" their own intellectual traditions.[17] Collectively these works are critical not only of an unspecified "Native American literature" category but also of a regionalist approach that would situate Native writing by Southeastern tribes in the South.

Just such a perspective, however, was available in the 1995 anthology by Daniel Littlefield and James Parins, *Native American Writing in the Southeast: An Anthology, 1875–1935.*[18] This collection of primary works by Cherokee, Choctaw, Chickasaw, Creek, and Yuchi writers attributes a regional coherence to this body of writing that already points forward to the idea of a Native South. The main goal of the anthology is to trace a "long history of cultural continuity" as the period under consideration was marked by a "tremendous literary energy and extensive production of a rich literature, which blossomed in the late nineteenth century and bore fruit in the twentieth."[19] Though they do not explicitly theorize the regional boundaries they draw, Littlefield and Parins sift through hundreds of texts by writers whose "ancestral homelands were in the American Southeast" to highlight their contribution to a legacy that inspired contemporary Native authors such as Linda Hogan (Chickasaw), Jim Barnes (Choctaw), Robert Conley (Keetoowah Band Cherokee), Joy Harjo (Cherokee/Muscogee), and others.[20]

In their introduction to the 2010 anthology *The People Who Stayed: Southeastern Indian Writing after Removal*, editors Geary Hobson, Janet McAdams, and Kathryn Walkiewicz argue that the title of Littlefield and Parins' anthology is "a misnomer, since only four, or possibly five, of the twenty-eight contributors were born in the Southeast prior to the Removal period of the 1830s and 1840s. All of the remaining writers were born in Indian Territory (later Oklahoma)."[21] The editors argue

INTRODUCTION

that the writers anthologized by Littlefield and Parins had a western geographical orientation since with the exception of four "they all lived their lives in Indian Territory."[22] Thus, strictly speaking, the writings of Reverend Israel Folsom, who was born in the Choctaw Nation in Mississippi in 1802, count in Hobson, McAdams, and Walkiewicz's book as Southeastern Indian literature, but not the contributions of Muriel Hazel Wright, a historian who was born into the Choctaw Nation of Oklahoma in 1889. This raises important geographical and historical questions: Where and when is the Native South to be found? Should Oklahoma, the former Indian Territory to which the Five Civilized Tribes were removed, be included or excluded? Does the term refer to any space where Native people originally from the South are now living? Or is it a template overlapping with mainstream geographical definitions of the US South? In insisting on a geographical US South and creating section headings by particular states and sub-regions, the editors of *The People Who Stayed* eliminate cultural connections and minimize continuities between people from the same tribe in the original Southeastern homelands and the new nations in Oklahoma—such as the Mississippi Band of Choctaw Indians and the Choctaw Nation of Oklahoma, or the Eastern Band of Cherokees and the Cherokee Nation of Oklahoma—but they effectively combat the pervasive idea of the Indian "vanished" from post-Removal southern space as they focus on "the South seldom seen."

If focusing on Native American writing of the South is helpful for freshly recontextualizing southern literature by modifying its entrenched black and white racial patterns, the question remains, what, if anything, can a regional framework add to Native American studies? What are the contributions that each literary community might be able to offer to the other? What are the theoretical and scholarly collisions and collaborations that might result from such an expanded cross-disciplinary framework? As Melanie Benson Taylor asserts in *Reconstructing the Native South* (2012), Native and non-Native southerners have much in common, and their literary efforts share topics and concerns "echoing one another's voices in kindred, unmistakable intimacy."[23] Taylor argues that "native and non-native southerners have arrived at a common meeting place: that very fixation on storied pasts and insurmountable loss forms a shared Lost Cause more present, prescient, and uncanny than we might imagine."[24] She proceeds to trace those points of conversion, including cultural narratives of abjection directed at southerners and Native people alike, poverty and economic deprivation, and haunting histories of material and cultural loss. Black southerners and Native Americans suffered long-term exposure to white supremacy and its "spectacles and illusions of opportunity and emancipation" that made

XII   INTRODUCTION

it difficult to maintain their cultures and communities.[25] Native and non-Native southern communities experienced an imposed economic order during Removal and Reconstruction that resulted in a profound and long-lasting sense of dispossession. Taylor suggests that "perhaps in the end, the tribes that remain in the South have the most to teach us about the hope of solidarity and the peril of compromise—and above all, about the haunted, insular, and frail foundations of contemporary tribal nationalisms and sovereignty."[26] As a trailblazer into the burgeoning field of Native southern studies, Taylor's book raises methodological problems, most critical among them the question of how already "frail" tribal national perspectives and claims to Indigenous sovereignty square with regional alliances. When should southern regional identity be subordinated to Native nationalism? By whom, how, and why? When and how does the cultural geography of the South become important for Native American writers? In other words, what does it mean for Native American writers to claim multiple homes, including the South? Scholarship on the South certainly stands to gain more nuanced insight and complexity by integrating Native American texts and perspectives, but what does the Native American scholarship gain by paying attention to the place and practices of a particular region? However we proceed in exploring these questions, Eric Anderson advises that the "radical nature of the difference [between Native and southern studies] needs to be acknowledged, respected, and foregrounded."[27] While Native and southern studies might have different disciplinary goals and ideological purposes in constructing their respective traditions, then, the fact is that being southern and Native American is a lived reality for many writers, including the sixty included in *The People Who Stayed*, and many more, like LeAnne Howe (featured in this collection) who are outspoken about embracing both legacies. While this introduction to *Faulkner and the Native South* can only gesture at the vexing complexity of these topics, we offer the chapters included here in the spirit of furthering discussion not only of Faulkner's Native South but of the intersections between Native and non-Native histories and methodologies more generally.

The Indians of Faulkner Studies

So, what do we mean by *Faulkner's* Native South? What, when, where, and who is it? If you were to go looking for Indians, or for the lineaments of Native histories and cultures, in Faulkner scholarship, you wouldn't run across much of note before the mid-1960s. Nor should you really expect to since the questions and methodologies that guided the first generations of Faulkner critics would not readily have directed them

INTRODUCTION   XIII

to this Native material. For the Marxist and sociologically oriented critics of the Depression years, who dismissed Faulkner as a minor figure squandering his literary gifts on grotesquerie, exoticism, and the macabre—figures like Granville Hicks, Maxwell Geismar, and Alfred Kazin—the writer's chief responsibility lay in exposing and exploring the social conditions of the modern era, a program best served by an aesthetic of social realism (or even naturalism) and by a historical focus on the nation's industrialized present rather than its Indigenous pasts, presents, or futures.[28] Similarly, the existential concerns that animated the French critics who were among Faulkner's earliest champions—Andre Malraux, Maurice Coindreau, Jean-Paul Sartre, Jean Pouillon, Jean-Jacques Mayoux, Claude-Edmond Magny, and others—also tended to privilege the narratives Faulkner set in his own time rather than in the nineteenth century: *Sartoris*, *The Sound and the Fury*, *Sanctuary*, *Light in August*.[29] It should also be said in defense of these early critics that most were formulating their thoughts about Faulkner's achievement *before* Native material had begun to play a significant role in novels such as *Go Down, Moses* and *Requiem for a Nun*, as distinguished from the US magazine fiction of the 1930s.

Turning to the coalition of southern New Critics and New York intellectuals who according to Lawrence Schwartz did the lion's share of the critical and ideological work of "creating Faulkner's reputation" as the leading American writer of the postwar period, we continue to find little interest in the role of the Native or of the Native South in the author's work. While both groups credited Faulkner with a historical consciousness that singled him out among his peers, for southern critics like George Marion O'Donnell and Robert Penn Warren, that consciousness found its focal point in a traditional plantation social order besieged by a succession of modernizing forces, from the Union Army, through Reconstruction-era carpetbaggers, scalawags, and upstart freedmen, to twentieth-century industrialization, commercialization, and a rising class of grasping poor-white arrivistes.[30] Meanwhile, for Malcolm Cowley, Irving Howe, Lionel Trilling, and other members of the *Partisan Review* set, it revolved around a Hawthornean vision of ancestral regimes whose originary crimes against humanity would haunt their descendants and place a curse on the land. Even here, however, the emphasis lay on slavery and land ownership, not Indian removal and land theft, as the unexpiated sins at the heart of the Yoknapatawpha chronicle.[31] Moreover, the methodological commitment of both groups to aesthetic formalism directed their critical attention toward questions of style and technique, criteria they used to install the difficult, idiosyncratic, restlessly innovative Faulkner as a paragon of American individuality and artistic freedom

XIV   INTRODUCTION

to be mobilized against Soviet totalitarianism in the cultural Cold War of the 1950s.[32] This critical agenda, however, was no more propitious than the ones that preceded it for a conscientious interrogation of what Toni Morrison might call the "Indianist presence" in Faulkner.[33]

It was instead, we suggest, the rise of American studies as an academic discipline and critical methodology that prepared the ground for a serious scholarly engagement with Faulkner's Indians. As the field emerged in the postwar years, American studies scholars shared a nationalist agenda with the New York intellectuals, but one predicated less on the global preeminence of American letters than on the exceptionalism of American history, society, and culture, including literature. That emphasis on exceptionalism, conspicuously on display in formative projects like Robert Spiller's multivolume *Literary History of the United States* (1948) and his companion monograph, *The Cycle of American Literature* (1955), sent critics in search of distinctive elements of national life and history that could explain the unique status and mission of the United States among nations; and one of the earliest and most lasting of these motifs to appear was the frontier.[34] Frederick Jackson Turner had laid the groundwork for this argument in his 1893 essay on the significance of the frontier in US history, where he posited the frontier encounter with wilderness as the defining crucible for the formation of US national character.[35]

And with the frontier came the Indian. Though the historical and ideological connection remained underdeveloped in Turner, D. H. Lawrence spelled it out with great brio in his 1923 volume, *Studies in American Literature*, another seminal work for first-generation American studies scholars. In Lawrence as perhaps never before the Indian stands front and center in the mythography—as opposed to the mythology—of America. "There has been all the time," Lawrence writes, "in the white American's soul, a dual feeling about the Indian."[36] In Benjamin Franklin we glimpse "the desire to extirpate the Indian," in Crèvecoeur "the contradictory desire to glorify him" and moreover to acquire and share his "dark mindlessness" and blood-knowledge (31), his "passionate love . . . for the soil" of the continent (51). Cooper attempts to resolve the impasse, only to reproduce the ambivalence, in Leatherstocking, the proverbial man who knows—and loves, and kills—Indians (52–63).[37] Melville maps the dilemma onto a new geography and its "savage" populations in his South Sea Island tales (136–37); Whitman characteristically introjects it, becoming in the process the "first white aboriginal" among American writers (173). For Lawrence, land and Native form an indivisible indigeneity that serves as both catalyst and stumbling block for the national literature of Anglo-America:

INTRODUCTION   XV

A curious thing about the Spirit of Place is the fact that no place exerts its full influence upon a new-comer until the old inhabitant is dead or absorbed. So America. While the Red Indian existed in fairly large numbers, the new colonials were in great measure immune from the *daimon*, or demon, of America. . . . At present the demon of the place and the unappeased ghosts of the dead Indians act within the unconscious or under-conscious soul of the white American, causing . . . the Orestes-like frenzy of the Yankee soul, the inner malaise which amounts almost to madness, sometimes. (35–36)

Primal, libidinal, and vanished (though Lawrence lived among Indians in New Mexico at the time he was writing *Studies in Classic American Literature*), Lawrence's mythic Red Indian is a fantastic and clearly problematic figure in its own right—but also a central and vital one for any reckoning with the defining mythoi of American literature.

Taking their cue from Turner and Lawrence, American studies scholars embarked on a quarter-century-long research effort that placed the frontier, and eventually the Indian, at the forefront of their investigations, a body of work that reaches from Henry Nash Smith's *Virgin Land* (1950), R.W.B. Lewis's *The American Adam* (1955), Leslie Fiedler's *Love and Death in the American Novel* (1960), and Leo Marx's *The Machine in the Garden* (1964), to Annette Kolodny's *The Lay of the Land* (1975).[38] This period coincides almost precisely with the rise of Faulkner studies from a cottage industry to international prominence, and it helped create the intellectual conditions under which Faulkner's Indians could surface as a research topic carrying scholarly legitimacy. Indeed, we can trace Faulkner criticism as, under the growing influence of American studies, it inches its way across the 1950s toward a scholarly reckoning with the Indians of Yoknapatawpha in the following decade. Four years before his sweeping account of "the ritualistic trials" of white American innocence in nineteenth-century US literature, for example, Lewis had already claimed the Ike McCaslin of "The Bear" for the mythic tradition of the American Adam, and Ursula Brumm also put Ike front and center in her essay of the same year on "wilderness and civilization" in Faulkner.[39] At the other end of the decade, Otis B. Wheeler again took up the question of "Faulkner's Wilderness," again with Ike and "The Bear" in the spotlight.[40] All three essays follow the American studies template of framing US literature in exceptionalist terms.[41] All pursue comparisons between Faulkner's vision and Cooper's, with Lewis additionally placing the Mississippian in the company of Hawthorne, Melville, and Twain, at the very heart of the classic American canon. Curiously, however, Lewis, Brumm, and Wheeler evince little interest in Sam Fathers's role in spiritually midwifing Ike as latter-day frontiersman

XVI   INTRODUCTION

and "new world hero"—and still less in the question of Sam's Native
lineage and how it might or might not inform his ceremonial and peda-
gogical functions as "wilderness" mentor.[42]

That changed in the 1960s, as the counterculture and the new social
movements of the era shook up literary studies. The same ten-year period
that witnessed the rise of the American Indian movement, the inception
of the Native American literary renaissance[43] with the 1968 publication
of N. Scott Momaday's *House Made of Dawn*, and the appearance of
American studies monographs by Roy Harvey Pearce, Leslie Fiedler,
and Richard Slotkin that tackled the representation of Indians in US
literature and intellectual culture, also saw the first significant efforts
by Faulkner scholars to assess the role of Southeastern Indians in his
fiction.[44] Leading the march was Elmo Howell, who published no fewer
than half a dozen notes and articles on the topic between 1965 and 1970.
M. E. Bradford, Beverly Young Langford, and Peter G. Beidler also contributed to the dialogue during this period. Fiedler addressed Faulkner's
work at least glancingly in *The Return of the Vanishing American* (1968),
repurposing some ideas first voiced in *Love and Death* in a new context
more sensitive to the Native's role in illuminating "that peculiar form of
madness which dreams, and achieves, and *is* the true [mythic] West."[45]
Duane Gage published on Faulkner in the inaugural issue of *American
Indian Quarterly* in 1974. Dissertations by Marc A. Nigliazzo (1973),
James Harvey Krefft (1976), and Lewis M. Dabney delved deeper into
the subject, and Dabney's project became the first, and to date still the
only, full-length monograph on Faulkner's Native southerners, published
by Louisiana State University Press in 1974 as *The Indians of Yoknapatawpha: A Study in Literature and History*. As Dabney's title indicates,
this first phase of critical work on Faulkner's Indians explored possible
sources for his interest in and representations of Mississippi Indians and
weighed the accuracy of those representations against the lives, experiences, characteristics, and customs of the Chickasaw, Choctaw, Natchez,
and other Southeastern nations as reconstructed from the historical and
anthropological record. Later essays by Howard C. Horsford (1992),
Patricia Galloway (2003), Robert Woods Sayre (2003), and Gene M.
Moore (2003) carried this primary excavation work forward, along the
way compiling an impressive inventory of source materials available to
Faulkner and situating his portraits and accounts of Indians within the
intellectual and popular culture of the novelist's era.[46] And as this scholarship was maturing, the rise of the so-called New Western History, with
its revisionist approaches to frontier ideology, US-Native relations, and
environmental challenges in the trans-Mississippi regions, combined
with an extraordinary multicultural flowering of US ethnic and border

INTRODUCTION   XVII

literatures during the 1980s and 1990s to further energize and sharpen critical inquiry into Native American histories and literatures.[47]

Since 2000, a second "wave" of scholarship has drawn on postcolonial studies and critical race theory to illuminate Faulkner's Indian fiction. Led by Édouard Glissant, who (unlike O'Donnell and Warren) singles out the expropriation of Native lands by white settler colonialism as "the original sin of the South" within the historical and moral scheme of the Yoknapatawpha fiction, this group of critics, which includes Bruce G. Johnson, Aude Lalande, Peter Lancelot Mallios (all 2003), Annette Trefzer (2007), and Lindsey Claire Smith (2008), stresses the destabilizing and often subversive forces that arise from the colonial, intercultural encounters among Indians, Europeans, and disasporic Africans in Faulkner's novels and stories.[48] Pointing to the fluid, hybrid subjectivities; the mimicry, masquerade, and misperformance; the parody and play; the strange pastiches and inevitable creolizations generated by these hemispheric exchanges, they come to differing conclusions about Faulkner's degree of control over this often uncomfortable material. Several of these scholars, for example, cite the work of Edward Said to call attention to the Orientalizing discourse at work in some of Faulkner's depictions of Native physique and temperament but do not reach a consensus about whether the author is colluding in this discourse or critically parodying it.[49] Other scholars such as Arthur F. Kinney (2000), Robert Dale Parker (2003), and Keely Byars-Nichols (2013) have turned to the work of Toni Morrison and other critical race and critical whiteness theorists to explore how Native characters and performances work by turns to unsettle and to prop up the color line in Faulkner's triracial US South, in the process triggering pervasive white anxiety.[50]

More recently, however, some Native scholars have expressed misgivings about these critical paradigms. They worry, for example, that the focus on cultural hybridity, race-mixing, and post-contact histories that dominates contemporary postcolonial studies approaches to literature diverts attention from more pressing issues of political sovereignty, cultural survival, land claims, community, and nationhood at the center of much Native activism and intellectual work today. As Lisa Brooks has put it,

> One of the central problems with the way hybridity theory has been applied to Native texts is that it does not seem to account for the relationship between community and land. Rather, culture and identity seem to rest within the individual "subject," who seems oddly out of place, displaced, caught between two assumed worlds or perspectives that are so intertwined that they no longer exist independently of each other. Okay, fine, but where does relationship to land figure into all this? Is this basically a way to say that we are all native to

XVIII INTRODUCTION

this land because Europeans and Native Americans are so intertwined as to melt together into a single multicultural mass? Has assimilation and extinction of aboriginal title been accomplished? Should we just drop our tribal delusions and go home? That is . . . if home could then ever be found.[51]

Jodi A. Byrd directs a similar skepticism toward the idea of "internal colonialism," which has proven to be an influential paradigm in postcolonial studies. "In the US context," Byrd writes, the concept has come to refer

primarily and originally to African American oppression that then over the course of time serves to erase indigenous peoples altogether as it is thought to account for the indigenous within the racial paradigms it creates. . . . It is this turn that finally allows [bell] hooks to reposition African American bodies as the foundational site of colonization rather than American Indian lands. . . ."Internal colonialism" becomes an empty referent that can be claimed by any marginalized group; to use it to describe the historical and spatial positionality of indigenous nations is a colonial violence that undermines sovereignty and self-determination.[52]

Jace Weaver points to a third reason why many Native scholars are leery of postcolonial theory: "There is a troubling temporal aspect to most postcolonial discourse—'postcolonial' truly means a time *after* colonialism, and for the indigenes of the Anglo-colonial settler colonies that time has not yet come."[53]

For these reasons many Native scholars have focused instead on developing their own theoretical paradigms and critical methodologies grounded in Indigenous intellectual traditions and cultural frameworks. Take the concept of Indigeneity itself, for example, which opts away from postmodern and postcolonial models of slippery, decentered "subjectivity" to anchor identity and community in the relationship to homeland. A third phase of scholarship on Faulkner's Indian tales is currently emerging in and around the work of Native critics bringing their own methodologies and "tribalographies" to the texts.[54] Weaver, for example, while noting that Faulkner's Yoknapatawpha is "from a Native standpoint . . . an ethnically cleansed landscape," has also called on Native studies to embrace the implications of the place name, which he translates from the Chickasaw as "split earth," as a "metaphor, indeed a powerful one, for Native existence in general and Native literature in particular," inasmuch as "Natives have been split from their lands" and "the land itself has been split, not only by the conqueror's plot, but by the conqueror's law" and regime of property

INTRODUCTION   XIX

ownership.[55] Taylor also mobilizes the "split land" motif to evoke the historical, social, and environmental predicament of the Native South, a country divided against itself and badly in need of healing.[56] Phillip Carroll Morgan opts for a slightly different translation of Yoknapatawpha, plowed or "furrowed land," by way of contextualizing his exciting discovery that the name designated not only a river in southern Lafayette County but also a nineteenth-century estate, Yakni Patafa, that stood on a pre-Columbian earthen mound just south of Pontotoc, Mississippi. Yakni Patafa was home to a prominent nineteenth-century Chickasaw family whose members, Morgan argues, were in all likelihood well known to Faulkner's paternal ancestors in Union, Tippah, and Pontotoc Counties. For Morgan, Faulkner's adoption of the term is less an arrogant appropriation of Native resources—a version of literary land theft—than an acknowledgment and enregistration of the human and environmental indigeneity that frames and infuses his Mississippi writings:

> It seems reasonable to argue that the astonishing popularity of Faulkner's work, along with its generally positive critical reception, reflect the power of the place in which his stories were conceived and written, and that the place is inseparable from its indigenous inhabitants and their traditions. . . . Faulkner exploited the Indian subject inaccurately, perhaps recklessly, but successfully. His stories are irrevocably framed by what he frequently called a "dark and nameless power" from the past. Perhaps Faulkner could not name it correctly, but neither could he ignore it. [57]

Yet Faulkner *did* name it—Yoknapatawpha—and that name has become perhaps the truest index of his achievement, in part for precisely the reasons Morgan lays out here.

In this light it is suggestive that Faulkner's earliest use of the Chickasaw phrase may have been to name a *person* rather than a place. In the autograph manuscript of Faulkner's story "Red Leaves," the Native character known in the published story (1930) as Louis Berry instead bears the name "Yo-ko-no-pa-taw-fa."[58] If there is any credence to the possibility cited by Theresa Towner and James B. Carothers that "Red Leaves" "may have been written as early as 1927, or perhaps in 1929," after Faulkner had christened his fictional county "Yocona" in the manuscript of *Flags in the Dust* (1927) but before he called it Yoknapatawpha for the first time in print in *As I Lay Dying* (1930), then the Native phrase may actually have entered the Faulkner lexicon in conjunction with living human Indigeneity rather than with indigenous landscape.[59] What might that choice—that difference—mean? Could it reflect

XX   INTRODUCTION

Faulkner's understanding, or maybe just his intuition, that the "plowed earth" of north Mississippi would take on the status—indeed, had all along borne the status—of a living, breathing entity, a life-force infused with the spiritual and ecological energies of centuries of Chickasaw and Choctaw living? If so, then Dabney is well within his rights to observe of the "Red Leaves" manuscript that "if there is a Yoknapatawpha saga, it begins here."[60]

What other interpretive riches might the Yoknapatawpha oeuvre be poised to yield to the critic approaching the work through Indigeneity or related Native paradigms? For one provisional answer, we might turn to one of the hand-drawn maps Faulkner made of his fictional territory. Not the famous maps of the county he drew for *Absalom, Absalom!* and Malcolm Cowley's *Portable Faulkner* volume, but the lesser-known one that he created for Cowley in the midst of their correspondence about the *Portable*. Asked about "factual discrepancies" that made it unclear to Cowley whether the Indians of "Red Leaves" and "A Justice" were Choctaws or Chickasaws,[61] Faulkner sent Cowley the following explanation, accompanied by a roughly sketched map of the region:

> The line dividing the Chickasaw and Choctaw nations passed near my home; I merely moved a tribe slightly at need, since they were slightly different in behavior. . . . The Indians actually were Chickasaws, or they may be so from now on. RED LEAVES actually were Chickasaws. A JUSTICE could have been either, the reason for their being Chocktaws [sic] was the connection with New Orleans, which was more available to Chocktaws, as the map herewith will explain.
>
> At this time the Tallahatchie, running from the Chickasaw across the Chocktaw nation, was navigable; steamboats came up it.[62]

Geographer Charles S. Aiken published a "corrected" version of this map in a 1979 article, but from a Native studies perspective, the sketch's degree of cartographic accuracy isn't really the point.[63] Rather, the map's significance lies in its forthright acknowledgment of the indigenous underpinnings of Faulkner's other maps, of his imaginary county, and of his literary project as a whole. (See figure 1.) Where the maps in *Absalom* and the *Portable* observe a strong rectilinear scheme, a Cartesian grid within which the county borders also assume nearly rectangular form, the unpublished map arranges space along undulating, serpentine lines defined by indigenous landscape features. The only straight line on the map, running northwest to southeast, is the border between the Chickasaw and Choctaw Nations. This is, moreover, the only human-devised boundary on the map. There are

INTRODUCTION   XXI

no county or state lines featured, nothing to indicate the legal jurisdiction and political reach of the settler-colonial nation-state except,
perhaps, the Indian agency located just south of the tribal border.[64]
The white villages of Jefferson and Memphis—rendered on the map
as small dots—are dwarfed by Native landmarks: the Mississippi, Tennessee, and Tallahatchie Rivers (with their Indian names, two in all
capital letters), Colbert's Ferry (an actual historical site along the Tennessee), the "Chocktaw" Agency, and the boundary line.[65] Where the
Yoknapatawpha County maps displace their Indian landmarks to the
county's northwestern corner (site of "ISSETIBBEHA'S CHICKASAW
GRANT" on the *Absalom* map, slightly modified to "ISSETIBBEHA'S
CHICKASAW PATENT" for the *Portable*), a peripheral area many
miles from Jefferson's municipal core, on the Cowley map Native space
is the environing medium and condition of possibility for Anglo settlement.[66] There is no land claim asserted here by an Anglophone authorial persona on his own behalf as "Sole Owner and Proprietor"—or
even, as in the *Portable*, as the surveyor and cartographer—of the territory represented. Yet neither is this "wilderness." It is instead a primal
field of indigeneity *and* Indigeneity out of which Yoknapatawpha can
and does emerge, something like a zero degree of Faulknerian space
and sociality. Sean Latham has suggested that the maps for *Absalom*
and the *Portable* point not to Philip M. Weinstein's concept of Yoknapatawpha as "a cosmos no one owns" but rather to what Latham calls
"a cosmos too diversely owned."[67] Yet on the Cowley map Faulkner
begins to peel back those layers of colonial proprietorship and state-
backed private ownership to leave a landscape defined primarily by
natural history and Indigenous sovereignty. If the author claimed to
have found in his fictional county "a kind of keystone in the universe,"
then this hastily improvised map depicts the keystone in that keystone,
reframing the territory it also founds.[68]

    A similar reframing effort is at work—not in the domain of space
but in the domain of time—in a second supporting document Faulkner
prepared for the *Portable* project, the celebrated Compson Appendix he
penned two months after drawing up his ur-map of north Mississippi for
Cowley. In the genealogical entries of the appendix, Faulkner believed
he had clarified and contextualized the meaning of *The Sound and the
Fury* in such a way that "the whole thing" would now fall seamlessly
"into pattern like a jigsaw puzzle when the magician's wand touched
it."[69] Significantly, then, his first bit of magic in the appendix was to
open the genealogy not as might have been expected with Compsons
but with a pair of figures whose inclusion works to resituate Compson
history within and against a *longue durée* of Indigeneity, conquest, and

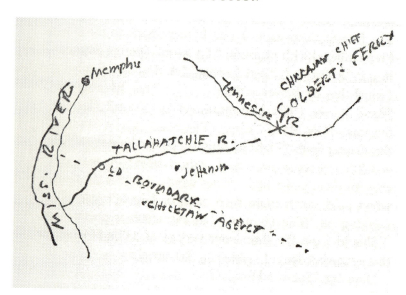

Figure 1. Hand-drawn map, William Faulkner to Malcolm Cowley, August 16, 1945. Malcolm Cowley Papers, Newberry Library. (c) Copyright 2018, Faulkner Literary Rights, LLC. Used with permission, the William Faulkner Literary Estate, Lee Caplin, executor.

expropriation, as "IKKEMOTUBBE. A dispossessed American king" meets "JACKSON. A Great White Father with a Sword."[70] For Faulkner to position Indian removal as the founding/framing event in the chronicle of one of Yoknapatawpha County's first (white) families, displacing even the Battle of Culloden from pride of textual/historical place, is once again to redirect and reinflect his project, from the perspective of midcareer, along Native lines.[71] If in 1948 Faulkner would backslide a bit on this stance, instructing his publisher to group four of his Indian tales under the heading of "THE WILDERNESS" for his *Collected Stories* volume[72]—as if to place Native life in/against a "virgin" setting like a dutiful American studies disciple—the retrospective view of his career occasioned by his collaboration with Cowley on the *Portable* seems to have awakened a new and deeper understanding of the indigenous wellsprings of his creative energies.

In addition to temporal and spatial reconsiderations of Yoknapatawpha, a Native southern studies lens provides another sort of politically anchored Indigeneity as an important informing context for "Lo!" Faulkner's 1934 short story about a delegation of Chickasaw Indians that travels to Washington to petition the president to help them resolve a violent dispute over rival land claims to a river ford not so unlike the actual Colbert's Ferry. Critics have made much of the levels of parody and mimicry at work between Natives and Anglos in the tale, where, for example, the Indians sport beaver hats, frock coats, and woolen underwear presented to them by the president as ceremonial gifts while neglecting to put on the shoes and, more to the point, the pants that would complete the outfits—and where, in a version of postcolonial potlatch that Bhabha would no doubt appreciate, the Chickasaw reciprocate and top the president's largesse by presenting *him* with his own ceremonial regalia, "a mass, a network of gold braid—frogs, epaulets, sash and sword—held loosely together by bright green cloth."[73] Almost the same as formal Western attire, but not quite.

As events unfold, however, these superficial hijinks yield to another mode of misperformance that carries subtler and more serious implications. When the president—clearly modeled on Andrew Jackson, the figure responsible more than any other for the Indian removal policies that would rob the Chickasaw and other Southeastern nations of their homelands—finally receives the delegation to begin deliberations over the dispute (in which a white land speculator has been killed), the leader of the Native party, Francis Weddel, expresses surprise over the venue for the inquest, which is being held in the chambers of one of the president's cabinet members, presumably the secretary of war (under whose jurisdiction, tellingly, Indian affairs fell at the time of Jackson's presidency). As the president explains to Weddel, he has appointed the secretary "to be the holder of justice between me and my Indian people" (*CS*, 395). To understand Weddel's confusion more fully, however, we need to review the forms of Native governance practiced along the eastern seaboard of North America during the colonial and early national eras. In the American South, by that time, the great hierarchical chiefdoms of the earlier Mississippian cultures had yielded to more egalitarian political systems of a more deliberative nature featuring town, tribal, and even intertribal councils. To the north, as the English colonists were slowly woven into the Covenant Chain of the great Iroquois Confederacy of the seventeenth and eighteenth centuries,[74] many expressed admiration for such Native governance systems, and some contemporary scholars have gone on to assert that the forms of participatory democracy and "forest diplomacy" practiced between and among tribal polities by means of such specific institutions as the Great Council of the Iroquois directly influenced the founders as they laid out the political architecture of the nascent United States.[75] It can be argued, then, that in council governance we see an indigenous foundation for New World republicanism as it would come to be practiced up and down the Americas in the eighteenth and nineteenth centuries.[76]

So when Weddel finds himself troubled as the president hands down a unilateral verdict purporting to settle the dispute over the ford, and moreover hands it down in the office of one of his own cabinet appointees, considerably more is involved than the mere comic obtuseness of a "simple" Native, the "poor Indian" of Alexander Pope evoked by the story's title. Rather, Weddel's assumption that the hearing would take place "in the big white council house beneath the golden eagle" (*CS*, 397)—in other words, at the US Capitol building, within the legislative rather than executive branch of government—makes sense in light of the governance procedures to which he would be accustomed as a member of an Indian nation from the continent's eastern woodlands.

Weddel's request, then—which the president hastily grants, moving the proceedings to the Capitol in his desperation to wrap up the matter and send the Indians home—should not simply be dismissed as the product of some amusing Native weakness for pomp and fanfare. Rather, a reader attuned to the political cultures of the Native South should be in a position to recognize the subtle way in which Weddel unmasks the president's dealings with Indians—and *this* president's dealings in particular—as illegitimate, by their rules *and* his. Indeed, the Chickasaw have managed to maneuver the president into acting precisely like the sort of tyrannical ruler—rash, imperious, given to unilateral decrees rather than collective deliberations—that the young nation supposedly broke away from England to gain independence from: a kind of latter-day George III, by this point in nineteenth-century history additionally notorious as a Mad King. It's the worst sort of colonial mimicry, all the more devastating because unsuspected, inadvertent: a monarchial sensibility masquerading as a presidential one. But the masquerade is so painfully awkward—much as the ludicrous spectacle Weddel corners the president into staging before Congress, a representative body that the president himself has acknowledged to be "a council of chiefs who are more powerful there [in the Capitol] than I am" (*CS*, 398), performs its own bad mimicry of the oratory and ritual that solemnized tribal council proceedings. By the time the president is done declaiming Petrarchan sonnets in the hope of passing off the Latin as lofty legal discourse, then punctuating his peroration with cannon fire, the colonial dynamic at work between Washington and Indian country has been thoroughly demystified, travestied, and unraveled—indeed reversed!

A Native studies reading of "Lo!" underscores how the Chickasaws trade on Indigenous political paradigms in order to destabilize any notion that they can expect justice from the United States, for all its vaunted democracy, republicanism, or love of freedom. Indeed, the specific, local issue of justice in the ford dispute is the Trojan horse within which the delegation smuggles a much more fundamental ethical question into the very heart of US political space: that of justice for Native nations in the context of removal. By getting the president to issue his decree in the public space of the Capitol, and to fire that artillery to seal the deal, Weddel rejiggers the whole ceremony to dramatize the thinly veiled threat of war that underlies every "diplomatic" overture made by the United States toward Native tribes. So it can hardly be a surprise when this threat comes out into the open at story's end. Alerted that Weddel and his people are on the march again for Washington after a second white speculator has been killed at the ford, the president reassumes his former office as "the Soldier"—the old Indian fighter showing his true colors—and sits down with the secretary of war to plot a military rather than political campaign against the invaders (*CS*, 402–3). By drawing on Indigenous models to tease out a deeper and more concrete set of subtexts from the tale's forays into parody and mimicry, a critical methodology grounded in Native studies can take us places with Faulkner's story that a postcolonial approach cannot reach on its own.

The chapters that follow offer new methodologies, perspectives, and interpretations as they engage Faulkner's Native South and the Native South's Faulkner. Like our Native studies–inspired reading of "Lo!" which takes us into a discussion of Native sovereignty and the potency of Indigenous political critique that reveals both the foundations and fissures of the national fabric of liberty, many of the readings that follow approach Faulkner's texts with a vocabulary central to Native studies, including the theory of "tribalography" and the concepts of political sovereignty, cultural authenticity, Native community, and land claims. We open, for instance, with an essay by the scholar who coined the term "tribalography," Choctaw/Cherokee writer, critic, and activist LeAnne Howe, who introduces us to some of the Indigenous ways of knowing that inform the methodology of Native South studies. "Faulkner Didn't Invent Yoknapatawpha, *Everybody Knows That*. So What Other Stories Do Chickasaws and Choctaws Know about Our Homelands?" blends poetry, fiction, historical documents, and personal commentary to illustrate how Choctaws and other Southeastern nations have turned to "core narratives as a survival strategy over millennia" of challenges posed both by the natural environment and by the "tired, hungry foreigners" who have sought refuge in Native homelands since the seventeenth century. Turning to the seemingly mundane subject of weather prediction, Howe cites a range of writings—from Bienville's correspondence of the early 1700s to Choctaw chief Ben Dwight's inquiries among leaders of other tribal nations in the 1950s—as evidence not only that the tribes possessed a diversity of Indigenous knowledge "about long-term weather

XXVI   INTRODUCTION

processes" but that they shared this knowledge intertribally, helping each other weather the threat of hurricanes, floods, droughts, and other forms of ecodisaster. Though Howe faults Faulkner for Native characterizations that trade on stereotype, she also, much like Phillip Carroll Morgan, finds his imagination to be "driven" and "enlivened" by Native stories. His own ways of knowing, then, were in some respects compatible if not entirely identical with the story-centered epistemologies that Howe explores.

For Chickasaw scholar Jodi A. Byrd, Indigenous methodologies also provide a way to work through a set of residual ambivalences about Faulkner's work and toward a more productive engagement with the Indigenous presences that figure there. In "Souths as Prologues: Indigeneity, Race, and the Temporalities of Land; or, Why I Can't Read William Faulkner," Byrd draws on Howe's tribalographic methodology, in which "family . . . is where one always starts," to reflect on her own genealogy as a lens onto Faulkner's world, where "the unspoken of family secrets" meets "the uneasiness of never quite having a—or being at—home" and where all human relations "hover between possession and dispossession." A related focus on land as "an agentive presence acting upon people and their losses to reorient them constantly into space and time" joins an Indigenous epistemology grounded in storytelling and open to "coincidence and speculation" to offer "ways of reading Chickasaws back into Faulkner." Among the narratives Faulkner gleaned from the oral culture of north Mississippi, for example, were tales of Native provenance such as the story of Yakni Patafa uncovered by Morgan, which illustrates how in both Mississippi history and the Yoknapatawpha fiction "the land holds and resists the violences humanity inflicts upon itself" through slavery and colonialism, how it "slowly reclaims and swallows the debris" of such histories, "resettling cultivated civilization through an agency that is a deep planetary temporality." Faulkner's work, Byrd finds, "denies Chickasaw sovereignty while requiring Chickasaw presence," even as it holds this very disavowal up for interrogation and critique in texts like *Absalom, Absalom!* where Thomas Sutpen's purchase of Chickasaw lands with Spanish coin takes its place in a history of conquest stretching at least as far back as de Soto, a "native/white encounter that frames the black/white one and forecloses the possibility of the native and black ever meeting at all." Despite her reservations, then, Byrd concludes that as an Indigenous intellectual she *can* read Faulkner after all, for the flawed but revealing window he opens onto "the alchemy of modern US race relations" and the land's claim upon all of the parties thereto.

Melanie Benson Taylor focuses on the "obscure, uncanny Indians" lurking in the family histories of Faulkner's major novels and in the

INTRODUCTION

author's treatment of the institution of slavery so fundamental to the history of Yoknapatawpha. She argues that when Indians appear in these contexts, they represent the opportunities and failures of the national promise. "Doom and Deliverance: Faulkner's Dialectical Indians" makes two crucial methodological moves. First, Taylor calls for new historical archives to be explored: for instance, did Faulkner model Sam Fathers on Sam Love, a Chickasaw Indian who owned slaves in Marshall County, Mississippi? Is there a connection between the historical Delilah Love and Faulkner's fictional Ikkemotubbe, both of whom apparently granted land to families in the area? May the postal rider Pettigrew in *Requiem for a Nun* have gotten his name from a school and a creek in Chickasaw County, Mississippi? Second, Taylor shifts from Indian characters to the signifier "red" in a move that opens up a rich textual field of fresh interpretive possibilities. Thus, in *Requiem for a Nun*, the settler community is "in the red" to the US government as a result of a stolen lock. Indians show up in the appendix to the Compson story in *The Sound and the Fury*, a story to which these characters are seemingly unconnected. Clytie of *Absalom, Absalom!* is "part Indian," Jewel in *As I Lay Dying* is described as a "cigar store Indian," and a man named "Red" is the sexual executor for the impotent Popeye in *Sanctuary*. In thus uncovering the astonishing pervasiveness of Indigeneity throughout Faulkner's canon, Taylor offers an expanding set of possibilities for the interpretation of his work.

Gina Caison also applies a Native studies methodology to Faulkner's work as she abandons the often-romanticized idea of a southern "sense of place" and heads for the water in two texts that present ecological disaster: Faulkner's 1927 Flood narrative "Old Man" (1939) and Monique Verdin's 2012 documentary film *My Louisiana Love*, which chronicles the aftermath of Hurricane Katrina and the BP oil spill. Both texts, Caison argues, propose not only shifting ground but complex temporal orders facing the past and the future at once from their postapocalyptic vantage points. In "Old Man," the tall convict with "Indian-black hair" who helps the pregnant woman give birth on an Indian mound in the midst of the flood is marked "lost" in the inventory of the prison system. But as he battles for survival on a river that runs crazily backwards, he is not lost at all but moving in synch with the cosmic swirls of time and place. This different, deeper sense of temporality links Faulkner's narrative with Verdin's film, the latter tallying loss in visual and verbal surveys of the ruined home of a Houma Indian family. Yet the film, too, pushes through the loss accompanying disaster as it focuses on the discovery of an armadillo, an ancient survivor and helpful reminder of the other temporalities and spatialities that rise into awareness during episodes of ecocatastrophe. Casting aside stereotypical images of "ecological

XXVIII INTRODUCTION

Indians" and the centrality of the Lost Cause in narratives about the South, Caison seems to ask: Is anything ever truly lost?

The next group of chapters draws on the archives, methodologies, and insights of ethnohistory in order to shed new light on Faulkner's work and world. Patricia Galloway turns to an element of Native culture that clearly captured Faulkner's imagination: clothing and adornment. In "Dressing the Part: Evolution of Indian Dress in Faulkner," Galloway employs a developmental and comparative approach to trace Faulkner's changing portrayals of Indigenous finery from the "Doom story" that unfolds over the two decades between "Red Leaves" and the prologues of *Requiem for a Nun*, through the "Weddel story" laid out in "Mountain Victory" and "Lo!" to the "Sam Fathers story" as traced from "A Justice" to "The Bear." Noting the fanciful affinity for French cultural trappings (including clothing, shoes, and other accessories) with which Faulkner endows his Mississippi Indians, Galloway goes on to distinguish the author's depictions of pre-Removal Indians as "free to wear canonical Euroamerican clothes as they chose" from the post-Removal figure of Sam Fathers, who typically sports work clothes also associated with African American slaves and freedmen, garments often described "as worn-out or second-hand to emphasize their lowliness." Deviations from this pattern tend to indicate meaningful differences of class or degrees of rank among Faulkner's Native characters. Other historical sources, however, including Galloway's own great-grandfather, a Methodist missionary to Indian Territory in the 1880s and 1890s, point to a greater degree of agency at work in Native clothing choices than Faulkner seems to acknowledge. Paintings, photographs, and written accounts all "suggest not only that Native people were fully capable of adopting Euroamerican clothing creatively to their own ends, in terms of what they found attractive or comfortable, but that they might also use this clothing as costume" for their own tactical purposes. Galloway's essay models a critical practice capable of reading Faulkner's descriptions of Native clothing habits against their own grain, as evidence of Indigenous resourcefulness rather than "a pathetic failure to understand European culture."

Complicating critical accounts of Yoknapatawpha County as "a primeval native ecology of place" incorporating Indians as "an inherent part," Annette Trefzer examines how Faulkner's key Indian texts of the 1950s, *Requiem for a Nun* and "Mississippi," go against their own nostalgic grain to tell a story of Mississippi Indigeneity that cannot be reduced to Native "obsolescence." "'A Valid Signature': Native American Sovereignty in *Requiem for a Nun*" finds a more nuanced account of Native modernity at work in Faulkner, focusing in particular on the "X" via which the Chickasaw matriarch Mohataha signs over legal title to her north Mississippi lands to the white settlers who found Jefferson. Drawing on the work of Ojibwe historian Scott Richard Lyons, Trefzer reads Mohataha's "x-mark" as a form of agency that creates a modicum of sovereignty and room to maneuver within conditions of severely limited choice. More than a concession to and retreat from Anglo modernity, Mohataha's mark, which Trefzer calls "the central organizing figure of Faulkner's novel," chiasmatically frames removal as at once a downward movement, a fall into dispossession, *and* an "ascent" that inaugurates "a new chapter in Chickasaw history." As a "gendered sign" and "a place-holder for a new identity" combining "property ownership, economic agency, cultural mobility, and transition to literacy," it finds an intriguing complement in Mohataha's clothing choices, which, as Galloway's chapter has helped prepare us to appreciate, put items of European finery to creative and cosmopolitan use as vehicles of authentic Native performance and Chickasaw cultural survival. Rather than confirming her marginality to modernity, then, Mohataha's performances link her at once to other important female figures in *Requiem* and to a historical legacy of sovereignty and modernity among real-life Chickasaw women. "'A Valid Signature'" offers a vital reassessment of "the limits of Faulkner's capacity to imagine Native American cultural survival in the South."

Starting from the premise that "both history and literature concern themselves with stories," historian Katherine M. B. Osburn employs a technique also found in some of Faulkner's greatest narratives—the interplay of contested stories, competing versions of the past—to interrogate the novelist's own representations of Mississippi Indians. Osburn's "'Brother: Is This Truth?': History, Fiction, and Colonialism in Faulkner's Mississippi" turns to the stories that Mississippi Choctaws were telling about themselves at the very time Faulkner was crafting his Indian fictions. These Native self-representations, argues Osburn, serve as a necessary counterpoint to the novelist's often-stereotypical evocations of Native southerners as ignoble and/or vanishing figures. In their efforts to win federal recognition for their tribe or to protect sacred sites, Mississippi Choctaws "strategically engaged the damaging images tossed about so casually by their non-Indian neighbors, including Faulkner." They used a narrative of Choctaw decline, for example, to hold the federal government accountable for broken treaty promises, and they put the vanishing Indian motif to work by presenting tribal history in tragic terms "as a form of moral suasion" directed at local, state, and federal officials. Deploying a fiction of their own noble savagery against the trope of the ignoble savage wielded against them, the Choctaws also sought and won press coverage for their efforts at political and cultural renewal in a variety of news outlets that reached into Faulkner's north

XXX   INTRODUCTION

Mississippi world, "performing Indianness" in order "to manipulate government officials" in a manner that Faulkner may well have recognized and worked into his story "Lo!" As evidence of "how subaltern peoples use historical narratives, even painful ones, for powerful political purposes," Osburn writes, the stories of the Mississippi Choctaws warrant "a place alongside Faulkner's work as a way to think about Native Southerners and that elusive and contingent thing we call truth."

The final chapters offer new interpretations of some of Faulkner's most classic texts from the vantage points provided by Native literature and scholarship. Three of these chapters are comparative, placing Faulkner's work in illuminating dialogue with writings and other creative works by Indigenous artists. Clearing a path to these comparative readings, Robbie Ethridge adds the fraught figure of "the Ecological Indian" to Osburn's inventory of hoary myths and clichés that a conscientious Native southern studies must seek to dispel. "The Wild and the Tame: Sam Fathers as Ecological Indian" follows historian Shepard Krech III in pronouncing the Ecological Indian, "connected to the wild and concerned about its preservation and conservation in ways that non-Indians can never be," more fiction than reality, noting that the "complex interplay between global economic forces, state-level political economies, indigenous knowledge and cultural practices, and local political economies" informed a variety of perspectives on the environment among Native peoples, leading to ecological mismanagement as well as to the healthy stewardship of land and other natural resources. In the character of Sam Fathers, Ethridge argues, Faulkner explores the implications of the Ecological Indian figure, setting up Sam as a wild and spiritually pure "counterpoint to the Euro-American world" only to complicate that scheme at the climax of the hunt for Old Ben in "The Bear," where "the ritual killing of the wild" orchestrated by Sam "goes awry," in "a surprised and botched ending" that allows Faulkner "to open up the moral ambiguities in the taming of the wild." Like Galloway and Osburn, Ethridge turns to historical examples from the Native and Global Souths in which Indigenous groups have been primitivized as "ecological" to their own detriment or have themselves attempted to leverage the "ecological" mantle, with mixed results. Cautioning against "framing social justice issues in terms of culturally defined identity" categories like the Ecological Indian, Ethridge finds in Faulkner's work a useful resource for contemporary efforts to think our way beyond the reductive binaries of wild and tame, pure and impure, that the stereotype has brought in its wake.

Eric Gary Anderson suggests that Faulkner's sense of the Native South is oblique, "as if hidden in plain sight." Anderson teases out the layers in the meaning of "Native southernness" in two ways: it is

INTRODUCTION

a reference to being Indigenous in the South and to being a native of the South. In Faulkner's novel *Light in August*, neither meaning of "native" is readily available because no character is originally from Jefferson. What should we make of this "hyper-foreign" nonnativeness? "Native Southern Transformations, or *Light in August* and Werewolves" reads Faulkner's 1932 novel through the lens of *Mongrel* (2016), a novel by Blackfeet writer Stephen Graham Jones, in order to bring into unexpected relation and productive conversation the issue of "nonnativeness" in the two works. The novels share an interest in the "transformative potential" of monstrosity that "in complicated, ambivalent, and at times deeply unsettling ways, annotates and re-conceptualizes both 'native' and 'southern.'" Anderson begins his chapter by following up on the reference to the town of Pocahontas in *Light in August* by which Faulkner seems to displace a historical town (possibly Pontotoc, Mississippi) and its Chickasaw Indians with a name that refers to John Smith's story set in Virginia. Noting that Faulkner composed *Light in August* at about the time when horror movies were being produced in Hollywood, including *The Werewolf in Paris* (1933), Anderson proceeds to read the monstrous transformations of the male orphan characters in both novels, outcasts in the South who function as feared metaphors of otherness. He shares with Byrd and Taylor the dramatic sense that the story of the New World is horror, and he argues that "Native Southern is not merely an interest group within southern studies, but rather a supple and productive methodology in its own right."

Melanie R. Anderson notes that William Faulkner and Louise Erdrich create vibrant communities and multigenerational sagas peopled by characters who reappear throughout their fiction. Although Erdrich writes about the Chippewa communities of North Dakota and Minnesota and Faulkner about the Choctaws and Chickasaws of Mississippi, the writers share an emphasis on the land, its connection to family history, and the racial dynamics of mixed-blood characters. In "From the Mausoleum to a Spider Web: William Faulkner's and Louise Erdrich's Takes on Hybridity," Anderson argues that the genealogies invented by the two writers point in different directions: Although Faulkner's Indian characters pervade his fiction from the 1930s to the 1950s, his narratives truncate Native genealogies in order to trace a non-Native southern heritage; by contrast, Erdrich "gives visibility to groups of characters that are elided in Faulkner's fiction." Both authors explore racial and cultural hybridity, but Faulkner "dooms" mixed-blood characters like Sam Fathers to vanish from the land, whereas Erdrich celebrates racially intermixed Indigenous family trees as an enduring source of flexibility and strength. Unlike Faulkner, who builds a stately mausoleum for his

Native characters, Erdrich weaves a delicate "spider web" symbolizing creativity and living continuity in the Native community.

Finally, John Wharton Lowe, a noted expert on humor writing in the literatures of North America, zooms in on the comic aspects of plot and character in two of Faulkner's Indian stories, "Lo!" and "A Courtship." "Red Laughter: Humor in Faulkner's Native Narratives" argues that Faulkner rejected the stereotypical silent and stoic Indian figure prevalent in the cultural imagination of his time and instead created funny and resourceful characters, "shifty operators who never cease to amuse" and have much in common with the trickster characters of Native American literature. Lowe reads the comic duel of David Hogganbeck and young Ikkemotubbe in "A Courtship" as a story in the pastoral tradition, with two courtiers who are rivals for the hand of a fair lady, in this case Herman Basket's sister. This rivalry, carried out in "Rabelaisian eating contests" and footraces, results in a growing bond and friendship between the men climaxing in their sudden joint realization that while thus occupied in determining the winner, another Indian, Log-in-the-Creek, courted and married their "lady-love." Faulkner shifts to another narrative strategy in "Lo!" where he relies on irony and comic reversal in his depiction of President Jackson as a "fool" outwitted by the Chickasaw delegation encamped at the White House. Lowe argues that Faulkner's use of "deceptive and self-reflexive humor" has much in common with Native American comedy. Was Faulkner familiar with humor in the Native American literary tradition? Had he heard of the Creek writer Alexander Lawrence Posey and his "Fus Fixico Letters" or read stories by Cherokee writer John Milton Oskison? Lowe's chapter raises provocative questions for intertextual and intercultural analysis centered on the trickster figure. After all, Lowe concludes, Faulkner may have understood his Native American characters better than we thought or that he let on when he infamously claimed to have "made them up."

Before proceeding to the chapters and other resources that follow, it might be useful to conclude here by pointing out some questions, challenges, and problems that potentially lie ahead for Faulkner studies and Native South studies as the fields move forward from their encounter in these pages. For one thing, the land-, tribe-, sovereignty-, or separatism-based approaches that distinguish current scholarship on Faulkner's Indians, and that energize several of the chapters here, are beginning to come under reassessment and critique in their turn, as part of the vigorous internal debate that has characterized Native American and Indigenous studies at least since the field's inception. What room or role, for instance, in an Indigenized disciplinary landscape does a Native studies grounded in literary nationalisms leave for non-Native scholars

INTRODUCTION   XXXIII

or for Native scholars less invested in identity as a critical paradigm and stance? And what in turn might the answers to those questions mean for future Faulkner scholarship—who does it, what it does, and how it gets done? Moreover, to what degree is Yoknapatawpha County or the oeuvre of its Anglo creator even worth engaging or appropriating for Indigenous scholars with far bigger critical, cultural, and political fish to fry? What are we ultimately after in excavating the Indigenous histories and redrawing the maps of this literary territory? Do we seek thereby to contribute to Native (South) studies in the same terms or to the same degree as to Faulkner studies? Can such contributions be pursued in the same ways at the same time? How will future generations of Native American literature *and* Faulkner scholars respond to the challenge posed by critics such as Jared Sexton—acknowledged by Byrd in her chapter here—to develop new and "unsovereign" sites and strategies for resistance to colonialism and capitalism that do not pit Native American and African American studies scholars, or Indians and diasporic Africans, against each other in mutual recrimination, comparative/competitive victimization, or rival claims to North American earth?[77] These are only a few of the ways in which the intellectual ferment and friction within the contemporary study of the Native South can and will challenge Faulkner scholars to reexamine the terms of their engagement with their subject. We hope and wager that the ferment within Faulkner studies already evidenced by this volume will help kindle similar and reciprocal reengagements among Native studies scholars, Indigenous and non-Indigenous alike.

NOTES

Many thanks to Eric Gary Anderson, Robbie Ethridge, and Melanie Benson Taylor for their comments and suggestions on draft material for this chapter.

1. Charles Hudson, *The Southeastern Indians* (Knoxville: University of Tennessee Press, 1976), 3. Hereafter cited parenthetically.

2. Grant Foreman, *Indian Removal: The Emigration of the Five Civilized Tribes of Indians* (Norman: University of Oklahoma Press, 1932); Angie Debo, *The Rise and Fall of the Choctaw Republic* (Norman: University of Oklahoma Press, 1934); David H. Corkran, *The Creek Frontier, 1540–1783* (Norman: University of Oklahoma Press, 1967); Arthur H. DeRosier Jr., *The Removal of the Choctaw Indians* (Knoxville: University of Tennessee Press, 1970); Arrell M. Gibson, *The Chickasaws* (Norman: University of Oklahoma Press, 1970).

3. Greg O'Brien, introduction to *The Native South: Histories and Legacies*, ed. Tim Allen Garrison and Greg O'Brien (Lincoln: University of Nebraska Press, 2017), xi.

4. Michael D. Green, *The Politics of Indian Removal: Creek Government and Society in Crisis* (Lincoln: University of Nebraska Press, 1982); Theda Perdue, *Cherokee Women:*

XXXIV INTRODUCTION

Gender and Culture Change 1700–1835 (Lincoln: University of Nebraska Press, 1998); and Theda Perdue and Michael D. Green, *The Columbia Guide to American Indians of the Southeast* (New York: Columbia University Press, 2001).

5. See the online description of the journal at http://unp-bookworm.unl.edu/product /Native-South,673964.aspx.

6. Clara Sue Kidwell, "American Indian Studies: Intellectual Navel Gazing or Academic Discipline?" *American Indian Quarterly* 33, no. 1 (Winter 2009): 1–17.

7. Ibid., 12.

8. Ibid.

9. Eric Gary Anderson, "Native American Literature, Ecocriticism, and the South: The Inaccessible Worlds of Linda Hogan's *Power*," in *South to a New Place: Region, Literature, Culture*, ed. Suzanne W. Jones and Sharon Monteith (Baton Rouge: Louisiana State University Press, 2002), 166.

10. Eric Gary Anderson, "Rethinking Indigenous Southern Communities," *American Literature* 78, no. 4 (2006): 732.

11. See also Roberta Rosenberg, "Native American Literature in the South," in *The Companion to Southern Literature*, ed. Joseph M. Flora and Lucinda H. MacKethan (Baton Rouge: Louisiana State University Press, 2002), 526–30.

12. Eric Gary Anderson, "South to a Red Place: Contemporary American Indian Writing and the Problem of Native/Southern Studies," *Mississippi Quarterly* 60, no. 1 (Winter 2006–2007): 6n4.

13. Craig S. Womack. *Red on Red: Native American Literary Separatism* (Minneapolis: University of Minnesota Press, 1999), 20.

14. Ibid., 191.

15. Daniel Heath Justice, *Our Fire Survives the Storm: A Cherokee Literary History* (Minneapolis: University of Minnesota Press, 2006).

16. Daniel Heath Justice, "'Go Away Water!' Kinship Criticism and the Decolonization Imperative," in *Reasoning Together: The Native Critics Collective*, ed. Craig S. Womack, Daniel Heath Justice, and Christopher Teuton (Norman: University of Oklahoma Press, 2008), 153.

17. Robert Allen Warrior, *Tribal Secrets: Recovering American Indian Intellectual Traditions* (Minneapolis: University of Minnesota Press, 1995).

18. Daniel F. Littlefield and James W. Parrins, eds., *Native American Writing in the Southeast: An Anthology, 1875–1935* (Jackson: University Press of Mississippi, 1995).

19. Ibid., xviii

20. Ibid., xxii.

21. Geary Hobson, Janet McAdams, and Katherine Walkiewicz, "Introduction: The South Seldom Seen," in *The People Who Stayed: Southeastern Indian Writing after Removal*, ed. Geary Hobson, Janet McAdams, and Katheryn Walkiewicz (Norman: University of Oklahoma Press, 2010), 15.

22. Ibid.

23. Melanie Benson Taylor, *Reconstructing the Native South: American Indian Literature and the Lost Cause* (Athens: University of Georgia Press, 2012), 2.

24. Ibid., 1.

25. Ibid., 116.

26. Ibid., 117.

27. E. Anderson, "South to a Red Place," 29.

28. Granville Hicks, *The Great Tradition: An Interpretation of American Literature since the Civil War*, rev. ed. (New York: Macmillan, 1935), 265–68; Maxwell Geismar, *Writers in Crisis: The American Novel, 1925–1940* (Boston: Houghton Mifflin, 1942),

INTRODUCTION   XXXV

141–83; Alfred Kazin, *On Native Grounds: An Interpretation of Modern American Prose Literature* (New York: Harcourt, Brace and World, 1942), 453–70.

29. Andre Malraux, "A Preface for Faulkner's *Sanctuary*" (1933), in *Faulkner: A Collection of Critical Essays*, ed. Robert Penn Warren (Englewood Cliffs, NJ: Prentice-Hall, 1966), 272–74; Jean-Paul Sartre, "*Sartoris*, by William Faulkner" (1938), in *Literary and Philosophical Essays*, trans. Annette Michelson (London: Rider, 1955), 73–78; Jean-Paul Sartre, "On *The Sound and the Fury*: Time in the Works of Faulkner" (1939), trans. Martine Darmon, in *William Faulkner: Three Decades of Criticism*, ed. Frederick J. Hoffman and Olga W. Vickery (1960; New York: Harbinger, 1963), 87–93; Maurice E. Coindreau, "William Faulkner," *Nouvelle Revue Française* 36 (June 1, 1931): 926–30; Maurice E. Coindreau, "Les principaux Romans de William Faulkner," *Aperçus de Littérature Américaine* (Paris: Gallimard, 1946), 111–46; Jean Pouillon, "Time and Destiny in Faulkner" (1946), in *William Faulkner: Three Decades of Criticism*, ed. Frederick J. Hoffman and Olga W. Vickery (1960; New York: Harbinger, 1963), 79–86; Jean-Jacques Mayoux, "The Creation of the Real in Faulkner" (1952), in *William Faulkner: Three Decades of Criticism*, ed. Frederick J. Hoffman and Olga W. Vickery (1960; New York: Harbinger, 1963), 156–72; Claude-Edmond Magny, "Faulkner or Theological Inversion" (1948), in *William Faulkner: Three Decades of Criticism*, ed. Frederick J. Hoffman and Olga W. Vickery (1960; New York: Harbinger, 1963), 66–78.

30. George Marion O'Donnell, "Faulkner's Mythology" (1939), in *William Faulkner: Three Decades of Criticism*, ed. Frederick J. Hoffman and Olga W. Vickery (1960; New York: Harbinger, 1963), 82–93; Robert Penn Warren, "William Faulkner" (1946), in *William Faulkner: Three Decades of Criticism*, ed. Frederick J. Hoffman and Olga W. Vickery (1960; New York: Harbinger, 1963), 109–24. From Warren we learn that the first families of Yoknapatawpha County "seiz[ed] the land from the Indians" (111) but little more.

31. Malcolm Cowley, introduction to *The Portable Faulkner* (1946), in *William Faulkner: Three Decades of Criticism*, ed. Frederick J. Hoffman and Olga W. Vickery (1960; New York: Harbinger, 1963), 94–109; Irving Howe, *William Faulkner: A Critical Study* (1951), 3rd ed. (Chicago: University of Chicago Press, 1975); Lionel Trilling, *The Liberal Imagination: Essays on Literature and Society* (1950; New York: Charles Scribner's Sons, 1976), 296–300.

32. Lawrence H. Schwartz, *Creating Faulkner's Reputation: The Politics of Modern Literary Criticism* (Knoxville: University of Tennessee Press, 1990). See especially chapters 3 and 4.

33. Here of course we are punning on Morrison's influential account of the "Africanist presence" in American literature, in her *Playing in the Dark: Whiteness and the Literary Imagination* (Cambridge, MA: Harvard University Press, 1990).

34. Robert E. Spiller et al., eds., *Literary History of the United States*, 3 vol. (New York: Macmillan, 1948); Robert Ernest Spiller, *The Cycle of American Literature* (New York: Macmillan, 1955).

35. Frederick Jackson Turner, "The Significance of the Frontier in American History" (1893), in *Annual Report of the American Historical Association for 1893* (Washington, DC: Government Printing Office, 1894), 199–227.

36. D. H. Lawrence, *Studies in Classic American Literature* (1923; New York: Viking, 1970), 36. Hereafter cited parenthetically.

37. For a magisterial intellectual genealogy of the "man who knows Indians" motif, see Richard Slotkin, *Regeneration through Violence: The Mythology of the American Frontier, 1600–1860* (Wesleyan, CT: Wesleyan University Press, 1973).

38. See Henry Nash Smith, *Virgin Land: The American West as Symbol and Myth* (Cambridge, MA: Harvard University Press, 1950); R. W. B. Lewis, *The American Adam*:

XXXVI INTRODUCTION

Innocence, Tragedy, and Tradition in the Nineteenth Century (Chicago: University of Chicago Press, 1955); Leslie Fiedler, *Love and Death in the American Novel* (New York: Criterion, 1960); Leo Marx, *The Machine in the Garden: Technology and the Pastoral Ideal in America* (New York: Oxford University Press, 1964); and Annette Kolodny's *The Lay of the Land: Metaphor as Experience and History in American Life and Letters* (Chapel Hill: University of North Carolina Press, 1975).

39. R. W. B. Lewis, "The Hero in the New World: William Faulkner's 'The Bear'" (1950), in *Faulkner: A Collection of Critical Essays*, ed. Robert Penn Warren (Englewood Cliffs, NJ: Prentice Hall, 1966), 204–18; Ursula Brumm, "Wilderness and Civilization: A Note on William Faulkner" (1950), in *William Faulkner: Three Decades of Criticism*, ed. Frederick J. Hoffman and Olga W. Vickery (1960; New York: Harbinger, 1963), 125–34.

40. Otis B. Wheeler, "Faulkner's Wilderness," *American Literature* 31, no. 2 (May 1959): 127–36.

41. Praising Faulkner for his "artistic conversion of specifically American materials," Lewis goes on to characterize "The Bear" as "a story . . . about the death of the frontier world and its possibility, of the new unspoiled area where a genuine and radical moral freedom—a kind of original innocence—could again be exercised" ("The Hero in the New World," 214, 215); Brumm's Faulkner presents "a genuinely American experience for which Europe has no counterpart: the destruction of the wilderness by civilization in one short, dramatic act taking less than a man's lifetime. . . . [Faulkner's] sorrow about the vanishing of the wilderness is as acute and more articulate than Cooper's, and he comes to a conclusion which to my knowledge no European has ever drawn with such severity" ("Wilderness and Civilization," 130); Wheeler adds that "almost from the first contact with the new world of North America white men have recognized in many ways that theirs is a unique kind of experience with the wilderness" ("Faulkner's Wilderness," 127).

42. For Lewis, Fathers is "foster parent," "tutor," and "spiritual guide" to Ike ("The Hero in the New World," 212); for Brumm, he is "old, illiterate but wise, solitary, kinless, childless, without property, and . . . held . . . in the veneration of an almost extinct species" ("Wilderness and Civilization, 128); for Wheeler, he is "spiritual father" and "priest of a primitive wilderness religion" ("Faulkner's Wilderness," 128). That he is Native, let alone Chickasaw, barely registers. Indeed, doubling down on this cavalier effacement of Indianist presence, Brumm compares Sam to Cooper's Leatherstocking—not to Chingachgook.

43. Scholar Kenneth Lincoln is credited with coining the term "Native American Renaissance" in his 1985 book of the same name (Berkeley: University of California Press, 1985).

44. Roy Harvey Pearce, *Savagism and Civilization: A Study of the Indian and the American Mind* (Baltimore: Johns Hopkins University Press, 1965); Leslie A. Fiedler, *The Return of the Vanishing American* (New York: Stein and Day, 1968); Slotkin, *Regeneration through Violence.*

45. Fiedler, *Return of the Vanishing America*, 7. See 116–17 and 142–45 for more on Faulkner specifically.

46. For full citation information on all of the Faulkner scholarship mentioned in this paragraph, see the further reading section that follows this introduction.

47. Among the seminal works of the New Western History are Donald E. Worster, *Rivers of Empire: Water, Aridity, and the Growth of the American West* (New York: Pantheon, 1985); Patricia Nelson Limerick, *The Legacy of Conquest: The Unbroken Past of the American West* (New York: Norton, 1987); Richard White, *"It's Your Misfortune and None of My Own": A New History of the American West* (Norman: University of

INTRODUCTION   XXXVII

Oklahoma Press, 1991); Patricia Nelson Limerick, Clyde Milner II, and Charles E. Rankin, eds., *Trails: Toward a New Western History* (Lawrence: University Press of Kansas, 1991); and William Cronon, *Nature's Metropolis: Chicago and the Great West* (New York: Norton, 1991). For a key text in the 1980s wave of US ethnic literatures that doubles as a pathbreaking work in the new western history (not to mention border studies and queer theory), see Gloria Anzaldúa, *Borderlands/La Frontera: The New Mestiza* (San Francisco: Aunt Lute Books, 1987).

48. Édouard Glissant, *Faulkner, Mississippi*, trans. Barbara Lewis and Thomas C. Spear (New York: Farrar, Straus and Giroux, 1999), 58.

49. See for instance Trefzer, *Disturbing Indians*, 158, 170–71; Patricia Galloway, "The Construction of Faulkner's Indians," *Faulkner Journal* 18, nos. 1–2 (Fall 2002–Spring 2003): 28; and Bruce G. Johnson, "Indigenous Doom: Colonial Mimicry in Faulkner's Indian Tales," *Faulkner Journal* 18, nos.1–2 (Fall 2002–Spring 2003): 105.

50. For full citations of all of the Faulkner scholarship mentioned in this paragraph, see the further reading section that follows this introduction.

51. Lisa Brooks, "Afterword: At the Gathering Place," in Jace Weaver, Craig S. Womack, and Robert Warrior, *American Indian Literary Nationalism* (Albuquerque: University of New Mexico Press, 2006), 240–41; see also Jace Weaver, "Splitting the Earth: First Utterances and Pluralist Separatism," in Jace Weaver, Craig S. Womack, and Robert Warrior, *American Indian Literary Nationalism* (Albuquerque: University of New Mexico Press, 2006), 28–29.

52. Jodi A. Byrd, *The Transit of Empire: Indigenous Critiques of Colonialism* (Minneapolis: University of Minnesota Press, 2011), 133, 135, 137.

53. Weaver, "Splitting the Earth," 39. See also Phillip Carroll Morgan, *Riding Out the Storm: Nineteenth Century Chickasaw Governors, Their Lives and Intellectual Legacy* (Ada, OK: Chickasaw, 2013), 58.

54. On the concept of tribalography, see LeAnne Howe, "Tribalography: The Power of Native Stories," *Journal of Dramatic Theory and Criticism* (Fall 1999): 117–25; and Howe, "The Story of America: A Tribalography," in *Clearing a Path: Theorizing Native American Studies*, ed. Nancy Shoemaker (New York: Routledge, 2001), 29–48.

55. Weaver, "Speaking the Earth," 58, 66–67.

56. Taylor, *Reconstructing the Native South*, 31.

57. Morgan, *Riding Out the Storm*, 111.

58. The manuscript passage, with Faulkner's excisions, reads as follows:

> "I know what we will find," the first Indian said. ~~His name was Three Basket.~~
> "What we will not find," the second said. ~~His name was Yo-ko-no-pa-taw-fa.~~ Tho [sic] it was noon, the lane was empty, the doors of the houses empty; no cooking smoke rose from the chinked and plastered chimneys.

William Faulkner, "Red Leaves," autograph manuscript, William Faulkner Foundation Collection, 1918–1959, Accession #6074, Box 8, Series IIA, Item 23a, Special Collections, University of Virginia Library, Charlottesville, VA.

59. Theresa M. Towner and James B. Carothers, *Reading Faulkner: Collected Stories* (Jackson: University Press of Mississippi, 2006), 164.

60. Dabney, *The Indians of Yoknapatawpha*, 24.

61. Malcolm Cowley to William Faulkner, August 9, 1945, in Malcolm Cowley, *The Faulkner-Cowley File: Letters and Memories 1944–1962* (1966; New York: Penguin, 1978), 23.

XXXVIII   INTRODUCTION

62. William Faulkner to Malcolm Cowley, August 16, 1945, in Cowley, *The Faulkner-Cowley File*, 25–27. See 27 for a reproduction of the map. Faulkner's claim regarding the boundary line between Choctaw and Chickasaw Nations is factually incorrect. The line was actually around one hundred miles south of Oxford.

63. Charles S. Aiken, "Faulkner's Yoknapatawpha County: A Place in the American South," *Geographical Review* 69, no. 3 (1979): 338.

64. Ironically, Aiken includes state boundary lines in his "corrected" version of the map.

65. In light of the fact that the Chickasaw queen Mohataha will place an "X" as her signature on the deed conferring title to her Yoknapatawpha lands to one of the county's white settlers in *Requiem for a Nun*, the fact that Faulkner indicates "Chickasaw Chief Colbert's Ferry" with an "X" on the Cowley map is nothing if not suggestive. On the far-reaching implications of the Native "X," see Scott Richard Lyons, *X Marks: Native Signatures of Assent* (Minneapolis: University of Minnesota Press, 2011).

66. See also Sean Latham, "An Impossible Resignation: William Faulkner's Post-Colonial Imagination," in *A Companion to William Faulkner*, ed. Richard C. Moreland (Malden, MA: Wiley Blackwell, 2007), 258. Latham suggests that the effect of this cartographic "clustering" may be "to set Jefferson off from a more hostile territory," but it could equally be viewed as the author's way of acknowledging and exposing the disavowal of Indigenous land claims and decentering of Native presence that accompanied colonialism in North America and throughout the hemisphere.

67. Latham, "An Impossible Resignation: William Faulkner's Post-Colonial Imagination," 254.

68. William Faulkner, interview with Jean Stein vanden Heuvel (1955), in *Lion in the Garden: Interviews with William Faulkner, 1926–1962*, ed. James B. Meriwether and Michael Millgate (1968; Lincoln: University of Nebraska Press, 1980), 255. Far more radically than the *Portable* frontispiece, the Cowley map revisits the imperial cartography of the *Absalom* map in a postcolonially inflected spirit of "'rechart[ing] and then occupy[ing]' spaces that have been appropriate by imperial regimes" (Latham, 256; citing Edward Said).

69. William Faulkner to Malcolm Cowley, October 18, 1945, in Cowley, *The Faulkner-Cowley File*, 36.

70. William Faulkner, *The Sound and the Fury* (New York: Vintage International, 1990), 325, 326.

71. As Aude Lalande perceptively observes of this startling move, "The writing—or the rewriting—of the origins invokes the Indians, absent in the first big genealogical novels sketching out the topography of the county, and who, much as in Lafayette County where Faulkner lived, have disappeared upon their entry into the narrative scene of the Yoknapatawpha created over thirty-five years of imaginary sublimation. The founding act of the county reappears at the center of the fiction: the Pontotoc treaty by which the Chickasaw ceded, in 1832, part of their territory, before accepting, one year later, to leave for Oklahoma" ("The Impossibility of Foundation: Native Americans in William Faulkner's Novels," *L'Homme*, 166 [2003], trans. Cadenza Academic Translations, viii).

72. Apparently the section heading was originally to be "The Indians," but Faulkner had second thoughts. On October 31, 1948, he wrote editor Saxe Commins, "I kept on thinking about the table of contents page: something about it nagged at me. I kept on thinking, why *Indians* when we had never said The Country *people* and the Village *people*, but only the *Country* and the *Village*. Then I thought, not *Indians* but *Wilderness*, and then suddenly the whole page stood right, each noun in character and tone and tune with every other. . . . [L]ike this:

INTRODUCTION   XXXIX

> The Country
> The Village
> The Wilderness
> The Wasteland
> The Middle Ground
> Beyond

I believe that's it." See Joseph Blotner, ed., *Selected Letters of William Faulkner* (New York: Random House, 1977), 277.

73. William Faulkner, *Collected Stories* (1950; Random House, 1995), 390. Henceforth cited parenthetically as *CS*.

74. See Joseph Roach, *Cities of the Dead: Circum-Atlantic Performance* (New York: Columbia University Press, 1996), 131–38. During this same period, English settler-colonists wove themselves into similar diplomatic and exchange networks with the Chickasaws as part of a multifaceted effort to check French influence in the southeastern interior while at the same time tapping into the lucrative potential of the Indian slave trade; see Robbie Ethridge, *From Chicaza to Chickasaw: The European Invasions and the Transformation of the Mississippian World, 1540–1715* (Chapel Hill: University of North Carolina Press, 2010), 167–68, 180–85, 192–200, 212–14, 230.

75. As such, we might consider the US political system to be an especially consequential example of what Roach calls circum-Atlantic intercultural performance. The specific question of Iroquois influence on the founders has sparked a lively and often contentious historical debate. See, for instance, Donald A. Grinde Jr., *The Iroquois and the Founding of the American Nation* (San Francisco: Indian Historian, 1977); Bruce E. Johansen, *Forgotten Founders: Benjamin Franklin, the Iroquois, and the Rationale for Revolution* (Ipswich, MA: Harvard Common, 1982); Kirke and Lynn Kickingbird, *Indians and the US Constitution: A Forgotten Legacy* (Washington, DC: Institute for the Development of Indian Law, 1987); Donald A. Grinde Jr. and Bruce E. Johansen, *Exemplar of Liberty: Native America and the Evolution of Democracy* (Los Angeles: American Indian Studies Center, University of California, Los Angeles, 1991); Alvin M. Josephy Jr., *500 Nations: An Illustrated History of North American Indians* (New York: Knopf, 1994); and Bruce E. Johansen, with Donald A. Grinde Jr. and Barbara A. Mann, *Debating Democracy: Native American Legacy of Freedom* (Santa Fe: Clear Light, 1998). For dissenting views, see Philip A. Levy, "Exemplars of Taking Liberties: The Iroquois Influence Thesis and the Problem of Evidence," *William and Mary Quarterly*, 3rd series, 53, no. 3 (July 1996): 588–604; and Samuel B. Payne Jr., "The Iroquois Confederacy, the Articles of Confederation, and the Constitution," *William and Mary Quarterly*, 3rd series, 53, no. 3 (July 1996): 605–20. And for Grinde and Johansen's rebuttal to Levy and Payne, see "Sauce for the Goose: Demand and Definitions for 'Proof' Regarding the Iroquois and Democracy," *William and Mary Quarterly*, 3rd series, 53, no. 3 (July 1996): 621–36.

76. On council governance among the Chickasaws specifically, see John R. Swanton, *Chickasaw Society and Religion* (1928; Lincoln: University of Nebraska Press, 2006), 41–46; James R. Atkinson, *Splendid Land, Splendid People: The Chickasaw Indians to Removal* (Tuscaloosa: University of Alabama Press, 2004), 26–28; and Ethridge, *From Chicaza to Chickasaw*, 201–2.

77. Jared Sexton, "The Vel of Slavery: Tracking the Figure of the Unsovereign," *Critical Sociology* (2014): 1–15. See especially 9–11.

XL INTRODUCTION

FURTHER READING

Bradford, M. E. "Faulkner and the Great White Father." *Louisiana Studies* 3 (Winter 1964): 328–29.

———. "That Other Patriarchy: Observations on 'A Justice.'" *Modern Age* (Summer 1974): 266–71.

Beidler, Peter G. "A Darwinian Source for Faulkner's Indians in 'Red Leaves.'" *Studies in Short Fiction* 10 (1973): 421–23.

Byars-Nichols, Keely. "On Precarious Footing: William Faulkner's Sam Fathers and the Specter of Slavery." In *The Black Indian in American Literature.* New York: Palgrave Macmillan, 2013. 55–72.

Byrd, Jodi. "A Return to the South." *American Quarterly* 66, no. 3 (2014): 609–20.

Cooley, John R. "Sam Fathers and Doom." In *Critical Essays on William Faulkner: The McCaslin Family*, ed. Arthur F. Kinney. Boston: G. K. Hall, 1990. 131–36.

D'Alessandro, Michael. "Childless 'Fathers,' Native Sons: Mississippi Tribal Histories and Performing the Indian in Faulkner's *Go Down, Moses*." *Mississippi Quarterly* (2014): 375–401.

Dabney, Lewis M. *The Indians of Yoknapatawpha: A Study in Literature and History.* Baton Rouge: Louisiana State University Press, 1974.

Doyle, Don H. *Faulkner's County: The Historical Roots of Yoknapatawpha.* Chapel Hill: University of North Carolina Press, 2001.

Erdrich, Louise. "Where I Ought to Be: A Writer's Sense of Place." *New York Times* (July 28, 1985). http://www.nytimes.com/1985/07/28/books/where-i-ought-to-be-a-writer-s-sense-of-place.html?pagewanted=all. Accessed July 19, 2017.

Gage, Duane. "Faulkner's Indians." *American Indian Quarterly* 1, no. 1 (Spring 1974): 27–33.

Galloway, Patricia. "The Construction of Faulkner's Indians." *Faulkner Journal* 18, nos. 1–2 (Fall 2002–Spring 2003): 9–31.

Gidley, Mick. "Sam Fathers's Fathers: Indians and the Idea of Inheritance." In *Critical Essays on William Faulkner: The McCaslin Family*, ed. Arthur F. Kinney. Boston: G. K. Hall, 1990. 121–30.

Glissant, Édouard. *Faulkner, Mississippi.* Trans. Barbara Lewis and Thomas C. Spear. New York: Farrar, Straus and Giroux, 1999.

Godden, Richard. "Reading 'Red Leaves': Mouths, Labor Power, and Revolutions." In *Faulkner and Mystery: Faulkner and Yoknapatawpha, 2009*, ed. Annette Trefzer and Ann J. Abadie. Jackson: University Press of Mississippi, 2014. 49–66.

Honnighausen, Lothar. "Faulkner Rewriting the Indian Removal." In *Rewriting the South: History and Fiction*, ed. Honnighausen and Valeria Gennaro Lerda. Tübingen: Francke, 1993. 335–43.

Horsford, Howard C. "Faulkner's Mostly Unreal Indians in Mississippi History." *American Literature* 64, no. 2 (1992): 311–30.

Howell, Elmo. "The Chickasaw Queen in William Faulkner's Story." *Chronicles of Oklahoma* 49 (1971): 334–39.

———. "President Jackson and William Faulkner's Choctaws." *Chronicles of Oklahoma* 45 (1967): 252–57.

———. "Sam Fathers: A Note on Faulkner's 'A Justice.'" *Tennessee Studies in Literature* 12 (1967): 149–53.

———. "William Faulkner and the Chickasaw Funeral." *American Literature* 36, no. 4 (1965): 523–25.

———. "William Faulkner and the Mississippi Indians." *Georgia Review* 21 (Fall 1967): 386–96.

———. "William Faulkner's Chickasaw Legacy: A Note on 'Red Leaves.'" *Arizona Quarterly* 26 (Winter 1970): 293–303.

Johnson, Bruce G. "Indigenous Doom: Colonial Mimicry in Faulkner's Indian Tales." *Faulkner Journal* 18, nos. 1–2 (Fall 2002–Spring 2003): 101–27.

Kinney, Arthur F. "Faulkner's Other Others." In *Faulkner at 100: Retrospect and Prospect: Faulkner and Yoknapatawpha, 1997*, ed. Donald M. Kartiganer and Ann J. Abadie. Jackson: University Press of Mississippi, 2000. 195–203.

Krefft, James Harvey. "Possible Sources for Faulkner's Indians: Oliver LaFarge's *Laughing Boy*." *Tulane Studies in English* 23 (1978): 187–92.

———. "The Yoknapatawpha Indians: Fact and Fiction." PhD diss., Tulane University, 1976.

Lalande, Aude. "The Impossibility of Foundation: The Indians of William Faulkner." *L'Homme* 166 (2003–2): 31–58.

Langford, Beverly Young. "History and Legend in Faulkner's 'Red Leaves.'" *Notes on Mississippi Writers* 6, no. 1 (1972): 19–24.

Latham, Sean. "An Impossible Resignation: William Faulkner's Post-Colonial Imagination." In *A Companion to William Faulkner*, ed. Richard C. Moreland. Malden, MA: Wiley Blackwell, 2007. 252–68.

LeCoeur, Jo. "William Faulkner's Two-Basket Stories." In *Songs of the Reconstructing South*, ed. Suzanne Disheroon-Green and Lisa Abney. Westport, CT: Greenwood, 2002. 149–57.

Mallios, Peter Lancelot. "Faulkner's Indians, or The Poetics of Cannibalism." *Faulkner Journal* 18, nos. 1–2 (Fall 2002–Spring 2003): 143–78.

Moore, Gene M. "Chronological Problems in Faulkner's 'Wilderness' Stories." *Faulkner Journal* 18.1–2 (Fall 2002–Spring 2003): 51–67.

———. "Introduction: Faulkner's Incorrect 'Indians'?" *Faulkner Journal* 18, nos. 1–2 (Fall 2002–Spring 2003): 3–8.

Morgan, Phillip Carroll. "Blizzards of Coincidence: Cyrus Harris and William Faulkner's Yoknapatawpha County." *Riding Out the Storm: Nineteenth-Century Chickasaw Governors, Their Lives and Intellectual Legacy*. Ada, OK: Chickasaw, 2013. 67–112.

Nigliazzo, Marc A. "Faulkner's Indians." PhD diss., University of New Mexico, 1973.

Parker, Robert. "Red Slippers and Cottonmouth Moccasins: White Anxieties in Faulkner's Indian Stories." *Faulkner Journal* 18, nos. 1–2 (Fall 2002–Spring 2003): 81–99.

Rhodes, Karen. "The Grotesque Economics of Tragicomedy: Cultural Colonization in Faulkner's 'Red Leaves.'" *Faulkner Journal* 18, nos. 1–2 (Fall 2002–Spring 2003): 69–79.

Sayre, Robert Woods. "Faulkner's Indians and the Romantic Vision." *Faulkner Journal* 18, nos. 1–2 (Fall 2002–Spring 2003): 33–49.

Smith, Lindsey Claire. "Legacy of 'Doom' on the Crossroads of William Faulkner's Yoknapatawpha." In *Indians, Environment, and Identity on the Borders of American Literature: From Faulkner and Morrison to Walker and Silko*. New York: Palgrave Macmillan, 2008. 75–107.

Taylor, Melanie Benson. "Reconstructing Loss: Native Americans, Nostalgia, and Tribalography in Southern Literature." In *Reconstructing the Native South: American Indian Literature and the Lost Cause*. Athens: University of Georgia Press, 2011. 26–71.

Trefzer, Annette. "Mimesis and Mimicry: William Faulkner's Postcolonial Yoknapatawpha." In *Disturbing Indians: The Archaeology of Southern Fiction*. Tuscaloosa: University of Alabama Press, 2007. 145–79.

Weaver, Jace, Craig S. Womack, and Robert Warrior. *American Indian Literary Nationalism*. Albuquerque: University of New Mexico Press, 2006.

Winston, Jay S. "Going Native in Yoknapatawpha: Faulkner's Fragmented America and 'The Indian.'" *Faulkner Journal* 18, nos. 1–2 (Fall 2002–Spring 2003): 129–42.

Note on the Conference

The forty-third Faulkner and Yoknapatawpha Conference, sponsored by the University of Mississippi in Oxford, took place Sunday, July 17, through Thursday, July 21, 2016. Eleven presentations on Faulkner and the Native South are chapters in this volume. Brief mention is made here of other conference activities.

The program began on Sunday with a reception at the University Museum for the exhibition *Gods and Men: Iconography and Identity in the Ancient World*. The exhibition took a closer examination of the image of ancient gods, kings, and the common man. The depictions contained a visual language, once easily understood throughout the ancient world. Following the reception, Robbie Ethridge presented "Mr. Faulkner's Indians: A Brief History of the Indians of Mississippi," followed by Melanie Benson Taylor's lecture, "Faulkner's Dialectical Indian: Modernity, Nativity, and Violence in the New South."

Following a buffet supper at Rowan Oak that evening, George "Pat" Patterson, mayor of Oxford, and Lee Cohen, dean of the College of Liberal Arts, welcomed participants, and Ted Atkinson, president of the William Faulkner Society, introduced winners of the 2016 John W. Hunt Scholarships. These fellowships, awarded to graduate students pursuing research on William Faulkner, are funded by the Faulkner Society and the *Faulkner Journal* in memory of John W. Hunt, Faulkner scholar and emeritus professor of literature at Lehigh University. James G. Thomas Jr., the Center for the Study of Southern Culture's associate director for publications, presented the 2016 Eudora Welty Awards in Creative Writing. Annalee Purdie, a student from Jackson Academy, won first place for her short story "A Summer in the Heat," and Kallye Smith, a Magee native who attends Simpson Academy in Mendenhall, won second place for her short story "Monster, Monster." The late Frances Patterson of Tupelo, a longtime member of the Center's advisory committee, established and endowed the awards, which are selected through a competition held in high schools throughout Mississippi. A lecture by LeAnne Howe, "Faulkner Didn't Invent Yoknapatawpha, *Everybody Knows That.*

NOTE ON THE CONFERENCE

So What Other Stories Do Chickasaws and Choctaws Know about Our Homelands?" rounded out the evening.

Monday's program began with Charles A. Peek and Terrell L. Tebbetts leading the first "Teaching Faulkner" session, "Faulkner's Native Aliens: Placed, Misplaced, Displaced," followed by Eric Gary Anderson presenting a lecture titled "Native Southern Transformations, or, *Light in August* and Werewolves." The day's program also included a Brown Bag Lunch Presentation by Maureen S. Meyers; a keynote lecture, "Another Mississippian's Indians: The Missionary Hope, 1886–1909," by Patricia Kay Galloway; and papers on "Yakni Patafa: Faulkner, Land, and Indigenous Critical Perspectives," presented by John Wharton Lowe, Kirstin L. Squint, and Gina Caison.

Tuesday's program included the second "Teaching Faulkner" session, "Faulkner's Native Humor," led by James B. Carothers and Theresa M. Towner. Katherine M. B. Osburn presented a lecture on "'Brother: Is This Truth?': History, Fiction, and Colonialism in Faulkner's Mississippi," which was followed by John Corrigan, Ren Denton, and Theresa M. Towner presenting a progress report on the Digital Yoknapatawpha project at the University of Virginia. That afternoon Annette Trefzer presented a lecture on "Indian Axle-Grease: Re-Imagining Removal," and Angela Jones, Melanie R. Anderson, and Phillip Gordon presented papers on the topic of "Native Soil North: Louise Erdrich's Reconfigurations of Faulknerian Space." A cocktail party at the Oxford Depot completed the day.

Wednesday's program began with the third "Teaching Faulkner" session, "Faulkner in the AP/IB Classroom," led by Brian McDonald. Leslie Walker Bickford, Lin Bin, Robbie Ethridge, and Anne MacMaster then presented papers on the topic of "Tricksters and 'Fathers': Native Figures in Faulkner and US Literature." The morning ended with the lecture "A Chickasaw Homecoming," by Brad Prewitt. Robert W. Hamblin spoke on "William Faulkner and Evans Harrington: A Study in Influence" at the J. D. Williams Library, followed by Jodi A. Byrd's lecture "Souths as Prologues: Indigeneity, Race, and the Temporalities of Land; or, Why I Can't Read William Faulkner" and a panel on "The Mississippi Choctaw Today: Language, Culture, and Contemporary Life," which included presentations by Amanda Bell, John Hendrix, and Fred Willis. A late-afternoon walk through Bailey Woods ended at Rowan Oak, where the annual picnic on the grounds concluded the day's events.

Guided tours of North Mississippi, including Oxford and Lafayette County, the Mississippi Delta, and the Chickasaw homelands around the Tupelo area, took place on Thursday, and the conference ended with a closing party at Square Books. The University Press of Mississippi exhibited Faulkner books published by members of the American Association of University Presses.

The Faulkner and Yoknapatawpha Conference is sponsored by the University of Mississippi Department of English and the Center for the Study of Southern Culture and coordinated by the Division of Outreach and Continuing Studies. The conference planners are grateful to all the individuals and organizations that support the Faulkner and Yoknapatawpha Conference annually. In addition to those mentioned above, we wish to thank the College of Liberal Arts, the Office of the Provost, Square Books, the City of Oxford, and the Oxford Convention and Visitors Bureau.

Faulkner and the Native South
FAULKNER AND YOKNAPATAWPHA

2016

Faulkner Didn't Invent Yoknapatawpha, *Everybody Knows That*

So What Other Stories Do Chickasaws and Choctaws Know about Our Homelands?

LeAnne Howe

Today I begin my talk by giving thanks to the Indigenous people whose land this is. I also want to thank University of Mississippi scholars Jay Watson and Annette Trefzer and all the others responsible for inviting me to the 2016 Faulkner and Yoknapatawpha Conference, "Faulkner and the Native South." It's good to be back in Oxford, Mississippi, where I lived for an academic year as the John and Renee Grisham Writer-in-Residence in 2006–07. It's great to see so many friends gathered together to celebrate Yakni Patafah, Choctaw for "Land That Spreads Out," or "Land That Is Open." As anthropologist Robbie Ethridge has said, "really the word is complex with multiple Indigenous meanings." I'm going to read from some removal poems that I wrote for the journal *Cutthroat*. They're based on one of the Choctaws' darkest moments in history: Removal.

"Upon Leaving the Choctaw Homelands, 1831, The Major Speaks"

> AFTER DEPARTURE, TICKET IS NON REFUNDABLE
> NO SHOW MEANS NO REFUND, FORFEITURE
> PENALTIES AND CANCELATIONS APPLY AT WILL
> CHANGES SUBJECT TO FINES—AND
> DEATH

"Nakfi, Brother, As He Helps Sister Load the Cart"

Our leaving will be sung in every church pew like a hymn.

"Intek, Sister, As She Helps Brother Pack"

Our leaving will be sung by every President, every Supreme Court Justice, every hang-around-the-fort lawyer, every cavalry officer, every merchant, every Wall Street nymph, every thief among thieves, every hazardous waste CEO, every medical waste CEO, every stockholder of the new wasted lands, every rat that shimmied off the ships from Spain, Italy, France, Alsace, Germany, Norway, Denmark, Sweden, every pox that crawled off English blankets and onto our hands.

Our homelands will sing a heart song of sorrow,
And sing,
And sing,
And sing,
She is singing still.

"Ishki, Mother, Looks Homeward"

(Pause.)

They moved into our log cabin yesterday.

Yelping like young puppies at play, they tore down the center pole of our Chief's dance ground, the one with the gar carved atop. Burned it for firewood. Joyous barking. But we could hear the gar roiling in the flames, close to the surface as if he were still in Atchafalaya. Gar, he moves slowly except when striking at prey. Now he soars high on a draft of air carried on wings of cedar ash.

Heading west.

"Intek, Sister, Fingers Her White Apron"

Brother, before you strap the burden basket to *Naholla's*° cart, who will we become now that we are leaving *Yakni Achukma?*°°

°*Naholla is "stingy" in Choctaw. It's a word reference for "white people."*
°°*Yakni Achukma is "good land" in Choctaw.*

"Chukchu Imoshi, Maple Tree Uncle, Helps Brother and Sister"

Some may say we are a people who left our mother, our homelands, for a linen promise. But I like it that even though we leave, the habits of our diligence on the land will remain private. Anonymous. Hidden to foreigners. *Hatak okla hut okchaya bilia hoh-illi bila. We are ever living, ever dying, ever alive.*

Yummak osh alhpesa, that is it.

"Intek, Sister, Runs to Catch Up"

But how long wills the connection between land and people, in which direction will we look to imagine our past? Our future?

"Ishki, Mother, One Step Ahead"

See Hilo-hah, Thunder,
See Malla-tha, Lightning,
We will be as they,
Our season will return
And return,
And return,
Is returning still.

All sing.
Hatak okla hut okchaya bilia hoh-illi bila.

Faulkner didn't invent Yoknapatawpha, everybody knows that. Truly they do. Here I refer you to Phillip Carroll Morgan's insightful chapter "Buzzards of Coincidence: Cyrus Harris and William Faulkner's Yoknapatawpha County" in *Riding Out the Storm: 19th Century Chickasaw Governors, Their Lives and Intellectual Legacy* (2013). Morgan (Choctaw-Chickasaw) nicely details how Faulkner took the Chickasaw place name of a home he and his ancestors were familiar with and used it in his fiction. Yes, Faulkner lied when he said he made up the word, but I understand why. Knowing what a litigious bunch the Choctaws *and* Chickasaws are, Faulkner didn't want his literary estate sued for libel.

So What Other Stories Do Chickasaws and Choctaws Know about Our Homelands?

The Choctaws and Chickasaws know about being refugees from Yakni Patafah, land that spreads out;

The Choctaws and Chickasaws know about genocide, starvation, dying from diseases from leaving Yakni Patafah, land that is open;

But the most important story Choctaws and Chickasaws, and other tribes of the Southeast know about Yakni Patafah, land that is split, furrowed, is how to offer refuge to the tired, hungry foreigners who've been coming to our homelands for the last three hundred years.

I should acknowledge that I know the title of my talk is perverse. Mainstream people in the United States seem to know next to nothing about the histories of the Choctaw and Chickasaw Nations, where we come from (Mississippi), or where our tribes are located today. This peculiar symptom gripping the entire population of the United States is called "willful amnesia." Sadly, there's no cure.

Yet so much has changed since I began writing. I have a community of writers and scholars that I imagine I'm writing to whether it's fiction or scholarship: Eric Gary Anderson, Jodi Byrd, Annette Trefzer, Robbie Ethridge, Kirstin Squint, John Wharton Lowe, Patricia K. Galloway, and all the rest of you, it feels good to be in the company of so many friends and colleagues and people working diligently to teach our tribes' rich and diverse histories even if we still have so much willful amnesia amongst us. Although lately people at my lectures sometimes ask me if I get monthly checks from Indian casinos—revealing that they do know about Indian gaming.

True Stories

On July 5, 2016, I was visiting the Eastern Band of Cherokee Indians in North Carolina at the tribal complex. I was co-producing a new documentary film, *Searching for Sequoyah*, and part of the story is told by members of the Eastern Band of Cherokees in North Carolina and members of the Cherokee Nation in Tahlequah, Oklahoma. We're following Sequoyah's journey to Mexico and to the Wichita Mountains. I'd just spoken to the tribal council about the documentary project and was in the waiting room of the tribal headquarters filling out paperwork for the request to film on the Qualla Boundary.

A woman about my age walked into the tribe's reception office and said she wanted to see the chief. She said she needed money and told the tribe's receptionist that while she didn't look Indian, she was. She said she was Cherokee. She again asked to see the chief or someone who could help her. I looked down at my fingers, thinking to put them in my mouth. This wasn't my tribe or my business. The woman continued to plead for help. She kept repeating that she didn't look Cherokee, but her mother did: "My mama was always ashamed of being Cherokee; that's why I don't know my own culture. My mama was afraid people would know she was Indian."

The tribe's receptionist finally had had enough. "That is offensive, ma'am," she said. "What about the people who couldn't pass for white? You're insulting everyone here."

"I know," said the woman, "I'm an ignorant. I don't mean anything by it; I'm just explaining why I'm here asking for help. Please help me?"

The Cherokees also know a lot about offering refuge to the tired, the hungry, and the poor, disparate peoples that have landed on their doorstep these past three hundred years. As a result, the tribal receptionist for the Eastern Band of Cherokee Indians told the woman to take a seat, and she would contact someone who *might* help her. Later that afternoon, I was told this kind of thing happens every day, fifty-two weeks a year.

This story is emblematic of what white people expect from Southeastern Indians. Tribal people must give land, give money, and give refuge.

I ask you to imagine that today a foreigner, a Frenchman, comes to the Mississippi State House in Jackson and asks to see the governor. The Frenchman says he's hungry and that he needs food and shelter, and to please give him some free land. While this is a bit absurd, in a way, that's exactly what happens to the Choctaws. Beginning as early as 1699, the French, under the direction of Pierre Le Moyne d'Iberville, then later his brother Jean Baptiste Bienville, began to settle in the Lower Mississippi Valley. French colonists, the majority of whom had no experience as farmers, were unable to feed themselves and nearly starved in the early years of the French colony. Hurricanes destroyed the new settlements in 1722 and 1723. But hurricanes are only a part of weather-related disasters. New Orleans was always going to be a site of great danger in terms of the weather and weather-related diseases because rivers flood and replenish the soils, nourish the lands. Yet as we all know these floods are a violent weather-related event. Witness Katrina in 2005.

Bienville's decision to place the capital of French Louisiana near the mouth of the Mississippi River reflected his calculation of the river's economic promise for the city of New Orleans and his hubris. As historian Ari Kelman has stated, "He saw only a magnificent system of watery roads, a tapestry of commercial empire woven from the strands of the river system's watercourses. Bienville read the geography of the Mississippi Valley as surely as we might read a map, and he saw the unmistakable imprint of divine providence. Viewing God and what he called 'Nature' as parts of a whole, Bienville perceived the river as a gift, a treasure map carved into the continent."[1]

A year after its establishment, spring floods delayed work on the construction of the city, and Bienville was forced to build a new fort in Biloxi, Mississippi, instead. Historian Leslie Harris has stated in her

8 LeAnne Howe

2010 essay, "SubAltern City, Subaltern Citizens: New Orleans, Urban Identity, and People of African Descent," that by 1722 there were 5,400 foreigners, or non-Indians, living in New Orleans.[2] More important to the story I'm telling is that the Choctaws could no longer provide food to the French since our tribe was at war with the Chickasaws. Here I want to pause, take a breath, and linger over the possible causes of the war between the Choctaws and the Chickasaws.

Bienville writes in August 1723,

> The things that are opposed to my proposal are the general sickness, the want of provisions since we are without bread and meat, and a very small number of troops, all great obstacles to such an enterprise, but the welfare of the colony, and the honor of the nation are too dear to me, *not* to surmount them.[3]

The background for this letter is that the Tunica have killed three Natchez, although "they are allied," he writes. Bienville believes the Tunica did it because the French told them to, which may or may not be correct. The Natchez that were killed were relatives of the Tattooed Serpent, a well-known Natchez leader in 1723. Bienville argues that the French should go and wipe out the Natchez before they kill all the Frenchmen in the area. Farther down in the letter, Bienville says that due to the rains, flooding, and rotting wood of the forts and houses, the French are having a hard time of it. In fact, he repeats it again and again in much of the correspondence of 1718–1723.

Later on, Bienville writes from New Orleans about his own illness:

> It was known to everybody that I was at the time on the brink of death and that on the ninth the surgeons went and found the Reverend Father Bruno to notify him to come and confess me since I was already in the throes of death, and I received the last sacrament on the next day.[4]

The French are sick and dying from all kinds of illnesses as a result of hurricane season. Throughout this period, two of the subjects that return again and again are the weather and the fact that the tribes are raiding each other's villages for provisions. Food. Choctaws, Chickasaws, Natchez, Tunicas, even a band of Wichitas some fifteen leagues upriver—and tribal men were stealing cattle and horses of the French. I suggest when these documents are read through the lens of the weather-related events during this chaotic time, 1718–1723, a bigger story emerges about the effects of the weather on Southeast Indians. How were the tribes' medicine people reading the weather signs? Here I must quote one of William Faulkner's most famous lines: "The past is

Faulkner Didn't Invent Yoknapatawpha, *Everybody Knows That* 9

never dead. It's not even past."[5] To understand the warfare and historic events during 1718–1723 in the Lower Mississippi Valley, we must consider tribal practices in the twentieth century.

One of our more brilliant Choctaw chiefs, Ben Dwight, was born near Mayhew, Indian Territory, on November 24, 1890. He was the son of Simon Timothy Dwight, a Choctaw, and Mary Jane Hunter. Ben's father, supervisor of Public Instruction for the Choctaws, instilled in his son the need for an education. Ben Dwight had a better Western education than any of the chiefs before him. He attended Jones Academy, Armstrong Academy, and Caddo Public Schools and graduated with honors from Honey Grove, Texas High School in 1908. He received a Bachelor of Arts degree from Columbia University in 1913. His postgraduate work was completed at the University of Michigan and the University of Oklahoma. Dwight continued his education, earning a law degree from Stanford University.

Ben Dwight was the first chief of the Choctaw Nation to be appointed by the president of the United States and then elected by the Choctaw Nation. During his tenure, he represented the tribe in Washington DC on many occasions. Like two Choctaws before him, Peter Pitchlynn and the first Indian lawyer in the United States, James McDonald (Choctaw), Dwight's two main concerns were to protect the property rights of the Choctaws and to ensure that the federal Indian policies would alleviate the social welfare on our people. After his term as chief concluded, Dwight became an attorney for the Choctaw Nation. In 1942 he was selected as administrative assistant to then-governor Robert S. Kerr. When Kerr was elected United States senator, former chief Ben Dwight went to Washington, DC with him. Again, like principal chief Peter Pitchlynn a century before him, Dwight remained in Washington. It's clear by studying the careers of Chiefs Peter Pitchlynn, Ben Dwight, and the *fani miko* James McDonald that our leaders kept our friends close but our enemies in DC closer.

You may be asking how the story of Choctaw chief Ben Dwight connects to the weather patterns in the 1700s. In 1950 Ben Dwight began writing a series of letters asking other tribal nation leaders about how they predicted the weather. The questions he asked not only show that tribes had Indigenous knowledge about long-term weather processes, but they show intertribal relationships between Indigenous peoples sharing what they know: observations about the weather made over long periods of time, perhaps eons. Here I want to stress that this Choctaw strategy concerning weather predictions is a window on the eighteenth-century worlds in which the Choctaws and Chickasaws were living. Not only did the weather impact their ability to feed themselves, but it perhaps adversely affected their intertribal trading relationships, leading to war. The weather patterns in the early 1700s may have been a long-term process that our medicine leaders had been concerned with since the coming of the Europeans. If we don't look for these patterns in the historic record, we may miss a larger story at work between the Choctaw and Chickasaw Tribes. Our two tribes hadn't been at war with each other for eons. In fact, our stories tell us something different and more profound: we are peoples that are intimately connected through kinship through the eons, not warfare.

Ben Dwight writes that he and Kerr had a "high regard for the old Indian ways of determining such things—because they are practical and have always been able to make some accurate predictions."[6] This sentence suggests that Choctaws had always had medicine people to predict the weather patterns based on long-term scientific observations.

Roly Canard, principal chief of the Creek Nation in Oklahoma, wrote back in 1951, "When lots of spider webs are in the air and on lots of trees such as we now see, means we will have a hard cold winter."[7] Letters from other tribal communities indicated that it would be a hard winter as well. The Chippewa Tribe in Cass Lake, Minnesota, said that "if the muskrat or beaver built an unusually high and large house the winter will be severe."[8] The Pima-Maricopa Council in Scottsdale, Arizona, reported that a wandering Gila monster was found in town, a sign of a long and very cold winter. The Navajo tribal council in Window Rock, Arizona, reported in 1951 that many signs, including the food-gathering behavior of small animals; the color and thickness of fur; insect behavior; the disappearance of bees, rabbits, birds, and eagles, were used to determine the weather. One of the old-timers of the Pottawatomie said he could no longer give good weather predictions since the atomic tests. "I believe," he said, "that the chemicals have interfered with the air and clouds, the clouds I used to see are no longer in the skies, it must be the atomic experiments have bothered them because I can't give you a good prediction."[9]

Oklahoma geographer Randy Peppler notes, "It is clear that one of Kerr's primary interests was harnessing the water resources of Oklahoma for the economic good of the state. And he was keenly inquisitive about the natural world as reflected in his rural upbringing and his own writings; as such, he may have sought information on the Indian weather forecasts simply because he was fascinated by what the forecasts offered and how they were informed."[10] Having Dwight, a respected former tribal chief, vouchsafe for Kerr amongst Indians was smart for obtaining weather advice. Kerr was also interested in harnessing the weather as a "strategy" for protecting Oklahoma farmers and ranchers. Kerr and Dwight's report is an example of "Indigeneity" in practice. They hoped to rely on Indigenous people to help farmers and ranchers in the 1950s and in the foreseeable future. It is hard to imagine the current US administration asking American Indians about Indigenous weather predictions. The twentieth-century story I just related is a window into practices of the Choctaws in the 1700s. Choctaws were very prescient about the weather, which helped them survive hurricanes, floods and other forces of nature.

Choctaws have used core narratives as a survival strategy over millennia. Faulkner was also driven by Native stories, and they enlivened his imagination, although his Native characters are mere stereotypes. In my own work, I'm motivated by Choctawan histories, by our core beliefs such as "giving refuge" and by Chief Ben Dwight's work on weather predictions that would help all farmers, Choctaw and non-Choctaw, working the land.

I'm also compelled to tell stories that have become a part of my life. For example, I've lived in Jordan off and on over the past twenty years, and my current novel, *Memoir of a Choctaw in the Arab Revolts*, is set in Bilaad Ash Sham (geographical Syria), or Sham, and in Allen, Oklahoma, a border town between the Choctaw and Chickasaw Nations. As my Middle East research continues, I've learned that weather patterns affected both the Arab Revolt in 1917 and the Arab Spring in 2011. Quoting from a 2013 article in *Smithsonian* magazine by Joshua Hammer:

> In Syria, a devastating drought beginning in 2006 forced many farmers to abandon their fields and migrate to urban centers. There's some evidence that the migration fueled the civil war there, in which eighty thousand people had died by 2013. "You had a lot of angry, unemployed men helping to trigger a revolution," says Aaron Wolf, a water management expert at Oregon State University, who frequently visits the Middle East.[11]

Hammer writes that history might suggest a way to solve conflicts. He says, "The world's first international water treaty, a cuneiform tablet now hanging in the Louvre, ended the war between Lagash and Umma."[12] The treaty is forty-five hundred years old.

Part of this research on drought in the Middle East will end up in my novel. As for Bienville and the eighteenth-century French in the Lower Mississippi Valley, who knows what the Choctaws told him about the weather predictions that he either ignored as foolish Native savagery or kept tucked away in the back of his mind. After all, what could savages teach the erudite French, or so they may have thought at the time.

I'll close with a few short excerpts from my new novel.

"The Weather Five Years Ago"

A sand storm last night, yesterday, from the Arabian Desert so fierce it left mountains of dust in the city, on everything, even in the air we breathe. My apartment—the floors, covered in a fine red powder. Very scary, the squall came across the city of Amman like a red hand from Allah. God is Red, after all. Vine Deloria Jr. would be proud.

"Camel Trek, 1993, Southern Jordan"

Does he have fleas? Is it nerves? Or does he really have fleas?

Ten minutes into a freaking heavy rain shower in the Naqub desert in southern Jordan, numerous waterfalls begin to roar over the sandstone mountaintops and into the aqueducts the Nabataeans made before Cleopatra's reign in Egypt. After 2,000 years the cisterns still hold water. It's the damnedest thing.

Does he have fleas? Is it nerves? Or does he really have fleas?

My camel refuses to say, but he stops, then heads toward the cistern. He must be remembering a thousand treks, his ancestors, the taste of rain. Now I understand his attack of nerves. A bath.

"Joy Ride, Midnight of the Cooling Winds, Amman 2010"

Above, the elongated Milky Way, stars like shingles deck the horizon, good weather, 87 degrees. Driving through the streets of Amman at midnight, winds cool my face, sunburned by the desert sky. I stop and traipse in and out of small shops, open until dawn. One on every block. A guy selling water and nuts. Another juices and colas. Still another has dates from Iraq and baklava, a Lebanese delicacy of honey, pistachios, the thinnest of filo dough. Small pharmacies dot the neighborhood hills, easy walking distances for *Sitt* and *Jiddo*. Shops are attached to the houses and remind me of the streets in West Ada, Oklahoma. As a kid, I would walk with Granny to the local shops searching for vegetables that she could not grow in her garden. What did we trade for, I don't recall now. But tonight, I find Queen Noor Street, and King Talal Street, and Trader Vics, the bar in the Regency Hotel. Trader Vics doesn't sell vegetables at midnight. Not ever. What am I looking for?

Joy riding home, I see my grandparents standing under a lamppost on Al WiFaq Street. What are they doing out so late? Both long dead, then suddenly alive on Harmony Street in Amman, and I know I don't understand the pull of

Bilaad ash sham, but my life here, yes. That it plays out in two places at once, that the climate marks me with small details of the weather five years ago. Yes.

"What Images Live On?"

A March rainstorm is the image I carry of my life in Jordan. I'm shopping at the corner market one block from my apartment in Amman. It's 2011 and hasn't rained for nearly a year. Then suddenly the clouds open and sheets of raindrops the size of silver dollars fall on the dusty streets. Mr. Farhan, the green grocer, is the first to dart outside followed by his customers, their families, even a truck driver delivering oranges. Like giggling children, we hold our hands up to catch the rain. Others chant *alhamdulillah* and weep openly. So do I. The downpour continues for almost an hour. Later, dripping wet, we return inside to shop for zucchini, potatoes, and onions. The cash register remains open·just as Mr. Farhan left it. Jordanian dinars and coins are tossed across the top of the drawer in haste. No one cares about money when you can drink the rain.

Early in 1992 I took my first trip to Jordan and Israel, and the experience marked me in ways I'm still ferreting out, from the major floods I lived through in southern Jordan in 1993 to the ongoing drought in 2011. I was a Fulbright scholar at the University of Jordan in 2010–11. One memory that stands out concerns a class I was teaching on American Indian literatures and climate change. I was explaining that in the 1830s, Southeastern tribes were being removed by the thousands to Indian Territory and that they, too, were experiencing climate changes. In my lecture I was soft-pedaling today's climate change when a Jordanian graduate student auditing the class finally raised his hand. He said, "Professor, we know about global warming. Look around. We live in the desert and our country is full of refugees. Thousands of Syrians are crossing our borders daily to escape being killed. There is no water in Jordan. Unless we manage rainfall, we will all die." The student was from the tribe of Beni Ḥassān, one of the larger tribes in Jordan. He was well spoken and polite but troubled. Many Beni Ḥassān clans still depend on grasslands for raising sheep. The drought had wiped out much of the open grasslands and the sheep were dying. The price of a single sheep had more than doubled in 2011.

I carry hundreds of memories of Jordan. I can say without hesitancy that in some ways when I return to Jordan, I always feel at home, although it isn't "home." Perhaps the reason is that Jordan is a nation of tribes and immigrants. In that respect, Jordan is much like Oklahoma, my homeland. I am a woman of Yakni Patafah—land that spreads out, splits open, becomes furrowed in order to cultivate new growth.

Hatak okla hut okchaya bilia hoh-illi bila. We are ever living, ever dying, ever alive.

NOTES

1. Ari Kelman, *A River and Its City: The Nature of Landscape in New Orleans* (Berkeley: University of California Press, 2003), 4.

2. Leslie Harris, "Subaltern City, Subaltern Citizens: New Orleans, Urban Identity, and People of African Descent," in *Subaltern Citizens and Their Histories: Investigations from India and the USA*, ed. Gyanendra Pandey (New York: Routledge, 2010), 111.

3. Quoted in *Mississippi Provincial Archives: French Dominion*, vol. 3, *1704–1743*, ed. Dunbar Rowland and A. G. Sanders (Jackson: Press of the Mississippi Department of Archives and History, 1927–1984), 361.

4. Ibid., 369.

5. William Faulkner, *Requiem for a Nun* (1951; repr., New York: Vintage, 1975), 80.

6. Randy A. Peppler, "'Old Indian Ways' of Predicting the Weather: Senator Robert S. Kerr and the Winter Predictions of 1950–51 and 1951–52," *Weather Climate and Society* 2, no. 3 (2010): 200.

7. Ibid., 201–2.

8. Ibid., 202.

9. Ibid.

10. Ibid., 207.

11. Joshua Hammer, "Is a Lack of Water to Blame for the Conflict in Syria?" *Smithsonian Magazine*, June 2013, http://www.smithsonianmag.com/innovation/is-a-lack-of-water-to-blame-for-the-conflict-in-syria-72513729/#PEctY6Y06GgpAVhJ.99.

12. Ibid.

Souths as Prologues: Indigeneity, Race, and the Temporalities of Land; or, Why I Can't Read William Faulkner

JODI A. BYRD

As excited as I was to be in Oxford, Mississippi, for the "Faulkner and the Native South" conference, to hear the 2016 conference papers and keynotes, and to share in the collective thinking-through of the meanings of Southeastern Indian presences and absences within the archives that have conditioned our understandings of race and colonialism in this country, I found myself at moments apprehensive and perhaps even a bit uneasy given the ongoing state-sanctioned violence that has permeated our society and rendered black lives less livable than other lives in this nation. And if I were honest, I was then and remain now somewhat disconcerted by the implications of what it might mean to think of Native Souths at a moment when nativism in this country aligns with white supremacy and US empire doubles down on regressive racism, spectacular gun violence, and the rife xenophobia of building walls and casting-outs. This is not to say I am not grateful to have had time and space to focus on the centrality of Chickasaw and Choctaw presences in the lands that nurtured us into being for thousands of years, and, at times, the 2016 conference also had the cast and hue of an old-home week, not least because of the opportunity to reconnect with my former colleague, LeAnne Howe, after the recent dispersal of Indigenous faculty from American Indian studies at the University of Illinois. There are lessons in removals and returns, and Howe's work, knowledge, and stories (I might have meant to write directives to be precise) have always reminded me of the deeply rooted relationalities that tie Chickasaws and Choctaws to ourselves and to our lands through time, through leaving and through coming back home again and again.

Setting foot in Mississippi for the first time in my life, then, has been akin to a kind of nostalgic homecoming for me, albeit one that has had more than its fair share of ambivalences. Driving through southern

Illinois into Arkansas with stops in Memphis before pushing farther south into Mississippi is a road-tripping experience inflected by the scales of injustice and precariousness to which we have all become conditioned. Though I have the privilege of my mixed-blooded Chickasaw and white ancestries to move freely through the world in ways more unmarked than the black, brown, and Native men made hypervisible in the profiling of police surveillance, I am always deeply cognizant of possibilities for violence that might emerge from the unexpected encounter should one of my taillights fail or should I stop to use the wrong bathroom along the way. As a precaution, I had my car in the shop before I left to make sure everything mechanical was in working order, I drove down in a long-sleeved shirt to hide my Southeastern Ceremonial Complex–inspired tattoos, and I considered investing in an entire new wardrobe to ensure my gender performance aligned properly with my biology in magical-thinking gestures of hypervigilance that such foresight might alchemically stave off unpleasant or worse confrontation.

Such preparations, though, could not fully address the underlying sense of temporal disjointedness that was really the source of my disquiet about journeying to Oxford for a Faulkner conference, perhaps because, deeply engrained in my psyche, are the violences of Removal, however much they are also couched and softened through the privileges of class and race that mark my genealogy. I have always been aware of the erasures that have accompanied the loss of lands for my Chickasaw relatives and ancestors in Mississippi no matter how much time has passed and no matter how successful we have been as a Nation in recent years at reasserting our presence through reclamation, rebuilding, and self-fashioning. At some level, I think I half-expected some epic dark-matter implosion to occur the moment I set foot in Mississippi to disrupt the space/time continuum. Or if not that, then at least some slight cosmic breeze to acknowledge what to me felt illicit or unsanctioned about the crossing of state lines into the heart of pre-Removal Chickasaw territory as a small fanfare of return. To be of and from a place so deeply and to have no claim or presence in the temporality of the here and now should have some consequence. Alas, and despite my addiction to *Doctor Who*, *Star Trek*, and videogames, including *BioShock Infinite*, there was nothing that ripped apart the boundaries of space and time to lay bare the multiple realities layered into the place toward any kind of righteousness. Turns out, only a couple unexpected rainstorms greeted me instead, so, where reality might have failed imagination, what I found instead was a deeper sense of justice as I remembered that the land itself bears the acknowledgment of Chickasaw history and presence. There in the dirt, the mounds, the rivers, and the trees and lakes, at least, the land

Indigeneity, Race, and the Temporalities of Land

retains the signs of its own remembrances, its own significances, and its own burdens, including the names of places along the way: Marshall and DeSoto Counties, Hernando, and of course, Love's Travel Stops.

In preparing for the keynote over the months leading up to the midsummer conference, as perhaps is becoming evident, I was surprised by the ways I was confronted with the various stages of what I can only describe as grief: from the denial of procrastination that the conference was closing in after the imperial pomp of the Fourth of July, to bargaining just to find ways to break the summer hiatus and push myself to grapple with the southerly formations of racism and colonialism that are so horrifically manifest in our current socially remediated digital and political lives. I even had moments of despairing as I found myself stymied by a deep sense of lack in the face of the expectation that I find something cogent to say about William Faulkner, an author I have read only reticently and sparingly, and even then, primarily as a high school student staging performances of "A Rose for Emily" or struggling to make sense of "The Bear." I found I much preferred Austen, the Brontës, and Dickens to Faulkner's southern tales, and while a love of the wordy and the literary propelled me to graduate school, it also pointed me to train first as a British Victorianist and then as a twentieth-century postcolonial theorist. By design, I managed to avoid almost all of American literature. And with good reason—I much preferred my empire distant, my racism stiff upper lipped, and perhaps I retained some of my ancestral proclivities for Anglophilia that signaled I descended from a group of people who today insist we remain unconquered and unconquerable despite all the expulsions, removals, and dispossessions that followed us from our homelands in northern Mississippi to Indian Territory.

Though I obtained my degree in literature, my career has taken me into the interdisciplinary terrains of political science and, more recently, technology studies. As a result of those disciplinary shifts, I struggled in the writing of this chapter with the insidious suspicion that I lack the disciplinary background to tackle Faulkner and do him justice. That, somehow, anthropology and history would be more adept and appropriate fields—or perhaps even better, archaeology and linguistics—to mine the depths of layered significances to reveal the phonemes and sediments of truth and stereotype embedded in his narratives. Disciplines more connected to the social end of the humanities and sciences rather than the literary or the digital. What could an Indigenous studies scholar of the contemporary now, a Chickasaw intellectual whom some might characterize as a presentist cultural and political theorist, really have to offer to this conversation in search of authentic Native Souths to counter the ellipses and elisions of Faulkner's crumbling facades haunted by curses, the decomposing dead, and, as Eric Gary Anderson ably demonstrates in these pages, werewolves? God, can I just say how much I wish I had sent an abstract promising werewolves or at least a zombie or two?

Here again was LeAnne reminding me that Faulkner is not about anthropology, and reading him is not a matter of replacing apocryphal Indians with the real through cultural performances and authentic embodiments. Tribe, she said, means family, *iksa*, and clan—and family, she reminded me, is where one always starts. As it turns out, family has a rich and deeply vexed connection within Faulkner's storied landscapes—and I love that Patricia Galloway begins her *Faulkner Journal* essay on Faulkner's Indians with the observation that "everyone with a Mississippi background has a Faulkner story."[1] With no small amount of irony, it is through Faulkner that there is some occasion to sift through remembrances to qualify and quantify Indigenous kinship and belonging in these lands despite the longevity of our own persistence and continuance of knowledge about the place. I tend to think of Faulkner as one of the greatest gossips in American literature—not a fan, remember—and apprehending the kernel of the real in his stories requires a nuanced patterning of readings attuned to the many Souths that exist simultaneously in the lands that are now named Mississippi. As readers of this collection know better than me, his work grapples with the unspokens of family secrets, the undercurrents of racial impurities, and the uneasinesses of never quite having a—or being at—home. There is in Faulkner a deeply ambivalent push-pull within the dialectics of love and hate for the South and its histories and identities that are marked by brutal and intimate violence. Stalled in the past as it bends toward the present, Faulkner's characters, their lives, and their relations hover between possession and dispossession, and the moral quandaries they ponder center on the processes of violent inclusion and exclusion that produced whiteness and blackness as the ontological consequences of slavery and conquest in the South.

Narrating his fictive Yoknapatawpha County into being alongside his imagined and displaced Chickasaws, Faulkner himself not only recognizes the centrality of the Native South to his work but in fact requires our prior presence to locate his own authority to write convincingly and compellingly about the place. When once asked a question about where he got his representational authority and knowledge to write about the Chickasaws, Faulkner notoriously responded, "There are records there, but I never did much research. I would—I probably got my information about Indians as I've got it about most of the other things I know, from listening to people and adding a little imagination to it. I suspect that—that no Chickasaw would recognize my Chickasaws, but people that do know more about Mississippi's history don't quarrel too much with my picture of Chickasaw Indians. And also, I have known some of their descendants."[2] From my side, I suspect much could still be written about settler and masculinist mastery that never needs much research to convey the truth, and the taken-for-grantedness of the authority of the author's imagination to fill in the gaps is the privilege of never having to actually research it.

Whether I recognize Faulkner's Chickasaws, at least some of his readers have insisted on his figurations of Indians as symbolically useful and have argued that his imaginative prowess provides insights into southern pasts and presents as prologue for US anxieties about whiteness, blackness, and the quotidian violences of slavery and colonialism. Echoing a long list of scholars who have critiqued Faulkner's representation of Chickasaws and Choctaws—many of whom gave keynotes at the 2016 conference—it seems to me that the antediluvian, stoic, and simple inhabitants of the wilderness that Faulkner imagines as hapless targets for fraud and abuse by white settlers might, simply, be a manifestation of what Geonpul Australian Aboriginal scholar Aileen Moreton-Robinson has discussed as the ontological basis for white patriarchal possessiveness in Canada, the United States, Australia, and New Zealand. "The regulatory mechanisms of these nation-states," Moreton-Robinson writes, "are extremely busy reaffirming and reproducing this possessiveness through a process of perpetual Indigenous dispossession, ranging from the refusal of Indigenous sovereignty to overregulated piecemeal concessions."[3] Erasure and inclusion function as dialectically balanced processes through which Indigenous presences, knowledges, epistemologies, and relationalities continue to be overwritten and undermined to further settler colonial occupation of indigenous lands. That Faulkner's work denies Chickasaw sovereignty while requiring Chickasaw presence helped codify certain ideas about whiteness and property in the South. For Moreton-Robinson, the process of settler colonialism produced the conditions through which "a new white property-owning subject emerged and became embedded in everyday discourse as 'a firm belief that the best in life was the expansion of self through property and property began and ended with possession of one's body.'"[4] Whiteness, in other words, acquired its possessive and ontological power through relationship with the original peoples of the lands and those forced into labor upon it, producing race and Indigeneity as signs of difference to mark and affirm the supremacy of dominance afforded to those who identified themselves as the ruling elite. Within such a system, Indigenous peoples must not only be dispossessed of their lands to provide the expansive rationale for participatory democracy as the best articulation of egalitarianism, but they must be evoked and acknowledged as the proprietary source-code for belonging insofar as that belonging can then be transferred to whites exclusively.

If there might be anything for me to recognize in Faulkner's Mississippi and his Chickasaws, then, it is perhaps exactly the degree to which his work ruminates on the tense and fragile binds that link families, bodies, and lands into the possessive logics of white subjectivity confronted by the horror and tragedy of colonialism, slavery, and racialization that produced the South as ruined from the start. These things have lately been on my mind in part because of rising concerns that Indigenous studies and settler colonial studies as fields are both imbricated in an intellectual antiblackness. In a recent essay, African American studies scholar Jared Sexton asserts that the failure of Indigenous studies has been its insistence on land, sovereignty, identity, self, resistance, and resurgence. His concern is that scholars in the field circulate elements that "draw from and contribute to the discourse of post-racialism by diminishing or denying the significance of race in thinking about the relative structural positions of black and nonblack populations, not in order to assert the colorblind justice of American or Canadian society or to extol the respective virtues and vices of 'model' and 'problem' minorities, but rather to establish the contrasting injustice of their settler colonial relations with indigenous peoples." Instead of prioritizing land as the site of sovereignty and decolonization, Sexton suggests that "disabusing ourselves of antiblack racism would . . . enable us to see that black struggles against slavery are *ultimately* struggles against colonialism."[5]

Importantly, I think Sexton raises key questions about the critical purchase of Indigenous studies within the circulation of whiteness and the production of racial difference, whether in his own collapse of Indigenous critical theory into settler colonial studies or in his observation that

Native Studies scholars mis-recognize 'the true horror of slavery' as de-culturalization or the loss of sovereignty because they do not ask what slavery is in the most basic sense—its local and global histories, its legal and political structures, its social and economic functions, its psychosexual dynamics, and its philosophical consequences. . . . Slavery is not a loss that the self experiences—of language, lineage, land, or labor—but rather the loss of any self that could experience such loss. (591)

The radical site of resistance, he concludes, is selflessness. "No ground for identity, no ground to stand (on). Everyone has a claim to everything until no one has a claim to anything. No claim. This is not a politics of despair brought about by a failure to lament a loss, because it is not

Indigeneity, Race, and the Temporalities of Land

rooted in hope of winning. The flesh of the earth demands it: the landless inhabitation of selfless existence" (593). In thinking with Sexton, his turn to selfless and landless inhabitation makes a radical kind of sense within the dialectical embrace of the opposite as politically ethical. The Enlightenment liberal notion of self-possession, that sense of being able to expand self through the acquisition of property through one's land, one's body, one's history, and one's kin that Moreton-Robinson theorizes as "the white possessive" provides the context for Thomas Sutpen's patriarchal hubris and final disintegration into the violence he himself originates in his pursuit of land and unimpeachable patrimony. Slavery and Removal produced profound losses of self that cannot be won through archives or claims; therefore, losing one's being and inhabiting that loss rather than pursing reparative justice in the form of self and property is the ultimate form of resistance. But what might happen to Sexton's formulation if the land was understood not as the ground upon which one stands or the claim through which one loses or possesses selfhood, but rather as itself an agentive presence acting upon people and their losses to reorient them constantly into relationship with space as well as time? Beyond the contaminations of miscegenation and incest that threaten to reveal family resemblances across color lines, the land still persists in Faulkner and bears the violence: *the rotting shell with its sagging portico and scaling walls, its sagging blinds and blank-shuttered windows, set in the middle of the domain which had reverted to the state and had been bought and sold and bought and sold again and again and again.*[6] Even though claiming, owning, and selling land are often the sources of the curses within Faulkner's geographies, the land holds and resists the violences humanity inflicts upon itself, and while structures crumble, decay, and burn, the land slowly reclaims and swallows the debris, resetting cultivated civilization through an agency that is a deep planetary temporality.

In the midst of such structural fragilities and the concomitant anxieties that have helped orient social and state power toward maintenance of the colonial and propertied supremacy of selfhood, many Indigenous scholars and activists across North America have started to break institutional, community, and familial silences about the systemic violences that permeate the network of lives across North America. Their work speaks to the stigma and fear that leave us unable, for instance, to talk about missing and murdered Indigenous women and the state-enabled ethnic purging that began with removal policies and continues into the present with tar sands, oil spills, and pipelines. Kwakwaka'wkaw First Nations scholar Sarah Hunt is one of those voices rising up to explain that were we to "take the time to look underneath and beyond the map of Canada, underneath the cities we now live in, Indigenous knowledge has much to teach us about where we live and how we might better live together on these lands." And as she further reminds us, "in many Indigenous teachings, it's not only *people* who have agency but also plants, animals, the land and the ocean—every living thing has agency. Each living thing has an important role in the order of the world. The teachings that emerge from our longstanding relationships upon the land and the ocean have allowed us to live with each other for thousands of years."[7] Those longstanding relationships are the basis for Indigenous law, and living with the vibrant agencies of life that surround us provides the ethical frameworks through which to transform violence. Family and kinship connection continue to remain a vital source for decolonial resistance, and the acknowledgement of relationality—to land, to people, to every object and thing—is a key component within Indigenous epistemologies no matter how transformed our cultures and societies become through the complicit innovations and accommodations settler colonialism requires and produces.

It is here that I want to return to LeAnne Howe's insistence on family as a methodology for any tribalography and follow the proper protocols to locate myself within the networks and agencies of geographic, kinship, and temporal coordinates.[8] I was born in Nebraska, not far from the Oglala Pine Ridge Indian Reservation, and I spent most of my childhood into my teenage years in a small border town six miles south of Sicangu Lakota Rosebud Indian Reservation. We were a Chickasaw family in a world defined by white and Lakota cowboys and cattlemen—to say that race and Indigeneity were an entangled mess in that place would be an understatement. My enrollment in the Chickasaw Nation derives from the Byrd side of the family, and my father, John Byrd, was a family doctor. His father, Roy Neal Byrd, was a Presbyterian minister who helped establish and build the church in Valentine, Nebraska. Though I grew up knowing that my relatives, ancestors, and living family on my dad's side were all Chickasaw, I had no depth of context to understand what that might even mean in a place like Valentine. It took me a long time to put together the story of how a thoroughly southern Byrd family ended up in rural Nebraska of all places and who exactly my Chickasaw relatives were beyond the brief and highly romanticized gestures my white mother would make when trying to help my brothers and me with homework and to explain both why we were not related to many of the folks in that small town like everyone else in the community and why my dad insisted on growing okra and eggplant in his Sandhills backyard garden to batter and fry on warm summer evenings. Grits, black-eyed peas, and

Indigeneity, Race, and the Temporalities of Land   23

cornmeal-battered fried green tomatoes were staples at our house, much to the horror of friends and neighbors brave enough to stay for dinner.

My route to knowledge about family history has often been circuitous and often required an undoing of settler imagination, story, and fiction to read between the lines and cohere something resembling a possible truth. Over time, I've found that genealogy and family require a reading praxis not unlike sifting through Faulkner's stories and novels to separate speculation from fact, rumor from truth, and desire from reality. Mom, translating stories she heard from my dad to us kids, always insisted that my great-great-grandfather was a Chickasaw chieftain and that another great-great was a medicine man. That we descended from men in service roles was supposed to explain why every single man in the family pursued careers dedicated to the spiritual and physical health of others. It was not until I got to graduate school at the University of Iowa that I started to push back against my mother's settler nostalgia about my dad's side of the family. My uncle and my grandfather helped clarify the genealogical tree: my great-great-grandfather, Benjamin "Frank" Byrd, was neither a chief nor a medicine man; he was, most unromantically, a postman and occasional treasurer for the Chickasaw Nation in the late 1880s and early 1890s. His brother, my great-great-grand-uncle, was William Leander Byrd, the firebrand Pullback governor of the Chickasaw Nation who served two terms from 1888 to 1890 and again from 1890 to 1892 during the contested debates surrounding the implementation of Indian Territory allotment policies that almost tore our nation out from underneath us for a second time. As a Pullback Party member allied with traditional Chickasaws, Governor Byrd stringently argued against allotment, against both black and white noncitizen intruders, and for Chickasaw national sovereignty. He was a staunch nationalist, an unrepentant Chickasaw Confederate soldier, and a deeply antiblack racist.[9]

While Frank Byrd was born post-Removal in Doaksville, Choctaw Nation, Indian Territory, in 1849, his older brother, William Leander, was born in 1844 in Marshall County, Mississippi, just three months before the family started their removal process westward. The lineages of their parents and my multiple great-great-grands, John Byrd and Mary Moore, are where the family line, I hope, gets a bit more interesting within the annals of Mississippi history and perhaps within Faulknerian geographies. Mary Moore was the daughter of Delilah Love Moore, and her aunt was Elizabeth "Betsy" Love Allen, the Chickasaw woman whose 1837 court battle to protect her property in the form of a slave named Toney from her husband's debt collectors helped establish property rights for women in the state of Mississippi through assertions of Chickasaw matrilineal customary rights.[10] Their mother, Sally Colbert, was a half-sister of George Colbert and was one of many Chickasaw women to marry British Loyalists in the mid-to late 1700s. Her connection to Thomas Love helped ensure the prominence of the family within both Chickasaw and southern plantation societies. Indeed, when the widowed Delilah Love Moore and her affiliated families and households left Holly Springs for the Chickasaw District in late October 1842, their party, according to research by Amanda L. Paige, Fuller L. Bumpers, and Daniel F. Littlefield, consisted of 188 travelers, 138 of whom were slaves, and 10 of whom were free black family members recognized by the Chickasaw nation.[11] At some level, Delilah's stature as a Chickasaw matriarch speaks to the continuance of Southeastern Indian cultural norms that located power in women, but what is also interesting is the degree to which she becomes matriarch within settler geographies in and around Marshall County. One story I have been able to find in circulation here in Mississippi is that she is believed to have deeded a fifty-acre plot to serve as the city square for Holly Springs over 175 years ago.[12]

John Byrd's lineage is a bit murkier, and his line of descent traces to Alabama before going cold within one generation, as if he emerged a bit like a sui generis Sutpen to make a fortune and an empire through marriage, property, and male progeny. That's not to say that folks have not told stories about his Byrd family lineage, and William Leander Byrd often maintained that his grandfather, Michael Byrd, was the disowned son of Commodore William Byrd III, who was himself the son of William Byrd II, author of *The History of the Dividing Line betwixt Virginia and North Carolina* and a man who is recognized as one of the founding fathers of Richmond, Virginia. If there are stories about Chickasaw families that linger in this place, I suspect that the Colbert, Allen, Love, and Moore family lines provide their fair share of secrets, losses, violences, and human frailties to serve as source material for any enterprising writer willing to pay attention.

I think one of the reasons I was drawn to postcolonial literatures and theories rather than American literature as a Chickasaw graduate student was the way in which writers throughout the Global South have used literature to write back against empire. Jean Rhys's *Wide Sargasso Sea* reimagined Charlotte Brontë's *Jane Eyre* through the perspective of creole Bertha Mason's romance with and imprisonment by Mr. Rochester. Wilson Harris's *Palace of the Peacock* revised Conrad's *Heart of Darkness* by placing it in the hinterlands of Guyana to grapple with Amerindian presence and absence in the Caribbean, and Aimé Cesaire offered a more modest *A Tempest* to give Caliban agency as an anticolonial intellectual and freedom fighter. With the rise of Indigenous critical theory

Indigeneity, Race, and the Temporalities of Land

alongside American Indian literary studies, Indigenous intellectuals such as Mohawk scholar Audra Simpson, Dene scholar Glen Coulthard, and others in the academy and in their communities are lately validating refusal instead of engagement as an affect of resistance, rejecting the terms of participatory dialogue altogether as acts of anticolonial resentment against filiation and reconciliation.[13] In her famous critique of Wallace Stegner, Dakota scholar Elizabeth Cook-Lynn argues with every aspect of his literary genius, observing, "Stegner and Indians, then, (no pun intended) are worlds apart. He simply took them as his culture gave them to him, though it is possible for those of us who read his works to wonder whether or not he grasped the final immorality of such a position."[14] I had a brief moment when I initially set out to provide a title for this piece where I considered following Cook-Lynn's lead and perhaps a little resentfully announcing a manifesto along the lines of "Why I Can't Read William Faulkner." But in approaching his work symptomatically and fitfully, I find I can indeed read him and, in the process and along the way, discern in the margins and in the differentiations of black and white space that carve out meaning on the page some semblance of Chickasaw presence after all. It is a matter of method.

And for that method, I've taken my cue from Choctaw-Chickasaw intellectual and novelist Philip Carroll Morgan whose scholarship and writing provide one possible approach for Indigenously reading Faulkner by taking the author at his word. If we believe Faulkner when he says he did no research but instead relied upon the stories he heard on the wind, from people in the community, and through the land, then coincidence and speculation serve as ways of reading Chickasaws back into Faulkner—not toward recovering the truth within the fictionalized histories of Faulkner's imaginative terrains, necessarily, but perhaps toward understanding the difference Indigenous presences make whether we are acknowledged as inhabiting the archive, as having lived upon the land, as having knowledge about our own history, language, culture, and traditions, or, finally, as being fully capable reading subjects from the future with familial and cultural ties to the very peoples represented and mischaracterized within the pages of his beloved southern tomes.

For Morgan, there comes an "Aha!" moment, a moment of making connection between a Choctaw-Chickasaw sense of Mississippi histories and the ones distortedly reflected back to us by accounts and stories written by settlers. For Morgan, such a moment occurred while he was researching the first Chickasaw governor, Cyrus Harris, and his birth, life, and experiences growing up in his ancestral home near the Ingomar Mounds, not far from where Faulkner was born over eighty years later. H. F. O'Beirne's 1885 account that a thirteen-year-old Harris came home from boarding school in 1830 to find "that his family had 'vacated the old Yoc-ne-put-tah-fah home, and in three day's slow travel reached their new home'" provided Morgan a possible epiphany that what is assumed to be Faulkner's fictive genius might be merely appropriative instead.[15] Additional insights came from puzzling out the linguistic origins of the transliterated "Ingomar" Mounds to show the word's phonic similarities to In-cun-no-mar, the house clan of Sally Colbert and her daughters Betsy and Delilah. There is, of course, no preponderance of evidence in the record that might prove these linkages beyond a reasonable doubt to colonial authorities knowledgeable in the matter, and such moments have little more credibility than a felt sense of familiarity to Chickasaws. But, Morgan points out, Ingomar and In-cun-no-mar, when spoken out loud, bear a striking resemblance to Ikoni Homma' Iksa, Red Skunk Clan. Between Yokni Patafa—whether we translate it as split, furrowed, plowed, or open land—and Ingomar, Morgan speculates, there is a possibility that the spirit of the land itself works with an agency of its own on the imagination of settlers, arrivants, and Natives alike, influencing us and actively inflecting which stories we tell and how we tell them.

This sense of the interconnectedness between story and land is something central to Chickasaw epistemologies no matter how much we change through time. As Lakota scholar Craig Howe says, Indigenous oral traditions are multidirectional, hypertextual, and depend upon interactive dynamics that draw on social, spatial, experiential, and spiritual elements to function.[16] In thinking with the provocations that Morgan's argument offers, and drawing on Hunt's assertion that for many Indigenous peoples agency exists beyond the human, within relations, and from lands and oceans, I want to return to Jared Sexton's concerns about how the field of Indigenous studies has failed to grapple with blackness and slavery in our insistence on sovereignty and self-determination, lands and nations. His assertion that the truly radical positionality in the New World is the ungrounded selflessness that comes from embracing the historical consequences of slavery as an undoing of identity, family, connection, and place resonates with Saidiya Hartman's discussions of the afterlives of slavery and the impossibilities of archives in her memoir, *Lose Your Mother*.[17] For Chickasaws, the experience of removal and colonialism was also a removal of our selves—our kin and kind—despite the fact that southern Indians are the most well-documented peoples in North America. But it was also an experience of loss mitigated by the slaves who were forced to remove with us, who bore the labor of rebuilding with and for us, and who remain unrecognized still within our communities. One of the problems in taking up the Native South as a viable conversation has been, I think, a tendency for us to theorize our Souths

Indigeneity, Race, and the Temporalities of Land 27

through the bite-sized boundaries of binaries: black/white, white/Indigenous, but never black/Indigenous. By centering land alongside family within discussions of race and colonialism, though, I am hoping it might be possible to triangulate racializations across whiteness, Indigeneity, and blackness and disrupt the quagmires of binaries and competitions for a purity of oppression within our theorizations of possible resistances. At the very least, apprehending relationship to land as agentive in itself, as more than just a claim to the ground through which history is staged and more than just property one owns, might help us talk across the disciplinary divides that inform the recent intellectual sparring between Indigenous studies and afropessimism. Finally, I hope it might provide us with ways to think about colonialism in the New World without casting all nonnatives, regardless of how they arrived here, as either settlers themselves or foils within the structures that whites built to capture, contain, and destroy black and Indigenous lives.

In *The Erotic Life of Racism*, Sharon Holland theorizes that the black/white binary in America is impossible to move beyond because of the "persistent problem inherent in the black/white encounter: namely, that this crossing seems impossible; that this crossing almost never happens." She goes on to ask, "What happens when someone who exists in time meets someone who only occupies space? Those who order the world, who are world-making master time—those animals *and* humans who are perceived as having no world-making effects—merely occupy space . . . [I]f the black appears as the antithesis of history (occupies space), the white represents the industry of progressiveness (being in time). It is possible to surmise that resistance to this binary might be telling a truth about our sense of time and space instead of a truth about the meeting itself."[18] If resistance to such a binary reveals a truth about our sense of time and space rather than a truth about the black/white encounter— here Holland uses Rosa's command to Clytie on the stairs in *Absalom, Absalom!* to exemplify this possibility—how can we think about space and time at Sutpen's Hundred without also thinking about Southeastern Indians whose world-making temporal presences also merely occupy space within the Native/white encounter that frames the black/white one and forecloses the possibility of the Native and black ever meeting at all?

For Faulkner, possession itself marks the means through which whiteness achieves its temporality as world-making potential, and *Absalom, Absalom!*'s repeated and mnemonic shorthanding of Sutpen's nefarious acquisition of his hundred miles of land is in itself a microcosm of the foreclosure of the possibility that native and black could ever meet within the contextual frameworks for thinking about time and space within settler colonialism. Repeatedly throughout the novel,

Faulkner links Sutpen's acquisition of his fortune, name, and power to the force of his will to manifest his domain temporally if not legally through, in Rosa's telling, land "which he took from a tribe of ignorant Indians, nobody knows how, and a house the size of a courthouse where he lived for three years without a window or door or bedstead in it and still called it Sutpen's Hundred as if it had been a King's grant in unbroken perpetuity from his great grandfather" (Faulkner, *Absalom, Absalom!* 10). It was "some of the best virgin bottom land in the country," we learn a few pages later, that Sutpen acquired from the Chickasaw through their agent and patented with the last of the Spanish coin in his possession (26). The Spanish coin that Sutpen uses to file his land patent carries multiple meanings in the novel, but one of the things it does is to fix Chickasaw dispossession temporally to a conquest rooted in the 1540s with De Soto's expedition along the Mississippi. However, he came by the land, virgin or Chickasaw, Sutpen's possession enshrouds Rosa's command to Clytie on the stairs of the house years later and helps set the stage for how the Native/white and black/white binaries shape the way we might think race, Indigeneity, space, and relationality throughout the South.

There are many things we could say about the intersections of slavery and conquest, antiblack racism and white possession in the South, how civilized society came to be synonymous with slave owning, how property and landownership signified freedom and selfhood, and how many mixed-blood and ruling families in the Chickasaw and Choctaw Nations enthusiastically pursued plantation slave economies not just to survive invasion but because it was economically lucrative to do so. Barbara Krauthamer, in her book *Black Slaves, Indian Masters*, demonstrates how "Choctaw and Chickasaw slaveholders clearly embraced a racial and gender ideology of black inferiority that informed their relationships with each other, with their slaves, and also with nonslaveholding Indians."[19] In the face of such unvarnished truths about the historical and modern complicities and realities of Indigenous antiblack ideologies, it is tempting to agree with settler colonial studies scholar Patrick Wolfe when he suggests that "a major implication for antiracist collaboration is the need to recognize the shared provenance of such differences in the White man's imposition of the colonial rule of private property. Yes, some Indians were involved in Black slavery, and, yes, some Blacks participated in Indian dispossession, but neither Indians nor Blacks were the originators and collective beneficiaries of these systemic crimes."[20] No matter how civilized and slave owning the elite ruling families became in the Chickasaw and Choctaw Nations, settler colonialism most assuredly dispossessed us of our lands, and it also disposed of our presence, rewrote our histories, and reimagined our relations through frames of blackness and whiteness that obscured our own genealogical and geographical relationalities, often leaving traces and crumbs to claim and rearrange along the way.

But there is, it seems to me, something a bit recursive when we juxtapose Wolfe with Faulkner, and doing so keeps returning me to a quote from Édouard Glissant that I've become obsessed with since I first read it. "Faulkner's depiction of Blacks is 'rural,'" Glissant writes.

> It claims no perspective or verisimilitude. Rather, it stems from an absolute source: the moment when the land suffered a split between the Indians, its first inhabitants, and the Whites who appeared from Europe (or from nowhere). To this the Blacks, introduced into this land as slaves, were silent and suffering witnesses. The "situation" of Blacks is thus emblematic of this beginning: they were but living witnesses, not a responsible party, to the original sin of the South (whether or not you call it expropriation). This "situation" will not accompany them throughout History, for they do not make History. As for the Indians, they have almost completely disappeared, at least from within the county borders (through the murderous exodus to Oklahoma). So it is only to White people that the question—the nagging question of original responsibility—is addressed.[21]

In his read of Faulkner, Glissant captures the commonsense logics of race and colonialism that haunt us in the present and inform Wolfe's insistence on the centrality of white agency even in black and Indigenous antiracist collaboration beyond whiteness. What Faulkner gave us in his work was the alchemy of modern US race relations: Indians vanish into timelessness, Blacks are living witnesses to that disappearance and to their own historical oppressions that leave them occupying space without making history, and whites not only bear the burden of their responsibility for both but in doing so ensure their own world-making supremacy by being the only ones through whom grievances can ever be addressed and then reconciled. Within such a framework, Southeastern Indian participation in slavery disappears, their occupation of space is projected backward through time but never forward, and the historical roots for antiblackness within articulations of Indigenous sovereignty remain not only unchallengeable but unthinkable.

Moreton-Robinson has suggested that one of the failures of Indigenous studies has been our inability to take up whiteness studies as a field to consider how the Indigenous ontological relationship to land produces "a doubleness whereby Indigenous subjects can 'perform' whiteness while being Indigenous. . . . There is always a subject position that can be thought of as fixed in its inalienable relation to land."[22] I agree with Moreton-Robinson that the doubleness of performing whiteness while Indigenous resides in our relationship to land—the nomenclature of the Five Civilized Tribes aptly demonstrates that—but I want to push back just a bit against her formulation to argue that, within the triangulations of race in North America at least, Indigeneity as whiteness exists in dialectical tension with how whiteness uses claims to Indigenous ancestors to assert the racial purity of its self-produced status as the ruling race and class. As an example of this dialectic, the Pocahontas exception to Virginia's 1924 Racial Integrity Act allowed descendants of the first families of the state to maintain their claim of descent from Pocahontas, to continue policing miscegenation, and to achieve in their claim to Indianness the fulfillment of the purity of white possession of the land.[23]

Given such dynamics, Faulkner's remnant and degraded Indians signal an innocence destroyed by contact with whites that is to be lamented by settlers as an echo of the "lo, the poor Indians" remixed with an "alas, they had to go so that we could take their place." But there is also, it seems to me, a fundamental anxiety in Faulkner surrounding the implications of Sam Fathers's black Indian identity, which threatens to achieve for blackness a grounded relationality that will finally supersede whiteness as the true inheritor of the vacuum left with the removal of Indians. If Indigeneity exists on both sides of the black/white binary and establishes both the impenetrability of the divide as well as the means to breach it, then it either makes the world-making of whiteness meaningless, or it provides the means through which blackness achieves both space and time. To resolve this anxiety, Faulkner abandons Sam to a kinless purgatory in the claimless wilderness of natural man in which he has no substantive community, no relations, and no possibility of futurity; despite the possessive verbing of his last name, Sam remains an ambivalently impotent vessel through whom Indigenous knowledge might safely be reinterred into white possession in the hopes that the black/white binary will remain intact.

Within many of the recent critiques raised about whether Indigenous insistence on land, sovereignty, and self-determination can ever achieve a truly radical decolonial transformation that resolves the breach between the racializations of (black) space and (white) time, there remains, I think, a persistent misunderstanding about how land functions for Indigenous peoples. The assumption is that land acquires meaning in the ways in which it is made to exist in relation to humans, to the claims made to it and on it over time. As Elizabeth Povinelli has explained, there is an assumed certain priority of the prior that provides Indigeneity its force of signification to assert dominion over lands even when they

Indigeneity, Race, and the Temporalities of Land

have been stolen through colonization.[24] Here I think Donna Haraway's recent work on the planetary effects of the Anthropocene, the "capitalocene," and the "plantationocene" might be helpful. Haraway offers a feminist and queer promise of multispecies assemblages in which "ongoingness is at stake" for every thing of us on the planet—bacteria, fungi, plant, human, mineral, and animal. She names the compostable, tentacular pasts, presents, and to comes the Chtulucene and exhorts us all to take up refugees and build connections with her sloganistic conclusion, "Make kin, not babies! It matters how kin generates kin."[25] Her formulation draws in Spider-Woman and Medusa, Gaia and Naga, and demands a capacious exogamy as a speculative feminist practice to ensure optimal survival, and it resonates with Southeastern Indian philosophies and epistemologies of making relations. Within the Native Souths that Chickasaws and Choctaws still imagine, know, and inhabit, the land is not something we claim; instead, it claims us, generates us in relationship to it, not as selfless or claimless, but as kin, as family, *iksa*, home. Embracing that home and telling the full truth of those Native Souths and how they are complicit with antiblackness might, I hope, help us move toward the open and the vulnerable modes of disrupting the binaries of space and time that have removed Chickasaws from ourselves and from our relationality to others.

NOTES

1. Patricia Galloway, "The Construction of Faulkner's Indians," *Faulkner Journal* 18, nos. 1–2 (Fall 2002–Spring 2003): 9.

2. "Writing and Literature Classes, tape 2," May 2, 1958, *Faulkner at Virginia*, http://faulkner.lib.virginia.edu/display/wfaudi026_2.

3. Aileen Moreton-Robinson, *The White Possessive: Property, Power, and Indigenous Sovereignty* (Minneapolis: University of Minnesota Press, 2015), xi.

4. Ibid., 113.

5. Jared Sexton, "The *Vel* of Slavery: Tracking the Figure of the Unsovereign," *Critical Sociology* 42, nos. 4–5 (2016): 591.

6. William Faulkner, *Absalom, Absalom!* (1936; New York: Vintage International, 1990), 173. Hereafter cited parenthetically.

7. Sarah Hunt, "In Her Name—Relationships as Law," TEDxVictoria 2013, https://www.youtube.com/watch?v=XmJZP21iqKI.

8.. For more on LeAnne Howe and tribalography, see *Choctalking on Other Realities* (San Francisco: Aunt Lute Books, 2013).

9. For more genealogical work on Chickasaw governor William L. Byrd, see Phillip Caroll Morgan, "Maze of Colonialism," in *Riding Out the Storm: 19th Century Chickasaw Governors, Their Lives, and Intellectual Legacy* (Ada, OK: Chickasaw, 2013), 19–66.

10. LeAnne Howe, "Betsy Love and the Mississippi Married Women's Property Act of 1839," *Mississippi History Now*, September 2005, http://www.mshistorynow.mdah.ms.gov/articles/6/betsy-love-and-the-mississippi-married-womens-property-act-of-1839.

11. Amanda L. Paige, Fuller L. Bumpers, and Daniel F. Littlefield Jr., *Chickasaw Removal* (Ada, OK: Chickasaw, 2010), 158.

12. Sue Watson, "Happy Birthday, Holly Springs!" *South Reporter Online*, November 29, 2012, http://archive.southreporter.com/2012/wk48/happy_birthday_holly_springs.html.

13. Glen Sean Coulthard, *Red Skin, White Masks: Rejecting the Colonial Politics of Recognition* (Minneapolis: University of Minnesota Press, 2014); Audra Simpson, *Mohawk Interruptus: Political Life across the Borders of Settler States* (Durham, NC: Duke University Press, 2014).

14. Elizabeth Cook-Lynn, *Why I Can't Read Wallace Stegner and Other Essays: A Tribal Voice* (Madison: University of Wisconsin Press, 1996), 30.

15. Morgan, *Riding Out the Storm*, 86.

16. Craig Howe, "Keep Your Thoughts above the Trees: Ideas on Developing and Presenting Tribal Histories," in *Clearing a Path: Theorizing the Past in Native American Studies*, ed. Nancy Shoemaker (New York: Routledge, 2002), 161–79.

17. Saidiya Hartman, *Lose Your Mother: A Journey along the Atlantic Slave Route* (New York: Farrar, Straus and Giroux, 2008).

18. Sharon Holland, *The Erotic Life of Racism* (Durham, NC: Duke University Press, 2012), 10.

19. Barbara Krauthamer, *Black Slaves, Indian Masters: Slavery, Emancipation, and Citizenship in the Native American South* (Chapel Hill: University of North Carolina Press, 2015), 5.

20. Patrick Wolfe, *Traces of History: Elementary Structures of Race*, Kindle ed. (London: Verso Books, 2016), location 519.

21. Édouard Glissant, *Faulkner, Mississippi*, trans. Barbara B. Lewis and Thomas C. Spear (Chicago: University of Chicago Press, 1996), 58.

22. Moreton-Robinson, *The White Possessive*, 11.

23. For more on Virginia's Racial Integrity Act, see Arica L. Coleman, *That the Blood Stay Pure: African Americans, Native Americans, and the Predicament of Race and Identity in Virginia* (Bloomington: University of Indiana, 2013), and Kevin Noble Maillard and Rose Cuison Villazor, eds., *Loving v. Virginia in a Post-Racial World: Rethinking Race, Sex, and Marriage* (Cambridge, UK: Cambridge University Press, 2012).

24. Elizabeth Povinelli, *The Economies of Abandonment: Social Belonging and Endurance in Late Liberalism* (Durham, NC: Duke University Press, 2011), 34.

25. Donna Haraway, "Anthropocene, Capitalocene, Plantationocene, Cthulucene: Making Kin," *Environmental Humanities* 6 (2015): 160, 161.

Doom and Deliverance:
Faulkner's Dialectical Indians

MELANIE BENSON TAYLOR

Faulkner's Indian characters are all a little bit ridiculous—colorful fabrications based loosely on popular assumptions and unspoken ideologies: they are either grotesquely ruined by the excesses of capitalism or, like the sage black-Indian Sam Fathers, mystically immune to it. When asked about his flamboyant Natives, Faulkner famously admitted that he "made them up."[1] Of course, as numerous critics and historians have noted, Faulkner was far too shrewd a student of Mississippi history to have ignored the facts entirely. But continuing these debates over the "accuracy" of his creations seems to me a dangerous dead end, a critical red herring (if you'll pardon the pun); as with anything in Faulkner's world, the reality lies somewhere in the murky in-between—and appropriately so. As the Comanche critic Paul Chaat Smith puts it, "The true story [about American Indian history] is simply too messy and complicated. And too threatening. The myth of noble savages, completely unable to cope with modern times, goes down much more easily."[2] Faulkner's savages aren't always noble, but they are strikingly "unable to cope with modern times." Faulkner's non-Native protagonists are often similarly ill-equipped, as was Faulkner himself at times. His is a dialectical dance, caught at the crossroads of colonial and capital development: he was (if often only rhetorically) tilling the earth one week, and lifting off it in an airplane in another; basking in the bright dazzle of Hollywood, or seduced back to the sanctuary of home; shuttling back and forth between the disparate worlds he "doesn't hate" in equal measure.[3]

The way we typically read Faulkner's Indians places them at one extreme in these dialectical equations: lost creatures in the purgatory of American history, tragic victims of avarice and assimilation. Faulkner is, in fact, almost shrill in his insistence that the Indian world becomes "obsolete," "vanished"—not slowly and inevitably, but abruptly "swept, hurled, flung"[4] out of a world careening toward its "destiny." This would be a fine postcolonial elegy if it were true, but, of course, it's both premature and overdone. Collapsed in the ideology of extinction is the Cold War Faulkner of the Nobel Prize acceptance speech pondering "When will I be blown up?"[5] Atomic anxiety merges here with a more abiding refrain, an American anthem of sorts: an unshakable fear of being expunged by the steamroller of progress. Here, Indians surface as a shattering episteme, a sort of ground zero for a profoundly personal dread of annihilation—and an irrepressible, uniquely American, and pointedly savage desire to strike back and survive at all costs. His Indians lie in the dialectical space between the "ravishment" of the colonial past and the rapacities of the capitalist future; they are despicably "other" even as they are uncannily, frighteningly kindred; and when we confront them more fully and soberly, those outlandish Indians look a little more dreadfully real. Faulkner actually got it right in ways we have hardly begun to appreciate.

The first step in doing so requires charting a less-traveled path straight through the heart of Yoknapatawpha. The "Indian canon" within Faulkner's oeuvre is relatively small, consisting of about six stories; *Go Down, Moses*; and the prologues to *Requiem for a Nun*. Truthfully, most of it is too overwrought with stereotypes to be interesting—at least to this reader—and more importantly, continuing to focus our attention on the most blatant representations simply perpetuates our tendency to misread the extent of Faulkner's knowledge and intentions. Paradoxically more illuminating are the obscure, uncanny Indians that lurk unseen in his major texts, boiling in the veins and the shadows of his most prominent families and novels; in what follows, I'll suggest a few of the more palpable, along with a sampling of the less apparent. Collectively, these Indians comprise a surprisingly active and pertinent contingent in Faulkner's modern South, and Faulkner seems keen to keep them so—not as Indians per se, but as specimens of America's most luminous possibilities and the most haunting failures. This is not Faulkner's project alone, of course: in the words of Paul Chaat Smith again, "[Americans and Indians] are hopelessly fascinated with each other, locked in an endless embrace of love and hate and narcissism. Together we are condemned, forever to disappoint, never to forget even as we can't remember. . . . We are the country, and the country is us."[6] Indians have long represented at once our best selves and our most vicious demons; the very incarnation of freedom and its dangerous obverse; emblems of deliverance on the one hand, and doom in the final reckoning. Faulkner's Indian is not a relic of history but a terrifying mainstay of modernity: an unsettling emblem of what might have been and what could never have been otherwise.

Faulkner's Dialectical Indians

To smoke out these Indians, we need first to radically revise our view of where the Native fits in the chronicle of Mississippi history, and it's not exactly at the margins or in the somber ether of Removal. In reality, Indians were deeply ensnared in the institution of slavery—as slaveowners and, later, as Confederates—and were often supportive of the idea of Removal for the same reasons as their white peers.[7] Many used their Removal payoffs to purchase more slaves once they arrived in Oklahoma and fought bitterly to preserve the chattel economy. This is one of those messy truths that we prefer not to acknowledge, even (and especially) in Indigenous studies, where we tend to loft our own battle flags for a more justified lost cause of radical, redemptive solidarity and sovereignty. Why wouldn't a writer like Faulkner find irresistible the haunting figures who so stunningly mirrored the ambivalence of the South and its own attempts to straddle the unbearable gulf between anticapitalist transcendence on the one hand and economic seduction on the other?[8]

It is our well-intentioned narrow-mindedness as critics that prevents us from seeing the extraordinary realities and consequences of Faulkner's Indian world. Most Faulkner critics are aware of Sally Wolff's recent discovery (published in 2010 as *The Ledgers of History*) that Faulkner was profoundly influenced by a set of plantation account books he encountered and studied in the home of a childhood friend, Edgar Wiggin Francisco, in Holly Springs. Specific names and events from Francisco's great-grandfather's diaries and ledgers reappear exactly throughout Faulkner's fiction, as does the revelatory power of this other [capital B] Book itself as a kind of southern birthright deeply internalized but infrequently deciphered. Somewhat incidentally in her study, Wolff tells about the family stories that Faulkner also heard while perusing these books in his friend's ancestral home, McCarroll Place; one such tale involved a prominent local Chickasaw Indian named Sam Love,[8] who helped to build the original log house of the plantation in the 1830s. Sam's "help" reportedly came not in sweat but rather his "approval or blessing," which he doled out along with requisite lessons in land stewardship and the notion that "behavior based on notions of ownership would not only be selfish, it would be self-destructive and would destroy the land";[9] indeed, Sam Love's admonishments reportedly inspired covert abolitionist sympathies in the family's white patriarch, John Ramsey McCarroll.[10] The very existence of the plantation ledgers reveals Sam's failure to successfully deter his friend from the sins of slavery and its attendant fortunes, but nonetheless, tales of his wisdom were quietly passed down within the family, and finally to Faulkner, until "the story of Sam disappeared."[11]

It's an extraordinary story mainly because it's almost certainly not true; or, at the very least, its essential components have been burnished to a high, narcissistic sheen throughout the generations. It is, in fact, a conspicuous example of white southern nativist fantasy, complete with an Indigenous permission slip to settle the land, and a heaping dose of spiritual wisdom to provide a self-flagellating but ultimately self-serving moral compass. It is thus terrifically ironic that Sam Love was most likely related to a woman named Delilah Love, a mixed-blood Chickasaw who married two wealthy white settlers and was one of the largest landowners in Holly Springs, apparently "donating" fifty acres for the founding of the downtown square.[12] A Sam Love turns up in the records as a slave-owning landowner himself; and in an appropriately Faulknerian turn, an apparent descendant also bearing the name of "Sam Love" appears on the Dawes Rolls as a Chickasaw Freedman, meaning that, like Sam Fathers, he was the mixed-race product of congress between an Indian and a slave. These genealogical traces would need further investigation to be corroborated, but for our purposes here, I merely want to pause and suggest that such threads of inquiry exist and beg for further investigation but that Wolff elects not to raise them, instead merely passing along the skeleton story as a transparent text unworthy of further analysis or applications to Faulkner's thinking. Most surprising, in a project that so thoroughly sleuths out the fingerprints of these rich new archives on Faulkner's writing, Wolff stops short of suggesting that the story of Sam Love might have inspired the similarly named and motivated Sam Fathers who, in *Go Down, Moses,* tutors and inspires Ike McCaslin, the reluctant white heir, to repudiate his own plantation legacy. The missed connection is not necessarily Wolff's fault: her omission is typical of the still overwhelmingly bifocal, biracial narrative that governs our cultural and critical perceptions. Indians provide the otherworldly instruction to interpret the ledgers, so to speak, plot devices who serve a symbolic purpose and then "disappear." Except, of course, that they don't.

From the very beginning, Faulkner's "postage stamp of native soil" had an Indigenous pedigree that goes far beyond the Choctaw etymology of "Yoknapatawpha" or the fact that Ikkemotubbe (like Delilah Love) apparently "granted" small parcels of land to every major family in the county. Faulkner tells a subtler story in *Requiem for a Nun* (published in 1951) about the founding of Jefferson, which begins, importantly, with the twin structures of an Indian trading post and a jail. The town is named after a man named Thomas Jefferson Pettigrew, a mail rider who contributes the lock from his delivery pouch to secure the county jail. When the lock is stolen, the founders contemplate simply charging it to the federal government: "'You could call that lock "axle

Faulkner's Dialectical Indians 37

grease" on that Indian account,'" one suggests, "'to grease the wagons for Oklahoma.'"[13] "'Put it on the Book,'" another declares, "the [capital B] Book: not a ledger, but *the* ledger."[14] It is Pettigrew, however, who deviously persuades the founders that it would be unethical to so shamelessly defraud the American government. To secure Pettigrew's allegiance and silence, the founders name the fledgling town "Jefferson" in his dubious honor. Jefferson, of course, is the obvious choice over his actual surname, "Pettigrew," the Scots-Irish evolution of the French for "little man"—fitting for a character repeatedly described as a scrawny windbag who works for the post office (much like the slightly built Faulkner himself, who had worked at the Ole Miss post office for nearly three years). Not incidentally, though, Pettigrew is actually a common name among the Chickasaw, no doubt due to the mixing of settler and Indigenous cultures in the early Southeast. Even more suggestively for Faulkner, it was the name of both a school and a creek in Chickasaw County, Mississippi (and we know how he loves Indigenous names for slow-moving streams).[15] But probably most importantly, Pettigrew as "little man" echoes Ikkemotubbe's moniker of "Doom," an anglicization of a French term for "*The* Man." Faulkner's world is filled with little men and big men, cowardly tricksters and brazen leaders: as conjoined allegories of sorts, Faulkner tacitly twins Pettigrew and Ikkemotubbe at the inception of his fictional world but names the town neither. He dramatizes instead the fetish operations of nationalism: the elevation of myth over the untidy reality. Choosing the patriotic Thomas *Jefferson* rather than, say, Andrew *Jackson*, appropriately deepens the artifice, because Jefferson epitomizes the stunning contradiction of democratic liberalism: fountainhead of freedom's virtues on the one hand, and on the other, designer of the Indian Removal policies executed by Andrew Jackson. His is the most suitable legacy for a universe where a prison "lock" and "Indian axle grease" are interchangeable; or, more precisely, where a *missing* lock, and therefore an apparently free society, silently lubricates the wheels of Indian extermination. As the man who runs the trading post justifies it, "it was the United States itself which had voluntarily offered to show them how to transmute the inevictable lock into proofless and ephemeral axle grease."[16] This is the pedagogy of citizenship in the settled world, recorded in "the" national ledger, the sacred ur-text of American economics that transcends and obliterates the dark secrets and exchanges held "proofless" in its pages.

In Faulkner's hands, this civic foundation narrative is most important as a signifier not of what the Indians lost, but what the *white* settlers forever sacrificed in the exchange: Jefferson earns the dubious glory, and the founders get nothing. Their plan to swindle the American government is halted by Pettigrew, that pesky, quasi-Indian conscience broker: the lock "could" be but never actually *is* registered as axle grease, and the men are permanently plagued by the tragedy of missed opportunity: "That lock," one grumbles, "that Indian axle grease." They "knew, understood. . . . It was neither lock nor axle grease; it was the fifteen dollars which could have been charged to the Indian Department on Ratcliffe's books and nobody would ever have found it, noticed it, missed it."[17] They mourn not the symbols or the things they conceal, nor even the money per se, but the squandered opportunity to *get something for nothing*, to profit effortlessly, unnoticed, and get away with it. The loss amounts to a kind of insurmountable debt for the founders, "leaving in fact the whole race of man, as long as it endured, forever and irrevocably fifteen dollars deficit, fifteen dollars in the red."[18] "In the red" is a pun that allows Faulkner to evoke both tangible debt and the abstract notion of the dispossessed "red" men who are the very signifier of deficit. Yet it also suggests that the haunting notion of loss is a direct result of America's removal strategies, that ordinary citizens would be forever in debt *to* the Indians for such grievous theft—or, more insidiously, that the Indians themselves took something away from humanity ever afterward, with their perceived pettiness and greed. They didn't just collect their pride and cultural memories for the road trip to Oklahoma, but in many cases, tidy sums of money and shotguns and the promise of new land and opportunities. According to the trading post ledgers in *Requiem*, the Indian accounts list, "with the United States as debtor . . . a crawling tedious list of calico and gunpowder, whiskey and salt and snuff and denim pants and osseous candy."[19] The Chickasaw purchases escalate quickly from practical items to apparent luxuries like whiskey and snuff and "osseous" candy, with "denim pants" interposed to suggest the craving for specifically Western trappings, much like the gaudy purple silk dresses, parasols, and too-small red shoes other Faulkner Indians sport. To describe the candy they buy, he uses the abstruse word "osseous"— meaning fossilized, like bone—to evoke its unpleasant rigidity (and thus, the Indians' indiscriminate appetites), but perhaps also to connote cannibalism, an apt metaphor for the self-devouring ends of participation in a consumer economy. Faulkner, of course, makes some of his Indians actual cannibals in the story "Red Leaves," a cultural fabrication but a metaphorical bullseye: they are ravenously hungry for commodities, flesh, and power, even if they don't quite know or admit it. Ikkemotubbe, of course, kills his nephew to usurp his place as heir, using poison that he keeps suggestively in a gold snuff box. Faulkner returns again and again to the candy, the whiskey, the myriad poisons concealed in gold—the material hungers that kill. The story that haunts the founders is one that reduces all men to the condition of savages, of the dispossessed, of the inveterately hungry victims "in the red" of the national accounts—a state about which the forever financially stressed Faulkner certainly had occasion to wax hyperbolic.

Requiem for a Nun comes relatively late in Faulkner's career. But by then, he had already seemed to develop a habit of looking back at the structures of his own fictional world and seeing the colonial parables and Indigenous mirrors lurking behind and within them. Take, for instance, the appendix to *The Sound and the Fury*, which Faulkner wrote in 1945, sixteen years after the novel itself, whose very first entry is devoted to Ikkemotubbe, "a dispossessed American king . . . who granted out of his vast lost domain a solid square mile of virgin north Mississippi dirt." The second entry is "Jackson: A Great White Father with a sword . . . who patented sealed and countersigned the grant with his own hand in his gold teepee in Wassi Town."[20] Critics have disagreed about the relevance of this odd appendix to the novel proper, but Faulkner insisted it was "the key to the whole book," causing the rest to "[fall] into pattern like a jigsaw puzzle."[21] As the apparent decoder ring for a novel containing no ostensible Indian themes or subtext, these entries resound: they yoke together the Natives and their ouster in the same golden teepee of avarice; Ikkemotubbe voluntarily "grants" the land that is always already "lost," no longer his at the moment when he realized he could get something for it in exchange. Faulkner includes a snide reference to oil, too: the discovery of black gold in Oklahoma, which probably would have prevented Jackson from sending the Indians there if he had foreseen it. But the Indians are distinctly not bettered by their fortune, saying that "one day, the homeless descendants of the dispossessed would ride supine with drink and splendidly comatose above the dusty allotted harborage of their bones in specially built scarletpainted hearses and fire-engines."[22] These twin villains at the start of the Compson story make theirs a national allegory, preparing us for a world undone by both too much and too little and peopled by "splendidly comatose" individuals riding around and around their respective squares of land in Indian-red vehicles meant for corpses and conflagrations.

The scathing totality of Faulkner's critique persists throughout his career, where Indian spirits haunt the bodies of characters poised most ambivalently within the economic structures that suffocate them. In the 1930 story "Evangeline," a warm-up to *Absalom, Absalom!* (another family tragedy rising out of land "granted" and doomed by Doom himself, Ikkemotubbe), the Clytie-figure Raby—Thomas Sutpen's miscegenated daughter—appears as not just part black but Indian as well: "'part Indian and part Sutpen, spirit and flesh' . . . still as granite, and as cold . . .

her whole face . . . perfectly blank, like a mask in which the eyesockets had been savagely thumbed and the eyes themselves forgotten."[23] "Part black" is omitted from the equation entirely: the haunted Indian and the striving Sutpen together form an exclusive dyad of human frailty and wayward desires. Significantly, Raby is the one who burns down the Sutpen mansion, with herself and Henry inside it, "in a silent and furious scarlet . . . among the wild and blazing branches of the cedars."[24] The very landscape itself seems to consume the house, exacting its revenge on the white man's transgression even as it safeguards its putrefying corpses—and we can all but hear the echo of those "scarlet" hearses and fire engines circling the charred ground forever after.

The dramatic function of the Indian in these narratives is to reify the self-immolating effects of colonial enterprise, of the desire to raise and tend big houses and dynasties not meant for human habitation. Other Indian bastards surface in subsequent texts as equally fretful figures on the margins of the social and economic order in ways both menacing and alluring. In *As I Lay Dying*,[25] written the year before "Evangeline," we have Addie's illegitimate love child, Jewel, described repeatedly as a "cigar store Indian" (14) with a "high-blooded face" (17), "pale, wooden eyes" (18), and a "harsh, savage voice" (19). He is markedly different from his brothers and sisters and favored by Addie for that reason: he is the product of her affair with Whitfield, the preacher, and thus her ironic, secret redemption. His very name implies that he is a priceless gem apart from the deadening economies of the rural South (unlike, say, his suitably named brother Cash, who labors relentlessly and falls meaningfully off of church rooves). "Jewel" is in fact resoundingly the very first word and image of the novel, as he walks behind his brother Darl but looms "a full head above" him (3), transcendent and ethereal. They come upon a dilapidated cotton house, quite clearly a signifier for the structural collapse of the Old South: Darl skirts it while Jewel barrels straight through, "in four strides with the rigid gravity of a cigar store Indian . . . endued with life from the hips down . . . [With] Jewel now in front, we go on up the path" (4). Jewel's superhuman power to surmount the cotton house puts him ahead of Darl, the Indian leading the way into the New South—fueled not by his mystical immunity to what the structure represents, but, more insidiously, by his knowledge that the route to the future runs directly *through* the detritus of slavery, and not around it. As a distinctly erotic, backwoods Elvis writhing with life from the hips down, this "cigar store Indian" belies its aggressive reproductive capacity: the Indian totem comes alive; the annihilation narrative will not stick. Removal is no bracketed genocide narrative sequestered from the explosion of the cotton kingdom, of chattel slavery, of transatlantic commodity markets. They have always been of a piece: the first cigar store Indian carvings actually resembled black slaves more than Natives, and Faulkner would likely have known that they were often referred to as "Black Boys."[26] Jewel's figuration thus exposes the coiled histories of the mystified plantation South, and his ironic paralysis at the threshold of America's earliest economic institutions will not do: Jewel bursts through and forward in a fit of erotic violence, unleashed significantly upon his beloved horse—a fitting symbol of Indigenous and rural culture in tense synergy. He "kicks [the horse] in the stomach," "strikes him across the face with his fist," and then proceeds to feed him vigorously: "'Eat,' he says. 'Get the goddamn stuff out of sight while you got a chance, you pussel-gutted bastard. You sweet son of a bitch,' he says" (13). In beating and overfeeding his "bastard" horse, the bastard Jewel abuses this mirror of the primal appetites of man as well as the Indian, refracting his own shameful longing to consume not just for subsistence, but to overconsume for pure pleasure.

Perhaps the most famous line in the novel—Vardaman's declaration "*My mother is a fish*"—overshadows Darl's equally cryptic pronouncement that "*Jewel's mother is a horse*" (196). In this semiotic substitution, Addie Bundren becomes not just horse but proxy Indian: the desired, loving, and lost mother of all Americans—consumed by temptation, corroded by labor, and finally decaying—the empty cipher and failed promise at the center of the text and the American family. In her deathbed reckonings, she muses on the notion that her children "were of me alone, of the wild blood boiling along the earth, of me and of all that lived; of none and of all. Then I found that I had Jewel. When I waked to remember to discover it, he was two months gone" (175). Jewel is clearly the apex of this wild blood, the thing she "found" she already had within her; but "two months gone" as a gestational term implies that he is the living dead, killed at the moment of "discovery" like the Indians who didn't exist either before or after the white man laid eyes on them. In our waking realities, it is always already too late for this kind of mythology. Addie's prehistoric, postcoital fantasy is extinguished along with her will to live, and it can't be an accident that her coffin is constructed meticulously by Cash, unstinting instrument of capitalism; but just as significantly, her casket evokes Jewel's wooden body, the box become a second skin through which Vardaman drills air holes so she might breathe, her body penetrated over and over again by the "wild" offspring who both slay and resurrect her.

Faulkner returns almost compulsively throughout his career to this idea of aborted deliverance—of the ambivalent Indian spirit that both sustains and slaughters, the stillbirth of new life in the necrotic environment of the modern South. One brief but vivid example occurs in the Old Man section of *The Wild Palms* (*If I Forget Thee, Jerusalem*), where a pregnant woman delivers in the middle of a raging flood, serendipitously atop an Indian mound. She is shepherded through the water by the reluctant tall convict—a man described as having "Indian-black" hair and an obligatory aversion to "crass and stupid money."[27] He also seems to have an Indigenous blood memory of "the firm earth fixed and founded strong and cemented fast and stable forever by the generations of laborious sweat, somewhere beneath him, beyond the reach of his feet."[28] Sure enough, a deer bobbing through the water practically leads them to the unseen mound and then vanishes—and Faulkner uses five variations of the word "vanish" in close succession here to underscore the point: this stereotypical emblem of Indian culture yields to the floodwaters, but the *land* endures—hopefully: "'Land!' [the convict] croaked. 'Land! Hold on! Just hold on!'" He is speaking to the woman, of course, but also to the earth; still, that faith is summarily snatched out from under him, perhaps because the "generations" of "laborious sweat" presumed to have cemented it "fast and stable forever" are what actually shattered it, sending him "plunging at the muddy slope [of the Indian mound], slipping back, the woman struggling in his muddy hands . . . as if his own failed and spent flesh were attempting to carry out his furious unflagging will for severance at any price, even that of drowning, from the burden with which, unwitting and without choice, he had been doomed."[29] He is not trying to hold onto the woman anymore, but to let her go: his burden, the inexorable doom, is the social organism and its attendant lusts, humanity's endless capacity to hunger, stumble, repeat, and reproduce, even in the midst of apocalypse. This quasi-Indian, this metaphorical convict, is sprung only briefly from that elemental prison at the epicenter of Faulkner's metaphorical universe, only to find freedom the cruel obverse of incarceration. In the final reckoning, Indigenous blood memory surfaces only to withdraw, to affirm the innate subjection crippling all humankind, not because they are bound but precisely because they are free.

This seductive darkness—this conjoined hunger and violence, what we know we are but still pretend not to be—runs potently through many of Faulkner's narratives where his most secret Indian characters appear. In his professed potboiler, *Sanctuary* (1929),[30] for example, violent sexual appetites are epitomized by the gangster Popeye, who infamously kidnaps and rapes the well-to-do, willful coed Temple Drake. Not incidentally, Faulkner based Popeye on the real-life Memphis criminal Popeye Pumphrey, son of a prosperous cotton planter and an attorney general's daughter—a shadow pedigree that makes the fictional Popeye's target of the affluent Temple even more deeply perverse, an attack on his own occluded elite heritage at the nexus of the South's economic and juridical systems. Because he is impotent—a figurative deflation of systemic power and its infertility—he uses two suggestively Indigenous props to achieve his assault on Temple: the infamous corncob has immediate applications to Native peoples, its first cultivators; but perhaps even more provocatively, Popeye sends in another gangster as sexual proxy—a man named "Red," a mysterious and seductive man who speaks in clipped one and two-word phrases that mimic stilted Hollywood Indian speech, and like another cigar store Indian, he does so "in a level tone, without moving" (236). The Native here is the red alter ego of the criminal American upper class, executing a kind of latent vengeance and self-contempt all at once.

Rather than cower under the advances of this exotic other, Temple becomes uncontrollably "wild" for more (237). Her violent physical yearning paralyzes her "with the blank rigidity of a statue" and "when [Red] touched her she sprang like a bow" (238). Mere proximity to Indigenous power renders her first stationary, and then, the very incarnation of Native weaponry; but he spurns her advances, leaving her arrested in pageantry and want, with "three savage spots of rouge" below her "blank eyes," a mouth "painted into a savage and perfect bow" (284), and of course, her suggestively "red" curls. Temple clings to the potential that Red represents but refuses to share: "It was not too late; Red was still alive" (237), she thinks desperately at one point. When Popeye assaults Temple, the best way she can think to torture him back is to say, "Dont you wish you were Red? Dont you? Dont you wish you could do what he can do?" (232). Of course, this means that Popeye will eventually murder Red—a symbolic slaying of the primal, satiating life force by the dead, perverted spawn of the elite whose own sense of virility is deeply challenged by the trauma of economic competition.[31] But Red's loss only further elevates his stock: he is extoled as a true "American"—"You may not be," one character says, "but [Red] was" (244–45). At one pole of American experience are Temple and Popeye, perversely matched vessels of boundless desire and insipid futility, fixated only on the getting; at the other is Red, actor and agent and liberator of terrible, excessive, satisfying violence. To be "Red" is to be "American," our best and worst selves irrevocably twinned, unleashed, and eliminated at will.

Irrepressible in all of these stories is a splinter of hope, a desperate but fleeting effort to conjure the untarnished aspect of the true Indigenous spirit, the primordial keeper of ancient, exculpatory ideals. Indian healers or nurses thus lurk quietly in several texts, conveying temporary relief to emphatically modern ills. In *Flags in the Dust*,[32] for instance, old Bayard Sartoris, founder and president of Merchant and Farmer's bank, has a cyst treated by Will Falls, a ninety-three-year old inmate of the local poor farm, with a remedy that Will's grandmother learned from a Choctaw woman 130 years before: "'Aint none of us never told what hit air, nor left no after trace,'" he says (227). Will's poor grammar befits his station, but it proclaims more than mere poverty: instead of saying that "none of us was ever told" the recipe, his turgid formulation implies "none of *us* never told nor left no after trace"—a deliberate safeguarding of ancient knowledge inherited and protected by simple country folk, a kind of clandestine birthright owned and defended by the meekest of the land. Will, deputy Indian here, has a face that is "browned and cheerful . . . with the simple and abounding earth" (226), and he tells long, nostalgic stories about the Civil War, his voice creeping "among ancient phantoms of the soul's and body's tribulations, into those regions of glamorous and useless strivings where such ghosts abide" (229). This all happens significantly in the back room of Bayard's bank, where he suffers from the bloated boils of his rank; and Will Falls is every bit the captive of capitalism who has traded one jail for another, the ghostly but "glamorous" soul of the precancerous, striving South bearing a secret, smelly antidote. But a Confederate is a Confederate after all, and so is an Indian—and thus, Will apologizes profusely for indulging in his weakness, a few pieces of his beloved, osseous hard candy—"I never did relish" the "soft" kind, he admits (228), and as he tells his "useless" stories, he chuckles and "mouthed his peppermint again" and again. Like the sweets-loving Chickasaws of *Requiem for a Nun*, Will's restless spirit circles seductively around the drain of memories and loss, of survivance and sorrow, and of hungers that lead to intractable debt. The Choctaw remedy does eliminate the blemish on Bayard's face, but the real shackles of the world remain: Will Falls hobbles back to the poor farm, and Bayard dies from a heart attack induced by another vessel of modernity, a too-fast automobile careening fatally out of control.

"Idyll in the Desert," another story published in 1931, takes place in a camp for tuberculosis patients in southwest Arizona. The narrative centers on the aftermath of an extramarital affair that leaves the woman, Addie Bundren-like, expiring slowly, in a sanctuary beyond the boundaries of settled civilization, that place where one contracts the quite literal disease of *consumption*. Her husband periodically sends money, which she believes comes from her lover, along with an "Injun" nurse who "couldn't talk enough of any language to tell her better than a rich man sent her to wait there. And there she waited."[33] The Indian woman's role is not to heal but only to "wait" for the inevitable to happen; she helps sustain the illusion of love, of comfort, of escape and survival, but that

Faulkner's Dialectical Indians

delicate apparatus collapses in the end with her inevitable death. At the close of the story, the man who has been telling her tale—significantly, the only other mail carrier in Faulkner's fiction besides Thomas Jefferson Pettigrew—jokes that he is actually the ghost of Sitting Bull. "I got killed one day a while back. Didn't you read it in the paper?"[34] This is the story's abrupt and absurd last line, Faulkner's striking reincarnation of the slaughtered Indian legends at the boundaries of the American narrative, not in the newspaper or the history books but in these tall tales and romantic fictions; these creations are not "real" but they are the mouthpiece of our world—some are silent like the nursemaid, harboring secrets both nutritive and noxious that they won't divulge, while others are covert marshals of communication—small-sized postal carriers and struggling novelists anxious to expose a world stricken with consumption, and perhaps to gain a bit of fame and fortune along the way.

For Faulkner, it is the ubiquitous Indian mounds, again, that serve as manifest expressions of the dialectical tension between the living and the dead, the uncanny meeting point between our most fervent ideals and our most devastating vulnerabilities: they are both elevated spaces of liberation and the malignant eruptions of an intrinsically despoiled earth. Fittingly, Lucas Beauchamp hides his whiskey still there and returns habitually seeking gold, the elusive buried treasure Faulkner's most bereft characters eternally pursue. *Sanctuary*'s Horace Benbow craves the "bumps of dirt the Indians made to stand on when the River overflowed" and thinks, with such "a hill to lie on for a while . . . then I would be all right."[35] He is never "all right," of course, but the chimera of release gives him the will to persist. A more overtly portentous Indian mound appears in Faulkner's short story "A Bear Hunt," published in 1933. The action of the story—told by Ratliff, the ubiquitous traveling salesman who oversees and tells all—is set significantly near an Indian mound "profoundly and darkly enigmatic" with "inferences of secret and violent blood, of savage and sudden destruction . . . what dark power still dwelled or lurked there, sinister, a little sardonic, like a dark and nameless beast lightly and lazily slumbering with bloody jaws."[36] The story itself is yet another Indigenous backdrop to a black-and-white narrative—a darkly comic revenge tale involving hiccups and fancy shirt collars (it's true—go read it if you haven't). But it's the Indian mound that disturbs this levity with tantalizing whispers of obliteration, of the "bloody jaws" that might at any moment awaken and attack. One of the most enduring archetypes in American culture is, of course, the savage Indian killer who returns to avenge the crimes committed against the innocent aborigine: watch any late twentieth-century horror movie, and you're likely to see an Indian burial ground from which restless

46 MELANIE BENSON TAYLOR

spirits explode with terrifying regularity and rage. Most iconically, in the appropriately named Overlook Hotel of Stanley Kubrick's *The Shining*, cascades of blood erupt within the opulent structures built brazenly on Indian lands, a container for the histories of violence that we know and commemorate but somehow still "overlook," the Indian killers too ambient and all-encompassing to be visible or even locatable. Faulkner's Overlook Hotel is the Jefferson jail, whose unlocked door and delusion of freedom and opportunity sent a deluge of blood, a sea of red, coursing through Yoknapatawpha County, where living "in the red" is not alleviated but only exacerbated by the erasure of debt, the cure that kills. As Faulkner's career moves forward, through the Depression and beyond, what is left then for his secret Indians but to infect more widely, to grow more furtive and famished, more grotesquely and ruthlessly hungry?

I want to end here, as Faulkner ends *The Town* (1957), the second novel in the Snopes trilogy, with Faulkner's own Indian killers. They are Byron Snopes's four half-Apache offspring, insidious hybrids of modernity and Indigeneity, the South and elsewhere (they are Jicarilla Apaches out of "Old Mexico," after all, and not Chickasaws, not even American Indians). They are walking collisions of the crass materialism of the infamous Snopes lineage on the one hand, and the sneaky, silent, wealth-hating Indian on the other. In a blatantly symbolic act, the children steal and kill (and probably eat) a rich woman's spoiled Pekinese dog; in other moments, they swill Coca-Cola and gobble candy, insatiable for emblems of Americanness. They are both eager consumers of capitalism and its cold executioners. They are walking signifiers of the dialectic of modernity—collapsing in small, incipient bodies the ceaseless reproduction of the will to ascend at all costs and to savagely assault the prosperous and their vapid, yapping accessories along the way.

The horrifying children are summarily deported from Jefferson, herded onto a train and sent back to Byron Snopes, while "we—all of us; we represented Jefferson—watched them mount and vanish one by one into that iron impatient maw: the girl and the two boys in overalls and [the] least un in its ankle-length single garment like a man's discarded shirt made out of flour-or meal-sacking or perhaps the remnant of an old tent. We never did know which it was."[37] The novel ends here, with all of Jefferson's citizens watching with outrage in their eyes and axle grease in their souls, witnessing the spawn of modernity "vanish" like Indians always do into the hungry maw greased for the *new* New World. And they go, like pieces of mail with shipping tags wired to their garments, errant letters from out of Thomas Jefferson Pettigrew's forever unlocked mail sack. Late in Faulkner's career, they are the perverse pinnacle of

Faulkner's Dialectical Indians

the mobile, malleable Indians shuttling in and out of his world and ours; small parcels of real knowledge forever unclaimed, unopened, and untranslatable but speaking volumes anyway; devoured by modernity but somehow flourishing, fierce, and perennially in motion. They are walking embodiments of the dissembling dialectics of modernity, bathed "in the red" of empire, clothed in either the empty sacks of consumer capitalism or in the shelter of an old, old world—"We never did"—or will—know which."

NOTES

1. Lewis M. Dabney, *The Indians of Yoknapatawpha: A Study in Literature and History* (Baton Rouge: Louisiana State University Press, 1974), 11.

2. Paul Chaat Smith, *Everything You Know about Indians Is Wrong* (Minneapolis: University of Minnesota Press, 2009), 20.

3. At the end of *Absalom, Absalom!* Shreve asks Quentin: "Why do you hate the South?" His response has been widely understood as expressing a passionate ambivalence that Faulkner may have shared (not just about the South): "'I dont hate it,' Quentin said, quickly, at once, immediately; 'I dont hate it,' he said. *I dont hate it* he thought, panting in the cold air, the iron New England dark: *I dont. I dont! I dont hate it! I dont hate it!*" (New York: Vintage, 1990), 303.

4. William Faulkner, *Requiem for a Nun*, in *Novels 1942–1954*, ed. Joseph Blotner and Noel Polk (New York: Library of America, 1994), 174.

5. William Faulkner, "Address upon Receiving the Nobel Prize for Literature," in *The Portable Faulkner*, ed. Malcolm Cowley, rev. ed. (1946; repr., New York: Penguin, 2003), 649.

6. Smith, *Everything You Know about Indians Is Wrong*, 6.

7. In fact, Faulkner pointedly used the little-known historical fact of slaveholding Indians to pitch his 1930 story "Red Leaves" to Scribner's: "Few people know that Miss. Indians owned slaves," he informed them, "That's why I suggest you all buy it. . . . I need the money." From *Selected Letters of William Faulkner*, ed. Joseph Blotner (New York: Vintage, 1977), 46–47. For recent scholarship on slaveholding among the Southeastern tribes, see Barbara Krauthamer, *Black Slaves, Indian Masters: Slavery, Emancipation, and Citizenship in the Native American South* (Chapel Hill: University of North Carolina Press, 2013); Tiya Miles, *Ties that Bind: The Story of an Afro-Cherokee Family in Slavery and Freedom* (Berkeley: University of California Press, 2005); Theda Perdue, "Cherokee Planters, Black Slaves, and African Colonization," *Chronicles of Oklahoma* 60, no. 3 (1982): 322–31; and Christina Snyder, *Slavery in Indian Country* (Cambridge, MA: Harvard University Press, 2010).

8. In his *Faulkner's County: The Historical Roots of Yoknapatawpha* (Chapel Hill: University of North Carolina Press, 2001), Don Doyle mentions a Sloan Love, a mixed-blood Chickasaw who operated a ferry on the Tallahatchie River (72). And "old Sam Love," a farmer, is mentioned in the recollections of John Malcolm, an Oklahoma ferryman; see http://digital.library.okstate.edu/Chronicles/v016/v016p302.html. In the account of a former slave named Kiziah Love, a "Sam Love" is identified as the slave-owning master of a nearby plantation, owner of Kiziah's husband; see http://www.african-nativeamerican.com /kiziah_love.htm. A man named "Sam Love" appears on the Dawes Rolls #3480 (lists of

people accepted between 1898 and 1914 by the Dawes Commission as members of the so-called "Five Civilized Tribes") as a "Chickasaw Freedman," indicating that he may have been the half-slave offspring of the Sam Love referred to in the McCarroll family stories; see http://www.okhistory.org/research/dawesresults.php?cardnum=835&tribe =Chickasaw&type=Freedmen. He may also have been one of the prominent pioneer settlers in Indian Territory, and eventually a judge in the Chickasaw courts; see http://digital .library.okstate.edu/Chronicles/v005/v005p400.html.

9. Sally Wolff, *Ledgers of History: William Faulkner, an Almost Forgotten Friendship, and an Antebellum Plantation Diary* (Baton Rouge: Louisiana State University Press, 2010), 175–76.

10. McCarroll soon decided that "a slave culture will enslave the owner more than the slave, since it enslaves the mind and soul of the owner" and began to promote a process of emancipation through indentured servitude, thus cloaking his abolitionist ideologies in a more palatable guise for the time and context (Wolff, 176).

11. Faulkner and his friend "discussed these family stories as current events," and Faulkner apparently "got very angry reading some old farm journals and cursing the writer . . . [and these] eighty-year-old events as if they happened that morning" (Wolff, 176, 177).

12. Sue Watson, "Happy Birthday, Holly Springs! Chickasaws, Settlers Forged Alliances; Love Donated Land for County Seat," *South Reporter*, November 29, 2012, http://archive.southreporter.com/2012/wk48/happy_birthday_holly_springs.html.

13. Faulkner, *Requiem*, 24.

14. Ibid., 17.

15. "Yoknapatawpha" is generally agreed to derive from the Chickasaw language and translates roughly as "water runs slow through flat land." This was Faulkner's response to a class at the University of Virginia, anyway, though Chickasaw sources give slightly different, darker translations: the word is actually a combination of two—"*Yakkni*" and "*Patawpha*"—which together refer to "land or earth that has been ripped or cut open for disemboweling." The editors of *The Critical Companion to William Faulkner* resolve the disagreement by claiming, perhaps too summarily, that "Faulkner, however, who is the sole creator of this fictional land, can make of the term what he likes" (A. Nicholas Fargnoli, Michael Golay, and Robert W. Hamblin, eds., [NY: Facts on File, 2008], 458).

16. Faulkner, *Requiem*, 29.

17. Ibid., 28.

18. Ibid., 29.

19. Ibid., 17.

20. William Faulkner, *The Sound and the Fury*, rev. ed. (1929; repr., New York: Modern Library, 2012), 317–18.

21. Blotner, *Selected Letters of William Faulkner*, 205.

22. Faulkner, *The Sound and the Fury*, 318.

23. William Faulkner, "Evangeline," in *Uncollected Stories of William Faulkner*, ed. Joseph Blotner (1979; repr., New York: Vintage, 1997), 595.

24. Ibid., 607–8.

25. William Faulkner, *As I Lay Dying*, rev. ed. (1930; repr., New York: Vintage International, 1990). All references cited parenthetically hereafter.

26. As Philip Bellfy documents, early carvers of the cigar store Indian (especially those common in Britain in the seventeenth century) used African slave boys as models; hence, the carvings were often referred to as "Black Boys" or "Virginians" (33). See Bellfy, "Permission and Possession: The Identity Tightrope," in *Walking a Tightrope: Aboriginal People and Their Representations*, ed. Ute Lischke and David T. McNab (Wilfred Laurier University Press, 2005), 29–44.

Faulkner's Dialectical Indians

27. William Faulkner, *The Wild Palms* [*If I Forget Thee, Jerusalem*] (1939; repr., New York: Vintage International, 1995), 20–21.

28. Ibid., 122.

29. Ibid., 148.

30. William Faulkner, *Sanctuary*, rev. ed. (1931; repr., New York: Vintage International, 1993). All references cited parenthetically hereafter.

31. This anxiety was no doubt experienced viscerally by Faulkner himself, who famously claimed to have written this apparent potboiler for the sole purpose of making money. For more on the relationship between Faulkner's economic anxieties articulated in the novel's preface and its theme of rape, see Sondra Guttman, "Who's Afraid of the Corncob Man: Masculinity, Race, and Labor in the Preface to *Sanctuary*," *Faulkner Journal* 15, no. 1 (Fall 1999–Spring 2000): 15–34.

32. William Faulkner, *Flags in the Dust* (1929, as *Sartoris;* 1973, as *Flags in the Dust;* repr., New York: Vintage International, 2012). All references cited parenthetically hereafter.

33. William Faulkner, "Idyll in the Desert," in *Uncollected Stories of William Faulkner*, ed. Joseph Blotner (1979; repr., New York: Vintage, 1997), 409.

34. Ibid., 411.

35. Faulkner, *Sanctuary*, 15–16.

36. William Faulkner, "A Bear Hunt," in *Collected Stories of William Faulkner*, ed. Joseph Blotner (1950; repr., New York: Vintage International, 1995), 65.

37. William Faulkner, *The Town* (1957; repr. New York: Vintage International, 2011), 390.

"Land! Hold On! Just Hold On!"

Flood Waters, Hard Times, and Sacred Land in "Old Man" and *My Louisiana Love*

GINA CAISON

Despite William Faulkner's best attempts to "hold on" to the mythology of the landed South via a "sense of place," a planetary deep time of Indigeneity pervades his work. To borrow a term from Wai Chee Dimock, this alternate temporal order creates a "double threading" of how we might read Faulkner under a rubric of a Native American studies methodology. Pulling together threads from southern networks of place and Indigenous understandings of land claim, a planetary time of Indigeneity appears stretched across Faulkner's landscape, not simply on the surface of Delta fields or buried beneath riverbank mud but as a coterminous, simultaneous universe, one that appears in his work even when the author himself seems only tacitly aware of its presence. As Dimock describes, "This double threading thickens time, lengthens it, shadowing in its midst the abiding traces of the planet's multitudinous life."[1] Calling this phenomenon "deep time," she explains how it "highlights [. . .] a set of longitudinal frames, at once projective and recessional, with input going both ways, and binding continents and millennia into many loops of relations, a densely interactive fabric."[2] Working from this idea of deep time, I think not so much of Faulkner's Native South as I do the Native South's Faulkner, positioning the author's work as one thread among many in the interactive fabric of the region. In many cases, Faulkner takes liberties and makes mistakes in his use of Native history, but to catalogue his successes or failures means to remain fixed upon Faulkner's tapestry alone, imagining that the "Native" runs through his fictional Yoknapatawpha like a single thread. Rather, I posit that we focus our critical attention on the ways in which Faulkner's work forms part of a larger fabric of a region still deeply imbued with the concerns of Indigenous land claim. Or even that we recognize, like Dimock, the ways in which these threads may appear as doubled, going both ways, pulling at our sense of temporal order rather than our sense of place. Simply put, the fact that Faulkner may not have always known, represented, or acted upon the region's Indigenous connections in his work does not mean that the region's Indigeneity did not act upon him.

For far too long, many scholars have understood Native American studies as an object-focused discipline, one that pursues Indigenous people and culture as objects of study. However, Native American studies offers an epistemological approach to the world. As a discipline, it draws from Indigenous knowledges to construct methods of analysis that can be applied to a diverse set of materials. Rather than taking from the discipline of Eurocentric literary studies and then applying those standards to Native literature, scholars such as Jodi Byrd, Daniel Heath Justice, Craig Womack, and others demonstrate how to take Native American studies as a disciplinary framework that allows us to read beyond Native-authored texts.[3] This distinction remains important for understanding how and why Native American studies is more than an amalgamation of traditional Western disciplines. Collectively, these critics produce scholarship that conceptualizes the Native South beyond the literary object and instead outlines new ways to approach literary criticism as a discipline. In this spirit, this chapter does not attempt to find the Native object in Faulkner's universe but to reread Faulkner within an epistemology of Indigenous land claim and temporality within the South. Within this framework, I interrogate William Faulkner's "Old Man" section of *The Wild Palms* (1939), with its depiction of the 1927 flood, alongside Houma filmmaker Monique Verdin's documentary *My Louisiana Love* (2012), which recounts Hurricane Katrina and the BP oil spill, to examine the ways that the two texts present ecological disaster in the Native South.[4]

For instance, in one climactic scene from the "Old Man" cycle of the contrapuntal novel, Faulkner depicts a scene of unlikely life as the "tall convict" thrusts the rescued pregnant woman upon a prodigiously appearing "Indian mound," so she can give birth during the flood. Just before dragging her from the boat to the mound, he exclaims, "Land! Land! Hold on! Just hold on!"[5] This moment might signal paradoxically both a rebirth for those trapped in the cycle of the prison-industrial complex of the Deep South, as the woman literally gives birth on a sacred site while being held by a convict who is believed by the authorities to be "lost," and a foreclosed set of possibilities as the convict desires nothing more in this scene than to return to his familiar imprisoned life.[6] This nameless Indian mound, likely near the Atchafalaya basin, directs the reader to a much older South all but consumed by Faulkner's biblical flood waters. However, as the site of the novella's one moment of futurity in birth, it points the reader forward to a time beyond the characters' present crises. This Indian mound, however, is not simply a mystical savior. Likewise, Indigenous-based approaches to Faulkner, literature, or the environment are not meant to offer non-Natives romantic solutions to questions about the future of southern studies, the humanities, or our contemporary ecological problems. Instead, the Indian mound—as active agent rather than passive setting—intrudes upon the narrative, I argue, because Faulkner simply could not get around it. When evoking the epic scale of flooding, the sheer failure of US infrastructure, and the destruction wrought by generations of settler-colonial land abuse, the novel— and perhaps by extension its author—was confronted by the inconvenient fact of the remaining land: it belongs to Indigenous people. When cast against the liquidity of nearly everything else, the Indian mound remains, adjusting the readers' measure of southern time and reminding them that narratives such as Faulkner's represent but a blip of Gregorian calendar time imposed on the region as settlers attempted, and in this case failed, to remake the landscape in their own image. The phrase "hold on" offers a double-threaded meaning, signaling both space and time. On the one hand, one can "hold on," to the physical object—the land or silt that slips through one's grasp. On the other hand, one can "hold on" by adjusting one's timing—by slowing down, waiting, or changing the pace of the expectant event. In this scene, the tall convict's utterance pulls both threads together, suggesting that the flood adjusts the understanding of land and temporality of the characters and, by extension, the reader.

Following this vein, this chapter theorizes a furrowed temporality of the flood. As water creeps or rushes over land, it erodes the very dirt long romanticized within southern frameworks of place. Rising water generates its own time signature. It can come quickly, gathering soil into its current and leaving earth-bound scars behind, or it can rise at a slower pace, roiling down the path of the river, gaining momentum and pulling under all that it sweeps across. The tension between the quick and slow creates its own faultlike trench where different temporal orders bump against one another. As a result of this friction, a space opens up where we might attempt to gaze into the deep time created by the clash of geological and man-made processes. The flood asks that we hold multiple temporalities in view. This chapter examines what happens when floodwaters furrow the earth, and it interrogates the epistemological claims that such moments entail for both Faulkner and Verdin. I focus on those moments when the presumably solid earth becomes liquid in order to illustrate how the heuristic of landed space draws our attention away from climatic and human abuses. As Steve Mentz argues,

Flood Waters, Hard Times, and Sacred Land 53

"We have begun to recognize that planet-sized ecological questions are really questions about the ocean."[7] I would add freshwater and brackish ecosystems to his cogent point, as with or without salt, the planet's health—and by extension ours as humans—lives and dies by the water.[8]

This focus on floods and water-based ecosystems encourages critical perspectives that link past events such as the 1927 flood with later disasters including Hurricane Katrina and the BP oil spill.[9] However, despite the seductive narrative links among these ecodisasters, they are not interchangeable occurrences. They each represent a particular set of actions and reactions, global and local frameworks. The flood of 1927 seemed to work in slow motion, with man-made factors such as vast deforestation and river flow manipulation and seemingly natural factors including unusually high yearly precipitation colliding to bring about a catastrophic result.[10] By contrast, Hurricane Katrina and the BP oil spill have come to represent a comeuppance for our willful ignorance on the climate change produced by our insatiable need for oil. Each disaster, however, revealed to many the deep inequalities of the US social networks and material infrastructure along racial and class lines.[11] Furthermore, as Susan Scott Parrish explains, the disasters of the early twentieth and twenty-first centuries share more than superficial similarities:

> Though these disaster-intensive periods . . . are associated with different immediate causes, they can both be places along a continuum within the planetary epoch that scientists have recently dubbed "the Anthropocene," a term meant to indicate the scope, intensity, and irreversibility of human alteration of planetary life begun around 1800 with intensive agriculture and deforestation, pollution, the combustion of fossil fuels, and other modern practices.[12]

This planetary scale, meant at once to adjust our spatial and temporal thinking, works in both Faulkner and Verdin's narrative constructions. Even though both works remain somewhat narrow in geographic scope—Faulkner barely leaves the Mississippi River, and Verdin stays within miles of the Gulf—they each signal larger networks of connection beyond their immediate settings. As each text deals with disaster, we see examples of Parrish's explanation that the Anthropocene "indicates that we have started to conceptualize the human, the human's relationship to nature, and the human's relationship to historical periods anew."[13] It is this melding of periods that bears most directly on my argument as I attempt to think through southern literature and literary studies' tendency to dwell on a periodization bound up with old and new Souths determined by settler-colonial societies and Lost Causes rather than on Indigenous presences and temporalities that trouble those received heuristics.

"Old Man" pushes and pulls against an understanding of the Native South within southern literary periodization. We are told in the opening passage of the story that our would-be protagonist possesses "a sunburned face and Indian-black hair" (*WP*, 20). This is not to argue that this character is secretly, covertly, or even implied as Native. He just has black hair, yet the inclusion of this opening physical description signals to the reader an idea of Indian-ness ahead of the subsequent action. More interestingly, to me, are the twin issues of the convict's "adventure" on the river: one, that he unwittingly travels in circles before collecting the stranded woman from the tree, and two, that he is simultaneously rendered as "lost" by the bureaucratic system of the prison even though we know very well that he is in fact not lost. Caught in currents he doesn't understand, the convict initially passes the woman stranded in the tree. Almost simultaneously, he ruminates that he has "accidentally been caught in a situation in which time and environment, not himself, was mesmerized" (*WP*, 124). When he unknowingly returns, the woman notes that she wasn't sure if he was "aiming to come back" (*WP*, 125). Here, Faulkner posits that the convict's time is moving in a circle without his being aware. As he later travels on rivers flowing backwards, again the convict ponders his race against time as the current rushes towards him: "Time: that was his hitch now, so his only chance was to stay ahead of it as long as he could and hope to reach something before it struck" (*WP*, 143). This moment creates an ironic counter to the novel's opening line, in which Faulkner places the reader directly (and parenthetically) in Gregorian calendar time: "It was in Mississippi, in May, in the flood year 1927" (*WP*, 20). Against this assured timeline, the convict loses his bearings in the flood's own temporality. Or simply put, the planet neither knows nor cares that it is 1927. Thomas McHaney notes. "Birth and death, departure and return, the waxing and waning of the flood come into the novel not only as theme but as form, too,"[14] and Matthew Wynn Sivils succinctly offers, "Faulkner's Southern ecology is a broken timepiece with hands pointing towards a troubled past."[15] Sivils's evocative argument focuses primarily on the social injustices of enslaved and conscripted African American laborers' relationship to the land. However, I posit that the addition, even intrusion, of Indigenous land in the novel via the Indian mound not so much breaks Faulkner's timepiece as sends those arms spinning, pulled by something larger than the author understands. While McHaney attributes this phenomenon to "[a] cyclic movement that suggests the unceasing round of generation and decay to which all Nature is subject," I see the novel as caught up in the Indigenous temporality of its setting, not simply unable to control an abstract "Nature" but rather signaling a tacit awareness that the very marks on the land in the form of the surviving Indian mounds scoff at the tall convict's, and perhaps Faulkner's, opening establishment of Western calendar time.[16] In this way, the novel's focus on water rather than on land challenges a progressive temporal order, broken or otherwise. It asks us to see spiraling patterns and returns, ebbs and flows that do not march off in linear fashion towards the past or the future.

Within this narrative order, it is important to examine the "meanwhile" of the convict's time adrift on the floodwaters while the prison officials ponder what to do about his disappearance. After his original companion, "the plump convict," is rescued following the initial run-in with the strong current, the deputy comes to the warden with the supposed news of the tall convict's demise, asserting, "We've lost a man." "Lost him?" the warden replies, then notes, "Well. Here I haven't lost a prisoner in ten years, and now, like this" (*WP*, 65). But he concludes, "The main thing is to get his name off the books as dead before some politician tries to collect his food allowance" (*WP*, 66). Desiring a neat end to the bureaucratic crisis, the warden pronounces the tall convict lost, completes the paper work, and moves on. The warden's response to the crisis of the lost convict is like many a reaction to environmental catastrophe in its desire for boundedness and order achieved via the discrete beginnings and endings of the unusual occurrence. However, as Mentz argues, "historical and contemporary experiences suggest that departure from stability—catastrophes—constitute the new normal."[17] Significantly, Faulkner's novel presages Mentz's remarks on sustainability, for as Robert Jackson explains, the US South and its authors have long engaged in what he terms the "Southern disaster complex," where "the full sense of tragedy that so many Southerners have perceived in their culture seems a particularly apt response to living in an environment where disasters of whatever origins occur with alarming frequency."[18] Jackson's southern disaster complex works to describe the aesthetic and psychological uses of tragedy in examining the Confederate Lost Cause. I argue that by employing a Native studies framework, we might imagine the temporal landscape of the South differently and thus more fully interrogate the appearance of the Indian mound as challenging the scope of catastrophe.

In *Reconstructing the Native South: American Indian Literature and the Lost Cause* (2011), Melanie Benson Taylor attempts to synthesize elements of the Confederate Lost Cause with the region's Native American literature and history in order to make sense of the contemporary forces of global capitalism. Taylor ask us to "confront difficult questions: in the aftermath of Removal and colonial devastation, what remains—for either group—to be recovered?"[19] While she asserts that she does not wish to "forge a false harmony between historically antagonistic groups" or "deny the necessity and the reality of tribal sovereignty and nationalism," much of her analysis may unintentionally do just that.[20] Whereas Taylor looks to examine the convergence of lost-cause narratives across southern and Native contexts, I seek to pull them apart a bit—to show their vast dissimilarities. When Taylor asks, "Is it acceptable to identify an Indian 'Lost Cause,' much as we have acknowledged the futility of the white South's tribalism and nostalgia?" I am prompted to turn towards Robert Warrior's remarks on the lost cause's currency in American Indian studies.[21] Drawing on the work of Edward Said, Warrior points out that "a cause seeming lost or not is a matter of many things, including the juncture in history at which the determination is being made, the sort of narrative the determination is part of, and the perspective from which judgment on the cause is being pronounced."[22] He then reminds us that "American Indians have never lost some fundamental things, like the relationship to their homelands" and that for Said, "no cause is ever finally lost until its hope is extinguished in the last person who holds it in his or her consciousness."[23] I agree and would like to extend this idea to zero in on the fact that these "determinations" are often based on a belief in a linear temporality. The benefit of thinking past and through the lost cause is exactly the type of new consciousness that emerges in the creativity of survival that sees a future beyond linear time. Taylor's analysis stays firmly within the twentieth century, and thus it might be difficult to examine the contours of the long discursive terrain of loss. She acknowledges this in proposing that "the important thing is to keep digging deeper, and to try and locate both the awful and beautiful stories that unearth themselves along the way."[24] Despite her use of the problematic archeology metaphor, given the long history of non-Native archeologists literally unearthing Native bodies and possessions without the consent of collaboration of Native people, I agree with her call to look more closely at how southern and Native worlds have been constructed with one another in active mind, and in doing this, I argue that neither the temporality nor the language of loss has to be determined exclusively by the region's Confederate history. Further, I assert that looking for the convergences among what scholars pronounce "losses" might very well do more harm than good in its continued centering of *objects* as the focus of Native studies within the South. As Warrior demonstrates, there are other ways to think about loss, and within southern studies we might do well to think with our colleagues in Native American studies or, as Jay Watson argues, environmental studies, to interrogate not simply the language of loss or lost objects but also the ontological and epistemological frameworks embedded in different conceptions of

Flood Waters, Hard Times, and Sacred Land 57

"lost-ness."[25] This is all the more true if we are to think ourselves out of the continued destruction wrought by Anthropocene projects, many of which are themselves extensions of settler colonialism in the Americas. In other words, we might not put so much pressure on the various *losses* identified by scholars as on the *causes* behind those identifications.

To return to Faulkner's novel, the convict is not lost. Instead, the pronouncement is made by a bureaucratic agent at a premature juncture. Readers know that he is out on the river caught up in the planetary time of the "Old Man" who never dies. But what does it mean that a convict protagonist with Indian-black hair rescues a woman after circling around floodwaters and manages to save her and her immanent infant only upon the appearance of an Indian mound out of a flooded river basin? And what to make of the fact that this same convict protagonist is rendered "lost" on paper just like those Native people, nations, knowledges, and causes pronounced as "lost" when they are in fact incredibly present? Might it be that the idea of "loss" does not fit the Native South at all and instead that its continued currency in scholarly circles results from bureaucratic and academic determinations unwittingly preoccupied with the constantly receding object? And more tellingly, might not a constant focus on "lost" people and objects buttress a supposed need for the scholar-savior, either assisting in the "search" for presumably Native items, characters, and plot points within authors such as Faulkner or patronizingly measuring the authenticity of Indigenous stories and worldviews against an undeniably more damaging mythos of the Confederate Lost Cause? If nothing else, "Old Man" makes clear the danger in believing everything one reads, as the tall convict is in jail because he followed the logic of the dime-store novels and attempted—incredibly unsuccessfully—to rob a train. In other words, he is not lost, but he certainly does not know where he is.

Within a Native studies framework, these scenes from "Old Man" push readers of the novel to disarticulate the romantic southern "sense of place" from Indigenous land claim. The affective realm of the "sense of place" can tend to move us all too easily into a material attachment to the physical land, without remembering that, as Eric Gary Anderson notes, "Native southern ground is not lost (or preliterate) ground, not simply a mistily nostalgic pre-southern place, situated in some other culture's bracingly chronological order and largely defined against the canonical non-Native South, the post-southern non-Native South."[26] Instead, the Native South is past, present, and future, and the land claim upon it does not terminate just because non-Native southerners feel attached to their own homes. This disjoining of a sense of place from a material land attachment is important for then considering the geographic and temporal fantasies that undergird much of white southern exceptionalism. In a way, this attempt at detangling echoes Martyn Bone's *The Postsouthern Sense of Place in Contemporary Fiction* (2005), in that each project remains invested in interrogating how place continues to work as a signifier within a southern studies that has become increasingly skeptical of a solid South. However, because the Native South is no more "postsouthern" than it is in Anderson's words "presouthern," the work needs attention from a specifically Native studies perspective.[27] The Native South exists alongside these pre- and postmarkers without adhering to their temporal determinations. While for Bone the Agrarian invention of and reliance on place represents a ground zero of sorts for southern studies, my emphasis on land claim attempts to recognize the material theft of Indigenous lands from sovereign Native nations that exist in practice and policy even as "the South" covers over this history with affective and sensory myths. This distinction between narrative place and material territory creeps up on the edges of Faulkner's novel and ultimately rises up through the flood, reminding the reader that when it comes to Indigenous land claim in the South, all is not lost.

I contrast my reading of the flood in "Old Man" with the floods and rebirths in Sharon Linezo Hong and Monique Verdin's *My Louisiana Love*.[28] Like Faulkner's novel, the documentary shows the destruction of rising water and consequent land loss. Despite this deep sense of loss and its recognition of our contemporary collective complicity in petroculture, the film points towards resilience through its construction of an Indigenous temporality that continues to "hold on." The film signals a distinct time signature against and behind the linear temporality of what might appear to be a lost cause of the "dying Delta." However, this is not the Lost Cause of the Confederate South. Rather, it is a lost cause as conceived by Robert Warrior—one signaling the emancipation of future possibility that comes with having already lived through one's own apocalypse. These causes do not deal in linear time, where one may look backwards and forwards down the line, but rather evoke a spiral, a looping back where every end marks another beginning. Yet this spiraling temporality is just one among many possible temporal frameworks that emerge when we begin to consider letting go of, rather than holding on to, our land-based narratives of region. These narratives deal in what Mentz calls fantasies of sustainability whose focus on stasis imagines that we "persist in time."[29] Instead, Verdin's narrative lives through and pushes past apocalypse. It represents what Jay Watson calls for within

> current efforts to rehabilitate nostalgia, utopia, apocalypticism, and other discourses of temporal alterity as bases for environmental activism and critique

. . . [that] can guide southern studies scholars to a deeper consideration of which pasts to claim and which forms of change to interrogate or contest in the field's ongoing work of negotiating tradition.[30]

Following its own temporality of the flood, Verdin and Hong's film navigates tradition as innovation through both content and form.

My Louisiana Love follows Verdin, a young Houma Indian woman who has returned to Louisiana to live with her father's family. The chronicle begins around 2004, and the film follows her and her family through Hurricanes Katrina and Rita (2005) as well as the BP oil spill (2010). Over the course of the film, which chronicles six years, viewers learn about Houma tribal history and culture as revealed through conversations between Verdin and her grandmother Matine, and they witness the profound personal and collective losses of Bayou people as a result of the region's entanglement with the oil and gas industries. The losses of the film are almost too numerous to count. From the literally disappearing land to the destruction of homes, and from the losses deriving from mental illness to the physical sickness resulting from the exposure to leaked crude oil, the film may seem to deal only in loss. It is bleak, and it is difficult to determine what hope there might be in the drama of petroculture writ small onto one Native American community in the South. Despite this amassed sense of loss, I argue that the film points towards resilience through its positing of an Indigenous temporality. Whereas the southern disaster complex described by Jackson "depends upon the unimportance of fixing blame or, to be more accurate, upon the importance of *not* fixing blame on any specific persons or decisions," *My Louisiana Love* lays the blame squarely at the feet of the oil and gas industries, which frequently target Native nations and their land.[31]

The United Houma Nation of Louisiana represents a Native southern community in which the temporality of a lost cause can be re-examined from a Native perspective rather than from an overdetermined (neo) Confederate one. As a tribe that has been repeatedly denied federal and cultural recognition through the lingering effects of Jim Crow–era policies, and as a community unduly affected by Louisiana's infamous "football field per hour" land loss, the Houma may seem to be continually fighting losing battles.[32] As a tribal people that live connected by waterways and depend upon coastal economies, they also represent a community that can teach the rest of the world about how to survive beyond what may seem like points of finality. Such survival, however, requires recognition—cultural, intellectual, and political. And it would also require a recognition of alternate ways to conceive of time and region and the real and imagined losses that inform these conceptions.

The Gulf South homelands of the Houma, with tides controlled by the temporality of planetary time, offer a potential space in and about which to think past Mentz's stasis of sustainability and instead to think through the options of the prolonged and ongoing.

Verdin attempts to form a chain of recognition across these concepts through her autobiographical approach in the film. Working backwards through her own personal history, she comes to construct a narrative that queries the temporal pace of belonging for tribal peoples in Louisiana. About half an hour into the film, Verdin is finally able to return to her grandmother's home after Hurricane Katrina. The destruction is overwhelming, with a visible flood line at approximately five feet high around each room. Photos and furniture are molded, mildewed, torn, and tarnished. Verdin's boyfriend and artistic partner, Mark Krasnoff, turns the camera on Verdin and asks her what she will miss about the house. In response, she chronicles both the joys and small hardships, from looking out the kitchen window to collecting water from the cistern. Each shot moves slowly from room to room and then back outside where Verdin surveys the land. At first there is no music, and the viewer only hears the buzzing insects who have managed to survive through the storm. A seemingly lone bird chirps while Verdin holds a ventilator mask to her face. At this moment, she points to something in a pile of wreckage and says, "An armadillo—it's right there," to which Krasnoff responds in pleasant surprise, "It's alive?! Yes. Oh my God. He made it." Verdin observes in reply, "Because he's a dinosaur." The camera zooms in on the animal, and a slow banjo tune begins to play as Verdin takes photographs of the scene.

The pace of this scene, juxtaposing the movement of the visual and verbal survey of profound loss with the still frame of photography, leaves the viewer to contemplate growth and stasis. As the banjo picks a melody that slowly reverberates across the visual image, the viewer is invited to consider the natural processes of land healing alongside the man-made disaster of oil rigs that float off their bases. The collocation is made even more evident by the shot of the armadillo—"the dinosaur" as Verdin calls it—next to a ruined Yamaha motorbike. The armadillo serves as an apt metaphor for unlikely survival as the species belongs to the last remaining biological families in its order *cingulata*. Its name in Nahuatl, *āyōtōchtli*, means "turtle-rabbit," thus signaling the possibility of a shift in temporal perspective between that which is at once very quick, even hopping when startled, but also armored to live and survive very slowly. Though the Houma language is closely related to Choctaw and not Nahuatl, as an embedded metaphor that carries significance, the armadillo's appearance in the visual image calls up multiple meanings

Flood Waters, Hard Times, and Sacred Land   61

across the Indigenous Americas. It is this very ability to shift in pace, to adjust the temporality, that can allow something to exist beyond its own supposed apocalypse or evolutionary extinction, and this is what the film demonstrates.

Additionally, the Gulf South, as a space where the rapid geological rise of petroculture crashes against the otherwise slow geological processes of tidal flux, erosion, and river flows, allows us to think through what's at stake in linking alternate temporalities and periodizations to our regional studies. As Lisa Brooks asks:

> What would it mean to privilege place when discussing periodization, to consider, as the geographer Davis Wishart does, that "period" and "region" are deeply linked narratives? What different shape might literary history take if we account for distinct conceptions of time that arise simultaneously from particular places? How might indigenous methodologies help answer some of the vexing questions that literary historians ponder in our present world?[33]

This rethinking of time from Indigenous methodologies gives us the space to think not only about the vexing questions literary historians ponder but also about those confronting all of us in this age of ecological change. The film does not provide answers, and indeed these questions are big ones, not likely to be solved by a single literary or cultural text. However, our shift from privileging land-based regional histories to ones that examine waterways also allows us to shift from literary histories of the region that privilege old and new Souths as a priori categories. In thinking with these different temporal constructions, we may assemble an archive that looks messy, incoherent, or even vaguely disjointed. However, this new thought-work may allow us to see new archives that emerge from the continually revised logics of the region we examine rather than from the inevitable story of their presupposed functions as elements of national narrative making. It asks that we forego the Lost Cause in favor of postapocalyptic futures that, rather than breeding misplaced nostalgia, enliven some form of future possibility for the region.

Towards the end of the film, after Verdin has experienced the suicide of her partner, Krasnoff, and the death of her father from cancer, she travels through the swamp on a boat. Through voice-over narration, she offers, "Since losing my father and Kras, I can see how the illness of our land and waters breeds illness on our people." "But," she continues, "our love ties us to this place and makes us feel responsible to care for it." The camera then follows her into a dark room as she explains, "It was by instinct that I first picked up a camera and began documenting my family." We watch her develop black-and-white film—a slow process to be sure in this age of digital photography—as she continues, "And now these images and stories bear witness to a disappearing Louisiana." However, her very act of documenting this way of life ensures at least some measure of its continuance, and her act of developing the film literally renders the appearance of her community before the viewer's eyes, battling a logic of "loss" and invisibility. Significantly, the film then cuts to a scene of Matine's ninety-sixth birthday party as she blows out the candles on her cake. This scene is juxtaposed with a direct cut to the burning flames atop the tall stacks of a refinery, leaving the viewer with an uneasy realization of the stakes of life lived in the age and shadow of oil. Notably, after this scene, the shot cuts to Verdin carrying plants for her grandmother's new garden, signaling to the viewer that an exclusive focus on perpetual loss serves no use for future growth.

There is resilience in *My Louisiana Love*, which closes with Verdin planting new crops with Matine and building her own home out of a repurposed shipping container. Not all is romantic hope, however. As Verdin does literally within her new home, we too live metaphorically inside the material conditions of our present-day container-shipping global economy of petroculture, and the change in our intellectual conceptions of time and region will affect little without large and small real-life actions.[34] Verdin does not simply offer a romantic remedy (Indigenous or otherwise) for the problems of the Anthropocene. Earlier in the film, she shows herself literally pumping gas as she and Krasnoff flee Hurricane Katrina, bound in escape to the very commodity they must resist. *My Louisiana Love* does not rewrite a romantic narrative about a nostalgic Houma identity; instead, it proposes Houma sovereignty as at least one concrete means of active legal protection for the tribe, its members, and the land. The issues of Native American national sovereignty should remain paramount, as these policy avenues offer at least some possibility of land protection even in the most vulnerable environments, but individual humans must also start the hard work of examining their own habits in the age of petroculture.

Despite the film's success in avoiding the representation of clichéd "Ecological Indians," it is also possible that some viewers might read it as squarely within the literary tradition of Jackson's southern disaster complex.[35] For, as Jackson explains, "this native Southern discourse has succeeded in imagining a history that becomes not just a resource for environmental protection, a political tool, a portentous spiritual and aesthetic wellspring, but a restorative environment in itself. Welcome to Dixie."[36] As the tone of his closing sentence suggests, such projects should be read skeptically for the old southern ideologies they uphold

Flood Waters, Hard Times, and Sacred Land

through embedded narratives of traditionalism. This formulation would render *My Louisiana Love* not so much different *from* as a clear descendant *of* Faulkner's "Old Man." I think, though, that the difference between the lowercased "native" of Jackson's critique and the uppercase "Native" of the Native South *does* matter here. There must be a way to recognize exclusive Native rights to Indigenous lands without dismissing all critiques of settler-colonial structures and practices via the appeal to Indigenous knowledges, myths, and histories as "romanticizing." This is why political, material Indigenous land claim matters over and above a southern "sense of place." This is why we need to think about the Native South's Faulkner rather than Faulkner's Native South.

By way of closing, I would like to return to the double threading of the deep time in both texts. As Keith Cartwright proposed recently in his *PMLA* manifesto on the future of southern studies, "We need a reconfigured disciplinarity open to undisciplined knowledge from beyond accredited time-space."[37] This "from beyond" might very well find a space in a southern studies that begins to take Native studies seriously as a discipline with its own methodological frameworks. There is a way forward—in practice and in policy—without romanticizing the Native object and without adhering to the hard time set down in "the chronological organization of anthologies and coursework [that] keeps the peculiar institutions of planters and founders at the center of the master narrative."[38] Texts such as *My Louisiana Love* perhaps answer the questions left unanswered by Faulkner's "Old Man." Together they pull that double thread, looped in an unlikely pairing that reveals southern studies' assumptions about lost causes. Their respective floods draw them into a dialogue across deep time as each text wrestles with a watery planet seemingly beyond human or authorial control. As Cartwright observes, "Cross-cultural authority draws from a different temporality (seasonal, musical, ritual, and deep time) in counterclockwise dialogue with eternity. We can move to the time signatures of our own spaces, which turn at their own angles to the sun."[39] Rather than keep Faulkner's Native objects securely within his own Yoknapatawpha universe, I want to advocate for more Native studies approaches to Faulkner, for a bit less "holding on" to our discipline's dear objects, for seeing what new horizons emerge when we let go.

NOTES

Portions of this chapter appear, in different form, in Caison's forthcoming book, *Red States: Indigeneity, Settler Colonialism, and Southern Studies*, to be published by University of Georgia Press in 2018.

1. Wai Chee Dimock, *Through Other Continents: American Literature across Deep Time* (Princeton, NJ: Princeton University Press, 2006), 3.

2. Ibid., 3–4.

3. For example, see Jodi A. Byrd, *The Transit of Empire: Indigenous Critiques of Colonialism* (Minneapolis: University of Minnesota Press, 2011); Daniel Heath Justice, *Our Fires Survive the Storm: A Cherokee Literary History* (Minneapolis: University of Minnesota Press, 2006); and Craig Womack, *Red on Red: Native American Literary Separatism* (Minneapolis: University of Minnesota Press, 1999).

4. As many scholars have noted, Faulkner preferred his original title for the work, *If I Forget Thee, Jerusalem.*

5. William Faulkner, *The Wild Palms [If I Forget Thee, Jerusalem]* (1939; repr., New York: Vintage Books, 1990), 148. Henceforth cited parenthetically as *WP.*

6. Cynthia Dobbs offers a compelling reading of the novel's investment in gender and geography as it relates to the convict's experience of the flood and Parchman prison. See Cynthia Dobbs, "Flooded: The Excesses of Geography, Gender, and Capitalism in *If I Forget Thee, Jerusalem,*" *American Literature* 73, no. 4 (2001): 811–35.

7. Steve Mentz, "After Sustainability," *PMLA* 127, no. 3 (2012): 587. Mentz's quote parenthetically references Sylvia Earle, *Sea Change: A Message of the Oceans* (New York: Ballatine, 1996).

8. This idea has been rendered highly visible in 2016 with the water crisis in Flint, Michigan, the Standing Rock protest against the Dakota Access Pipeline in South Dakota, and, most pressingly for the present argument, the proposed Bayou Bridge Pipeline that would cut through the Atchafalaya Basin.

9. Anthony Dyer Hoefer, "'They're Trying to Wash Us Away': Revisiting Faulkner's *If I Forget Thee, Jerusalem [The Wild Palms]* and Wright's 'Down by the Riverside' after the Flood" *Mississippi Quarterly* 63, nos. 3–4 (2010): 537–54.

10. John Barry, *Rising Tide: The Great Mississippi Flood of 1927 and How It Changed America* (New York: Touchstone, 1997).

11. Susan Scott Parrish, *The Flood Year 1927: A Cultural History* (Princeton, NJ: Princeton University Press, 2017).

12. Ibid., 5.

13. Ibid., 5–6.

14. Thomas L. McHaney, *William Faulkner's* The Wild Palms: *A Study* (Jackson: University of Mississippi Press, 1975), 40.

15. Matthew Wynn Sivils, "Faulkner's Ecological Disturbances," *Mississippi Quarterly* 59, no. 3 (2006): 500.

16. McHaney, *William Faulkner's* The Wild Palms, 40.

17. Mentz, "After Sustainability," 587.

18. Robert T. Jackson, "The Southern Disaster Complex," *Mississippi Quarterly* 63, nos. 3–4 (2010): 559.

19. Melanie Benson Taylor, *Reconstructing the Native South: American Indian Literature and the Lost Cause* (Athens: University of Georgia Press, 2011), 21.

20. Ibid.

Flood Waters, Hard Times, and Sacred Land

21. Ibid.

22. Robert Allen Warrior, "Native Critics in the World: Edward Said and Nationalism," in *American Indian Literary Nationalism*, ed. Jace Weaver, Craig S. Womack, and Robert Warrior (Albuquerque: University of New Mexico Press, 2006), 218.

23. Ibid., 219.

24. Taylor, *Reconstructing the Native South*, 205.

25. Jay Watson, "The Other Matter of the South," *PMLA* 131, no. 1 (2016): 157–61.

26. Eric Gary Anderson, "On Native Ground: Indigenous Presences and Countercolonial Strategies in Southern Narratives of Captivity, Removal, and Repossession," *Southern Spaces* (2007). Accessed May 13, 2010.

27. Martyn Bone, *The Postsouthern Sense of Place in Contemporary Fiction* (Baton Rouge: Louisiana State University Press, 2005).

28. Sharon Linzo Hong, dir., *My Louisiana Love* (Cambridge, MA: Within A Sense, LLC, 2012).

29. Mentz, "After Sustainability," 586.

30. Watson, "The Other Matter of the South," 159.

31. Jackson, "The Southern Disaster Complex," 557.

32. Mark Edwin Miller, *Forgotten Tribes: Unrecognized Indians and the Federal Acknowledgment Process* (Lincoln: University of Nebraska Press, 2004), 156–207.

33. Lisa Brooks, "The Primacy of the Present, the Primacy of Place: Navigating the Spiral of History in the Digital World," *PMLA* 127, no. 2 (2012): 309.

34. See Boris Vormman, *Global Port Cities in North America: Urbanization Processes and Global Production Networks* (New York: Routledge, 2016), and Marc Levinson, *The Box: How the Shipping Container Made the World Smaller and the World Economy Bigger* (Princeton, NJ: Princeton University Press, 2008).

35. See Shepard Krech III, *The Ecological Indian: Myth and History* (New York: W. W. Norton, 1999). Several scholars have critiqued Krech's work as reductive and shortsighted in its descriptions of Indigenous knowledges regarding ecological practices. See, for example, Michael Harkin and David Rich Lewis, eds., *Native Americans and the Environment: Perspectives on the Ecological Indian* (Lincoln: University of Nebraska Press, 2007).

36. Jackson, "The Southern Disaster Complex," 569.

37. Keith Cartwright, "Tar-Baby, Terrapin, and Trojan Horse—A Face-the-Music Cosmo Song from the University's Hind Tit," *PMLA* 131, no. 1 (2016): 178.

38. Ibid.

39. Ibid.

Dressing the Part:
Evolution of Indian Dress in Faulkner

Patricia Galloway

Problems with Faulkner's Indians

More than ten years ago I wrote a piece about Faulkner's portrayal of Indian people in the "Wilderness" stories and in *Go Down, Moses*, attempting to use the lens of ethnohistory to take a more seriously anthropological look at what was plausibly portrayed by Faulkner and what was fiction.[1] It seemed clear to me, as it has to many others, that Faulkner's portrayals of Indian people in the "Wilderness" stories made them into Others who could entertain a popular readership while enacting a kind of adoption of some white preferences as well as an unbelievable performance of those preferences that had nothing to do with the known behaviors of Chickasaw or Choctaw leaders either before or after the Removal to Oklahoma of the 1830s. As for Sam Fathers, clearly a sympathetic figure in his tutelage of Isaac McCaslin in the mysteries of the land, his role as a trusted employee was to enact with dignity the inevitable declension of the Indian in Yoknapatawpha as Faulkner in his later work was troubled by "changes in the land" brought about by agriculture that exhausted the land and by logging that destroyed the virgin forests of the Delta.[2]

When I thought about what I might contribute to the Faulkner and Yoknapatawpha Conference on Faulkner and the Native South, what immediately sprang to mind was a document that I had recently discovered written by my great-grandfather, Charles Betts Galloway, who, as a newly made bishop of the Methodist Episcopal Church South in 1886, was assigned to conduct the annual conferences of the church in Indian Territory, as the not-yet-state of Oklahoma was then known. As was usual with Galloway, he wrote a report on his travels that year and on other trips to the Territory in 1887 and 1892. I had begun to transcribe the document and to look into Galloway's connection with Indian missions after Removal, and in doing so I had turned to the considerable body of documentation of

Evolution of Indian Dress in Faulkner 67

missionary efforts to Southeastern Indians.[3] Since clearly the missionaries' goals of converting as many Indians as possible did tend to counter the theme of the vanishing Indian that is so prominent in Faulkner's work, I thought the discourse of the missionaries who did have contact with Native people in Mississippi and Oklahoma could be valuable.

But I also had a real curiosity about why Faulkner seemed to revel in constructing his oddly non-Indian Chickasaws as fancying French culture (when the real Chickasaws were strong allies of the English) and did not allow that the creative use of artifacts from an alien European culture (including pants) might be an assertion of agency and not a pathetic failure to understand European culture. Why, for that matter, did Faulkner choose likewise to victimize a foppishly dressed French architect and darkly hint at French ties for Sutpen in *Absalom, Absalom!*? Here we have a clue to a way of comparing the two discourses by focusing on described artifacts, a clue that begs to be looked at if only through the lens of hybridity through which it comes back to Faulkner's treatment of Indians.[4] Bishop Galloway, too, was fascinated by Indigenous dress—both in the Americas and when he made missionary travels to Asia and the Middle East.

Finally, it is clear that Faulkner wasn't trying to understand what Indians thought about anything. Most commentators agree with him that he "made them up" so that they could speak to issues that increasingly interested him, to situate the "curse" of slaveholding and the beginnings of environmental degradation. And although missionaries did make an effort to understand at least how Indian beliefs contradicted the beliefs they were trying to inculcate, they were nevertheless sure that they knew best for the people they sought to proselytize, because they were offering them, after all, eternal life. So, neither in the discourse of Faulkner's oeuvre nor in much of that of missionaries to the southern Indians do we find an effort to understand how the Indian people who lived the outcomes of colonization, of "storms brewed in other men's worlds," had experienced those drastic changes.[5] Ethnohistorians are prone to moaning about the dearth of primary sources for Indian perspectives, but most of us these days have adopted seriously critical readings of the observations of outsiders. Also, by now, several generations of Native American scholars have gone farther, using their scholarship and the understandings they own from having mastered subtle gestures and non-Anglo habitus. It may therefore be possible to approach a third perspective, that of Indian people who became actors in Faulkner's work and of those who were proselytized by missionaries.

How can one begin to bring these very different perspectives together? Interestingly, as hinted above, clothing can provide an initial ground for observation. Historically, we know that the earliest trade goods coveted by Southeastern Indians included woven cloth and clothing made from it.[6] Cotton and linen clothing would be cooler in summer, wool perhaps warmer in winter, and garments from both would be far less laborious to make when the work did not include scraping hides or weaving cloth of fibers from mulberry bark. As a result, Indians had been wearing articles of European clothing and modifying them to their own tastes since at least the seventeenth century, eventually causing a demand that led to European manufacture of the clothing styles they actually wanted.[7] But Faulkner's constant reiteration of the alleged Indian reluctance to wear pants, which I will elaborate upon, touches on a second issue: although enslaved Africans might be forced to wear European-style clothing, it took a good while for Indians to decide whether and when to wear European clothing as Europeans wore it, and some Europeans took an adoption of it as an attestation of inward change, although Indian people clearly often performed it as masking.

If we consider how Faulkner dresses the pre-Removal Chickasaws and the "remnant" sage Sam Fathers, there is quite an interesting contrast: his Chickasaws choose exotic European clothing at first, while Sam Fathers is always shown as wearing the practical work clothes of black laborers and the white hunting men he serves almost as an equal. At the end of the nineteenth century, Protestant missionaries and Bishop Galloway made a distinction between the "blanket Indians" of the Plains, who had not begun much behavioral transition except to adopt fragments of white dress in "inappropriate" ways that suited them, and the Five Civilized Tribes of the Southeast (and the lands of Yoknapatawpha), who had already been allies and enemies of Europeans for three hundred years. Like the black slaves some of them owned, the Five Civilized Tribes had by the time of Removal in the 1830s and afterwards adopted some Euroamerican behaviors and especially, under some circumstances, their soberer habits of dress. But it is in comparing the details of descriptions from different Anglo observers—and hopefully some sense of meaning from the original Mississippians—that we can perhaps cast more light on Faulkner's understanding of Indians through an examination of the portrayal of different clothing practices, as written by Faulkner and observed by others.

Falkners and Galloways as Mississippians after Removal

Neither the Falkners nor the Galloways started as Mississippians, but both founders came to Mississippi indirectly or directly from the Carolinas shortly after the Removal of Mississippi's Indians, at a point when large numbers of the Choctaws had gone to Oklahoma, and almost all the Chickasaws, in spite of having started later, were also gone. Both of the family founders eventually settled in the middle of Mississippi, in Lafayette County for the Falkners and in Attala and Madison Counties for the Galloways, the Old Black Belt where Choctaws and Chickasaws had farmed and hunted and where mid-nineteenth-century white settlers made their plantations before the thin soils were exhausted.[8] Both family founders owned slaves. The Galloways began with twelve enslaved people brought from North Carolina in 1837, but, by 1860, the head of the family, Alfred, had fifty-two slaves to farm his land outside Canton, while his son Charles Betts had eighteen near Kosciusco, where practiced medicine until 1863, when he moved his family to Canton. William Clark Falkner started on his own with nothing in Ripley, married a well-to-do wife who brought slaves with her into the marriage, and was listed as having six mulatto slaves in 1860, by which time he also had multiple businesses apart from farming.[9] Both families therefore were prosperous enough to establish landholdings and to see one or more of their sons into professions—law on the Falkner side and medicine and the clergy on the Galloway side—while at least one Falkner established himself in emerging railroads. Both families served in the Civil War, one Galloway participant as a military surgeon (Charles), another (George) as a private in Harvey's Scouts.[10] Falkners served as field officers: William allegedly rode with Nathan Bedford Forrest's cavalry—as did E. B. Willis, the father of bishop Charles Galloway's wife.

Both families were interested in education, and both were of the Methodist faith. In the third generation, the two families established acquaintance at the University of Mississippi after the Civil War. Charles Galloway followed an academic track from 1865 to 1868, while John Wesley Thompson Falkner graduated in 1869 in law; both studied with L. Q. C. Lamar, who taught ethics and law.[11] In the fourth generation, Ethelbert Galloway became a doctor like his grandfather, while Murry Falkner pursued his father's businesses, including railroading and shipping. In the fifth generation, Ralph Muckenfuss (son of the bishop's daughter, Margaret Galloway Muckenfuss) and William Faulkner shared a double desk in the sixth grade at the white public school in Oxford and knew each other to speak to through their pre-college schooling.[12] The likenesses we see here between the two families are not unusual, given the fact that neither family ultimately established vast plantations and both families eventually turned to a more professional, urban existence. Thus, the attitudes of family members toward the Native people on whose lands they lived might be expected to be similar, allowing for differences in personal experience and generation after Removal and the Civil War.

70 PATRICIA GALLOWAY

Faulkner's Portrayal of Indian Dress

What was Faulkner's relationship to Indigenous Mississippians? Faulkner does not seem to have spent much time in southeastern Mississippi, where the remaining Choctaws lived and were beginning to rebuild their communities, and by his time the remaining Chickasaws had come to occupy a nearly legendary status. Faulkner places Indians at several important nodes of his work: questioning race, race-mixing, and interracial relationships; and providing the land that would be exploited by the white dwellers in north-central Mississippi once they were gone. Their portrayal in the stories provided a small group of inaccurate pictures of Indian life and culture that have, nevertheless, become canonical Faulknerian authority on these topics.

In working through Faulkner's use of the description of dress to characterize Indian behaviors, it is important to consider the sequence of composition of the Indian stories in order to follow the development of this aspect of Faulkner's writing. Table 1 follows Blotner in attempting to trace this sequence.[13]

There are really three thematic threads that have already been recognized by many scholars and that are also significant when it comes to clothing. First is the dominant Doom story that begins in "Red Leaves," then is traced through "A Justice," "The Old People," "A Courtship," and two chapters in *Requiem for a Nun.* Second comes the Weddel story that manifests in "Mountain Victory" and then flashes back in "Lo!" Third is the Sam Fathers story that begins in "A Justice" with Sam's origin story but is significant in "The Old People" and "The Bear." These threads are woven together in complex ways as Faulkner both reused and revised materials in order to expand Yoknapatawpha. But by keeping one's eye on clothing, we see him establish over time sets of clothing that are worn in specific ways by specific people.

Doom Story

The earliest and generally the most complex of the Indian stories, "Red Leaves" (1930), begins with the first Doom story of a Choctaw chief who went to New Orleans and fell in with the Frenchman Chevalier Soeur Blonde de Vitry (*CS*, 317) gambling and becoming involved with a young West Indian woman with "Negro blood" (*CS*, 321).[14] Doom returns home to Mississippi and in some way becomes chief, his uncle and cousin having died. A woman arrives in Mississippi heavily pregnant with Doom's child; he marries her, and Issetibbeha is born. Doom acquires African slaves, spends five months with his slaves dragging a steamboat stuck in

Evolution of Indian Dress in Faulkner 71

Table 1.

Historical year	Year of publication	Work	Stories
18--	1930	"Red Leaves"	Doom
1820	1931	"A Justice"	Doom, Sam Fathers
[1865]	1932	"Mountain Victory"	Weddel
[1829–37]	1934	"Lo!"	Weddel
	1942	Go Down, Moses	
		"The Old People"	Doom, Sam Fathers
1883		"The Bear"	Sam Fathers
	1948	"A Courtship"	Doom
	1951	Requiem for a Nun	
1833		"The Courthouse"	Doom
[1830s]		"The Jail"	Doom

Table 1. Faulkner chronology for Indian stories mentioning dress (historical years from *Portable Faulkner* or from contemporaneous [historical events]; dates of the works from Blotner; elements gathered under collections where relevant).

river mud to his house site to serve as a mansion, sets up a plantation, and dies. Issetibbeha visits Soeur Blonde de Vitry in Paris and brings back a gilt bed, girandoles belonging to Madame de Pompadour, and a pair of red-heeled slippers.[15] After the death of Issetibbeha, his son Moketubbe (borne by one of his slaves) apparently requires the slippers to prove his having inherited his dead father's rank of "the Man," but they are far too small to fit him. Nevertheless, while assisting with the pursuit of Issetibbeha's body servant, who is to be killed to join his master in death, Moketubbe occasionally puts the slippers on only to fall into a faint from the pain of wearing them while being carried on a litter.[16] Further, Moketubbe is portrayed as wearing "a broadcloth coat and no shirt" as well as the "bottom piece of a suit of linen underwear" (*CS*, 325). The nearly one hundred guests for the funeral are described as "decorous, quiet, patient in their stiff European finery," while the Indians who are helping in the chase (and wondering whether slaves are worth the trouble) begin it wearing "shirts and straw hats, carrying their neatly rolled trousers under their arms" (*CS*, 331), although the slave, catching sight of them, imagines that they will roll up all their "Sunday clothes" and wedge them "into tree crotches" (*CS*, 334) in the course of the chase. At the beginning of his escape, the fugitive slave wears "dungaree pants bought by Indians from white men, and an amulet slung on a thong about his hips" consisting of half a lorgnon from France and the skull of a water moccasin (*CS*, 330). Most of these clothing descriptions will be seen again.

The second of the stories in this series is "A Justice" (1931), which has been simplified to become the canonical Doom (du Homme or—incorrectly translated—the Man) story; the men portrayed are still Choctaw (*CS*, 344).[17] The story traces Issetibbeha's nephew Ikkemotubbe's trip to New Orleans, from which he returns having been tutored by a French companion, wearing "a coat with gold all over it, and he had three gold watches" (*CS*, 345). We are given to understand that Ikkemotubbe poisons the existing Man (Issetibbeha?) and his son (Moketubbe?) and claims the title before their funerals, after which he organizes slaves he brought from New Orleans to work with his Indian subjects to move a stranded steamboat to join onto his house. The woman slave that he brought with him gives birth to Sam Fathers, later in "The Old People" said to be the son of Ikkemotubbe (*GDM*, 159), though in this story the woman is married by order to a slave whom Ikkemotubbe had brought from New Orleans. In "A Justice," however, Sam identifies his "pappy" as an Indian already living on the plantation whose "name was Crawfishford, but usually it was Craw-ford" (*CS*, 347) and who was suspected of having relations with his mother (*CS*, 357).[18] Sam is thus named by Ikkemotubbe as "Has-Two-Fathers."

The third Doom story is told in "The Old People" (originally published in 1940), in which the story is revised somewhat as a background for Sam Fathers's story: Ikkemotubbe (now designated Chickasaw) comes from New Orleans with "the quadroon slave woman who was to be Sam's mother, and a gold-laced hat and coat" and Chevalier Soeur Blonde de Vitry.[19] He finds Issetibbeha dead and Moketubbe in succession, whereupon Ikkemotubbe poisons Moketubbe's son and Moketubbe promptly abdicates. Ikkemotubbe marries the pregnant quadroon to one of his slaves and two years later sells the whole family to Carothers McCaslin. Later on, after the Civil War, Sam continues to work for McCaslin, living among McCaslin's ex-slaves and "dress[ing] like them and talk[ing] like them" (*GDM*, 163).

The final Doom story is in "A Courtship" (1948), for which it forms an abbreviated back story. After an agreement with Andrew Jackson, Issetibbeha's plantation border is agreed to be a straight line on the other side of which is America; and here also we learn that the Colberts, an influential mixed-blood Chickasaw-English family related to the object of the courtship, consider Issetibbeha and his kin to be "mushrooms" (*CS*, 365): in some way inferior. The "courtship" of the title is a contest that takes place between David Hogganbeck (the steamboat captain) and Ikkemotubbe

Evolution of Indian Dress in Faulkner 73

for the hand of Herman Basket's sister. During the several phases of the contest, Ikkemotubbe tries to impress the girl by wearing "his flower-painted weskit and pigeon-tailed coat and beaver hat in which he looked handsomer than a steamboat gambler and richer even than the whisky-trader" (CS, 364) and, another time, by donning "the used general's coat which General Jackson gave Issetibbeha" (CS, 370). In spite of his looks, fine clothing, and feats in competition with Hogganbeck, the girl marries neither of them. In a single paragraph, we learn that, after the contests, Ikkemotubbe goes to New Orleans and returns with his French friend wearing "fine gold-trimmed clothes" (CS, 379) and with a supply of poi-son with which he gets his way in everything.

Yet this is not the last of Issetibbeha and Ikkemotubbe. In two chap-ters of *Requiem for a Nun* (1951), in which the emergence of Jeffer-son is outlined, we have another portrait of the Chickasaws. First in "The Courthouse," set at the beginnings of Jefferson when a Chickasaw agency is set up there, Issetibbeha's activities are described as "pattern-ing the white people" (PF, 45) by creating the plantation mentioned in the earlier Doom stories, where the men wear "white man's denim and butternut and felt and straw" (PF, 33) except when they wear "Sunday clothes" for travel, including pants rolled up and not worn "or perhaps tied by the two legs around their necks like capes or rather hussars' dol-mans" (PF, 42). In this story Mohataha is identified as Issetibbeha's sister and Ikkemotubbe's mother, and she signs off on everything the Chicka-saws buy at the store in Jefferson. Then, in "The Jail," where most of the information about Indians is set around Removal and the descriptions of clothing are much expanded, Ikkemotubbe's Chickasaws no longer wear moccasins or deer-hide leggings and jerkins but "Eastern factory-made jeans and shoes sold them on credit . . . walking in to the settlement on the white man's Saturday, carrying the alien shoes rolled neatly in the alien pants under their arms" until they get near town, when they wash themselves and put the pants on (PF, 670–71). At Removal, they dress in

> the formal regalia of the white man's inexplicable ritualistic sabbaticals: broadcloth trousers and white shirts with boiled-starch bosoms (. . . and car-rying the New England-made shoes under their arms too since the distance would be long and walking was better barefoot), the shirts collarless and cra-vatless true enough and with tails worn outside, but still board-rigid, gleam-ing, pristine. (PF, 671)

In addition, both here and in the earlier chapter, we see the Indians led by Mohataha, riding in a wagon, seated in a "gilt brocade empire chair" in "Courthouse" (PF, 42) and in a rocking chair in "Jail" (PF, 667). At

74   PATRICIA GALLOWAY

Removal, she follows her son to Indian Territory in the wagon after having signed away the Chickasaw land. As the wagon departs, she is

> barefoot as always but in the purple silk dress which her son, Ikkemotubbe, had brought her back from France, and a hat crowned with the royal-colored plume of a queen, beneath the slave-held parasol still and with another female slave child squatting on her other side holding the crusted slippers [the red-heeled ones?] which she had never been able to get her feet into, and in the back of the wagon the petty rest of the unmarked Empire flotsam her son had brought to her [the gilded bed and girandoles?] which was small enough to be moved. (*PF*, 667–68)

The dress is also described as being one of "the cast-off garments of a French queen" (*PF*, 668).

Weddel Story

The first of the Weddel stories, "Mountain Victory" (1932), portrays a mixed-blood French-Choctaw Civil War officer, Saucier Weddel, returning with his black body servant from the war and passing through the mountains of Tennessee on the way back from Virginia to the Mississippi Delta. They seek shelter from the cold with a mountain family that fought for the Union and that believes them both to be black; both are dressed in threadbare uniforms as well as coats, Jubal the servant in a huge Federal private's coat, a blue forage cap, and fur wrappings for his legs (*CS*, 746, 754–55) and Saucier in a "broad slouched hat bearing the tarnished wreath of a Confederate field officer" and a "cloak [that] was weathered, faded about the shoulders where the light fell strongest. The skirts were bedraggled, frayed, mudsplashed: the garment had been patched again and again, and brushed again and again; the nap was completely gone" (*CS*, 747). Weddel is invited to have dinner with the family and dons a shirt and a pair of "thin dancing slippers," the uppers of which are cracked (*CS*, 752)—perhaps an echo of the red-heeled French shoes we have seen before. During the dinner, Saucier tells his story (*CS*, 759–60), remarking also on his father's trip to Washington from his "Contalmaison" plantation, which has already been described at greater length by Jubal in the kitchen. The older one of the sons threatens Saucier, and the father tries to persuade both Saucier and Jubal to leave, but they take shelter in the barn instead. In the morning, trying to get away, both are shot by the older son.

The second of the stories, referred to in the first as having taken place well before the Civil War (presumably sometime between 1829 and

Evolution of Indian Dress in Faulkner 75

1837), is "Lo!" (1934), in which Saucier's (now) half-Chickasaw father travels to Washington to clear another of his sons for killing a white man who tried to take control of a ford controlled by the family; he and a large body of his people travel in a coach and on foot and demand to see the president, never specifically named but clearly Andrew Jackson. Within two days after their arrival, Jackson presents all the Indian men with a set of "proper" clothing that they choose how to wear:

> They wore beaver hats and new frock coats; save for the minor detail of collars and waistcoats they were impeccably dressed—though a little early—for the forenoon of the time, down to the waist. But from here down credulity, all sense of fitness and decorum, was outraged. At a glance one would have said that they had come intact out of Pickwickian England, save that the tight, light-colored smallclothes ended not in Hessian boots nor in any boots at all, but in dark, naked feet. On the floor beside each one lay a neatly rolled bundle of dark cloth; beside each bundle in turn, mute toe and toe and heel and heel . . . sat two pairs of new boots. (*CS*, 382)

Weddel also wears lace at his neck and cuffs, repeatedly described as "dingy" (*CS*, 389) or "soiled" (*CS*, 393). Faulkner observes that in return for these clothes, the Indians gave Jackson "a costume . . . a mass, a network, of gold braid—frogs, epaulets, sash and sword—held loosely together by bright green cloth" (*CS*, 390). The Indians are put up in army tents (through the roofs of which they cut holes so as to have fires inside) and do their own hunting of deer. They drive the government mad by their polite but settled presence, such that Jackson pardons the son to persuade them to leave.

Sam Fathers's Story

Sam Fathers's story begins with the tale of his name in "A Justice" (1931), where it connects with the Doom story, in which Sam's name is explained. But in "The Old People" Sam is seen as wearing "nigger clothes" (*GDM*, 166). What this means is further elaborated upon in "The Bear" (1942), where Sam is at one point referred to as wearing "battered and faded overalls and the frayed five-cent straw hat which had been the badge of the negro's slavery and was now the regalia of his freedom" (*GDM*, 197) and, while hunting, as wearing "battered overalls and rubber boots and a worn sheepskin coat and a hat which had belonged to the boy's father" (*GDM*, 210–11).[20] Yet, in spite of these clothes, Sam is identified in "Old People" as "the old dark man sired on both sides by savage kings" (*GDM*, 159).

76 PATRICIA GALLOWAY

Weaving the Threads

The first difficulty to point out is the chronology of Yoknapatawpha itself, which is at best confusing and was apparently not thought out by Faulkner until he was well into telling its story as a linked one; even in the second edition of *The Portable Faulkner*, Cowley doesn't break down all the stories as covering specific times. But it is useful to try to follow the order in which the stories were written in order to try to see how Faulkner modifies the segments that continue to be reused. If the pattern of clothing in "Red Leaves" had not introduced the theme of Indians carrying instead of wearing their European-style pants, and if Moketubbe had not been portrayed wearing a jacket and underwear pants, there would not have been clear links to the gift of clothing sets from Andrew Jackson to Weddel and his men in "Lo!" where the Indians dress much like Moketubbe (except with shirts) and wear underwear and carry their pants instead of wearing them. Nor would the portrayal of European clothing as "Sunday clothes" and the preservation of those clothes by carrying pants instead of wearing them have turned up in the two episodes in *Requiem* where Ikkemotubbe and his people depart in removal to Indian Territory. Finally, the connection of Sam Fathers to Ikkemotubbe in "A Justice" allows the contrast between Sam's "nigger" or "hunter" clothing and that of his Indian forebears.

The complete clothing outfit as detailed in "Lo!" seems to make up what Faulkner considered appropriate for a European of Andrew Jackson's day to wear. But from whence comes the notion in "Lo!" of Indians wearing, below their beaver hats and frock coats and shirts, underwear in place of pants (a motif already seen in "Red Leaves")? I think one clue is in Faulkner's observation in the text that "at a glance one would have said that they had come intact out of Pickwickian England, save that the tight, light-colored smallclothes ended not in Hessian boots nor in any boots at all, but in dark, naked feet" (*CS*, 382). In one of Robert Seymour's illustrations in Dickens's *The Posthumous Papers of the Pickwick Club* (1847), Pickwick is standing on a chair to address the members of the club, wearing skin-tight, light-colored pants and Hessian boots as well (see figure 1). Doubtless, these are the form-fitting pantaloons (see figure 2) of the turn of the nineteenth century (not the earlier knee-length "smallclothes" which Faulkner in any case took for underwear) made of "fabrics that were knitted or, like kerseymere and nankin, cut on the bias, so that the garment would hug the leg. Pantaloons were recommended for men whose legs were both slim and muscular. The idea was to show off a good leg."[21] One can only assume that Faulkner had some familiarity with the Dickens illustrations without understanding the

Evolution of Indian Dress in Faulkner   77

style; though the pantaloons could be knitted, they were not underwear. And when the term "pantaloons" is used in Faulkner's text, it seems to refer to ordinary pants to go with the frock coats. A second clue may come from the multiple portrayals of Andrew Jackson in military uniform and on horseback, which show him wearing such light-colored, form-fitting pantaloons with boots (see figure 3). Finally, in a photograph of First Nations chiefs together with Methodist pastors that Charles Betts Galloway brought back from a visit in the 1890s to a Canadian Methodist Conference, one of the chiefs, James Goodstoney, is wearing tight, light-colored pants much like pantaloons, along with a jacket and vest, while the other two Native chiefs wear traditional blankets and leggings (see figure 4). I have yet to discover where Faulkner got the idea of the Indians' reluctance to wear trousers, especially during the nineteenth century and especially since he only once (*PF*, 670) mentions the breechcloths and leggings that were worn in the eighteenth and nineteenth centuries in the Southeast and on the plains.

The term "Sunday clothes" seems to apply to something less formal or more recent than the suits of clothes in "Lo!"—shirt, pants, and shoes—while something even less formal—the materials for which are "denim and butternut and felt and straw" (*PF*, 33)—comes to occupy the slot of "Saturday clothes." It is clear, however, that from "Red Leaves" to Removal in *Requiem*, even according to Faulkner, Choctaws/Chickasaws were free to wear the canonical Euroamerican clothes as they chose, whether for comfort or to make them last longer. In a matter of chronology, Sam Fathers and first slaves and then freedmen are portrayed in work pants or machine-made dungarees, sometimes portrayed as worn-out or secondhand to emphasize their lowliness. Although it may not be wrong to attribute "dungarees" or jeans as garb for workers in the very late nineteenth century, it seems pretty clear that the "dungaree pants bought by Indians from white men" (*CS*, 330) were not really available as manufactured goods until the 1870s.

Marked departures in clothing clearly come at both ends of a spectrum of class or rank. In "A Courtship," Doom adds a gold-laced coat or cloak and chooses a flowered weskit and "pigeon-tailed coat" on one occasion (*CS*, 364); on another, he tries to impress by wearing a cast-off general's coat given to Issetibbeha by Andrew Jackson (*CS*, 370). At the other end of the spectrum are the garments of slaves: the dungarees worn by the fleeing slave in "Red Leaves," the "nigger clothes" worn by Sam Fathers in "Old People," and, more specifically, Sam's "battered and faded overalls" and "frayed five-cent straw hat which had been the badge of the negro's slavery and was now the regalia of his freedom" (*GDM*, 197). In "The Bear," Sam wears hunting clothes and rubber boots and a

Figure 1. "Mr. Pickwick addresses the Club," by Robert Seymour, from *The Posthumous Papers of the Pickwick Club*, by Charles Dickens. From Victoria and Albert Museum, original etching, museum number E.822–1972.

worn sheepskin coat; even the swampers who lived on trapping and small plantings have clothes a little better, though "any town negro would have thrown away or burned" them (*GDM*, 226). The white hunters wear khakis, rubber boots, coats, and hats, which are implicitly better. Trying to understand the patterns here is difficult because Faulkner's view of his characters changes over time, as does his concept of Yoknapatawpha, and, so far, we have only his words to work with.

There have been, as I suggested, other witnesses. Choctaws and Chickasaws had been missionized in Mississippi, first under the American Board of Commissioners for Foreign Missions, funded by the American government, and then by individual churches, including Methodists and Baptists. Under the American Board, much work had been done preparing Native-language dictionaries, catechisms, and hymnals, clearly grasping the need for Indian people to be able to understand Christian religion in their own languages. The Methodists had founded a

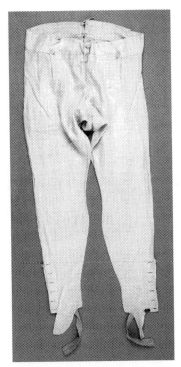

Figure 2. Pantaloons dated to 1830–40. Metropolitan Museum, purchase, Irene Lewisohn bequest, 1970, accession number 1970.281.6.

Choctaw mission in Mississippi under William Winans in 1825 and had been particularly effective when Alexander Talley converted Greenwood LeFlore, one of a few major Choctaw leaders.[22] By 1830, it was reported that there were some four thousand church members among the Choctaw compared to the fifteen thousand total population.[23]

Meanwhile, however, government plans had shifted toward removal west of the Mississippi River so as to open up the eastern part of the country to white settlers. Some missionaries were opposed to removal, but others felt it would be protective. Talley, for instance, assisted the Choctaws in evaluating the lands offered in Indian Territory and resettled with them, as did many missionaries to the Five Civilized Tribes. Those Choctaws who stayed behind in Mississippi had to make their way as small farmers if they had managed to hold on to land, or to subsist on hunting, selling baskets, or seeking wage labor.[24]

Figure 3. *Andrew Jackson with the Tennessee Forces on the Hickory Grounds (Ala) AD 1814.* Breuker & Kessler Co., lithographer, Philadelphia. Library of Congress, reproduction from original print, http://hdl.loc.gov/loc.pnp/pga.03127.

In 1887 Galloway once again went to Indian Territory, first to Eufaula in the Muskogee District to meet with the International Indian Council, June 5–10 and later to conduct the Indian Mission Conference in Vinita, Cherokee Nation, October 12–17. At the International Indian Council, he met for the first time with the "wild tribes" who had been placed on reservations in western Oklahoma only ten years before, as well as the Five Civilized Tribes, who were long settled. At this meeting, he heard

Figure 4. Photograph of Methodist ministers and First Nations Indians at Canadian Conference of Methodist Episcopal Church, September–October 1886, by J. Fraser Bryce, Toronto. Men identified left to right as Reverend John Chantler McDougall, Samson (Cree chief), Pakan or James Seenum (Cree chief), Reverend R. R. Steinhauer, and James Goodstoney (Stoney). Photographed by Karen Pavelka, from collection of the author.

what had brought the two groups together as a council: the threatened intention of the US government to force the tribes into holding their land in severalty rather than in common as tribes. Fifty years on from Removal, what had been considered Indian Territory was to be partly confiscated to settle restless whites from east of the Mississippi.[25] It was as a witness to this council that Galloway mentioned most fully his ideas

82   PATRICIA GALLOWAY

about the Indian people he had met during the previous nine months on his trips to Oklahoma. In his notes for an article in the *Christian Advocate*, his fascination with the differences in dress between "Wild" and "Civilized" tribes, and the symbolic conclusions he drew from them, are evident:

> A more remarkable body of men I had never seen. Eighteen tribes were represented. In dress, manners, etc. they presented a striking object lesson of the power of the gospel and the influence of our Christian civilization. Among the representatives of the five civilized tribes were men who would fill creditably a seat in either house of our National Congress. But their brethren of the far west, without education and the gospel, dressed after the manner of their fathers in the wildness of the wilderness, presented a picture that ought to stir the missionary fire of the Church. Their painted faces, hair dressed with feathers, ears strung with immense and numerous rings and bodies wrapped in blankets or other material of loud color, were in striking and sad contrast to their well-dressed and educated brethren of the five civilized tribes.[26]

A strong speech Galloway heard from a Kiowa spokesman made a distinct impression, perhaps because of the contrast between dress and speech:

> A speech by "Poor Buffalo," a Kiowa chief, impressed me as no other appeal I ever heard in life. He was an elderly man, tall, with strong features, painted cheeks, and plaited hair decked with feathers. He wore a red shirt trimmed with yellow, beaded moccasins, elaborate leggings, and had his body wrapped in a scarf of white domestic. He spoke with animation and emotion. His references to their ignorance of our religion and earnest desire that missionaries and teachers might be sent to his people as to the Five Civilized Tribes were eloquent beyond description. How I longed for the men and money to go up and possess a land so white unto harvest. If the picture of that aged chief, with his facial expression, tone of voice, and pleading manner could be reproduced in the eyes of every congregation, not a poor son of the forest would be denied the privileges of the gospel within the next few years. I became so interested in the chief and his people as to induce a friend—a prominent Creek—to interview him and ascertain the facts of his history. Once a man of blood, he now pleads for the gospel of peace.[27]

Clearly, Galloway saw the dress of the Indians he met as a much clearer comparison of extremes than Faulkner did: the Five Civilized Tribes he judged to be dressed normally for a formal occasion, probably in suits much like the group of white and Indian ministers portrayed in Tash Smith's book (see figure 5) and indeed like his own normal attire,

Evolution of Indian Dress in Faulkner 83

so he did not describe them. I suggest that such clothing thus constituted a metaphor for restrained, modern Christian behavior, that the sobriquet "wild tribes," which was widely used for the Plains Indians, could not accord to the Kiowa (see figure 6).

Dressing the Part: Native American Dress and Agency

Both Faulkner and Galloway and historical evidence from the eighteenth and nineteenth centuries provide a sort of trajectory from Indian clothing to an adoption of European clothing elements to a full adoption of European clothes for formal ("Sunday clothes"), informal ("Saturday clothes"), and work occasions in the nineteenth century, but this is only true depending on the degree of exposure that Native groups had had to whites and on *what they were doing when observed*. To Faulkner, this trajectory meant a slavelike declension, set out through specific practices, that he apparently considered inevitable; to missionaries it seems to have signaled a spiritual change. But neither of these observers had a full picture. The glimpses we get through historical sources suggest not only that Native people were fully capable of adopting Euroamerican clothing creatively to their own ends, in terms of what they found attractive or comfortable, but that they might also use this clothing as costume. Faulkner seems to suggest this in "Lo!" when he has one of the Indians say, "So long as we are here, we'll have to try to act like these people believe that Indians ought to act. Because you never know until afterward just what you have done to insult or scare them" (*CS*, 383). But this jest on Andrew Jackson, if it plays out in the way the gift clothes are worn, may be just as operative in the apparently unthreatening Euroamerican dress of a Choctaw preacher in Oklahoma who might also be a participant in the Plains peyote ceremony.[28]

In "Lo!" Faulkner's portrayal of the dress of Chickasaws setting off for Oklahoma was, as it happens, far too conservative and dependent on the patterns of dress he depicted as evidence of their "taming." Certainly, they rode their famous Chickasaw ponies—not mentioned by Faulkner. This 1836 description of Chickasaws trading their land allotments in Mississippi for money usable in Oklahoma shows them falling, gaudily bedecked, into the hands of Pontotoc speculators, sounding more like an account of Ikkemotubbe trying to impress Herman Basket's sister than like Faulkner's sober description of Sunday clothes:

> Hundreds of these [Indians] are now in the streets. Many drunk and most of them wasting their money as fast as they can. It is amusing to see their displays of finery. The dress are all of the most fanciful kinds—of every variety of cut

Figure 5. "A mixed group of Indian workers and leaders among the Indians on the east side of Okla. In the Methodist Church . . . ," ca. 1900. J. J. Methvin is seated in the second row behind an unidentified woman. From the Oklahoma Historical Society, Mrs. C. M. Coppage, collection, photographs, box 1, #560.

and colour. Some of them are ridiculously gaudy, while others are rich and tasty—giving the wearer a martial and splendid appearance.[29]

And here, from an account of the first large exodus of Chickasaws to Oklahoma, is a description of Chickasaw dress on the trail from a Louisville merchant who watched their crossing of the Mississippi at Memphis, an even farther cry from Sunday clothes:

> I do not think that I have ever been a witness of so remarkable a scene as was formed by this immense column of moving Indians, several thousand, with the train of Govt waggons, the multitude of horses; it is said three to each Indian & beside at least six dogs & cats to an Indian. They were all most comfortably clad—the men in complete Indian dress with showy shawls tied in turban fashion around their heads—dashing about on their horses, like Arabs, many of them presenting the finest countenances & figures that I ever saw. The women also very decently clothed like white women, in calico gowns—but much tidier & better put on than common white-people—& how beautifully they managed their horses, how proud & calm & erect, they sat in full gallop. The young women have remarkably mild & soft countenances & are singularly decorous in their dress &

Figure 6. "In Summer-Kiowa-No. 1042," photograph of three Kiowa delegates to the 1898 United States Indian Congress of the Trans-Mississippi and International Exposition, Omaha, Nebraska. Men are identified as Kim Ah-Keah-Boat, Frank Tobah or his brother Doyebi, and Jimmy Hummingbird. Courtesy of National Museum of the American Indian, Smithsonian Institution, catalog number P27503A. Photo by Frank A. Rinehart.

deportment.... It was a scene to paint, not describe with words—civilized society is so uniform & tame in the dress & manner & equipage that a crowd has no life in it. Here however no man was like another, no horse caparisoned like another. Their clothing was of all the bright colors of the rainbow & arranged with every possible variety of form & taste—but all *flowing* & fantastic & *untailorlike*.[30]

In other words, these are not the staid Five Civilized Tribes of 1880s Oklahoma whom Galloway met at Methodist Conference meetings nor yet the barefoot marchers dressed well (down to their bare feet) that Faulkner invented. They were always more complex than that.

Figure 7. Portrait of Peter Pitchlynn: *Há-tchoo-túc-knee, Snapping Turtle, a Half-breed*, by George Catlin, 1834. From Smithsonian American Art Museum, gift of Mrs. Joseph Harrison, Jr., catalog number 1985.66.296.

This becomes clear for the post-Removal period when we look at two portraits of Peter Pitchlynn (see figures 7 and 8). Pitchlynn was born in Mississippi as the son of Scottish trader John Pitchlynn and his Choctaw wife, Sophie Folsom. The first portrait was painted by George Catlin, portraying Pitchlynn in a matchcoat, shirt, leggings, and moccasins, with a scarf across his chest and a knot of feathers in his hair. He made many

Figure 8. Portrait of Peter Pitchlynn: *P. P. Pitchlynn, Speaker of the National Council of the Choctaw Nation and Choctaw Delegate to the Government of the United States*, by George Finderich, 1849. From the Library of Congress, photograph number 3b06312.

trips to Washington to negotiate for his tribe and served as overall governor of the Choctaw in Oklahoma from 1864 to 1866. The second portrait by a German artist portrays a recognizable Pitchlynn, allegedly in his persona as Choctaw leader and representative to Washington, as something of a romantic poet, with European shirt, jacket, and neckerchief. We know that Pitchlynn was the recipient of a fine education for his day from boarding school and university, so it is not surprising that he could play both roles with equal competence. In fact, when he met Charles Dickens on an Ohio River steamboat, and Dickens expressed disappointment not to see Pitchlynn in Native dress as Catlin had portrayed him,

Figure 9. *Wi-jún-jon, the Pigeon's Egg Head (the Light), Going to and Returning from Washington*, by George Catlin, 1832, published by Currier & Ives. From the Library of Congress, reproduction number LC-DIG-pga-05077.

Pitchlynn replied that "his race were losing many things besides their dress . . . but he wore it at home, he added proudly."[31] He also noted that he found Catlin's likenesses in the gallery "elegant."[32] Do we need to ask which was the "true" Pitchlynn? From his matrilineal identity, he was certainly Choctaw.

Catlin is more famous for a painting he did of Assiniboin chief Wi-jún-jon, a "before and after" portrayal of a trip to Washington that magically transformed him from serious, traditionally dressed chief to dressy Regency beau (see figure 9). This painting might well be an intertext for Andrew Jackson's failed intention in "Lo!"—had it not failed—though of course we know nothing of what Wi-jún-jon thought of his Euroamerican dress. We might have wished that Faulkner's Chickasaws in that story, rather than Andrew Jackson, had commented not just on what they thought of Jackson and Washington, but also on their wearing of the clothing that Jackson had provided.

Faulkner's representations of Indians certainly had their purposes. Faulkner, of course, had no obligation to depend on anything but his own imagination to create his odd Indians, and he makes them carry the burden of miscegenation combined with a foolish aping of whites' destruction of the environment, a combination of tall tale and dark vision, in an atmosphere where an elderly Ike McCaslin in "Delta Autumn," realizing the race and ancestry of Roth Edmonds's lover, thinks to himself, *"Maybe in a thousand or two thousand years in America. . . . But not now! Not now!"* (*GDM*, 344), and where Sam Fathers allegedly welcomes death because, as Ike also tells himself, *"for seventy years now he had had to be a negro. It was almost over now and he was glad"* (*GDM*, 206). These were the problems that Faulkner wanted to address as he imagined Indians' weaknesses (gambling, sex, greed) as somehow at the origin of American problems of race and environmental destruction—never mind that the vast majority of Mississippi Indians who intermarried did so with whites and that Chickasaw ponies were unbeatable over rough ground.[33]

NOTES

1. Patricia Galloway, "The Construction of Faulkner's Indians," *Faulkner Journal* 17, nos. 1–2 (Fall 2002–Spring 2003): 9–32.

2. William Cronon, *Changes in the Land: Indians, Colonists, and the Ecology of New England* (New York: Hill and Wang, 1983). Sam Fathers's father is identified in "A Justice" as Choctaw but as Chickasaw in Malcolm Cowley's *Portable Faulkner* volume. Compare William Faulkner, "A Justice," *Collected Stories of William Faulkner* (1950; repr., New York: Vintage International, 1995), 344, and Malcolm Cowley, ed., *The Portable Faulkner* (New York: Viking Portable Library, 1977), 4. *Collected Stories* hereafter cited parenthetically as *CS*; *The Portable Faulkner* hereafter cited parenthetically as *PF*.

3. See Clara Sue Kidwell, *Choctaws and Missionaries in Mississippi, 1818–1918* (Norman: University of Oklahoma Press, 1995); Tash Smith, *Capture These Indians for the Lord: Indians, Methodists, and Oklahomans, 1844–1939* (Tucson: University of Arizona Press, 2014); Katherine M. B. Osburn, *Choctaw Resurgence in Mississippi:*

Race, Class, and Nation Building in the Jim Crow South, 1830–1977 (Lincoln: University of Nebraska Press, 2014); Barbara Krauthamer, *Black Slaves, Indian Masters: Slavery, Emancipation, and Citizenship in the Native American South* (Chapel Hill: University of North Carolina Press, 2013).

4. Unfortunately, the only article I could find that foregrounded the theme of clothing in Faulkner ignored both Indians and historical dress entirely in favor of dress contemporary to the time when Faulkner was writing. See Sylvia J. Cook, "Reading Clothes: Literary Dress in William Faulkner and Erskine Caldwell," *Southern Literary Journal* 46, no. 1 (Fall 2013): 1–18.

5. This is the wonderful title of Elizabeth A. H. John's marvelous book, *Storms Brewed in Other Men's Worlds: The Confrontation of Indians, Spanish, and French in the Southwest, 1540–1795* (Norman: University of Oklahoma Press, 1975).

6. For a look at the English trade that reached the Chickasaws, see Kathryn E. Holland Braund, *Deerskins and Duffels: Creek Indian Trade with Anglo-America, 1685–1815* (Lincoln: University of Nebraska Press, 1993), 122–25. The Louisiana French lists of goods for Indians similarly included much in the way of woven cloth. A recent article by Jessica Stern points to the distinctly Native and often-surprising choices made from the stocks of cloth and clothing maintained by English and Scottish traders in the southeastern settlements. See "Native American Taste: Re-evaluating the Gift-Commodity Debate in the British Colonial Southeast," *Native South* 5 (2012): 1–37. In the Southwest, the Navajo were quick to adopt sheepherding as another source of fiber.

7. We also know that Benjamin Hawkins, as government agent to the southern tribes at the beginning of the nineteenth century, introduced the farming of cotton, cotton gins, and spinning wheels to make cloth manufacture easier. See Florette Henri, *The Southern Indians and Benjamin Hawkins, 1796–1816* (Norman: University of Oklahoma Press, 1986).

8. Faulkner's "Delta Autumn" reminds us that the Delta was not cleared until railroads were put in. See Mary Evelyn Starr, "Logging Out the Delta: From Mosquitoville to the Sardis and Delta Railroad," in Patricia Galloway and Evan Peacock, eds., *Exploring Southeastern Archaeology* (Jackson: University Press of Mississippi, 2015), 282–316.

9. See Joel Williamson, *William Faulkner and Southern History* (Oxford: Oxford University Press, 1993). Williamson claims that William Clark Falkner had a "shadow family" with the slave Emeline after the death of his wife, the sale of four of the slaves from his wife, and even during his marriage to Lizzie Vance (22–29). One of his perhaps two daughters from this relationship, Fannie Forrest Falkner, he sent to Rust College, where she met and married Matthew Dogan, who became president of Wiley College in Marshall, Texas, serving from 1895 to 1942 (64–71). Even in this respect there was a likeness between the Falkner and Galloway families, since Abraham Galloway, escaped slave and abolitionist who helped other enslaved people to escape and join Union African American regiments, shared a great-grandfather with Bishop Galloway. See David S. Cecelski, *The Fire of Freedom: Abraham Galloway and the Slaves' Civil War* (Chapel Hill: University of North Carolina Press, 2012).

10. John Francis Hamtramck Claiborne, *A Sketch of Harvey's Scouts, Formerly of Jackson's Cavalry Division, Army of Tennessee* (Starkville, MS: Southern Live-Stock Journal Print, 1885).

11. *Historical Catalogue of the University of Mississippi, 1849–1909*, Bulletin of the University of Mississippi, series 8, no. 4 (Nashville: Marshall and Bruce, 1910).

12. Joseph Blotner, *Faulkner: A Biography* (Jackson: University Press of Mississippi, 1984), 33, 39.

13. Ibid., passim.

14. The name is spelled "Soeur" in all editions, which means "sister" rather than the "lord" ("'Sieur") that seems to have been meant.

Evolution of Indian Dress in Faulkner
91

15. I cannot help pointing out that *Madame Pompadour*, a film about Madame de Pompadour with Dorothy Gish in the lead, was very popular in 1927, when Faulkner could have been working on this story.

16. The practice of retainer death is a Natchez one, not Choctaw as this story implies.

17. In *The Portable Faulkner*, however, the Choctaw identity is revised to Chickasaw (4).

18. Where this name comes from is a mystery, though it might be worth mentioning that the name of the Chakchiuma people, an Indian group originally from the confluence of the Yalobusha and Yazoo Rivers but allied with the Chickasaws during the French colonial period, means "red crawfish" (or rather "crawfish red") in both Choctaw and Chickasaw and had been mentioned in John Swanton's *Indian Tribes of the Lower Mississippi Valley and Adjacent Coast of the Gulf of Mexico* (Washington: Smithsonian Institution, 1911), 292–96. See Patricia Galloway, "Chakchiuma," in Raymond Fogelson, ed., *Southeast*, vol. 14 of *Handbook of North American Indians* (Washington: Smithsonian Institution, 2004), 496–98.

19. William Faulkner, *Go Down, Moses*, rev. ed. (1942; repr., New York: Vintage International, 1990), 160. Hereafter cited parenthetically as *GDM*.

20. Presumably the boy is Isaac McCaslin.

21. See Vic, "Regency Fashion: Men's Breeches, Pantaloons, and Trousers," https://janeaustensworld.wordpress.com/2013/06/21/regency-fashion-mens-breeches-pantaloons-and-trousers.

22. LeFlore, son of trader Louis LeFleur, stayed in Mississippi and became a legislator. It is his plantation, Malmaison, that was the model for the "Contalmaison" of "Mountain Victory" (and perhaps also for Ikkemotubbe's steamboat/house), and his carriage was the model for the one in "Lo!" For LeFlore's legend in Mississippi as told by teacher Allene DeShazo Smith, complete with photographs of both Malmaison (88–90, 92) and the elaborate carriage (78), see Smith, *Greenwood Leflore and the Choctaw Indians of the Mississippi Valley* (Memphis, TN: C. A. Davis, 1951).

23. For details on the missionization of the Choctaws and Chickasaws, see Rev. Thomas Smith and Rev. John O. Choules, *The Origin and History of Missions*, vol. 2 (Boston: S. Walker and Lincoln & Edmonds, 1834), 368–81. For Mississippi, see Kidwell, *Choctaws and Missionaries.*

24. Kidwell, *Choctaws and Missionaries*, 163.

25. See Frederick E. Hoxie, *A Final Promise: The Campaign to Assimilate the Indians, 1880–1920* (Lincoln: University of Nebraska Press, 1984), which is a classic source on the federal push for allotment.

26. Bishop Charles Betts Galloway Collection, Millsaps College Archives, M14, Box 5, Folder 68, "A Visit to the Indian Country," 3.

27. In Poor Buffalo's words, not fully presented here, one hears the formal expressions of Native American diplomatic speech. His role as a peace chief was based not on violent authority but on words alone. Nevertheless, he had been involved in the Red River War of 1874–75 after the Kiowa had agreed in the 1867 Treaty of Medicine Lodge to a reservation in western Oklahoma with the Comanche but then had been prevented from hunting buffalo as promised. See Paul H. Carlson, *The Plains Indians* (College Station: Texas A&M University Press, 1998), 159–60. The description of Poor Buffalo's speech comes from Warren A. Candler, *Bishop Charles Betts Galloway* (Nashville: Cokesbury, 1927), 90.

28. Andres Martinez ("Andele"), one of the preachers who worked with Galloway's appointed missionary to the Kiowa, Apache, and Comanche, participated in peyote rituals for years (Smith, *Capture These Indians*, 122).

29. Journal of Edward Fontaine, entry for November 23, 1836, Edward Fontaine Papers, 1809–1979, folder 1 (reel 1), Special Collections, Mitchell Memorial Library, Mississippi State University, Starkville; quoted in James Atkinson, *Splendid Land,*

Splendid People: The Chickasaw Indians to Removal (Tuscaloosa: University of Alabama Press, 2004), 232.

30. John E. Parsons, ed., "Letters on the Chickasaw Removal of 1837," *New York Historical Society Quarterly* 37 (1953): 280–81. This source presents a group of letters from the well-traveled Princeton graduate Bowes Reed McIlvaine. In fall of 1837, he was traveling in the Mississippi Valley on business and was present when thousands of Chickasaws crossed the Mississippi at Memphis on their way to Oklahoma. The extracts are from a long letter to his family in Louisville.

31. Charles Dickens, *American Notes for General Circulation* (New York: Harper & Brothers, 1842), 62.

32. Ibid.

33. Krauthamer argues that both Choctaws and Chickasaws adopted the white practice of positioning blacks low in the hierarchical ranking of races and that in the 1820s Choctaws adopted laws that forbade marriage and sexual relations with blacks (Krauthamer, *Black Slaves, Indian Masters*, 34–35).

"A Valid Signature"

Native American Sovereignty in *Requiem for a Nun*

ANNETTE TREFZER

In the wake of Malcolm Cowley's *Portable Faulkner* (1946), when the literary outlines of Yoknapatawpha County began to take chronological shape from its wilderness origins to 1945, William Faulkner began to take stock of his work, ordering and classifying stories.[1] In the process, the writer in the early 1950s set to work defining the long history of his "postage stamp of native soil." Two narratives in particular tell this story: the prologues to *Requiem for a Nun* (1951) contain the complete story of the founding of Jefferson in the first half of the nineteenth century, a story of the foundations of the white South intricately bound up with black slavery and predicated upon the expulsion of American Indian residents from the Mississippi Territory and shortly thereafter from Mississippi and Alabama when they assumed statehood in 1817 and 1819, respectively.[2] Three years later, the Nobel Prize-winning author wrote "Mississippi" (published in *Holiday* magazine in April 1954), an essay in which he addresses again the origins of Mississippi predicated upon the removal of southern Indian populations.

In both the prologues to *Requiem for a Nun* and the essay "Mississippi," Faulkner takes the long historical view to construct a narrative of Native American descent, dispossession, and disappearance. The history begins with the primeval land itself and subsequent inhabitants, including the "nameless though recorded predecessors who built the mounds to escape the spring floods and left their meagre artifacts: the obsolete and the dispossessed, dispossessed by those who were dispossessed in turn because they too were obsolete: the wild Algonquian, Chickasaw, and Choctaw and Natchez and Pascagoula, peering in virgin astonishment down from the tall bluffs at a Chippeway canoe bearing three Frenchmen."[3] The sentence reappears in the essay "Mississippi" in almost identical form with an homage to the "predecessors" with their "simple artifacts" who "built the mounds and vanished, bequeathing only the mounds in which the succeeding recordable Algonquian stock would leave the skulls of their warriors and chiefs and babies and slain bears, and the shards of pots, and hammer-and arrow-heads and now and then a heavy silver Spanish spur."[4] Faulkner's archeological dig into the Mississippian period in his semiautobiographical, mostly nonfictional essay is followed by his acknowledgment that the modern Chickasaws and Choctaws of the area who had lived through the violent colonial histories of Spanish, French, and Anglo-Saxon occupation had disappeared by the time he was a boy at the turn of the century. Only few had left traces in the local mixed-blood population, "looking occasionally out from behind the face of a white man or a Negro" (12).

The entrenched logic of the "vanishing Indian" inscribed in the conclusion that "the Chickasaw and Choctaws and Natchez and Yazoo were as gone as the predecessors" is familiar to scholars of Faulkner's work who have variously accounted for it (12).[5] Faulkner, critics argue, crafts a narrative of Yoknapatawpha that is about the loss of a primeval native ecology of place of which his Indigenous people are an inherent part.[6] The temporal and spatial displacement of cultures prior to the European settler culture is essential and integral to this origin myth.[7] Like James Fenimore Cooper, William Gilmore Simms, Ernest Hemingway, and other non-Native writers, Faulkner participates in a nostalgic discourse in which the Native American past functions "as a lost locus of ideals by allusion and implied antithesis" to modernity.[8] This antimodern strain in his fiction is part of a specifically southern regional resistance to modernity, a tradition carried into the twentieth century most famously by the Agrarians and the rhetoric of a "Lost Cause."[9] Whether Faulkner's voiding of Indigeneity is understood as part of an explicitly southern strategy of claiming access to land, or as a national pattern with long recourse to the colonialist/imperialist narrative of Manifest Destiny, these explanations illuminate Faulkner's understanding of the past. But what did he know of the Native American present?

I propose that Faulkner's discourses of Indian obsolescence correspond to Native American termination legislation of the post–World War II period. When Faulkner rewrites Indian Removal in *Requiem for a Nun* and returns repeatedly to the act of a Chickasaw woman's signature on a land deed that marks the birth of Jefferson, the city in the heart of Yoknapatawpha County, new legal efforts were underway aimed at dissolving Native American land trusts and relocating Native Americans yet again. After sketching the ironic echoes of this postwar context, I investigate the "X-mark" of Mohataha, Faulkner's fictional Chickasaw woman, as a gendered act and ask about the power and agency of Chickasaw and Choctaw women during the Removal period. What processes

Native American Sovereignty in *Requiem for a Nun* 95

of cultural reinvention and renewal were available to Mohataha and her real-life sisters? How did they preserve a sense of cultural identity and indigeneity after the tragedy of Removal? I follow Mohataha's wagon west to mobilize Native stories and epistemologies hoping to counter the narrative of Indigenous decline with spectacular stories of Indigenous women's continuity and cultural assent.

I

Faulkner's home in Oxford, Mississippi, is only 125 miles north of the Choctaw Indian reservation in Neshoba County and surrounding counties. Tribal members are descendants of the Choctaws who refused to be moved to Oklahoma during the Indian Removal of the 1830s, when approximately thirteen thousand Choctaws left for Indian Territory.[10] Historian Donna Akers estimates that three to four thousand Choctaws remained behind in their homes in the old Choctaw Nation in Mississippi, where each head of household was assigned 640 acres, communal landholdings were dissolved, and Choctaws became citizens of the state of Mississippi with limited rights.[11] In 1945, the remaining Choctaw tribal groups organized themselves into the Mississippi Band of Choctaws, the only federally recognized tribe in the state. Given Faulkner's sustained interest in Native southern history from his early Indian stories of the 1930s, including "Red Leaves" (1930), "Mountain Victory" (1930), "A Justice" (1931), "A Bear Hunt" (1933), and "Lo!" (1934), to *Go Down, Moses* and "The Bear" in the 1940s, to *Requiem for a Nun*, he very likely knew of the contemporary Choctaw presence and their cultural and political efforts. In fact, in his essay "Mississippi," Faulkner reveals his awareness of remaining Native populations in his state. After listing the towns of Columbus, Aberdeen, West Point, and the hamlet Shuqualak, the area where the Removal Treaty of Dancing Rabbit Creek was made with the Choctaws (33), Faulkner refers to Philadelphia, Mississippi, as a place "where the Neshoba Indians whose name the county bears still remain for the simple reason that they did not mind living in peace with other people, no matter what their color or politics" (32). Faulkner may have known of Article 14 of the Treaty of Dancing Rabbit Creek that allowed for Choctaws unwilling to leave for Indian Territory to stay behind on allotment lands in Mississippi, as is evident by this reference to the specific location where the treaty was made on September 27, 1830.

He was also clearly aware of the Choctaw presence in Neshoba County. Here the Mississippi Band of Choctaw Indians worked steadily toward tribal recognition and self-determination during the Indian

New Deal of the 1930s and the decades following. As Katherine M. B. Osburn writes, in order to attain tribal sovereignty, the Mississippi Choctaws worked with many different constituencies at the federal, state, and local levels, including, for instance, Mississippi's white supremacist governor and later US Senator Theodore Bilbo.[12] Faulkner's reference to the construction of alliances between Mississippi Indians and people "no matter their color or politics" may well refer to Bilbo, who is mentioned in the essay when Faulkner tells of the rise of the (fictional) Snopeses, "who were destroying that little which did remain" of a genteel South as they "elected the Bilboes and voted indefatigably for the Vardamans, naming their sons after both" (13). As Osburn fascinatingly documents, the Mississippi Choctaws repeatedly worked with Senator Bilbo to push petitions and bills on their behalf through the Committee on Indian Affairs in Washington. Bilbo's support of the Choctaws and his openly racist antiblack views were not the contradiction they may first appear but a long familiar nativist gesture by which whites claim descent from the Indians, the original owners of the land. Indians were not "black," and thus Bilbo's nativism and the Choctaws' efforts towards recognition of their racial identity as Native Americans were perversely complementary. Faulkner's pointed phrase "no matter their color or politics" reveals his awareness of these complex political connections and indicates that he was informed on Native politics in his state.

Faulkner would have also been culturally aware of the Mississippi Choctaws. He owned a copy of the 1938 *Mississippi Guide to the Magnolia State*, from which, as Noel Polk writes, he cribbed some of the history of Mississippi for the second prologue of *Requiem for a Nun*. Polk argues that since "the borrowing is certainly blatant and unobscured . . . there is a real sense in which Faulkner probably even wanted the reader to associate 'The Golden Dome' with the *Guide*."[13] Although most of the *Guide* styles the Native population as belonging to the remote history of the state, as evident in a chapter on "Archeology and Indians" written in a narrative voice that speaks of them in the past, there are three photos in the Tour section of the *Guide* presumably of contemporary subjects: they are of an older Choctaw woman weaving a basket, a young Choctaw girl in traditional dress, and a large Choctaw basket.[14] Osburn reports of the sustained efforts of the Choctaws to work with Mississippi Tourism and other state and county agencies to strengthen their communities by exhibiting their arts and crafts at fairs and thus drawing attention to their presence and distinct identity as Native Americans.[15] The *Mississippi Guide* features information on contemporary population numbers, citing Philadelphia, Mississippi, as the place of the Choctaw Indian Agency with "the greatest number of the 1745 Indians remaining in Mississippi."[16]

The *Guide* also refers to their contributions to the Neshoba County Fair, where in the 1930s one night of the fair was "set aside as Indian night, at which time the Choctaw give exhibitions of tribal games and dances."[17] Again, Faulkner likely knew of the Choctaws' contemporary cultural and political efforts towards self-government and sovereignty.

Why then, does he return to the pervasive logic of the "vanishing Indian" in his fiction? I propose that Faulkner's discourses of dispossession and "obsolescence" are fueled by Cold War anxieties that found their way into laws and policies advocating for Native American termination. In both the prologues to *Requiem for a Nun* and "Mississippi" Faulkner engages Indian dispossession not only of land but of a Native American identity no longer useful or used, in other words "obsolete." This language of "obsolescence" is resonant and even politically prescient from the vantage point of the early 1950s, when federal policies pursued the goal of "terminating" Indian land trusts, tribes, and identities. What is known as Termination was a series of political and legal efforts, beginning after World War II, to withdraw government services for Native Americans so as to integrate them into mainstream society as fully American.[18] Although Native Americans had been granted citizenship in 1924, their tribal identities conferred on them a legal and social status separate from other US citizens. To completely enfold Indians into the national polity was commensurate with the pressure to consolidate and strengthen an American Cold War identity.

This Cold War policy backdrop resonates in Faulkner's *Requiem for a Nun*, first in the preoccupation with legal settings, signatures, and federal control agencies such as the Bureau of Indian Affairs (BIA), and second, in the narrative's compulsive return to Indian Removal. Arguably, the 1950s saw yet another Indian removal rescripted in contemporary federal relocation programs that moved Native Americans off their reservations and into cities: "By late 1954 approximately 6,200 Native Americans of an estimated 245,000 reservation population had resettled in large cities. From 1952 to 1955, in Chicago alone some 3,000 reservation Indians, mainly from the Southwest, had relocated."[19] As Donald Fixico writes, "BIA publicity portrayed relocation as a 'New Deal' for Native Americans, one that offered them a chance to improve their economic status."[20] However, many Native Americans disagreed about the benefits of termination and relocation programs citing cultural loss and psychological trauma, as depicted, for instance, in N. Scott Momaday's *House Made of Dawn* (1968) and Leslie Marmon Silko's *Ceremony* (1977). Although these novels were published decades after *Requiem for a Nun* and "Mississippi," they are set after World War II, when Faulkner wrote his narratives during the years of intense policy debates surrounding Termination. These debates included arguments for liquidating the federal trust relationships and eventually dissolving the Bureau of Indian Affairs.[21]

Faulkner must have been aware of these efforts as congressional debates were broadcast in the media as well as in editorials and articles in the mainstream press, including the *Washington Post* and the *New York Times*. Many Indian advocates believed that the termination policies were a thin veneer for white greed and minority disenfranchisement. Former long-term BIA director John Collier, for instance, argued that the goal of the Eisenhower administration "has been to atomize and suffocate the group life of the tribes—that group life which is their vitality, motivation, and hope."[22] But despite Collier's advocacy of tribal sovereignty, Native American rights in the postwar era were debated in settings infused with the political ideologies of the Cold War, which, as Kenneth Philip points out, "contributed to a view among policy makers that Indian culture was deficient and an unwanted part of American life."[23]

Recent scholarly assessments of *Requiem for a Nun* place the novel in a Cold War context: Barbara Ladd calls it "the best example of Faulkner's post-Hiroshima engagement with the troubling potentialities of the State in the modern world,"[24] and several critics have followed suit, positing a "newly geopolitical inflection in Faulkner's spatial imagination during the Cold War"[25] and establishing a transpacific "network" that links the defeat of the Japanese at Hiroshima with New World genocide.[26] Leigh Anne Duck argues that the novel engages "domestic and global elements of US Cold War ideology" in terms of "oppositional temporalities" of nation and region that center on African Americans' political and economic disenfranchisement.[27] However, the contemporary ironies of Faulkner's engagement with Native American disenfranchisement during the period of Termination have not yet been noted. If the main theme in *Requiem for a Nun* is "America's survival as a sovereign nation," as Steven Weisenburger posits,[28] then we must add to these cogent arguments about state control, national sovereignty, and African American disenfranchisement Faulkner's preoccupation with Native American sovereignty as a historical and political issue inseparable from anxieties about the nation during the Cold War.

Native American disenfranchisement is the outcome of federal policy and the passing of laws whether in the period leading up to the 1830 Removal Act or to the 1950s termination legislation. Faulkner's emphasis, in *Requiem for a Nun*, on legislative locations and processes prompts Jay Watson to characterize the narrative as a prime example of "jurigenesis."[29] Indeed, Faulkner's historical narrator traces the legal origins of

Native American Sovereignty in *Requiem for a Nun*   99

Jefferson from its birth as a "Chickasaw Agency trading-post" through the town's legal documents recording the land grants, patents, and deeds that testify to the "simple dispossession of Indians [which] begot in time a minuscule of archive" (3). This legal archive is proof that Indian land was not "taken" or stolen but traded and legally sold. In Faulkner's fictional universe, several land transfers took place: the Chickasaw chief Ikkemotubbe sold the first square mile of land for a race horse in 1813. Then he sold to Thomas Supten a hundred-square-mile tract after the passage of the Treaty of Pontotoc in 1832. This was the treaty by which the Chickasaws ceded all their lands in and around Lafayette County. As Patricia Galloway explains, this treaty "provided all the formal allotments of land in Mississippi to individuals [few of whom were situated precisely in Lafayette County] who agreed to sell them in order to remove to Oklahoma, thus permitting speculators to buy up their lands."[30] It is in this way that the fictional Chickasaw woman Mohataha most likely acquired her parcel of land, the exact place where Jefferson's courthouse was going to be. Faulkner's narrative returns several times throughout the prologues to the moment when Mohataha sells her land by making her "X" on the land deed, as if to underline by repetition the legality and traumatic unreality of this act:

> then she said, "Where is this Indian territory?" And they told her: West. "Turn the mules west," she said, and someone did so, and she took the pen from the agent and made her X on the paper and handed the pen back and the wagon moved, the young men rising, too, and she vanished so across that summer afternoon to that terrific and infinitesimal creek and creep of ungreased wheels, herself immobile beneath the rigid parasol, grotesque and regal, bizarre and moribund, like obsolescence's self riding off the stage on its own obsolete catafalque, looking not once back, not once back toward home. (170–71)

Four pages later, the scene is self-consciously replayed with a vocabulary that highlights the dramatic significance of Mohataha's signature, this time inviting the reader to consider that all that was required to lose her land was "the single light touch of the pen in that brown illiterate hand, and the wagon did not vanish slowly and terrifically from the scene to the terrific sound of its ungreased wheels, but was swept, hurled, flung not only out of Yoknapatawpha County and Mississippi but the United States too" (174). Mohataha's X-mark on the deed testifies to the legally expedient displacement of Native populations until they were an "anachronism out of an old dead time and a dead age . . . until in a few more years that last of them would have passed and vanished in their turn too, obsolescent, too: because this was a white man's land" (32).

100 ANNETTE TREFZER

The nationalist motivation that drives this conclusion is applicable not only to the Native exodus from the South of the 1830s but also to Indian Termination of the 1950s.

II

Faulkner had the choice of making the signer of the land deed that later became the city of Jefferson the surviving Moketubbe (of "A Courtship," "Red Leaves," and "The Old People"), but he chose to make this figure a woman. Traditionally, Chickasaw women had control of the land and held property rights because the tribe was matrilineal, a fact Faulkner may have been aware of by the 1950s, when he properly reassigned his Indian characters to Mississippi's geography with Chickasaws in the northern parts of the state and Choctaws further south. Historian Don H. Doyle suggests that Faulkner was familiar with the story of a Chickasaw woman named Hoka "who had been allotted land under the terms of the removal treaties" and that she signed her "x" on the deed, "thereby transferring ownership to three white men": John Chisholm, John Martin, and John Craig.[31] Doyle speculates that Hoka must have been a family head and thus eligible for her own allotment, which she sold for eight hundred dollars. Like Doyle, I examined this document at the Chancery Court in Oxford to see how the deed was recorded. Her mark is certified as authentic and valid by James and George Colbert of the Chickasaw Nation, who wrote, "We the undersigned hereby certify that the above named Hoka is capable to take care of her own affairs this 13th day of June 1836." Chickasaw Agent Benjamin Reynolds also signed the deed (see figure 1). Doyle argues that for the white settler community, this "x," even one hundred years after it was made, symbolizes "legitimate ownership" of the land that was to become Oxford: "It was transferred, not as spoils of war or conquest but by way of legal treaties, deed transfers, and allotments of money—all rational market exchanges fully in keeping with the white rule of law."[32] Doyle is right about the importance of the legality of acts of Indian dispossession, but I question the conclusion that "the crude 'x' at the bottom of the deed and the guarantee of tribal leaders at the same time underscored the incapacity of Hoka and the Chickasaw to comprehend fully the rules of white civilization."[33] I like to imagine that the Indian woman's signature expresses neither her lack of comprehension nor, as Weisenburger suggests, a "carelessness in forfeit[ing] their homelands, hence their sovereignty."[34] A closer look at the actual land deed ledgers reveals that only signatures by Chickasaw women are certified by Native male witnesses, indicating a shift towards a patriarchal white legal system that does not

Native American Sovereignty in *Requiem for a Nun*   101

recognize the validity of women's signatures. Theda Perdue traces a similar shift among the Cherokees, whose government also became more centralized in the 1820s when power rested increasingly "in the hands of a few elite men who adopted the planter lifestyle of the white antebellum South."[35] Meanwhile, Cherokee women's access to political power was restricted when the "cult of domesticity" began to relegate them to their homes. However, this did not mean that Native women were unaware of the political and economic crisis. As Perdue writes, "The exclusion of women from politics certainly did not produce the removal crisis, but it did mean that a group traditionally opposed to land cession could no longer be heard on the issue."[36] I doubt that the historical Hoka was not capable of understanding the act of signing the land deed, and I imagine that the fictional Mohataha knew full well what she was doing.

Ojibwe historian Scott Richard Lyons reads the "x" on removal treaties and land transfer deeds as a "sign of the political realities of the treaty era," when native peoples, left with few choices, signified their agency with their signature.[37] He writes, "The x-mark is a contaminated and coerced sign of consent made under conditions that are not of one's making. It signifies power and a lack of power, agency and a lack of agency. It is a decision one makes when something has already been decided for you, but it is still a decision. Damned if you do, damned if you don't."[38] Lyons argues that although the "x" is a treaty signature legally signing land away, it also marks an "assent" into a new economy and lifestyle. The forced dispossession and migration of Mississippi Chickasaws and Choctaws produced new communities; it was not the end of the Trail as so often imagined. Removal, though by far not the same as migration, led to a new home.

Following Lyons's provocative interpretive lead, I read Mohataha's "x" on the land deed as a sign that sealed the Chickasaw exodus from Yoknapatawpha, marking in the downward vector of the "x" the descent of the Native South and the beginning of "that white man's land." But the upward vector traces an opposing trajectory of cultural ascent into a new chapter in Chickasaw history, mobilizing stories and Native epistemologies that counter the notion of Indian "obsolescence." Mohataha's "x" is also a gendered sign encoded with both the limitations and the possibilities of a character with many contradictory signifying possibilities. In my reading, the "x" of Mohataha's signature is not just a legal mark required to authenticate her deed; it is a placeholder for a new identity. Standing in for an unformed infinity of possibility, the "x" is a fantasy, an element of the imagination. Like the settlers' act of "jurigenesis" that germinates the new town of "Jefferson, Yoknapatawpha County, Mississippi" in "one conjoined breathing, one compound dream-state" in act 1, Mohataha's

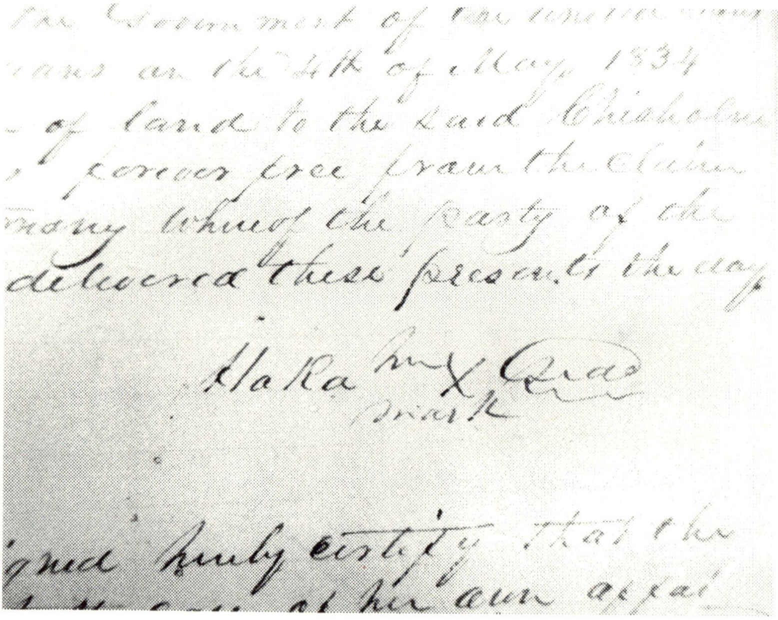

Figure 1. Hoka's recorded "x" in deed record A, page 125; Chancery Court, Oxford, Mississippi. Photograph by Annette Trefzer.

legal signature stands for something that will come into being that is of yet unknown (26).[39] In math, the "x" is an undetermined number, an independent variable; in Faulkner's novel, it expresses the unknowability of the Indian woman. Spatially, Mohataha's "x" marks the spot where things cross and come into being; temporally, it marks the transition to literacy, ushering in new definitions of Native cultural authenticity, Indigenous femininity, and racial sovereignty.

Finally, the "x" is the central organizing figure of Faulkner's novel. It is a chiasmus where the plot strands cross in the legal settings of the novel, thus linking the historical prologues featuring the Chickasaw woman, Mohataha, with the contemporary drama centering on the African American woman, Nancy Mannigoe. In act 1, Mohataha lounges in the shade to watch the building of the courthouse where more than one hundred years later Nancy Mannigoe is sentenced to death for the killing of Temple (Drake) Stevens's infant daughter. On the place of the "century-cold ashes of Choctaw camp-fires" rises the "golden dome" of the state Capitol in Jackson where Temple seeks clemency for Nancy in act 2. And the jail, where Nancy is imprisoned until her death, is the building that inaugurates non-Native space in the eviction of Mohataha

Native American Sovereignty in *Requiem for a Nun*   103

and her Chickasaw Tribe from Jefferson in act 3. Faulkner crosses plot strands in space and time, shuttling back and forth between historical deep structure and the contemporary moment to create ironic tensions and connections among the four female characters of the novel: Temple and Nancy, Mohataha and Cecilia Farmer. Constrained by patriarchal legal institutions—the courthouse, the Capitol, and the jail—the women have few options for resistance or escape, but they are by no means simply victims. Both story lines express minority women's entanglements with the legal foundations of white supremacy and white women's failure to engage the legal system successfully as they are pushed back into the private spheres of their families and homes.[40] The narrative highlights Cold War constrictions on women's access to the public sphere and their exclusion from full citizenship.

In the nineteenth century, white women's signatures on petitions against Indian Removal and slavery became marks of their claim to citizenship and their power to exercise their political rights. The women's signatures in Faulkner's text, however, do not gesture toward a collective political consciousness or a new shared subjectivity. On the contrary, the emphasis is on Cecilia Farmer's isolated identity. The "frail blond girl" who leaves her signature on the jail window before she gets swept away from Jefferson by her Confederate soldier provides only a "paradoxical and significantless name" (182). Her "frail and indelible" signature on the "old milky obsolete glass" (200) is her private "meditation" (180) or dreamy "musing" (185). Literally inscribed in and on her father's jail, her imprisoned signature is of no legal consequence except perhaps to speak of the unmarried status of "that tender ownerless obsolete girl's name" (200). The term "obsolete" links Cecilia and Mohataha as they leave Yoknapatawpha and recede in the memory of the citizens of Jefferson, who only have their signatures to contemplate. The continuing significance of Cecilia's signature is that of a "maiden muse" for historians intent on listening for the galloping horses of the Confederacy. Both Cecilia's and Mohataha's signatures inscribe them into Yoknapatawpha history, but only Mohataha's "x" triggers monumental historical change by setting loose a flood of settlers into southern Native lands: "instead of putting an inked cross at the foot of a sheet of paper, she had lighted the train of a mine set beneath a dam, a dyke, a barrier already straining, bulging, bellying, not only towering over the land but leaning, looming, imminent with collapse, so that it only required the single light touch of the pen in the brown illiterate hand" to burst (174). If there is any connection between Cecilia Farmer and Mohataha, it is their escape from the imprisoning legal structures of Jefferson, though Cecilia will only get as far as Alabama, where she is bogged down by the birth of a dozen

104 ANNETTE TREFZER

boys, all becoming farmers who contribute to the ascent of the white cotton South. Her signature, without legal ramifications, remains a sign of her private identity as a girl, wife, and mother.

Mohataha's "x" on the land deed, however, is a sign of her property ownership, economic agency, cultural mobility, and transition to literacy. Even the "x" is a sign that uses the alphabet, as opposed to nonliterary ways of making a treaty or contract. By the time Choctaws and Chickasaws moved to Indian Territory, literacy had spread because missions had been established among them for more than a decade.[41] Many Native leaders could write, not just the Anglo men who by marrying Choctaw or Chickasaw women of status hoped to access leadership lines for their male offspring.[42] "By 1818 both Choctaws and Chickasaws could attend the new Choctaw Academy established by the Baptist Mission Society of Kentucky," and around the same time in Mississippi, mixed-blood Choctaw chiefs Greenwood Leflore and David Folsom agreed to the Presbyterians' plans to build a school on the Yalobusha River, near present-day Grenada.[43] In the spring of 1819, missionary teachers opened the first literacy-based school, the Eliot School. What Morgan writes of the Choctaws is true for all Indigenous people of the Southeast: if they "failed to develop their own school curricula, much would be lost in terms of Native epistemology, belief and practice."[44] Keeping literate and nonliterate Native knowledge systems alive was and is crucial to cultural survival. As Eric Anderson reminds us, "Native people have for centuries been literate in earthworks, baskets, trade routes, petroglyphs, ecosystems, rhetorical performances, newspapers, treaties, books, and many other kinds of legible texts that they have created as well as, in some instances, received; Native knowledge has for centuries traversed space as well as time."[45] Mohataha's "x" marks a cultural contact zone, the transition point where Native and non-Native literacy systems meet.

Despite the signs of Mohataha's cultural and economic integration into the white South, her appearance in the history of Jefferson is literally bracketed three times in act 1. For instance, when the Indians watch the courthouse being built, Mohataha is introduced in parenthesis: the Indians watch "squatting or lounging in the shade, courteous, interested and reposed (even old Mohataha herself, the matriarch, barefoot in a purple silk gown and a plumed hat, sitting in a gilt brocade empire chair in a wagon behind two mules, under a silver-handled Paris parasol held by a female slave child)" (25). The image of the passive woman watching for her own oblivion to begin is in keeping with a Eurocentric patriarchal reading of the Native woman's cultural descent, doubly doomed by Andrew Jackson's Removal Act and her own adoption of southern black slavery. Yet the image is more complex, suggesting at once defeat and victory, Native American sovereignty and European royalty, elegance and tawdriness. Faulkner images his Indians as cosmopolitans—travelers to Paris, where Mohataha's son, Ikkemotubbe, bought the purple silk dress—and members of a community of modern commerce and exchange. Mohataha has incorporated European luxury clothing items into her life, marking her modern hybridized identity as she moves her household to a new place. This hybridity does not signal the loss of her Chickasaw identity. On the contrary, it is a sign of her creative ability to integrate and assimilate new items and objects in her own way. Acoma Pueblo poet Simon Ortiz creates a new definition for Native American cultural authenticity: "because in every case where European culture was cast upon Indian people of this nation, there was similar creative response and development, it can be observed that this was the primary element of a nationalistic impulse to make use of foreign ritual, ideas, and material in their own—Indian—terms."[46] Following Ortiz, we can read Mohataha as embracing her authentically "Native self" by wearing the French gown.

Mohataha's textiles signal a complex textuality, a crossing of respectability and cheap gaudiness as she dresses "in the cast off garments of a French queen, which on her looked like the Sunday costume of the madam of a rich Natchez or New Orleans brothel" (170). The suggestion of Mohataha's sexual tawdriness (but also her economic proprietorship, as madam of such an establishment) links her directly to the female figures in the main plot of the novel: Temple Stevens and Nancy Mannigoe, whose whorehouse experiences form a bond of motives and behaviors that are hard to pin down. Illuminating this opaque relationship, Susan Donaldson suggests "that Temple and Nancy recognize on some level the intertwined nature of whiteness and blackness and the literal and figurative violence that has gone into the making of narratives about black sexuality and white purity."[47] The reductive split of female sexuality into white purity and black licentiousness that has historically served the maintenance of segregation and white supremacy is complicated in the main drama of the novel. Temple distances herself from Nancy, whom she denigrates as "an ex-dope-fiend nigger whore" (124), but she also paradoxically identifies herself as Nancy's sister in "sin." The collusion of these female characters makes them "disturbing" and "illegible," as Donaldson suggests. Indeed, the women engage in actions driven by confounding and impenetrable motivations: Nancy murders Temple's child presumably in order to save the white woman's marriage. Temple's confession and appeal on behalf of Nancy attempts to give voice to these motivations, but the white patriarchal law literally cannot hear her contorted story. At the end of Temple's self-exposure, she discovers that the governor has left, and her husband has taken his place, thus containing the confession within the private framework of the family. The female characters cannot successfully appeal to the legal apparatus of the State. Even Temple, who, as Deborah Barker suggests, grows up believing that as a white upper-class woman "she had the power and force of law on her side," fails to stay the execution by asking the governor to invoke a state of exception.[48] These female characters are ultimately powerless to intervene in the laws regulating their lives and behaviors; however, they can disrupt the imprisoning regulatory codes applied to women's sexuality. Like Temple and Nancy, Mohataha appears as a matriarch *and* a madam, and Cecilia is a "demon-nun and angel-witch" (205) so that female sexual and moral conduct ultimately remains undecidable.

This undecidability also applies to Mohataha's relationship with the black slave girl shading her with the "silver-handled Paris parasol" on their shared journey west. Does her slave make her more respectable in the eyes of the contemporary spectators of Jefferson—more "civilized" because accepting of white ways, thus underlining the cruel irony of the removal of the Five Civilized Tribes? Or does the image show her moral depravity, the shared inheritance of the burden of slavery that the Chickasaws had to contend with? On the one hand, Mohataha appears to take care of her charges, including children and slaves. On the other hand, she is the sovereign demanding servitude of the African American girl who is her property. Her relation to African American slavery is at once protective and predatory. As commanding sovereign, she takes her movable human property with her; as a dispossessed Chickasaw woman, she is forcefully barred from property access like the black slaves in her charge. Together, the twinned figures of color throw into sharp relief the whiteness of the nation-building effort and its racial exclusions that persist for African Americans and Native Americans well into Faulkner's contemporary moment.

Faulkner's recurring image of Mohataha "beneath a French parasol held by a Negro slave girl" is his creative construction arising from a historical background that he embellished and transformed from the "actual into the apocryphal."[49] Faulkner was well read in the history of his home state and knew that Chickasaw Indians had slaves who traveled with the tribe to Indian Territory. He may also have been aware of a famous court case in Mississippi history involving Elizabeth "Betsy" Love Allen, a Chickasaw woman, and her slave, an event that could have sparked his iconic image. Betsy deserves our attention for her successful defense, in the highest appellate court in Mississippi in 1837, of her right to retain her individual property, Toney, a black slave. Betsy was married to a white man, John Allen. Phillip Caroll Morgan and Judy Goforth Parker, who brought her story to my attention, call this

Native American Sovereignty in *Requiem for a Nun*   107

landmark decision "a strategic affirmation of tribal sovereignty, and a breakthrough legal precedent in the struggle for equal property rights for married women."[50] Here is what happened:

> The issue at hand in the Monroe Country, Mississippi, Courthouse was the case being brought by John Fisher, an attorney, against Betsy's husband, John Allen, and so styled *Fisher v. Allen*. It seems that Mr. Allen had failed to pay an attorney's fee for Mr. Fisher's successful defense against another previous creditor. Fisher, in his petition, demanded payment for Allen's bad debt in the form of a slave named Toney, who was considered worth the sum owed according to Mr. Fisher's appraisal.[51]

However, Betsy Love entered the case in her own defense, arguing that Toney was a slave in her possession before she married Mr. Allen. Under Chickasaw law, a wife's property was not co-owned by her husband and could not be transferred.[52] Therefore, her properties could not be used to satisfy her husband's debt liabilities. The court ruled in Betsy Love's favor. This ruling is crucial for many reasons: first, it acknowledged Chickasaw matrilineal property law. As Justice Smith writes, "by the customs of the Chickasaws, the husband acquired no right to the property of the wife which she possessed at the time of marriage."[53] Second, the case placed Chickasaw law and American law into contradiction with each other. According to American law, which followed English common law, a wife's property became the husband's after marriage, because they were considered one unit. The status of what was called "coverture" made it impossible for wives to control their own property unless so stipulated in a premarital agreement.[54] And third, this case preceded and possibly led to the passing of the Married Woman's Property Act, passed two years after Betsy Love's success by the Mississippi legislature, "the first such legislation in the United States—perhaps in the world."[55] It gave non-Native women the same rights that Chickasaw and Choctaw women had enjoyed long before them. Maybe Betsy Love also wore a purple dress like her fictional sister Mohataha. In any case, it is not a stretch to read her court case as an early feminist victory resulting from an older matrilineal kinship system that considered Chickasaw men and women to be different but equally powerful human beings.

However, the positive ruling for Betsy Love is also disturbing and disheartening as the property in question was a human being. Toney had been in Love's possession since November 1829, before Mississippi state law was extended over Native Americans in January 1830. The court ruled that "upon the admission of Mississippi into the Union she [Betsy Love] became clothed with the attributes, and was vested with the power of sovereignty, and could exercise every right which attaches to that character."[56] The legal language, especially the words "clothed," "vested," and "sovereign," helps us see Mohataha clothed in her purple silk, a sovereign over her slaves.

What does this case reveal about Indian slavery in the South? The romantic idea that Indians would have been better and kinder masters to African American slaves is easily corrected by historical research. As Christina Snyder argues, at the time of Removal, "Native slaveholders, who included elites and an emerging middle class, had a good deal in common with white masters" in terms of economic surplus production of cotton and household help. They also used "legal codes and social mores to enforce racial hierarchies; white and Native masters alike worried over runaways, slave resistance, and protection of their private property."[57] The main difference may be that white slavery was based on a paternalistic culture that stipulated a fictive kinship with slaves (and often involved an unacknowledged biological kinship with them as well). This idea of slaves and later domestic African American labor as "kin" to a white family is illustrated in the novel by Temple's efforts to include Nancy in her family. But for Chickasaws slaves were not part of the clan or kinship structure. On the contrary, as Snyder writes, Chickasaw efforts at distinguishing themselves from African Americans at the time of Removal "rested on notions of aboriginal descent, race, and freedom from slavery" (212). And one hundred years later, when the Mississippi Band of Choctaws organized its tribal council, these notions of racial identity retained importance for membership.

But did Faulkner really know of Betsy Love when he created Mohataha? Could the conjoined historical pair of Betsy Love and her slave Toney be the inspiration for the fictional pair of Mohataha and "a Negro slave girl" (169)? Although there is no clear sign that Faulkner was aware of Betsy Love's court case, his knowledge of local history and his family connections indicate a probability. Phillip Carroll Morgan traces the entwined history of the Falkner family with Cyrus Harris, the first elected governor of the Chickasaw Nation (1856). Both William Faulkner and Cyrus Harris were born in New Albany, Mississippi, three generations apart, in 1897 and 1817, respectively.[58] Morgan posits that "the Faulkner and Harris families were known to each other, perhaps well known, and that Faulkner consciously, freely, and sometimes eloquently drew on Chickasaw mythos, personalities, and history to create his beloved Yoknapatawpha County."[59] Although Morgan does not mention Betsy Love in his account of Chickasaw intellectual and political leadership, Faulkner may have heard about her.[60]

Betsy Love had white and Native ancestry; she was the daughter of Thomas Love and (Imahota) Sally Colbert, both biracial families who

Native American Sovereignty in *Requiem for a Nun*   109

owned slaves.[61] The Loves and the Colberts were leading Chickasaw families in northern Mississippi, where the story of Betsy Love Allen was not forgotten. In 1954, only three years after *Requiem for a Nun* was published, the Mother's Study Club of Toccopola, a hamlet in Pontotoc County, erected a gravestone for her with the following inscription:

BETTY ALLEN
Dau. of
Thomas Love and Third Wife
a Chickasaw Indian
Wife of
Col John L. Allen
17??–1837
Noted for her role in the
establishment of property rights
of married women in the
Anglo-Saxon world.

Although her name is misspelled, and James Allen is referred to as "John Allen," this is clearly a tribute to Betsy Allen.[62] Thus, in the early 1950s, local women, not far from Faulkner's hometown, organized funds for a granite marker publicly memorializing Betsy Love Allen. This act points to the living memory and continuing significance of the Chickasaw woman whose story was known to local contemporaries of Faulkner, and we may assume that the writer may have been aware of her. Certainly, his persistent twinning of Mohataha and the slave child evokes this other historically conjoined pair and the Chickasaw woman who, in insisting on her right to her own property, changed legal history by setting a precedent for the Married Women's Property Act of 1839.

III

Faulkner alludes only briefly, and again parenthetically, to the Chickasaw experience in Indian Territory in the story of Old Doc Habersham's son "(now a man of twenty-five, [who] married one of Issetibbeha's granddaughters and in the thirties emigrated to Oklahoma with his wife's dispossessed people)" (7). Here he served as Chickasaw agent "until he resigned in a letter of furious denunciation addressed to the President of the United States himself" (5). Faulkner had imagined resistance to Indian Removal in his earlier story "Lo!" where a Chickasaw delegation occupies Andrew Jackson's White House, but in *Requiem for a Nun*, Chickasaw political agency is mediated by the intervention of the federal government in the figure of the white BIA agent whose letter reports of their hardships and protests the government's neglectful treatment of Chickasaws in the new territory.[63]

Faulkner does not follow Mohataha's wagon to Indian Territory; he does not record the dangers and disappointments she would have encountered on her way, the gnawing hunger, fatigue, self-doubt, and spiritual despair that we get in narratives by Cherokee writers John Milton Oskison and Diane Glancy, for instance. Mohataha would have reflected on her homeland left behind and all the stories connected to the places she knew and valued. And she would have carefully laid aside her purple silk dress, tattered and torn from the journey, for her daughters and granddaughters because it held the memories of the march. We learn from Chickasaw writer Linda Hogan that women who kept these dresses called them "tear dresses." The narrator of her novel *Mean Spirit* explains,

> Tear dresses were what the women wore during the removal of the Chickasaws from the Mississippi homeland. As they journeyed west, to Oklahoma, the women had been permitted to carry nothing sharp, no knives nor scissors, not even their tongues; nothing with the potential for being a weapon against the American army that herded the uprooted torn-away people from their beautiful rich woodlands in the south. Because they had no scissors or knives, cloth was torn by their blunt teeth and ripped apart by their hands. The resulting straight lines and corners of cotton were fashioned into dresses. Those women who survived renamed the dresses, calling them "tear" dresses, meaning "to weep and cry."[64]

Mohataha's torn silk dress, now mended with ripped squares of unmatched cloth, would have been her "tear dress," a reminder of her endurance, survival, and strength—in the words of Gerald Vizenor, her "survivance."[65] The dresses were artifacts from which new generations of women could draw inspiration and fortitude. "Tear dresses" taught lessons about the role of women in the history of the Removal and their contributions to the survival and continuance of the Chickasaw community. These dresses told stories of strong women.

Choctaw women who walked their Trail of Tears also kept these tearful memories; they too passed on traditions and survival techniques, as well as the Choctaw language, stories, and songs that continued into the new territory and are alive today. In the novel *Shell Shaker*, LeAnne Howe tells the story of Nowatima, who survives the terrors of the Removal experience and learns the traditions of grieving by singing the Choctaw funeral songs for all the people who died on the trail. More than one hundred years later, new generations come to learn "the old songs" from Nowatima, and this starts a revival of Choctaw music and

Native American Sovereignty in *Requiem for a Nun*   111

traditions.[66] As Choctaw historian Donna Akers writes, "the Choctaws' survival centered upon their ability to reform their society to accommodate necessary change, while simultaneously maintaining a cultural framework that set them apart, gave them comfort, and provided a permanent foundation on which to build."[67] This is equally true for all Native Americans who arrived in Indian Territory in the late 1830s, who would have needed a sense of comfort and stability to continue their lives. These stories of Native American women who survived and thrived work directly against political and literary discourses of Indian "obsolescence." For cultural continuity and social well-being, the centrality of powerful women is unquestioned, as Paula Gunn Allen argues in *The Sacred Hoop*, as Howe demonstrates in her novels, and as many Native American women proudly pronounce.[68]

In Oklahoma, Mohataha would have passed on those stories to her daughters and granddaughters, endowing them with her courage, daring, and spirit. Although not literally related to the fictional Mohataha, Pearl Carter Scott could have been one of her great-granddaughters. Pearl became an aviator in the early 1930s. Pearl was a Chickasaw woman who saw her first airplane at age eleven as it flew over her rural hometown of Marlow, Oklahoma; she first boarded an airplane in 1927, when Wiley Post landed his plane in her neighborhood.[69] Post's fame as the first aviator to fly around the world in seven days was still ahead of him that afternoon when he took Pearl up in the air for her first flying lesson.[70] Fascinated with aviation, fearless and talented, Pearl received her "Student Pilot's Permit" from the Aeronautics Branch of the United States Department of Commerce in June 1930, when she was twelve.[71] She owned her own plane, a Curtiss Robin monoplane that cost her father, the prosperous white businessman George Carter, more than $4,000, a considerable sum at that time. The plane had a range of 590 miles on a fifty-gallon tank—a whole new way of thinking about Native American mobility.[72] Thus, before Faulkner wrote *Pylon* (1935), a Chickasaw woman turned stunt girl and "youthful aviatrix" (as she was called in the press) thrilled audiences at air shows. Faulkner was able to image the blond Laverne, a mechanic and parachute jumper who is openly sexually involved with two men who are the fathers of her boy, but I dare propose that the sight of Mohataha's great-granddaughter in the air may have challenged everything he ever imagined about Native American women.

I conclude this chapter with a high-flying Chickasaw "aviatrix" because it is an image of sweeping cultural ascent into modernity and female Chickasaw agency that contrasts sharply with Mohataha's disappearance from the narrative and with the descending fortune of Nancy, who stays and dies in the prison cell in Mississippi. Though Nancy's singing voice can be heard through the bars of the jail, "African American agency," as Jay Watson argues, "triggers a special kind of censorship in Faulkner's imagination" that disavows a "dawning awareness" of southern civil rights activism as early as the 1920s and 30s—and certainly, I would add, by the early 1950s of the civil rights movement to come.[73] The trajectory of Mohataha's cultural descent into "obsolescence" is resonant with contemporary termination legislation, but it also signals the limits of Faulkner's capacity to imagine Native American cultural survival in the South.

Faulkner concludes "Mississippi" with a homage to Caroline Barr, who is "free these many years but . . . had declined to leave" her white family, which is indebted to her because she would never "accept in full her weekly Saturday wages" (16). Sketched as a matriarch in a rocking chair, like Cecilia Farmer and Mohataha, she is "imperial, and more: imperious" (41). Caroline is never truly sovereign in the way the word "imperial" implies, so Faulkner follows up with the more fitting term "imperious," which refers to her command to the family to lay her out her dead body according to her wishes. Faulkner's final admission of "loving all of [Mississippi] even while he had to hate some of it" (42) may refer to his appreciation of and guilt over Caroline Barr's lifelong service, which was both voluntary and involuntary. The dual sentiments of love and hate characterize Faulkner's relationship to the rise of the white South based on legal structures that supported Indian Removal and slavery. Writing of and against obsolescence, Faulkner ensures that the stories of Temple and Nancy, Mohataha and Cecilia are remembered because all are connected through the intersecting paths that weave the history of Mississippi in time and space.

NOTES

I want to thank audiences and presenters at the 2017 Faulkner and Yoknapatawpha Conference at the University Mississippi for their responses to an earlier version of my argument, especially Eric Anderson, LeAnne Howe, Jodi Byrd, Theresa Towner, Gina Caison, Kirstin Squint, Deborah Barker, Patricia Galloway, Robbie Ethridge, Katherine M. B. Osburn, John Lowe, and Melanie Benson Taylor. Thanks also to Katie McKee and Jaime Harker, who provided valuable feedback on earlier drafts and to Jay Watson for his evocative suggestions and discerning comments.

1. Malcolm Cowley, *The Portable Faulkner* (New York: Viking, 1946). For Faulkner's retrospective approach to his work, see Noel Polk, *Faulkner's Requiem for a Nun: A Critical Study* (Bloomington: Indiana University Press, 1981).

2. Mississippi was the twentieth state in the Union, and Alabama in 1819 was the twenty-second state.

3. William Faulkner, *Requiem for a Nun* (1951; repr., New York: Vintage, 1994), 81. Hereafter cited parenthetically in the text.

4. William Faulkner, "Mississippi," in James B. Meriwether, ed., *Essays, Speeches and Public Letters* (New York: Modern Library, 2004), 11–12. Hereafter cited parenthetically in the text.

5. See Lewis M. Dabney, *The Indians of Yoknapatawpha: A Study in Literature and History* (Baton Rouge: Louisiana State University Press, 1974), and the essays in the special issue on Faulkner's Indians edited by Gene M. Moore, *Faulkner Journal* 43, nos. 1–2 (Fall 2002–Spring 2003).

6. Thomas L. McHaney, "The Ecology of Uncle Ike: Teaching *Go Down, Moses* with Janisse Ray's *Ecology of a Cracker Childhood*," in *Faulkner and the Ecology of the South: Faulkner and Yoknapatawpha, 2003*, ed. Joseph Urgo and Ann Abadie (Jackson: University Press of Mississippi, 2005), 98–114.

7. Bruce G. Johnson, "Indigenous Doom: Colonial Mimicry in Faulkner's Indian Tales," *Faulkner Journal* 43, nos. 1–2 (Fall 2002–Spring 2003): 101–27.

8. Robert Woods Sayre, "Faulkner's Indians and the Romantic Vision," *Faulkner Journal* 43, nos. 1–2 (Fall 2002–Spring 2003): 38.

9. Melanie Benson Taylor, *Reconstructing the Native South: American Indian Literature and the Lost Cause* (Athens: University of Georgia Press, 2011).

10. Official website of the Mississippi Band of Choctaw Indians, http://www.choctaw.org/aboutMBCI/history/index.html.

11. Donna L. Akers, *Living in the Land of Death: The Choctaw Nation, 1830–1860* (East Lansing: Michigan State University Press, 2004), 92.

12. Katherine M. B. Osburn, *Choctaw Resurgence in Mississippi: Race, Class, and Nation Building in the Jim Crow South, 1830–1970* (Lincoln: University of Nebraska Press, 2014), 131.

13. Polk, *Faulkner's Requiem for a Nun*, 100. Polk mentions that Thomas L. McHaney first pointed this out in "Faulkner Borrows from the *Mississippi Guide*," *Mississippi Quarterly* 19 (Summer 1966): 116–20.

14. *Mississippi: A Guide to the Magnolia State* (New York: Viking, 1938): 465–67.

15. Osburn, *Choctaw Resurgence*, 170.

16. *Mississippi: A Guide*, 465.

17. Ibid., 468.

18. On Termination, see Kenneth R. Philip, *Termination Revisited: American Indians on the Trail to Self-Determination, 1933–1953* (Lincoln: University of Nebraska Press, 1999); Donald L. Fixico, *Termination and Relocation: Federal Indian Policy, 1945–1960* (Albuquerque: University of New Mexico Press, 1986); Vine Deloria, Jr., ed., *American Indian Policy in the Twentieth Century* (Norman: University of Oklahoma Press, 1985).

19. Fixico, *Termination*, 138.

20. Ibid., 139.

21. Ibid., 61.

22. John Collier, "Indian Takeaway: Betrayal of a Trust," *Nation*, October 2, 1954, 290–91.

23. Philip, *Termination Revisited*, 94.

24. Barbara Ladd, "'Philosophers and Other Gynecologists': Women and the Polity in *Requiem for a Nun*," *Mississippi Quarterly* 52, no. 3 (June 1999), n.p. Accessed electronically.

25. Spencer Morrison, "*Requiem*'s Ruins: Unmaking and Making the Cold War in Faulkner, *American Literature* 84, no. 2 (June 2003), n.p. Accessed electronically.

26. Wai Chee Dimock, "Faulkner Networked: Indigenous, Regional, Trans-Pacific," in *Faulkner and History: Faulkner and Yoknapatawpha, 2014*, ed. Jay Watson and James G. Thomas Jr. (Jackson: University Press of Mississippi, 2017), 15.

27. Leigh Anne Duck, *The Nation's Region: Southern Modernism, Segregation, and US Nationalism* (Athens: University of Georgia Press, 2006), 227.

28. Steven Weisenburger "Faulkner in Baghdad, Bush in Hadleyburg: Race, Nation, and Sovereign Violence," *American Literary History* 18, no. 4 (Winter 2006): 740.

29. Jay Watson, "Dangerous Return: The Narratives of Jurigenesis in Faulkner's *Requiem for a Nun*," *Modern Fiction Studies* 60, no. 1 (Spring 2014): 108–37. Watson borrows the term "jurigenesis" from legal scholar Robert Cover. See Martha Minow, Michael Ryan, and Austin Sarat, eds., *Narrative, Violence, and the Law: The Essays of Robert Cover* (Ann Arbor: University of Michigan Press, 1995).

30. Patricia Galloway, "The Construction of Faulkner's Indians," *Faulkner Journal* 43., nos. 1–2 (Fall 2002–Spring 2003): 14.

31. Don H. Doyle, *Faulkner's County: The Historical Roots of Yoknapatawpha* (Chapel Hill: University of North Carolina Press, 2001), 45.

32. Ibid.

33. Ibid., 46.

34. Weisenburger, "Faulkner in Baghdad," 752.

35. Theda Perdue, "Cherokee Women and the Trail of Tears," *Journal of Women's History* 1, no. 1 (Spring 1989): 20.

36. Ibid., 21.

37. Scott Richard Lyons, *x-marks: Native Signatures of Assent* (Minneapolis: University of Minnesota Press, 2010), 1.

38. Ibid., 2–3.

39. Thanks to Jay Watson for suggesting this parallel process of creating normative meaning in the town's beginnings.

40. See Ladd's reference to David Riesman's notion of "reprivatization."

41. As Theda Perdue writes of the Cherokees, the national newspaper, the *Cherokee Phoenix*, was bilingual, with type in English and Cherokee syllabary, thus accommodating Native and non-Native readers; it also boosted Cherokee pride and helped in their resistance to removal. The inaugural issue appeared in February 1828 under the editorial direction of Elias Boudinot, a Cherokee who was educated in mission schools. See Theda Perdue and Michael D. Green, *The Cherokee Removal: A Brief History with Documents* (Boston: Bedford/St. Martin's, 2005), 15.

42. See James F. Barnett, *Mississippi's American Indians* (Jackson: University Press of Mississippi, 2012), 164–207, and Clara Sue Kidwell, "Choctaws and Missionaries in Mississippi before 1830," in Greg O'Brien, ed., *Pre-Removal Choctaw History: Exploring New Paths* (Norman: University of Oklahoma Press, 2008), 200–20.

43. Barnett, *Mississippi's American Indians*, 182.

44. Phillip Carroll Morgan, "Who Shall Gainsay Our Decision? Choctaw Literary Criticism in 1830," in *Reasoning Together: The Native Critics Collective*, ed. Craig S. Womack, Daniel Heath Justice, and Christopher B. Teuton (Norman: University of Oklahoma Press, 2008), 137.

45. Eric G. Anderson, "The Presence of Early Native Studies: A Response to Stephanie Fitzgerald and Hilary E. Wyss," *American Literature* 45, no. 2 (2010): 251.

46. Simon Ortiz, "Towards a National Indian Literature: Cultural Authenticity in Nationalism," in *Nothing but the Truth: An Anthology of Native American Literature*, ed. John Purdy and James Ruppert (Upper Saddle River, NJ: Prentice Hall, 2001), 121.

47. Susan V. Donaldson, "Reimaging the Femme Fatale: *Requiem for a Nun* and the Lessons of Film Noir," in *Faulkner and Mystery: Faulkner and Yoknapatawpha, 2009*, ed. Annette Trefzer and Ann J. Abadie (Jackson: University Press of Mississippi, 2014), 157.

48. Deborah Barker, "Demystifying the Modern Mammy in *Requiem for a Nun*," in *Faulkner and Film: Faulkner and Yoknapatawpha, 2010*, ed. Peter Lurie and Ann J. Abadie (Jackson: University Press of Mississippi, 2014), 85.

Native American Sovereignty in *Requiem for a Nun*   115

49. Dabney, *The Indians of Yoknapatawpha*, 12.

50. Phillip Carroll Morgan and Judy Goforth Parker, *Dynamic Chickasaw Women* (Sulphur, OK: Chickasaw, 2011), 11.

51. Ibid., 13.

52. *Fisher v. Allen*, 3 Miss. 611; 1837 Miss. Lexis 29; 2 Howard 611.

53. Morgan and Parker, *Dynamic Chickasaw Women*, 15

54. Ibid., 14.

55. Ibid., 13

56. *Fisher v. Allen*, 2.

57. Christina Snyder, *Slavery in Indian Country* (Cambridge, MA: Harvard University Press, 2010), 211.

58. Phillip Carroll Morgan, *Riding Out the Storm: 19th Century Chickasaw Governors, Their Lives and Intellectual Legacy* (Ada, OK: Chickasaw, 2013), 67.

59. Ibid., 68

60. The only entry in Morgan's book on the Love family is for Overton "Sobe" Love (1823–1906), born in Holly Springs, Mississippi. He was a wealthy landowner and cattle rancher, and after Removal he became a Chickasaw judge in Indian Territory (44).

61. LeAnne Howe, "Betsy Love and the Mississippi Married Woman's Property Act of 1839," *Mississippi History Now*, http://www.mshistorynow.mdah.ms.gov/articles/6/betsy-love-and-the-mississippi-married-womens-property-act-of-1839.

62. Howe (ibid.) points out that the name of James Allen is often misattributed as John Allen in historical documents.

63. Charles Hudson writes that the Chickasaws had a difficult start in Indian Territory: they were attacked by Shawnees, Kiowas, and Comanches, whose land they were given by the federal government, and they suffered a smallpox epidemic and malnutrition because "the government did not supply them with the food due them by the treaty they had signed." See Charles Hudson, *The Southeastern Indians* (Knoxville: University of Tennessee Press, 1999), 462.

64. Linda Hogan, *Mean Spirit* (New York: Ivy Books, 1992), 81.

65. Gerald Vizenor, *Manifest Manners: Postindian Warriors of Survivance* (Hanover, CT: Wesleyan University Press, 1994).

66. LeAnne Howe, *Shellshaker* (San Francisco: Aunt Lute Books, 2001), 150.

67. Akers, *Living in the Land of Death*, 103.

68. Paula Gunn Allen, *The Sacred Hoop: Recovering the Feminine in American Indian Traditions* (Boston: Beacon, 1992).

69. Paul F. Lambert, *Never Give Up! The Life of Pearl Carter Scott* (Ada, OK: Chickasaw, 2007), 50.

70. Ibid., 41.

71. Ibid., 50.

72. Ibid. 46.

73. Watson, "Dangerous Return," 127.

"Brother: Is This Truth?"

History, Fiction, and Colonialism in Faulkner's Mississippi

KATHERINE M. B. OSBURN

The first thing that came to mind when Professors Watson and Trefzer invited me to contribute to this work was the C-minus I received on my oral presentation on *The Sound and the Fury* in my freshman literature class back in 1973. When I inquired as to the reason for my grade, my literature professor explained that I had "made the characters sound crazy." I was astonished at this remark and, in my eighteen-year-old cluelessness, said something equivalent to "did you *read* the book?"[1] Much later I realized that what I had dismissed as people being crazy was Faulkner's way of telling stories from multiple perspectives. Having been a practicing historian for twenty-three years, I now have much more appreciation for complex stories, but I was still terrified by the idea of addressing this gathering. How could I offer a fresh perspective on the Indigenous characters of this literary world? What could I, as a historian concerned with the material reality of rural Mississippi in the nineteenth and twentieth centuries, have to say to Faulkner scholars and aficionados, working in the realm of the imagination? Yet scholars of both history and literature concern themselves with stories, so I want to talk about what we can learn from comparing how these two disparate disciplines frame stories of Indigenous Mississippi.

To accomplish this goal, I will discuss shifting ideas about historical narrative and review what other scholars have said about Faulkner's Indigenous peoples. Beyond historiography, however, I hope to demonstrate the importance of stories crafted from historical documentation to understanding Faulkner's Mississippi. At the time that Faulkner was writing, Choctaws were engaged in their own storytelling. The tales Mississippi Choctaws spun over the course of Faulkner's life demonstrate how subaltern peoples use historical narratives, even painful ones, for powerful political purposes. Considering the actions of Mississippi's actual Indigenous peoples locates Faulkner's imaginary Indigenous

History, Fiction, and Colonialism in Faulkner's Mississippi   117

peoples in a critical historical context of colonialism. The stories that Mississippi Choctaws crafted about themselves, excavated from the archives, deserve a place alongside Faulkner's work as a way to think about Native southerners and that elusive and contingent thing we call truth.

Since stories are our focus, let us start with historians' ambivalent relationship with narrative. For the general public, history *is* a narrative—an allegedly accurate account of past events and people based on a careful examination of the documentary record and communicated objectively through stories with a beginning, a middle, and an end. Somewhere along the way, the historian explains how element "A" working in concert with element "B" "caused" the story to unfold as it did, and then everybody understands what *really* happened and *why* it occurred. Yet among professional historians, the role of narrative in historical interpretation has been in flux at least since the first decades of the twentieth century. The Annales school, founded by historians Lucien Febvre and Marc Bloch at the University of Strasburg in 1929, was one of the first groups to eschew narrative as its primary analytical device. Initially inspired by Marx's attempt to interpret history according to larger forces of economic change, Annales scholars wanted history to be more scientific. Some of them, however, found Marx's attachment to the Hegelian dialectic reductionist, so they turned to other social sciences to craft a new scientific approach to the discipline. Their methodology viewed history as a synthesis of "hard" data from the social and, in some cases, the natural sciences projected onto the past.[2]

The trend continued in the 1960s and 1970s when a "'New' Social History" argued for abandoning the traditional historical narrative, which tended to focus on the actions of elites, in favor of understanding the past "from the bottom up." This shift in emphasis birthed many of the schools of historical study that take racial and ethnic minorities, "ordinary" laboring people, and women as their subjects of study. Methodologically, these scholars sought wisdom in quantitative approaches that helped them determine larger patterns of social change, and they viewed both documentary evidence and narrative structures as potentially elitist and incomplete.[3] Following closely on their heels, literary theorists such as Michel Foucault and Jacques Derrida also regarded narrative histories not as objective reconstructions of the "actual" past but as a set of "codes" that represented little more than the views of elite power brokers.[4] Carrying the level of abstraction even further, some of the historical profession's most articulate philosophers, Hayden White and Louis O. Mink, have argued that historical narratives are suspect because they are not intrinsic to history per se but are imposed upon the documentary record by historians.[5] For many professional historians, then, narrative history has seemed quaint and antiquarian at best and elitist and oppressive at worst.

Yet narrative history did not perish, perhaps because storytelling is so universal to humans.[6] In fact, some influential historians have recently admonished their colleagues to respect well-written historical narratives as important analytical tools for understanding the past.[7] These scholars, however, are careful to note that all historical narrative is constructed according to our own agendas, and we may not always see things as they "really are." This is especially true of my field, ethnohistory, where a new generation of Indigenous scholars are challenging Eurocentric history. Some of these scholars propose a research methodology of decolonization, which privileges Indigenous wisdom over empiricism. For these scholars, Indigenous sacred stories are the starting point of all knowledge of their history and culture.[8] Historiographically, this gets us back to stories, the analytical focus of both history and literature, but philosophically, it still begs the question of what distinguishes historical narratives from fictional narratives.

The most obvious answer, from the perspective of Western empiricism at least, is content—one set of stories concerns what "actually happened" while the other set is "made up." This distinction is grounded in the idea that historical narratives are discovered in the archives while fictional narratives are fabricated from the imagination. Yet different historians can detect very dissimilar stories in the same archives and come to fundamentally contrary conclusions about any given historical event. For example, environmental historian William Cronon's comparison of two divergent narratives of the Dust Bowl—Paul Bonnifield's *The Dust Bowl: Men, Dirt, and Depression* and Donald Worster's *Dust Bowl: The Southern Plains in the 1930s*—reveals how two historians reading exactly the same primary sources can nonetheless write two very different historical accounts. For Bonnifield, the Dust Bowl resulted in a generation of farmers whose determination and ingenuity overcame ecological trials and created a better world for their descendants, while Worster views the same period as an unmitigated disaster that revealed the ecologically suicidal folly that is capitalism.[9] That two thoughtful and careful historians can come to such different conclusions about the same body of evidence suggests that perhaps historical stories are not something to be "uncovered" in the archives but are every bit as "made up" as Faulkner's stories.

Yet these opposing judgments about the meaning of a single ecological episode do not suggest that history is, in the words of historian David Carr, "a structureless sequence of isolated events" rather than a story. Instead, Carr argues, history is "a complex structure of temporal configurations that interlock and receive their definition and their meaning

History, Fiction, and Colonialism in Faulkner's Mississippi 119

from within the action itself."[10] Or, to put it more directly, real things happened to real people in the past, and the writing of history is about imposing meaning on both. Historians, however, do not operationalize the past in the same way that novelists do. Historians, unlike novelists and literary critics, are constrained by the boundaries of their historical evidence, at least in the paradigm of Western empiricism. As a historian of Indigenous Mississippi, I have some thoughts on what the evidence I discovered and the narrative I composed about it might tell us about Indigenous Mississippi in Faulkner's day. Let me quickly note, however, that I make no claims to speak for the Choctaw people; rather, I speak as a non-Indigenous historian who spent ten years working in archives of Choctaw history. But first, let us review what literary critics and historians have already said about Faulkner's Indigenous Mississippi.

Numerous scholars have analyzed Faulkner's literary treatment of Indians and found a range of problems, themes, and meanings. Faulkner's fiction is historical in nature, which leads some historians of the South to take Faulkner's tales seriously as a statement on, or at least an impression of, southern history and culture.[11] The historian who has studied Faulkner most extensively, Don H. Doyle, has written, "Faulkner wrote about the past with unusual sensitivity and understanding." Doyle also asserted that the purpose of his book *Faulkner's Country: The Historical Roots of Yoknapatawpha* was not "to burden readers with nitpicking corrections of various historical 'errors' or implausible stories" in Faulkner's work.[12] Rather, Faulkner's evocative prose had sparked a curiosity about the county in which the man lived and wrote, leading Doyle to tell what I, as a non-Indigenous historian, regard as the "real" story of Lafayette County (aka Yoknapatawpha), the historical story found in documentary evidence. Doyle regards Faulkner's "real" world as a "typical, even ordinary, portrait of the southern past."[13] Likewise, literature professor Annette Trefzer states that in analyzing Faulkner's portrayal of Indigenous peoples, "it is tempting to get caught up in questions of historical accuracy, ethnographic authenticity, and political correctness."[14] While she is careful to note the negative effects of long-standing harmful stereotypes on modern-day Indigenous peoples, Trefzer concludes that pointing out the inconsistencies and errors in Faulkner misses the larger importance of how he captured attitudes toward Indians that were commonly held by the people all around him.[15] Although it is true that Faulkner portrayed common stereotypes of Indians, he was notoriously uninterested in material reality.

William Faulkner made no claims to be an ethnographer, nor did he believe in research. He famously wrote to his friend and editor Malcolm Cowley that he did not "care much for facts, am not much interested in them, you can't stand a fact up, you've got to prop it up, and when you move to one side a little and look at it from that angle, it's not thick enough to cast a shadow in that direction."[16] Consequently, Faulkner preferred not to create his characters from historical documents but from his imagination, which was shaped by folk tales and readings in Mississippi history.[17] The result is a story unencumbered by the kinds of concerns that trouble historians—accuracy, consistency, evidence. Faulkner conflates Chickasaw and Choctaw history and culture, while distorting and misrepresenting both, and is not consistent in identifying his characters' tribal affiliations.[18] Faulkner justified his cavalier attitude toward material reality by noting that his work sought something nobler than a chronicle of historical events. "The poets are almost always wrong about the facts," he wrote. "That's because they're not interested in the facts, only in truth."[19] Which leads us to ask, what truth is Faulkner attempting to communicate in his Indian stories?

Faulkner sought to unsettle the moonlight and magnolias image of the South that was popular during the early twentieth century by doing what all great novelists and storytellers do—talking about subjects that people would prefer to ignore—or, as Doyle put it, crafting a "disturbing exploration of some of the region's more discomforting features."[20] However, while Faulkner may have undeniably rattled clichés about the South, his portrayal of Mississippi Indians rested comfortably on centuries of dehumanizing stereotypes, the most central of which is the notion that Indigenous peoples are either noble or ignoble savages. The general consensus of scholars who have examined Faulkner's treatment of Indians is that they lean toward the ignoble side of this continuum, especially in his early writing. They are obese, unkempt, lazy, corrupt, and sometimes ridiculous.[21] Some literary critics have interpreted this unflattering portrayal as Faulkner's way of underscoring the injustices Indigenous peoples faced and critiquing the corrupting influences of colonial culture on this once noble people. This is especially true of the scholars who see Faulkner's Indians as comic.[22] Other scholars construe these negative portrayals of Indians as axiomatic of anxieties that Faulkner and his contemporaries had about race, especially whiteness, and gender, specifically masculinity.[23]

The debased characteristics of Mississippi's Indigenous inhabitants are linked to the second major stereotype of Indigenous peoples found in Faulkner—the vanishing Indian, a perception that confines Indians to the past despite their obvious presence in the present.[24] Faulkner portrayed Mississippi's Indigenous peoples as a pathetic and degraded "remnant" of the once great Choctaw Nation, which is also how many white Mississippians at the time viewed them.[25] And it is to that remnant

History, Fiction, and Colonialism in Faulkner's Mississippi

that we now turn to examine the stories that Choctaws and their political allies were proclaiming even as Faulkner's prose denigrated them and dismissed their sustained presence.

Choctaws who remained in Mississippi following Removal had originally attempted to claim individual allotments of land under Article 14 of the 1830 Treaty of Dancing Rabbit Creek. The federal government botched the allotment process by appointing an agent who was a notorious drunkard, however, and the Choctaws were dispossessed. Following Removal, Choctaws were scattered across Mississippi from the Gulf of Mexico to the Tennessee border, but the majority of them lived in seven communities in the sand-clay hills in the east-central portion of the state—a desperately poor region about one hundred and twenty miles from Oxford.[26] They maintained distinct cultural boundaries around their communities with their persistent use of Choctaw language, dress, and customs, and they rarely married outside of the tribe.[27] Choctaws in Mississippi declared their identity as an Indian tribe holding unfulfilled treaty promises, and they worked tirelessly to get politicians at all levels to recognize them as such. As they did so, they strategically engaged the damaging images tossed about so casually by their non-Indian neighbors, including Faulkner.

By 1918 these efforts had led the Office of Indian Affairs (OIA) to open an agency in Philadelphia, Mississippi, where the federal government provided a hospital, schools, and vocational training for Choctaw farmers and their wives.[28] In 1933 John Collier became the Commissioner of Indian Affairs and proposed the Indian Reorganization Act (IRA), under which Indians were encouraged to form tribal governments. Soon after, Choctaw Agency superintendent Archie Hector appointed a Tribal Business Committee (TBC) to consider the IRA.[29] Around the same time, Joe Chitto, a TBC member, wrote to Collier asking if the Choctaws should form a tribal government before Congress approved the IRA. Collier replied that Chitto should draft a constitution, so as to be ready to institute a new tribal government when the IRA cleared Congress.[30] Choctaw leaders then met with their white allies and created the Mississippi Choctaw Indian Federation (MCIF). Simultaneously, state senator Earl Richardson and E.T. Winston—a newspaper editor and close associate of former Mississippi governor and newly elected senator Theodore Bilbo—founded the Mississippi Choctaw Welfare Association(MCWA), an "affiliate" of the MCIF, which existed to "assist the Indians in their very laudable undertaking toward self-government and self-expression."[31] There were now two Choctaw tribal councils, one called by the agent (the TBC), and one created by the Choctaws and their political allies in the MCWA (the MCIF). Not surprisingly, the majority of Choctaws preferred that the MCIF govern them, but Collier backed the committee that the agent had created. In their struggle to assert their political preferences, the Mississippi Choctaws engaged the stereotypes proffered by Faulkner and others and turned them to their political advantage. In performing an identity based on these stereotypes, Choctaws engaged in a form of literary-political jujitsu, turning the momentum of colonialism against the colonizers. An examination of the documents left by the campaign shows how Choctaw stories had powerful political resonance in Depression Era Mississippi.

I tell the extended political story of the Choctaws and their agency in my monograph, *Choctaw Resurgence in Mississippi: Race, Class, and Nation Building in the Jim Crow South, 1830–1977*. Here, I focus on the ways in which Choctaws and their allies framed their campaign to win acceptance of the MCIF. Choctaws interpreted the IRA as a means of reestablishing their political standing stolen from them by a duplicitous federal government. To make this case to Collier, Choctaw leader Joe Chitto engaged a declensionist narrative, much like the one represented by the Indigenous leader whom Faulkner named Doom, by quoting at length from a famous speech by the Choctaws' nineteenth-century headman Samuel Cobb. In 1843 Cobb had addressed one of the several commissions sent by the federal government to investigate the failures of Article 14.

> Brother: When you were young we were strong; we fought by your side, but our arms are broken now. You have grown large, my people have grown small.
>
> Brother: Our hearts are full. Twelve winters ago our chief sold our country. Every warrior that you see here was opposed to that treaty. If the dead could have been counted, it never would have been made; but alas, though they stood around they could not be seen or heard. Their tears came in the raindrops and their voices in the wailing wind, but the pale faces knew it not, and our land was taken away. . . .
>
> The Great Spirit loves truth. When you took our country, you promised us land. There is your promise in the book. Twelve times the trees have dropped their leaves, and yet we have received no land. . . . We dare not kindle our fires; but you said we might remain and you would give us land.
>
> Brother: Is this truth?[32]

Whatever the ultimate accuracy of these words, which may have been embellished in translation, they resonated with the Choctaws across nearly a century, for they engaged the vanishing Indian trope on Indigenous terms.

History, Fiction, and Colonialism in Faulkner's Mississippi   123

Furthermore, Cobb had employed a form of Native American oration known as treaty language, which was common to diplomatic protocol between Indigenous nations and the invaders. Native American treaty language sought to build understanding between polities by reference to a common humanity and by employing kinship terms. As Choctaw scholar Donna Aikers has argued, treaty relationships were not just legal constructs to Choctaws but instead were sacrosanct obligations of reciprocity between equals. Choctaws did not view these kin relationships metaphorically but literally—treaty partners *were* family. Thus, Cobb repeatedly used the term "Brother" and spoke in the paradigm of familial demands of reciprocity so crucial to Choctaw culture.[33] Choctaw activists thus refashioned Faulkner's vanishing Indian from a figure of degradation to a noble idealist victimized by the family he had fought for and trusted. If the Choctaws were impoverished and oppressed it was because they had expected white Americans to keep their word.

Building upon Cobb's words, Joe Chitto concluded his letter to John Collier by emphasizing what he considered to be the obvious parallels. "You see how the government treated our fathers, and now after more than one hundred years, the remnant of the once powerful Choctaws took Mr. Collier at his word [only] to be told by you that you would not recognize our federation," he wrote. "It makes us Choctaws wonder if the government ever makes its promises good to the Indians."[34] Chitto's reference to the "remnant of the once powerful Choctaw" declared his recognition of the general consensus regarding the Choctaw, which was reflected in Faulkner's writing. It did not, however, end with that image. Rather, it called upon the Choctaws' tragic history as a form of moral suasion. While Faulkner may have used his vanishing Indian narratives as a way to relegate Indians to the past, Choctaws took that same material as an inspiration to repair that damaged history in service of a better future.

The Choctaws had managed to convince some powerful politicians and civic leaders of the justice of their cause, and this led to extensive press coverage of their campaign. It is here that the Choctaws' drive for self-determination entered William Faulkner's orbit. To celebrate their tribal rebirth, the MCIF and its allies performed a ceremony to install its officials on September 27, 1934—the 104th anniversary of the signing of the Treaty of Dancing Rabbit Creek—at the home of Edmund Tobias (E. T.) Winston in Pontotoc, Mississippi, thirty-two miles east of Oxford.[35] Winston was the editor in chief of the *Sentinel*, a weekly newspaper in Pontotoc. He was also an amateur historian and a self-proclaimed expert on Mississippi Indians. He became good friends with then-governor Theodore Bilbo in the 1920s when Bilbo moved the governor's office from Jackson to Pontotoc to escape the brutal Mississippi summers, and he represented the governor in hearings before the

Senate Subcommittee on Indian Affairs in 1929.[36] Winston served as vice president of the MCWA and corresponded frequently with the Office of Indian Affairs on the Choctaws' behalf. His article on the installation ceremony got extensive coverage in the press, including the *Neshoba County Democrat*, the *Jackson Daily News*, and the *Memphis Commercial Appeal*.[37] If Faulkner read any of the state's major papers, he knew that the allegedly vanishing Choctaws were in the process of resurrecting their tribal government.

It is possible that Faulkner was aware of this campaign and responded to it in his 1934 short story titled "Lo!" In this tale the Chickasaw chief Francis Weddel (based loosely on the Choctaw leader Greenwood LeFlore) leads a delegation to Washington DC to address President Andrew Jackson. The ostensible reason for this visit is to ask Jackson to pronounce judgment on Weddel's nephew, who has killed a white man for installing a tollbooth blocking the Choctaws' access to a river, but Faulkner uses the occasion to allow the Chickasaws to present a broader set of grievances. Some literary scholars view Weddell as a more complex and sympathetic Indigenous character than those found in Faulkner's other stories, for he outwits Jackson, forcing him to make a public proclamation of the nephew's innocence. After the delegation leaves, Jackson also issues a declaration of support for the Chickasaws' right to use the river ford free of tolls.[38] Although Faulkner's description of Weddel as "the squat obese man with the face of a Gascon brigand and the mannerisms of a spoiled eunuch" is certainly in line with other insulting portrayals of Indians, Weddel's behavior in this story could be interpreted as evidence that Faulkner recognized that Indians were sometimes able to manipulate government officials to their own purposes by performing Indianness.[39] As Weddel remarks to one of his followers, "You don't understand white people. They are like children: you have to handle them careful because you never know what they are going do next. . . . So long as we are here [in Washington], we'll have to try to act like these people believe Indians ought to act."[40] Perhaps this acknowledgment of Indian savvy was sparked by what Faulkner had read or heard about the Choctaws' push for tribal rebirth.

George H. Ethridge, assistant justice of the State Supreme Court, swore in the new Choctaw government. The Mississippi Congressional delegation was invited, and the new representative from Pontotoc attended.[41] A close analysis of the press coverage of this ritual illuminates how the Choctaws and their allies wrestled the popular "Lo! The poor Indian" narrative of degradation and decline into a powerful call to action. "The ages of mankind have seen many nations destroyed; few restored," began Winston's article for the *Memphis Commercial Appeal*.

History, Fiction, and Colonialism in Faulkner's Mississippi 125

Winston noted that nations were generally destroyed by the sins of their people, but the Mississippi Choctaws "did not sin to lose their nationality. They were only the victims of a stronger race and the evident dupes of governmental diplomacy."[42] Faulkner's Indians were also largely dupes and victims, but his prose was generally less redemptive than Winston's.

Winston eschewed the ignoble savages of Faulkner's work and instead engaged the noble savage stereotype to chronicle the Indians' suffering, explaining that they "carried on with the courage, patience, and fortitude of their race. They are honest, loyal and true to every trust that is reposed in them."[43] The middle-and upper-class white men and women who worked with Mississippi's Indigenous peoples also confirmed that Choctaws were far closer to the noble savage ideal than the ones in Faulkner's stories. For over a century this motif appeared in virtually every piece of writing generated by the Choctaws' campaign for tribal rebirth. This included the Congressional Record, where the Mississippi Congressional Delegation held forth on the injustices that had driven this once-noble people into decline in language every bit as florid as Faulkner's.[44] Choctaws and their allies reclaimed stories of their decline, transforming them into a political tactic to invoke treaty obligations and to counter stereotypes of the ignoble savage.

In the end, the campaign to win recognition of the MCIF as the legitimate tribal council failed, but it significantly transformed the process of constructing a tribal government.[45] Perusal of the historical record thus demonstrates that the stories the Choctaws told about themselves over the years led to important political outcomes. They let powerful people know that they had not disappeared but remained in the land of their ancestors, which was symbolized by Nanih Waiya, their revered "Mother Mound" located in Winston County. To underscore this commitment to place, the MCIF and the MCWA hoped to advance the Smithsonian's stalled plans to create a national park at Nanih Waiya.[46] Which leads us to another subject found in Faulkner's Indian stories.

An important component of the vanishing Indian trope in Faulkner's writing is the presence of Mississippi's Indian mounds in his work. Trefzer encapsulates the meaning of these ancient burial sites in Faulkner's world: "The Indian mounds of his fiction are monuments of a bygone era and symbols of dispossession testifying to a 'vanished' population."[47] She grounds her insightful analysis of Indigenous peoples in southern literature in the metaphor of archeology, noting that the period in which Faulkner and others wrote was also a time of intense archeological exploration of southern mounds, whose presence on the land served to link the Indigenous peoples of the region to an ancient way of life long gone.[48] Faulkner's portrayal of Indian mounds as mysterious relics of the past and the interest of the

Smithsonian in excavating them to uncover the "prehistory" of Mississippi tell one set of stories; the Choctaws, of course, tell another.

Some Choctaws resisted removal in 1830 because of their reverence for their venerated Mother Mound.[49] One version of the Choctaw creation story told of a primordial migration in which the *fabussa*, a consecrated pole carried by their spiritual leader, led them to the site of a large earthen mound, Nanih Waiya. There they buried the bones of their ancestors that they had carried with them. Another version describes the Choctaws' emergence from the underworld at this Great Mother Mound. Either way, their Great Father Aba (the divine incarnation of the sun) established the Choctaws in this land and promised them a prosperous life if they remained on the bright path of His purposes.[50] For Choctaws, Nanih Waiya was not a relic of the past but a holy site on a par with the Vatican for Catholics or Mecca for Muslims, and the stories they told about it anchored that sacralization.[51]

Nonetheless, Choctaws did not own this place, and other Mississippians had plans for it, which leads to further tales about the Indian mounds in Faulkner's world. A man with the Faulknerian name of Munch Luke owned the land in Winston County where Nanih Waiya stood. In 1935, he was planning to level it, probably for agricultural purposes, when state and federal officials intervened, urging him to instead consider Nanih Waiya's potential for tourism. The Office of Indian Affairs and the Smithsonian joined the Mississippi Department of Archives and History and the Highway Department in calling for an excavation of the site and the creation of a park.[52] The curator of the State Archives, Moreau Chambers, proclaimed that the Choctaws were intensely interested in the preservation of their hallowed mound and predicted their collaboration when the time came to create a park.[53] With the backing of these organizations, Mississippi senator Pat Harrison won Works Progress Administration (WPA) approval to excavate Nanih Waiya.

Suddenly, however, uncertain congressional funding shut down the project.[54] Chambers warned the WPA administrator who scotched the plan that "the citizens of the immediate Nanih Waiya region have become so incensed at the slowness with which the WPA is handling this project that to show their disapproval there is a threat that the mound will be blown up."[55] His effort failed, however, and by January of 1937, Chambers declared the Nanih Waiya dig a "closed issue." Notwithstanding the threats of Winston County residents desperate for jobs, no one dynamited the mound in retaliation.[56]

These stories of the Nanih Waiya mound during the 1930s expand our understanding of its meaning beyond its role signifying the vanishing Indian for colonizing literary lights. To some degree, they echo Faulkner's

History, Fiction, and Colonialism in Faulkner's Mississippi 127

interpretation of the mounds as a place to hunt treasure developed in *Go Down, Moses*. Even if the mound did not come to life and chuck valuable artifacts at interlopers, Nanih Waiya and other mounds had economic value for non-Indigenous Mississippians. State officials cast the mound as a place to generate tourist dollars while poor residents nearby looked for work on the excavation. For Choctaws, however, the mound's meaning was much more esoteric. What Faulkner imagined as a symbol of cultural decline (if indeed that is what this signifier meant to him), they saw as an emblem of cultural renewal. Claiming their place in the park project as they celebrated their tribal rebirth, they imagined this sacred site as a celebration of their continuing indigeneity.

This brief summary of Mississippi Choctaw activism during the early twentieth century brings to light a buried set of stories about Mississippi's Indigenous peoples. These historical accounts reveal how a strategic engagement with unflattering categorizations and declension narratives was central to the Choctaws' political rebirth and highlight how Indigenous connections to the Mississippi soil fortified their efforts. Stories of dispossession and economic decline are also at the heart of Faulkner's metanarrative of Mississippi Indians, but he crafted these narratives by portraying Indians in a most unappealing light. As Gene Moore remarks in his introduction to the special issue of the *Faulkner Journal* focused on Indians, "In their mixture of the exotic, the grotesque, and the all too human, Faulkner's 'Indians' remain a troubling presence in his work."[57] This discomfort is exacerbated when one reads Faulkner's own words about the actual Indigenous people just down the road from him:

> There are a few of them still in Mississippi, but they are a good deal like animals in the zoo: they have no place in the culture, in the economy unless they become white men, and they have in some cases mixed with white people and their own conditions have vanished, or they have mixed with Negroes and they have descended into the Negroes' condition of semi-peonage.[58]

Speaking from this disparaging perspective, Faulkner dismissed and insulted the Indigenous peoples who engaged in very public displays of nation-building with some of the state's most prominent politicians and citizens. Once one knows the historical circumstances under which he was writing, Faulkner's work becomes even more "troubling."

Which brings us back to the question of truth. Faulkner asserted that he was not interested in facts but in truth, and he told his truth as he saw it, historical or cultural accuracy be damned: Indians were degraded beings, whose relationship to the surrounding community was like that of animals in a zoo. To his credit, Faulkner recognized that the duplicity of the federal government and the indifference of Mississippi citizens had created this situation. Nonetheless, Faulkner's truth was different from the Mississippi Choctaws' truth, and as a historian, I cannot help but declare the Choctaws' truth to be, well, truer. Although their story intersected with Faulkner's when they condemned their treatment by the US government, the Choctaws' metanarrative was very different. They asserted that they were a specific people, not an interchangeable stereotype of something called "Indian."[59] They were Choctaws—indigenous to their hallowed homelands—and, despite the tragedy of Indian Removal, they had not vanished. They used this historical truth to shame the settler colonial society: "When you took our country, you promised us land. There is your promise in the book. Twelve times the trees have dropped their leaves, and yet we have received no land. Brother: Is this truth?"[60] I cannot imagine anyone with any integrity arguing that it is.

For all his literary brilliance, Faulkner was a clueless colonialist who ignored the nuanced realities of Mississippi's Indigenous history in favor of ugly stereotypes. Is it unfair to this great writer to point that out? Perhaps. From the perspective of literary criticism Trefzer argues, "As a modernist writer, Faulkner privileges linguistic ambiguity, not political activism."[61] From the historian's perspective, judging the past by the standards of the present violates the most sacred shibboleths of historical thinking—objective historical relativism. Faulkner was, as we historians like to say, a "man of his times." Yet dismissing these dehumanizing stereotypes because they are an example of "the times" assumes that Mississippians in the early twentieth century were monolithically racist with regard to Indians. My research demonstrates that they were not. When the governor, the congressional delegation, local elected officials, and many members of the press proclaimed the Choctaws' virtues and fought for fulfillment of their treaty promises, it is clear that there were other models for portraying Indians available in Faulkner's "times."[62] Nonetheless, why should I, also a privileged white academic, insist on pointing this out? Because my mind keeps coming back to that very literal and thoroughly unsophisticated young woman that I was as an undergraduate and that I now see in class as a professor at Arizona State University; she did not "get it," and neither do today's undergraduates. They are more than likely to walk away from their encounter with Faulkner's Indian characters feeling pity and perhaps contempt for Mississippi's Indigenous inhabitants than they are to see those Indians as representing a critique of colonialism. Moreover, there is a voluminous literature on the material and psychic consequences of vicious stereotypes and how such stories support colonization.[63] Over the five hundred years since Europeans set foot in the Americas, settlers and policymakers

History, Fiction, and Colonialism in Faulkner's Mississippi 129

have deployed the same stereotypes that Faulkner embraced—Indians as lazy, cannibalistic, foolish, disappearing—to justify dispossession, military aggression, and programs of forced assimilation that included the removal of children from their families. But I am not proposing that we refrain from reading Faulkner. I also do not mean to say that we should scrub his prose of racism, as literary scholar Alan Gribben recently did with Mark Twain's work in the NewSouth Books' edition of *Huckleberry Finn*.[64] Rather, I end with a plea for all of you who teach Faulkner.

When you discuss his Indian lore with your students, remind them that Faulkner's portrayals of Mississippi's Indigenous peoples are part of a larger narrative of racism that justifies colonial dispossession and erases Indigenous peoples. Then tell them the story of how the Mississippi Choctaws, just down the road from Oxford, resisted that dispossession and erasure. Tell them how savvy Choctaw activists and their white supremacist allies lobbied federal officials for over a century, demanding that they fulfill their treaty promises and recognize the continuing Indigeneity of Mississippi's Choctaws. Tell that truth, and let it contextualize, critique, and confront Faulkner's troubling Indians.

NOTES

1. Yes, I was *that* student, and a quick glance at my Rate My Professor page demonstrates that I have received the appropriate karmic payback on this side of the desk.

2. The most famous work of this school is Ferdinand Braudel's epic *The Mediterranean and the Mediterranean World in the Age of Philip II*, 2nd ed., trans. Sian Reynolds (Berkeley: University of California Press, 1996), which interprets the king's life and times from a broad multidisciplinary perspective. For an excellent overview of the Annales school, see Michael Harsgor, "Total History: The *Annales* School," *Journal of Contemporary History* 13, no. 1 (January 1978): 1–13.

3. The insightful and important work done by this school is far too voluminous for a footnote, but a wonderful summary of this field can be found in Laurence Veysey, "The 'New' Social History in the Context of American Historical Writing," *Reviews in American History* 7, no. 1 (March 1979): 1–12.

4. Michel Foucault, *The Order of Things: An Archaeology of the Human Sciences*, reissue ed. (New York: Vintage Books, 1994); Hayden White provides a good overview of the idea of codes in "The Question of Narrative in Contemporary Historical Theory," *History and Theory* 23, no. 1 (February 1984): 1–33.

5. White, "The Question of Narrative," 21–27; Louis O. Mink, "History and Fiction as Modes of Comprehension," *New Literary History* 1, no. 3 (Spring 1970): 541–58.

6. A cultural universal is a trait, activity, or value held across cultures and times, and storytelling is one of them. There is a somewhat spotty literature on the idea of cultural universals. A succinct summary of the topic is George P. Murdock, "The Common Denominator of Culture," in Ralph Linton, ed., *The Science of Man in the World Crisis* (New York: Columbia University Press, 1945),123–42. Claude Lévi-Strauss addressed this topic from a structuralist perspective in *The Savage Mind* (1962; repr., Chicago: University

of Chicago Press, 1966). Two provocative new studies of this idea, one from the field of evolutionary biology and the other from anthropology, wrestle with the idea of a universal human nature rooted in human evolution. The anthropologist is Donald E. Brown, *Human Universals* (Philadelphia: Temple University Press, 1991), and the evolutionary biologist is Steven Pinker, *The Blank Slate: The Modern Denial of Human Nature* (New York: Penguin Putnam, 2002). Pinker's work has been rightly criticized for its reliance on Western models and, ironically, its lack of rigorous cross-cultural comparisons.

7. Some of the most persuasive calls for powerful storytelling and clear prose are William Cronon, "A Place for Stories: Nature, History, and Narrative," *Journal of American History* 8, no. 4 (March 1992): 1347–76; Patricia Nelson Limerick, "Dancing with Professors: The Trouble with Academic Prose," in *Something in the Soil: Legacies and Reckonings in the New West* (New York: W. W. Norton, 2000): 333–41; and Karl Jacoby, *Shadows at Dawn: A Borderlands Massacre and the Violence of History* (New York: Penguin, 2008). See also Claudio Saunt, "Telling Stories: The Political Uses of Myth and History in the Cherokee and Creek Nations," *Journal of American History* 93, no. 3 (December 2006): 673–97.

8. For the call to replace empiricism with Indigenous sacred stories in researching Indigenous peoples, see Devon Abbott Mihesuah and Angela Cavender Wilson, eds., *Indigenizing the Academy: Transforming Scholarship and Empowering Communities* (Lincoln: University of Nebraska Press, 2004); Devon Mihesuah, ed., *Natives and Academics: Researching and Writing about Native Americans* (Lincoln: University of Nebraska Press, 1998); Linda Tuhiwai Smith, *Decolonizing Methodologies: Research and Indigenous Peoples* (New York: Zed Books, 1999); and Alfred Taiaiake, *Peace, Power, Righteousness: An Indigenous Manifesto* (Toronto: Oxford University Press, 1999).

9. Cronon, "A Place for Stories," 347–48.

10. David Carr, "Narrative and the Real World: An Argument for Continuity," *History and Theory* 25, no. 2 (May 1986): 122.

11. The (arguably) most distinguished historian of the South, C. Vann Woodward, devoted an entire chapter to Faulkner as representative of southern history and culture. C. Vann Woodward, *The Burden of Southern History*, 3rd ed. (Baton Rouge: Louisiana State University Press, 1993), 265–80.

12. Don H. Doyle, *Faulkner's Country: The Historical Roots of Yoknapatawpha* (Chapel Hill: University of North Carolina Press, 2001), 12.

13. Ibid., 3.

14. Annette Trefzer, *Disturbing Indians: The Archeology of Southern Fiction* (Tuscaloosa: University of Alabama Press, 2007),151.

15. Ibid., 152.

16. William Faulkner to Malcolm Cowley, February 18, 1946, in Malcolm Cowley, *The Faulkner-Cowley File: Letters and Memories, 1944–1962* (New York: Viking, 1966), 89.

17. Cowley notes that Faulkner read "books about the Indians" (*The Faulkner-Cowley File*, 153). In the only book-length treatment of Faulkner's Indians, historian Lewis M. Dabney scours the biographical information on Faulkner to discern the scholarly influences on his work. He argues that Faulkner's library contained books and articles on Mississippi history that included the standard works on Mississippi's Indigenous peoples, and he finds evidence of many contemporary histories in Faulkner's work. Still, he concluded that "the scholarship was less a source than a stimulus of his work." See Dabney, *The Indians of Yoknapatawpha: A Study in Literature and History* (Baton Rouge: Louisiana State University Press, 1974), 37. For a more contemporary analysis of the scholarly works behind Faulkner's Indians, see Patricia Galloway, "The Construction of Faulkner's Indians," *Faulkner Journal*, 18, nos. 1–2 (Fall 2002–Spring 2003): 9–31.

History, Fiction, and Colonialism in Faulkner's Mississippi   131

18. For example, in the short story "A Justice," the protagonist, an Indian prophetically named Doom, is a Choctaw, but Faulkner later deems him a Chickasaw. Likewise, the Indian character Francis Weddell is a Choctaw chief in 1932 (in "Mountain Victory") but has changed tribes by 1934, becoming a Chickasaw in "Lo!"

19. Faulkner quoted in Don H. Doyle, "The World That Created William Faulkner," *Southern Review* 30, no. 3 (Summer 1994): 621.

20. Don H. Doyle, "Faulkner's Yoknapatawpha and the Southern History Narratives," *Quaderni Online* 6, 1996, http://www.library.vanderbilt.edu/Quaderno/Quaderno06/Doyle.pdf.

21. For the ignoble savage, see Doyle, "Faulkner's Yoknapatawpha," 83; Elmo Howell, "William Faulkner and Mississippi Indians," *Georgia Review* 21, no. 3 (Fall 1967): 394; Duane Gage, "William Faulkner's Indians," *American Indian Quarterly* 1, no. 1 (Spring 1974): 28; Howard C. Horsford, "Faulkner's (Mostly) Unreal Indians in Early Mississippi History," *American Literature* 64, no. 2 (June 1992): 317; and Robert Dale Parker, "Red Slippers and Cottonmouth Moccasins: White Anxieties in Faulkner's Indian Stories," *Faulkner Journal* 18, nos.1–2 (Fall 2002–Spring 2003): 82. Robert Woods Sayre challenges this idea in "Faulkner's Indians and the Romantic Vision," *Faulkner Journal* 18, nos. 1–2 (Fall 2002–Spring 2003): 33–49. Sayre argues that Faulkner's Indigenous characters are romanticized and sentimentalized.

22. Howell, "William Faulkner," 386; Gage, "William Faulkner's Indians," 30; Lothar Hönnighausen, "Faulkner Rewriting the Indian Removal," in Lothar Hönnighausen and Valeria Genaro Lerda, eds., *Rewriting the South: History and Fiction* (Tubingen: A. Francke Verlag, 1993), 335–43.

23. Gage, Horsford, and Hönnighausen explore these themes of race and gender. For a more contemporary perspective on Faulkner's Indian works, see Trefzer, *Disturbing Indians*, 145–79. Trefzer uses postcolonial theory to analyze Indians in the works of southern writers.

24. Trefzer, *Disturbing Indians*, 3–4, 13–14.

25. Horsford, Parker, and Galloway all note the proximity of the Mississippi Choctaws to Faulkner's home in Oxford, yet there is no record of his communicating with any of them. For the prevalence of the "degraded remnant" image with respect to the Mississippi Choctaws, see Katherine M. B. Osburn, *Choctaw Resurgence in Mississippi: Race, Class, and Nation Building in the Jim Crow South, 1830–1977* (Lincoln: University of Nebraska Press, 2014), passim.

26. Clara Sue Kidwell, *Choctaws and Missionaries in Mississippi, 1819–1919* (Norman: University of Oklahoma Press, 1995); John H. Peterson Jr., "The Mississippi Band of Choctaw Indians: Their Recent History and Current Relations" (PhD diss., University of Georgia, 1970), 42–45. Special Agent Douglas Cooper's 1853 census of the Choctaws remaining in Mississippi is available online at http://www.accessgenealogy.com/native/cooper/index.htm. The distance between Oxford and Philadelphia, Mississippi, home to the Choctaw Agency, was calculated using Google Maps.

27. Frances E. Leupp to President Theodore Roosevelt, March 16, 1908, House Committee on Indian Affairs; 63rd Cong, 2nd Sess.; *Hearings on Enrollment in the Five Civilized Tribes*; April 1, 2, 14, 16; May 14; June 2, 4, 9, 11, 13; August 4–7, 11, 12, 14, 15, 17, 24–27, 1913; Microfiche-Group 1A; SUDOC: Y4. In2/1: F58/3, 118. Hereafter cited as *Hearings on Enrollment*. Kidwell discusses the construction of these communities in detail in *Choctaws and Missionaries*.

28. Cato Sells, Commissioner of Indian Affairs (CIA), to Mrs. J.E. Arnold, September 10, 1917, Central Classified Files, Choctaw (hereafter CCF): 806–81856, National Archives and Records Administration, Washington, DC (NARA-DC). All references to the Central Classified files are found in the main archives in Washington DC.

29. Robert J. Enochs, Choctaw Superintendent, to CIA, May 14, 1927, CCF: 100–98178–1922; Archie C. Hector, Choctaw Superintendent, to John Collier, CIA, June 10, 1934, CCF: 150–54948–1933.

30. Joe Chitto to John Collier, April 30, 1934; Collier to Chitto, June 7, 1934, CCF: 150–54948–1933.

31. E. T. Winston to CIA, July 31, 1934, CCF: 150–54948–1933 and May 9, 1934, CCF: 068–9544A-1936. Mississippi Choctaw Indian Federation (hereafter MCIF) to the Honorable Senators Pat Harrison, Hubert D. Stevens, and Congressmen Ross Collins, Wall Doxey, W. M. Whittington, John E. Rankin, Jeff Busby, William M. Colmer, and Russell Elizey (hereafter cited as the Mississippi Congressional Delegation), August 21, 1934, CCF: 150–54948–1933; Archie C. Hector to CIA, August 21, 1934, CCF: 150–54948–1933. The quotation is from E. T. Winston, "Choctaws Turn to Friends among Pale Faces in Effort to Recapture Old Glories," *Memphis Commercial Appeal*, August 21, 1934, n.p., clipping with the file.

32. Joe Chitto to John Collier, August 20, 1934, CCF: 150–54948–1933. Chitto quoted Cobb's speech from Colonel J. F. H. Claiborne, *Mississippi As a Province, Territory, and State*, vol. 1 (Jackson, MS: Power and Barksdale, 1880; Baton Rouge: Louisiana State University Press, 1964), 512–13. The original speech may be found in *Niles Weekly Register* 64 (April 29, 1843), 131–32.

33. Donna L. Akers, "Removing the Heart of the Choctaw People: Indian Removal from a Native Perspective," *American Indian Culture and Research Journal* 23, no. 3 (1999): 129–30. On Indian diplomacy and treaty language, see Robert Williams, *Linking Arms Together: American Indian Treaty Visions of Law and Peace, 1600–1800* (New York: Routledge, 1999).

34. Joe Chitto to John Collier, August 20, 1934, CCF: 150–54948–1933.

35. The distance between Oxford and Pontotoc was calculated using Google Maps.

36. "Pontotoc County History, Typescript," WPA State-wide Historical Research Project; "E. T. Winston, Brief Biography," in part 2, 266–70, and "Interview with E. T. Winston," in part 3, 142–46, both in *The Story of Pontotoc* in three volumes (Pontotoc, MS: The Pontotoc Progress Print, 1931), 321. All volumes found in the Pontotoc Historical and Genealogical Society, Pontotoc, Mississippi; *Survey of Conditions of the Indians in the United States*, Hearings before the Subcommittee on Indian Affairs, United States Senate, 71st Congress, 3rd session, part 16 (Washington, DC: Government Printing Office, 1931), 7699–703.

37. Archie C. Hector to John Collier, August 21, 1934, CCF: 150–54948–1933. The letter includes press clippings from the *Jackson Daily News*, September 10, 1934, the *Meridian Star*, July 30, 1934, and the *Memphis Commercial Appeal*, August 21, 1934.

38. Speaking of "Lo!" Lothar Hönnighausen argues that the story "rewrites a tragic chapter of history as burlesque comedy and transforms the victims into the victors" ("Faulkner Rewriting the Indian Removal," 339). Similarly, Elmo Howell concludes that "the sight of a President, a battlefield hero, finally put to rout by an old effeminate half-savage is a most satisfying spectacle, which at the same time does no violence to the character of General Jackson or the dignity of his office" ("William Faulkner and Mississippi Indians," 392).

39. William Faulkner, *Collected Stories of William Faulkner* (New York: Random House, 1950), 389.

40. Ibid., 383.

41. Archie C. Hector to John Collier, August 21, 1934, CCF: 150–54948–1933. The letter includes press clippings from the *Jackson Daily News*, September 10, 1934, the *Meridian Star*, July 30, 1934, and the *Memphis Commercial Appeal*, August 21, 1934.

History, Fiction, and Colonialism in Faulkner's Mississippi   133

Hector noted the congressman who attended the ceremony; see Archie C. Hector to A. J. Shippe, Director of Extension Services, December 1, 1934, CCF: 150–54948–1933, NARA-DC.

42. A clipping from the *Memphis Commercial Appeal*, August 21, 1934, appears in Archie C. Hector to John Collier, August 21, 1934, CCF: 150–54948–1933.

43. Ibid.

44. For an overview of this motif across time, see Katherine M.B. Osburn, "Mississippi Choctaws and Racial Politics," *Southern Cultures* 14, no. 4 (Winter 2008): 32–54.

45. For a detailed explanation of how this occurred, see Katherine M. B. Osburn, "'In a Name of Justice and Fairness': *The Mississippi Choctaw Indian Federation v. the BIA, 1934*," in Dan Cobb and Loretta Fowler, eds., *Beyond Red Power: Indian Activism in the Twentieth Century* (Santa Fe: School for Advanced Research Press, 2007), 109–23.

46. R. L. Breland, "The Story of Neshoba," *Neshoba Democrat*, February 1, 1935, Vertical Files: Indians, Neshoba County Library, Philadelphia, MS.

47. Trefzer, *Disturbing Indians*, 147.

48. Ibid., 3–4, 82–84, 145–47, 154–56.

49. Samuel J. Wells, "Mixed-Bloods in Choctaw History," in Samuel J. Wells and Roseanna Tubby, eds., *After Removal: The Choctaw in Mississippi* (Jackson: University Press of Mississippi, 1986), 47–52. Over the years, the testimony of Choctaws who applied for Article 14 lands noted this motivation repeatedly. I do not mean to imply that those Choctaws who removed were less spiritual than those who stayed, only to note the reasons given by some Article 14 claimants for staying.

50. For the migration story see Donna Akers, *Living in the Land of Death: The Choctaw Nation, 1830–1860* (East Lansing: Michigan State University Press, 2004), 1–2, and Valarie Lambert, *Choctaw Nation: A Story of American Indian Resurgence* (Lincoln: University of Nebraska Press, 2007), 19–20. For the emergence story see Kidwell, *Choctaws and Missionaries*, 3, and James Taylor Carson, *Searching for the Bright Path: The Mississippi Choctaw from Prehistory to Removal* (Lincoln: University of Nebraska Press, 1999), 8.

51. For an insightful essay on the practical uses of oral history, see Julie Cruikshank, "Oral History, Narrative Strategies, and Native American Historiography: Perspectives from the Yukon Territory, Canada," in Nancy Shoemaker, ed., *Clearing a Path: Theorizing the Past in Native American Studies* (New York: Routledge, 2002), 3–27.

52. Dunbar Rowland to Brown Williams, September 30, 1935; Brown Williams to Munch Luke, October 2, 1935, Fabian Fraser Papers (Z789f), Mississippi Department of Archives and History, Jackson, MS. This entire collection is contained in one folder.

53. Moreau B. Chambers, Curator, to Fabian Fraser, November 25, 1935; Chambers to Fraser, March 5, 1936, Fabian Fraser Papers.

54. Moreau B. Chambers, Curator, to Fabian Fraser, December 20, 1935, February 7, 1936, and May 16, 1936, Fabian Fraser Papers.

55. Moreau B. Chambers to Mr. T. J. Bolster, Director, District #2, WPA, Meridian, Mississippi, August 10, 1936, Fabian Fraser Papers.

56. In 1939, the Greenville Chamber of Commerce in Washington County wrote the Commissioner of Indian Affairs for permission to place some Choctaws on the mounds in their county as a tourist exhibit. The commissioner replied that, in order to prevent the "exploitation" of the Choctaws, Greenville had to draw up a contract with specific instructions for the treatment of Indians. The project then fell through. Willard L. McIlwain, Greenville, Mississippi, to John Collier, September 28, 1939; William Zimmerman Jr., assistant commissioner of Indian Affairs, to McIlwain, November 2, 1939, CCF: 042–63719–1939.

57. Gene M. Moore, "Faulkner's Incorrect 'Indians,'" *Faulkner Journal* 18, nos. 1–2 (Fall 2002–Spring 2003): 1.

58. Faulkner quoted in Frederick L. Gwinn and Joseph L. Blotner, eds., *Faulkner in the University: Class Conferences at the University of Virginia, 1957–1958* (Charlottesville: University Press of Virginia, 1959), 43.

59. See note 18 above.

60. Samuel Cobb quoted in Claiborne, *Mississippi as a Province, Territory, and State*, 512–13.

61. Trefzer, *Disturbing Indians*, 153.

62. For an insightful critique of the "man of his times" perspective, see Robin Bernstein, "Signposts on the Road Less Taken: John Newton Hyde's Anti-Racist Illustrations of African American Children," *J19: The Journal of Nineteenth-Century Americanists* 1, no. 1 (2013): 97–119.

63. Acknowledgment of the harmful impact of stereotypes on Native Americans has been a staple of ethnohistorical literature since the 1970s. Robert F. Berkhoffer's classic work *The White Man's Indian: Images of the American Indian from Columbus to the Present* (New York: Alfred A. Knopf, 1978) is still useful as an overview of these damaging images, while Philip J. Deloria's *Playing Indian* (New Haven: Yale University Press, 1998) provides a more contemporary view from an Indigenous perspective. Two recent books that explore how these pernicious ideas become enacted in harmful policies are Margaret D. Jacobs, *White Mother to a Dark Race: Settler Colonialism, Maternalism, and the Removal of Indigenous Children in the American West and Australia, 1880–1940* (Lincoln: University of Nebraska Press, 2010), and Daniel H. Usner, *Indian Work: Language and Livelihood in Native American History* (Cambridge, MA: Harvard University Press, 2009). A recent overview of negative stereotypes by a team of sociologists is also useful. See Peter A. Leavitt, Rebecca Covarrubias, Yvonne A. Perez, and Stephanie A. Fryberg. "'Frozen in Time': The Impact of Native American Media Representations on Identity and Self-Understanding," *Journal of Social Issues* 71, no. 1 (2015): 17–38.

64. For an interview with Gribben and the editors at NewSouth Books, see Marc Shultz, "Upcoming NewSouth 'Huck Finn' Eliminates the 'N' Word," *Publishers Weekly*, January 3, 2011, http://www.publishersweekly.com/pw/by-topic/industry-news/publisher-news/article/45645-upcoming-newsouth-huck-finn-eliminates-the-n-word.html.

The Wild and the Tame

Sam Fathers as Ecological Indian

ROBBIE ETHRIDGE

According to oral tradition, when queried about where he got his portraits of Indians, William Faulkner quipped, "I made them up."[1] In a 2002 special edition of the *Faulkner Journal* devoted to exploring Faulkner's Indians, Patricia Galloway, in an effort to find out what Faulkner used to make them up, excavates his source material. After some digging, she surmises that Faulkner may have made up many things about his Indians, as he claimed, but that he did not do so whole cloth. Rather, Galloway concludes that as he began to imagine his Indians, Faulkner "assimilated both local and national popular thinking about Indian people."[2]

In this chapter, I would like to detail Faulkner's use of one of the popular notions about Indians that would have had currency at the time of his writing and that still does today. This is the popular conception that Indian people have a special relationship to the environment—that somehow, by virtue of being Indian, a person acquires a sense of oneness with the natural world; that Indians are connected to the wild and concerned about its preservation and conservation in ways that non-Indians could never be; that an Indian person is, as Shepard Krech has dubbed it, the "Ecological Indian."[3] However, Krech's premise is that the Ecological Indian is a myth and that Indian relationships to the land were not always ecological and were instead shaped by their histories in the larger world. Krech's book *The Ecological Indian* (1999) details case studies from the precolonial and postcolonial eras wherein Indian interactions with the environment were not sustainable and led to environmental change and degradation. Since its publication, *The Ecological Indian* has received much attention from both those arguing for and those arguing against Krech's thesis.[4] Today, environmental history and environmental studies are showing the Western world that both precolonial and postcolonial relationships between Indigenous peoples and their environments

135

are much more complex than the Ecological Indian myth would have it. These relationships include deep ecological knowledge derived from use of and production from local natural resources as well as mythical, religious, and familial connections. These studies also show that some Indigenous people manage their landscapes and keep them healthy and productive, but others mismanage them, resulting in environmental degradation. Numerous studies of contemporary Native people also detail the overexploitation of natural resources and land mismanagement by Native business people and governments because of commercial interests. In all, such studies demonstrate that the motives underlying both mismanagement and good management derive from a complex interplay between global economic forces, state-level political economies, Indigenous knowledge and cultural practices, and local political economies.[5] Still, the myth of the Ecological Indian persists.

The Western idea that American Indians, and really all Indigenous people, have an essential connection to the natural world is certainly as old as Rousseau's ruminations on the Noble Savage, wherein the Indian is identified as peaceful, carefree, unshackled, eloquent, and wise—an innocent living at one with the world of nature (*EI*, 16–20).[6] The Ecological Indian, then, begins with the Noble Savage, and, as outlined by Krech, the stereotype gained strength in the 1960s and '70s when the environmental movement appropriated the Noble Savage as an icon of the movement and as an exemplar of a pure, environmentally sound, and sustainable way to live (*EI*, 20–21). Into the twenty-first century, the Western image of the Indian is still of a person who intuitively understands the systemic environmental consequences of her actions, feels a deep sympathy with all living forms, and takes steps to conserve and preserve so that, to quote Krech, "the earth's harmonies are never imbalanced and resources never in doubt" (*EI*, 21). This image is a powerful one in the Western psyche because it is mostly used as a critique of Euro-American urban life where the "white man" is usually depicted as just the opposite of the Indian: full of conflict, strife, shackled, foolish, and destructive (*EI*, 20).[7]

Surely one of the most memorable and significant uses of the Ecological Indian trope in American literature is Faulkner's Sam Fathers in *Go Down, Moses*. For his portrait of Sam Fathers, Faulkner used a variant of the Ecological Indian that would have been in the national consciousness in the midtwentieth century. Under Faulkner's pen, Sam Fathers is the ultimate Ecological Indian. Faulkner uses Sam much as Western thought uses the Ecological Indian and the Noble Savage: as a counterpoint to the Euro-American world. In this case, Faulkner posits Sam as a binary opposite to white southerners. Sam is everything that Faulkner's

Sam Fathers as Ecological Indian

137

McCaslins, Edmondses, Compsons, Sartorises, and Snopeses are not. These white southerners are impure, foolish, tamed, morally compromised, and accountable for the sins of their kin. Sam, on the other hand, is pure, wild, wise, spiritual, and solitary, not linked by blood, love, or obligation to his forbearers and their sins. I should note here that not all of Faulkner's Indians are noble—some, including Sam's father, are quite ignoble. But Faulkner explains that those ignoble Indians had been corrupted by whiteness; some, such as Sam's father, Ikkemotubbe (or Doom), were corrupted when they adopted white sensibilities, including avarice and cruelty; others were corrupted by the "white blood" in them. Such closeness to whiteness accounts for their degeneration, decay, and descent into decadence. The ignoble Indians also serve as a counterpoint to Sam and to reinscribe Sam as "pure," noble Indian.[8]

In this imagining of Sam Fathers, Faulkner overlays the binary Indian/white onto the binary opposition between the wild and the tame (see table 1). And he decidedly places Sam on the wild side, thus rendering him the ultimate Ecological Indian, the quintessential Other.[9] Sam Fathers is actually of mixed descent; his father was a Chickasaw, and his mother was a "quadroon" slave woman, meaning she was part African and part Euro-American. So Sam is part Indian, part African, and part white.[10] But, as we will see, Sam sheds both his blackness and his whiteness when, following some inner spiritual beckoning, he recedes into the wilderness.

In the stories that comprise *Go Down, Moses*, the most famous of which is "The Bear," Sam acts as spiritual guide and mentor to the adolescent boy Ike McCaslin. Sam takes Ike into the Big Woods to first hunt deer and then later Old Ben, the bear. Faulkner introduces Sam in the story "The Old People," at which point Sam is about seventy years old. Ike's cousin McCaslin Edmonds introduces Sam thus: "He was a wild man" (*GDM*, 167). McCaslin goes on to delineate Sam's mixed genealogy, explaining that even though Sam is wild, he is also caged, not by being an ex-slave still working for the McCaslins, as Ike first presumes, but because of the taint of whiteness (*GDM*, 167–68). Whiteness was tameness, and Sam's white blood, while not altogether taming him, cages him. About midway through the story, Sam hears the call of the wild. And like a caged, wild animal with an open door, Sam instinctually heeds it. He leaves the McCaslin farm and moves to the bottomlands of the Tallahatchie River, Faulkner's Big Woods (*GDM*, 173).

As many critics have noted, the Big Woods and Old Ben, the bear, are symbols of the wilderness—a pure, untouched world imperiled and doomed by the advance of civilization and the sins of southern history. In fact, "The Bear" is probably the most famous wilderness story in American literature, and literary critics have dissected "The Bear," as well as

Table. 1.

Tame	Wild
Yoknapatawpha County	Big Bottom
human	nature
human-made laws (order)	laws of nature (chaos)
light	dark
open	closed
safe	dangerous
worldliness	spirituality
death	life
rationality	intuition
advanced	primitive
change	eternal
women	men
kinship	solitary
emotion	instinct
polluted	pure
science/reason	magic/mystical
property	unowned
whites	nonwhites (blacks and Indians)

Table 1. Binary oppositions between the tame and the wild.

the full collection of stories in *Go Down, Moses*, every which way. For our purposes, I will only point out two of their basic conclusions about Faulkner's treatment of wilderness. For Faulkner, wilderness has two roles: (1) it is the bearer and teacher of moral and spiritual truth, and (2) it is the victim of Western rapacity.[11] Faulkner juxtaposes these two roles so that Western rapacity and the destruction of the wilderness, which is completed not in "The Bear" but in a later story, "Delta Autumn," has ethical implications: the destruction of the wild is the destruction of the moral. Faulkner then synthesizes this moral tension with others, such as the moral tensions between black and white, past and present, and his own love and hate of the South, which lie at the heart of his work.

Faulkner again and again places Sam on the wild side. So Sam, too, is doomed, like the wilderness. Faulkner takes his cue from larger Western stereotypes—the Indian and the wild, both vanishing, both victims of Western wantonness.[12] Sam is also the bearer and teacher of moral and spiritual truth. Sam is savage priest, the only one pure enough, wild enough, magical enough to initiate Ike into the wild, to ready the boy for his sojourn to the pure, the eternal, the primitive.

Interestingly, Sam's whiteness also renders him just tame enough to be Ike's mentor. The one "full-blood" Chickasaw in Ike's childhood world is Jobaker, who lives by himself in the woods. Faulkner only gives us a fleeting glimpse of Jobaker. He has no past; in fact, "nobody knew his history at all." He, like a wild panther, is solitary and dangerous. He "consorted with nobody, black or white; no negro would even cross his path and no man dared approach his hut except Sam" (*GDM*, 172). Jobaker is pure, essential wildness—unapproachable, fearsome, and dangerous to the tame as well as to most wild things. He could not serve as spiritual guide to Ike because he is simply too wild, rendering him too dangerous and too disinterested. Sam, although certainly of the wild, can approach Ike without danger because of his hint of tameness, and because of his hint of tameness he can take an interest in Ike if only to understand the boy as a vase in which to plant a living memory of what Sam knows to be doomed: the pure, spiritual, moral wilderness.

Old Ben too is doomed. The bear, of course, is the object of Sam and Ike's hunt. But the motive of the hunt is not to destroy the wild but to appropriate the impending doom, to prevent the dishonorable rape and mutilation by the unworthy white man through the taking of the bear's life with honor and reverence by ritually pure priests (Wheeler, 131). Sam is careful to make sure that Old Ben is confronted only by worthy opponents, opponents who are also of the wild. Insuring worthiness and ritual purity is why only Sam can lead the hunt. It is why Ike has first to be initiated and tutored in the ways of the wild. It is also why Sam must first find the right dog, a dog from the wilderness itself, to assist in the hunt. The dog is Lion, and Sam is careful to train and tame him only minimally, so as to keep Lion's wildness intact (*GDM*, 216–20). Securing the purity of the sacrifice means not only that the priests have to be pure and worthy but that the hunt itself must be a ritual of the wild and, therefore, performed without the accouterments of the tame. They face Old Ben with things of the wild—instinct, intuition, and solitude. Obviously, Faulkner's wild is America's wild, a thing, a place untouched by humans. The Indian, then, because he is of the wild, is not human. The Indian is a wild, natural creature, at one with the environment. Sam Fathers is Old Ben is Lion is the Big Woods.

Using the tension between the wild and the tame, Faulkner sets up "The Bear" as the mythical struggle between the natural and the human. But he then inverts and subverts this tension in the denouement, the killing of Old Ben and Sam Fathers. Neither of them is killed by Ike or Lion, the ritually pure priests, but instead Lion is killed by the bear, and the bear is slain by Boon Hogganbeck, a shadowy, weird man of Euro-American and Chickasaw descent. In fact, Faulkner uses this death scene not as ritual but as an interruption of ritual. For one, it is not Ike, Sam, or Lion alone who confront the bear. Rather, while Ike and Sam are preparing for the fatal day's hunt with Major de Spain, Tennie's Jim, Boon, and all the mules, horses, and hounds needed for an ordinary killing, Lion detects the presence of the bear and bolts into the wilderness in pursuit. On his heels follow Sam, Ike, Boon, and a young hound with plenty of courage but little "judgment" or experience in the wild (*GDM*, 239), trailed by Major de Spain and the rest. Lion and the young hound meet the bear first, and Lion rips into the bear's throat, locking his jaws in what turns out to be a death grip for Lion, not the bear, because Old Ben guts Lion then and there. The full pack of hounds then rushes in, wildly circling when, with Ike as witness, Boon launches heedless into the fray, not to subdue the bear but to rescue Lion. Boon, too, latches onto Old Ben, stabbing him a single time, then "working and probing the buried blade" beneath the bear's flesh until the animal, along with the man and the dog gripping onto him, drops to the ground, "as a tree falls" (*GDM*, 241). Old Ben is dead, and Lion is mortally wounded.

The ritual killing of the wild, then, goes awry. The confrontation is not ceremonial but chaotic. For example, the young hound enters the wild with abandon, not reverence. The dog is also a female, a disruption in Faulkner's decidedly male wilderness. She approaches and even attempts to emulate Lion, which is sacrilegious because the young bitch is neither fully wild nor has she or could she have been initiated: she has not shed the blood of the wild. But Lion, too, contributes to the debauching of the planned ritual. Overwhelmed by the prey instincts of the wild, Lion preempts the ritual by chasing the bear on his own. And perhaps that is how it should have been—Old Ben killed not by ritually pure priests, but by one of his own, a wild animal—wild on wild. But perhaps because Lion bears a hint of taming at the hands of Sam Fathers, the confrontation opens a space for the impure to enter, whereupon Boon delivers the final blow.

Perhaps because he is born of a Chickasaw mother rather than a chief, as Sam was, Boon is not Indian enough for Faulkner.[13] Perhaps he has too much whiteness to be of the wild. Additionally, Boon does not have the wisdom that comes from the wild—Boon has the "mind almost of a child" (*GDM*, 220). He does not fully understand the wild, he does not know how to act in it, and consequently he violates the laws of the wild. In particular, Boon develops a loyal, indeed obsessive, attachment

Sam Fathers as Ecological Indian

to Lion, transgressing the solitary detachment that is one of the laws of the wild. By transgressing the laws of the wild, like an outlaw, Boon is rendered powerful, unpredictable, and hence dangerous. Boon's final deliverance of both the bear and Sam is not a pure, sacrificial act; it is a surprised and botched ending in both cases.

In the end, Old Ben is dead, Sam is dead, Lion is dead, and Boon is insane (*GDM*, 330–31). Ike himself comes away from the whole adventure not purified and glorified, but confused and dejected, unable to return to the wild and finally renouncing his own selfhood, leaving the desecration of the wild to his Edmonds cousins: first Cass, then Zack, and finally Roth, one of Faulkner's most immoral, devious, and degenerate characters (Wheeler, 133). So the sacrifice and the honorable death are botched; the wilderness is subjected to white rapaciousness after all. Faulkner sets up a binary opposition by using popular notions about Indianness and wildness to build a tension that he then subverts in order to open up the moral ambiguities in the taming of the wild as well as to open up the host of other moral ambiguities that is his Yoknapatawpha County.

Faulkner places his Indians on the wild side in order to move toward this denouement, this moral ambiguity. In so doing, he also makes them, in their pure, undegraded state, like natural creatures. He instantiates the Ecological Indian. In "making up" his Indians, Faulkner not only assimilates American popular notions, but he borrows from a concept so imbedded in the Western psyche that we barely even recognize it as a construct. Sam Fathers *is* the Ecological Indian. And none of the literary critics that I read in preparation for this chapter question Sam's Indianness on these grounds. In fact, some seek his authentication as Indian *because* he is one with the wilderness.[14]

In lesser hands, placing Indians on the wild side of the wild/tame binary results not in great literature exploring the burdens of southern history but in blatant stereotyping and haphazard identity constructions of Indianness. Even so, the binaries in "The Bear" persist today in insidious ways. Both non-Native and Native writers and scholars continue to extol the American Indian as having a special, ecological, and protective relationship to the natural world, and they typically juxtapose this stance against the white man's destructiveness. There are numerous examples, but I will cite only a few from some of the more well-known Native writers and thinkers. In 1970, Vine Deloria wrote that "the Indian lived with his land. The white destroyed his land. He destroyed the planet earth."[15] In 1976, N. Scott Momaday remarked that "the Native American ethic with respect to the physical world is a matter of reciprocal appropriations; appropriations in which man invests himself in the landscape, and at the same time incorporates the landscape into his own most fundamental experience," something Momaday seriously doubts that the non-Native can ever understand.[16] Famed environmentalist Winona LaDuke remarked in 1999 that the sense of commitment and tenacity that underlies the grass roots struggle of Native environmentalism "springs from our deep connection to the land," and she goes on to document innumerable cases of environmental racism and degradation at the hands of the white man.[17]

Such statements could have come directly out of "The Bear." They are familiar archetypes of Indians as ecologically responsible and the white man as detached from and destructive of the natural world. Clearly, there must be more to these statements by Native writers than essentializing and identity politics. But what exactly? To answer this question, we must broaden our focus to examine the experience and histories of Indigenous peoples beyond the Native South. Like Indigenous peoples throughout the world, Indians of the Native South have a long history of colonial entanglements that have resulted in myriad challenges as well as opportunities. Once incorporated into the global market system, Indigenous use of land and resources sometimes resulted in overexploitation and consequent serious ecological problems. In addition, questions of land ownership and resource rights have become tied to questions of tribal sovereignty and Indian identity, and there are numerous studies across the world of Native peoples' struggle over resource rights and tribal sovereignty. I will highlight three in which Indian identity was central to either Native or Western arguments. One case is from the historic Native South, and the other two are from the twentieth century and from places far distant from the American South. These latter two case studies, however, illustrate the pervasiveness of the Ecological Indian construct, and both were highly publicized events where what it meant to be "Native" was up for public debate.

In the early nineteenth century, the Creek Indians, who lived in present-day Alabama and Georgia, had segued from commercial hunting to successful farming and cattle and hog ranching when the deerskin trade collapsed after the American Revolution. At that point, they and other Indians in the Native South had already embarked upon a program of conscious acculturation, and although they retained much of Indian life and culture, many Indian people had established Western-style businesses, were multilingual, had converted to Christianity, were commercial farmers and ranchers, and generally resembled many of their American frontier counterparts.[18] However, when white southerners began eyeing their lands for cotton growing, the Creeks resisted the United States' attempts at land appropriations and insisted on their territorial claims as the rights of a sovereign nation. American officials countered by leveraging the Ecological Indian stereotype and argued that all Indians were "savages" who were at best childlike wood nymphs who did not understand how to best use the lands around them and that the value of this real estate could only be realized by elite white males.[19] In this case, southern Indians who had purposefully distanced themselves from Western "ecological" stereotypes and prejudices found American officials leveling those very same stereotypes against them. The result was the disastrous policy of Indian Removal.

On the other hand, Indigenous people have sometimes appropriated stereotypes and put them in service of their struggles against colonial oppression and for treaty rights. One of the most famous examples of this occurred in 1989, when the Kayapó Indians of the Amazon basin launched a protest against the Xingú Dam project by gathering, en masse, in the city of Altimira to confront prodam politicians and developers. The Kayapó, under the leadership of Payakan, a young, Western-educated Kayapó, devised a strategy to play on the urbanite's conception of wild Amazonian Indians. They showed up painted and in all their regalia, complete with their famous headdresses and lip rings. They demanded that the dam be halted to protect their "traditional" way of life. The Kayapó recognized that they could use the stereotype of the Ecological Indian in order to align themselves with the environmental movement, thereby connecting their struggle for treaty rights and natural resource rights to the worldwide environmental movement and garnering international media attention and celebrity advocates.[20] They did all of this to great success. Even Sting showed up. And they stopped the Xingú Dam project.[21]

In other cases, Indian groups fighting for treaty rights and sovereignty have deployed the Ecological Indian construct only to have it backfire. One well-known example occurred in the late 1990s, when the Makah Indians of North America's northwest coast petitioned to hunt whales on the grounds that by treaty they were entitled to continue their traditional livelihood. They further argued that in order to save Makah identity and culture, they had to hunt whales, for the Makah and the whale were one. The Makah soon found themselves pitted *against* the environmentalists, who then turned the stereotype against them. The environmentalists used their publicity connections to vehemently and vociferously lambast the Makah, accusing them of having no regard for conservation and no regard whatsoever for whale population recovery. They questioned the Makah's sincerity about being one with the whale and proclaimed that the tribe's real motive was to conspire with the International Whaling Commission in an attempt to open gray whales to commercial whaling.[22] The environmentalists concluded that the Makah were degraded

Indians, motivated by the white man's greed. They were not "real" Indians, because they were not ecological enough. The Makah succeeded in hunting a whale that time, but they suffered a devastating public relations blow and a loss of public support.

As the examples of the historic Creek Indians and the contemporary Kayapó and Makah show, playing with stereotypes can cut many ways. In some cases, powerful entities use stereotypes to justify abrogating treaty rights and tribal sovereignty. In others, Indigenous rights advocates such as Winona LaDuke or Payakan appropriate the stereotypes to further their causes. They opt to deal with the fallout later. And these cases also demonstrate that using stereotypes can open up dangerous ground because it hangs political, economic, and social justice issues on issues of identity construction, which in turn hang on the concept of culture.

Culture is in the eye of the beholder, and when the dominant society has defined the people it seeks to exploit in terms of cultural traits, it has usually resulted in stereotypes such as the Noble Savage and the Ecological Indian. It also means that when Natives quit acting according to the supposed cultural type, they are somehow less Native, less authentic, less real, and hence less entitled to their rights. If the Makah did in fact hope to open commercial whaling of gray whales, would this, as the environmentalists claimed, make them somehow less Makah? Was the half-white, half-Chickasaw Boon trespassing in the wilderness simply because his blood line made him somehow less Chickasaw? To my mind, framing social justice issues in terms of culturally defined identity is a risky strategy because it opens the door not only to questioning what "makes" an Indigenous person but also to questioning Indigenous peoples' rights to demand redress for years of social, economic, and political oppression.[23]

Another interpretation as to why Native writers and thinkers use the Ecological Indian is the very real possibility that American Indians do indeed have a close connection to the natural world: that they are at one with the whale, the buffalo, the salmon, the tulles, the deer, the bear; that their spiritual being is nourished by the natural world and hence that they have a deep reverence for the environment and concern for its health. If this is the case, then, did Faulkner have it right after all? Is Sam Fathers a real Indian? Or have we somehow entered a hall of mirrors? Obviously, pronouncements of what is or is not Indian by Native writers and others involve questions of identity, authority, and authenticity and are derived from any number of things, including the possibility that, as Phillip Deloria has shown, one is oftentimes reflecting back the reflection of the reflection of the reflection of the reflection.[24]

Although scholars have gone far in dismantling stereotypes such as the Ecological Indian, we sometimes fall back on tried and true Western constructs of binary opposites such as Native and non-Native, the wild and the tame, the Ecological Indian and the rapacious white man. In this chapter, I have endeavored to show that perhaps Faulkner, in his use and inversion of such binaries as the wild and the tame, has something to offer us in figuring out how to work with these binary constructs to explore the space in between.

NOTES

1. Lewis M. Dabney, *The Indians of Yoknapatawpha: A Study in Literature and History* (Baton Rouge: University of Louisiana Press, 1974), 11.

2. Patricia Galloway, "The Construction of Faulkner's Indians," *Faulkner Journal* 18, nos. 1–2 (2003): 10. Galloway briefly discusses some of the more infamous characteristics of Faulkner's Indians, such as retainer burial, patrilineal kinship, and so on. The other contributors in the special issue go on to investigate various metaphorical, literary, narrative, and tropic uses to which Faulkner puts his Indians. This body of work, along with a smattering of other articles, one book, two master's theses, and brief mentions of Faulkner's Indians in works devoted to other topics demonstrates that, while Indians are not central to Faulkner's fiction, they clearly function to introduce and push along many of the themes that play out in significant ways throughout his body of work. See Bruce G. Johnson, "Indigenous Doom: Colonial Mimicry in Faulkner's Indian Tales," *Faulkner Journal* 18, nos. 1–2 (2003): 101–28; Benjamin S. Lawson, "The Men Who Killed the Deer: Faulkner and Frank Waters," *Faulkner Journal* 18, nos. 1–2 (2003): 179–90; Gene M. Moore, "Chronological Problems in Faulkner's 'Wilderness' Stories," *Faulkner Journal* 18, nos. 1–2 (2003): 51–68; "Faulkner's Incorrect 'Indians'?" *Faulkner Journal* 18, nos. 1–2 (2003): 3–8; James Harvey Kraft, "The Yoknapatawpha Indians: Fact and Fiction" (master's thesis, Tulane University, 1976); Peter Lancelot Mallios, "Faulkner's Indians, or The Poetics of Cannibalism," *Faulkner Journal* 18, nos. 1–2 (2003): 143–78; Marc Anthony Nigliazzo, "Faulkner's Indians" (master's thesis, University of New Mexico, 1973); Robert Dale Parker, "Red Slippers and Cottonmouth Moccasins: White Anxieties in Faulkner's Indian Stories," *Faulkner Journal* 18, nos. 1–2 (2003): 81–100; Robert Woods Sayre, "Faulkner's Indians and the Romantic Vision," *Faulkner Journal* 18, nos. 1–2 (2003): 33–50; Annette Trefzer, *Disturbing Indians: The Archaeology of Southern Fiction* (Tuscaloosa: University of Alabama Press, 2007); and Jay S. Winston, "Going Native in Yoknapatawpha: Faulkner's Fragmented America and 'the Indian,'" *Faulkner Journal* 18, nos. 1–2 (2003): 129–42. Others have also corrected Faulkner's ethnographic and historical mistakes about Indians, of which there are many. See Dabney, *The Indians of Yoknapatawpha*, 11; Don H. Doyle, *Faulkner's County: The Historical Roots of Yoknapatawpha* (Chapel Hill: University of North Carolina Press, 2001); Galloway, "The Construction of Faulkner's Indians"; Howard C. Horsford, "Faulkner's (Mostly) Unreal Indians in Early Mississippi History," *American Literature* 64, no. 2 (1992): 311–30; Elmo Howell, "William Faulkner and the Mississippi Indians," *Georgia Review* 21 (1967): 386–96; "William Faulkner's Chickasaw Legacy: A Note on 'Red Leaves,'" *Arizona Quarterly* 26 (1970): 293–303; Kraft, "The Yoknapatawpha Indians"; and Moore, "Chronological Problems."

146 ROBBIE ETHRIDGE

3. Shepard Krech III, *The Ecological Indian: Myth and History* (New York: W. W. Norton & Company, 1999). Subsequent references to this book will be cited parenthetically in the text as *EI*.

4. For a collection of articles that, among other things, engage and critique many of Krech's case studies, see Michael E. Harkin and David Rich Lewis, eds., *Native Americans and the Environment: Perspectives on the Ecological Indian* (Lincoln: University of Nebraska Press, 2007).

5. See M. Kat Anderson, *Tending the Wild: Native American Knowledge and the Management of California's Natural Resources* (Berkeley: University of California Press, 2005); Keith Basso, *Wisdom Sits in Places: Landscape and Language among the Western Apache* (Albuquerque: University of New Mexico Press, 1996); Michael Dove, "A Revisionist View of Tropical Deforestation and Development," *Environmental Conservation* 20, no. 1 (1993): 17–24, 56; Robbie Ethridge, *Creek Country: The Creek Indians and Their World* (Chapel Hill: University of North Carolina Press, 2003); Harkin and Lewis, *Native Americans and the Environment;* Linda Hogan, *Dwellings: A Spiritual History of the Living World* (New York: W. W. Norton, 2007); Andrew C. Isenberg, *The Destruction of the Bison: An Environmental History, 1750–1920* (York: Cambridge University Press, 2001); Celia Lowe, "Global Markets, Local Injustice in Southeast Asian Seas: The Live Fish Trade and Local Fishers in the Togean Islands of Sulawesi," in *People, Plants, and Justice*, ed. C. Zerner (New York: Columbia University Press, 2000), 234–58; Shaylih Muehlmann, *Where the River Ends: Contested Indigeneity in the Mexican Colorado Delta* (Durham, NC: Duke University Press, 2013); Darrel A. Posey, "Indigenous Management of Tropical Forest Ecosystems: The Case of the Kayapó Indians of the Brazilian Amazon," *Agroforestry Systems* 3 (1985): 139–58; "Intellectual Property Rights and Just Compensation for Indigenous Knowledge," *Anthropology Today* 6, no. 4 (1990): 13–16; Paige West, *Conservation Is Our Government Now: The Politics of Ecology in Papua New Guinea* (Durham, NC: Duke University Press, 2006); and Paige West and David M. Ellis, "Local History as 'Indigenous Knowledge': Aeroplanes, Conservation, and Development in Haia and Maimafu, Papua New Guinea," in *Investigating Local Knowledge: New Directions, New Approaches*, ed. A. Bicker, P. Sillitoe, and J. Pottier (London: Ashgate, 2004), 105–28.

6. In Western philosophy since Rousseau, the Noble Savage was oftentimes in contrast to Western depictions of indigenous people as bloodthirsty savages.

7. J. Peter Brosius, "Analyses and Interventions: Anthropological Engagements with Environmentalism," *Current Anthropology* 40, no. 3 (1999): 277–309; Beth A. Conklin and Laura R. Graham, "The Shifting Middle Ground: Amazonian Indians and Eco-Politics," *American Anthropologist* 97, no. 4 (1995): 695–710; and Phillip Deloria, *Playing Indian* (New Haven: Yale University Press, 1998).

8. Of course, the notion of "blood" descent is widely discredited today, when we understand descent to be a matter of genetics, not blood. I have opted to keep the language of "blood" in the chapter as that is the language used by Faulkner in *Go Down, Moses* and his other works.

9. Sam is not the only character that Faulkner otherizes, and literary critics have examined Faulkner's otherizing of the many nonwhite characters that people his Yoknapatawpha County.

10. See William Faulkner, *Go Down, Moses* (1942; repr., New York: Vintage, 1973), 166–67. Subsequent references to this edition will be cited parenthetically in the text as *GDM*.

11. Otis B. Wheeler, "Faulkner's Wilderness," *American Literature* 31, no. 2 (1959): 127.

12. See Trefzer, *Disturbing Indians*, 172–78; Jace Weaver, Craig Womack, and Robert Warrior, *American Indian Literary Nationalism* (Albuquerque: University of New Mexico Press, 2006), 58–61.

13. This, of course, is one of Faulkner's misinterpretations about southern Indians. Indians of the American South, until the late nineteenth and early twentieth centuries, reckoned their kinship along matrilineal lines, meaning that individuals were not related to or descended from their fathers. Their "blood line" ran through the mother, so they were only considered consanguineous kin to their mother's side of the family. So, to southern Indians, Boon, not Sam, would have been considered Chickasaw.

14. See Trefzer, *Disturbing Indians*, 172–78; Johnson, "Indigenous Doom," 111–20; Lawson, "The Men Who Killed the Deer," 180; Sayre, "Faulkner's Indians," 40; and Winston, "Going Native in Yoknapatawpha," 134–35.

15. Vine Deloria, *We Talk, You Listen: New Tribes, New Turf* (New York: MacMillan, 1970), 186.

16. N. Scott Momaday, "Native American Attitudes to the Environment" (1976), in *Stars Above, Earth Below: American Indians and Nature*, ed. Marsha C. Bol (Newt, CO: Roberts Rinehart Publishers for Carnegie Museum of Natural History, 1998), 3.

17. Winona LaDuke, *All Our Relations: Native Struggles for Land and Life* (Cambridge, MA: South End, 1999), 4.

18. Ethridge, *Creek Country*, 140–214.

19. On the justifications for Indian Removal, see Jason Edward Black, *American Indians and the Rhetoric of Removal and Allotment* (Jackson: University Press of Mississippi, 2015); John P. Bowes, *"Land Too Good for Indians": Northern Indian Removal* (Norman: University of Oklahoma Press, 2016); and Tim Alan Garrison, *The Legal Ideology of Removal: The Southern Judiciary and the Sovereignty of Native American Nations* (Athens: University of Georgia Press, 2002).

20. See Michael Beckham, dir., *The Kayapó: Out of the Forest* (Chicago: Films, 1989); and Conklin and Graham, "The Shifting Middle Ground." Today, many Indigenous peoples around the globe use stereotyped notions of what a "traditional" person is supposed to look like to enact so-called "cultural shows" for tourists; see Amanda Stronza, "Anthropology of Tourism: Forging New Ground for Ecotourism and Other Alternatives," *Annual Review of Anthropology* 30 (2001): 261–83. They use these stereotypes intentionally to get tourist dollars and to make a living in areas of the world where transnational corporations are encouraging the development of extractive economies, resulting in extreme environmental degradation, displacement, and loss of local economic opportunities. For other examples of Indigenous people linking to and using the environmental movement, see Molly Doane, "The Political Economy of the Ecological Native," *American Anthropologist* 109, no. 3 (2007): 452–62, and West, *Conservation Is Our Government Now*.

21. The Kayapó managed to stop the dam for about twenty years; the project is now back on the developer's agenda.

22. Robert Sullivan, *A Whale Hunt: How a Native American Village Did What No One Thought It Could* (New York: Scribner, 2002), 59–65, 165–68.

23. Conklin and Graham, "The Shifting Middle Ground," 706.

24. Deloria, *Playing Indian*, 204.

Native Southern Transformations, or, *Light in August* and Werewolves

ERIC GARY ANDERSON

"Did I miss the werewolves in *Light in August*?" you might be asking yourself. You might also be wondering about *Light in August*'s more general relevance to a discussion of Faulkner and the Native South. But, as I will argue, if Native southern studies and Faulkner studies are to be methodologically useful to each other, they ought to be useful in a wide range of ways, some straightforward—Louise Erdrich joking about Faulkner in an interview or Indian characters appearing on the pages of Faulkner's texts—and some indirect and perhaps even surprising.[1] In this chapter, I build on and extend the important work that has been done on literary demographics ("Indians in Faulkner"), including assessments of his accuracy and artistry in representing Indigenous people, tribes, homelands, histories, and perspectives. But, in the main, I read *Light in August* (1932) alongside *Mongrels* (2016), a Native southern werewolf novel by Blackfeet writer Stephen Graham Jones, toward a different end. I demonstrate that both novels feature characters—human and monster alike—who embody and mark a transformative potential that, in complicated, ambivalent, and at times deeply unsettling ways, annotates and reconceptualizes both "Native" and "southern." I suggest that connections between Faulkner and Native southernness are sometimes oblique and sometimes as if hidden in plain sight. And, tracking "mongrels," monsters, and transformations in both novels, I also identify Native southern patterns and develop Native southern paradigms—ways of thinking and reading that point toward the transformative methodological value of Native southern studies.

There is plenty of room for such investigations. *The Oxford Handbook of Indigenous American Literature*, a landmark seven-hundred-page volume published in 2014, makes no mention of *Light in August* or, for that matter, of Faulkner. The editors of this volume, James H. Cox

Light in August and Werewolves   149

and Daniel Heath Justice, explain that "two new modes of inquiry" have transformed the field of Indigenous American literary study:

> Tribal nation specificity encourages a shift in critical focus from identity, authenticity, hybridity, and cross-cultural mediation to the Native intellectual, cultural, political, historical, and tribal national contexts from which Indigenous literatures emerge. American Indian literary nationalism works more explicitly to produce literary criticism that supports the intellectual and political sovereignty of Indigenous communities and tribal nations. Both literary critical modes affirm that these contexts, communities, and tribal nations are the first concern of the discipline.[2]

These methodologies do not necessarily exclude Faulkner, but they help underscore that the most challenging and complicated word in the phrase "Faulkner and the Native South" is "and." In her incisive essay "In Deep," Melanie Benson Taylor reflects on this "and" and presses us to foreground neither sovereignty nor tribal specificity but rather Native/southern inseparability: "It is time to do better at assessing the very tangible ways that Indians are deeply embedded in southern terrain, both as historical subjects and contemporary actors, as perpetrators and victims, as tutors and pupils. In deep, in more ways than one: a part of the soil, the history, the honor, and the hubris. Indians have shaped the South and been shaped by it in turn."[3] Exactly as Taylor says, "All of us, in deep together"[4] are radical, and at times unwilling, kindred, a network of relations uneasy enough that it opens up space for us to read not only "Indians . . . in southern terrain" but also, I would add, southernness on Native ground. In figuring out how to be counterintuitively "in deep together," it could therefore be helpful to work up a counterintuitive reading of *Light in August* that starts with Pocahontas and proceeds to werewolves.

On the seventh page of this five-hundred-page novel, the narrator makes a fleeting reference to a road that *"goes to Pocahontas"*—Pocahontas, Mississippi.[5] Granted, Pocahontas in this novel might well stand in for Pontotoc, in Chickasaw territory some 33 miles east of Oxford and a plausible route for Lena Grove's travels from Alabama. But Faulkner explicitly identifies the place Grove visits as Pocahontas, a small town in Choctaw territory some 158 miles south of Oxford. The "kind and nameless faces and voices" that tell Lena Grove about this road do not mention that Pocahontas's points of interest include two Native earthworks: a platform mound and a burial mound. These anonymous, disembodied people simply agree with her that it is yet another place where the most interesting man in her world, Lucas Burch, might be. Not long after, we're told that Lena remembers another group of "nameless kind faces and voices" saying, "*You say you tried in Pocahontas? This road? It goes to Spring-vale*" (8). When Lena Grove "tried in Pocahontas," what did she do? Did she see the earthworks? Did she think about Native girls and white male colonizers? Did she understand herself to be on Choctaw ground?

And when Faulkner added "Pocahontas" to the manuscript of his novel, did he? Of all the Mississippi places Faulkner could have mentioned, including of course Pontotoc, why did he decide to mention *this* place? Of all the ways he might have added Indigenous presences to *Light in August*, why does he instead offer a quick and second-hand reference to an absence? Maybe he liked the interplay between Lena Grove's story and the Pocahontas story he was most likely to have known and given credence to: John Smith's story about an Indian girl, the daughter of the paramount chief, Powhatan, who steps in and apparently rescues Smith from execution at the hands of Indians, including her powerful father. But, for me, this quick reference to something Native, the most explicit such reference in the novel, is most interesting because Pocahontas was not from Mississippi. She was a Powhatan who lived in Virginia and then England in the early seventeenth century, several centuries after Mississippian (800–1600 CE) architects, artists, engineers, and laborers designed and built the earthworks in present-day Mississippi. I also wonder why the late nineteenth-century founding fathers of Pocahontas, Mississippi, decided to give their town a name that is "Indian" but not Choctaw. Maybe they did so out of respect for their Choctaw neighbors, but I think it is at least as likely that they wanted to avoid being mistaken for Choctaws. So Pocahontas, Mississippi, was (and still is) Indigenous, in a manner of speaking, but not *too* Indigenous.

For a "Faulkner and the Native South" gathering, Pocahontas might appear to be an Indian in an unexpected place, to borrow Philip Deloria's apt phrase.[6] But her name in this context also raises a familiar topic in Native American and Indigenous studies: the ways and means by which Indigenous people, histories, and land have been dispossessed, displaced, misrepresented, and/or rendered absent by non-Native settler-colonists. Throughout *Light in August*, Faulkner does not write about Choctaws or about Indians of any other Native southern tribal nation. And if he indeed substitutes Pocahontas for Pontotoc, he manages to vanish Chickasaws *and* Choctaws in a single place name. But he also pushes a hypervisible non-Nativeness to extraordinary extremes. If the absence of Indians is excessive in *Light in August*, so too is the presence of non-Natives and a hyperbolic, startlingly varied, and often startlingly weird non-Nativeness that destabilizes and undercuts the efficacy of settlement. As Jodi Byrd suggests, it might be productive "to read the cacophonies of colonialism as they are rather than to attempt to hierarchize them into coeval or causal order."[7] In the next part of my chapter, I look somewhat more narrowly at the cacophonies of non-Nativeness as they are, and as it is, in *Light in August*. Throughout the book, unexpected non-Native outsiders just keep turning up, both from and in unexpected places.

My reading of destabilized non-Nativeness also takes guidance and inspiration from Leigh Anne Duck's excellent essay on peripatetic modernism in *Light in August*, in which she argues,

> If . . . we seek not only to situate Joe and other new arrivals to Yoknapatawpha County in relation to its norms, but also to understand how these individual wanderers . . . excite these small-town and rural locales, the social space of *Light in August* begins to look more chaotic. Although far smaller in scale than the migrations shaping the cities of the early twentieth century, these movements nonetheless create conceptual or social crisis, forcing residents to reassess their beliefs, plans, or forms of behavior—or, of course, to try to eradicate the disruption through violence.[8]

While these migrations are potentially transformative for migrators and residents alike, they also reveal an alarmingly fine line between migration as an opportunity for reimagining communities and migration as a threat that needs to be policed if not violently eradicated. In *Light in August*, Faulkner repeatedly restages the uneasy arrival of someone or something excessively non-Native—so much so that when two characters who *are* native to Jefferson, Percy Grimm and Gavin Stevens, enter for the first time near the end of the novel, the effect is disorienting. Who are these Jeffersonians, and what in the world are they doing in Jefferson? For just about everyone in the book, these arrivals serve up what the narrator of Stephen Graham Jones's werewolf novel calls "a constant reminder of what I wasn't becoming"[9]—or they *could* serve up such reminders, if they were not so ruthlessly and ironically suppressed. As Heidi Kim explains, "Faulkner sweeps all his characters together in a common tangle of race relations that acknowledges immigration from the North, the Caribbean, or China, with the exception of Native Americans who have always been in Yoknapatawpha. All (except perhaps Sam Fathers) are foreigners from this long-sighted historical perspective, Brown no less than Christmas, or the Snopeses no less than the unnamed Chinese laundryman."[10] But many of these characters do not realize that they are "in deep together" in this way.

In fact, all the major characters in *Light in August* are both non-Native and nonnative. That is, they are neither Native Americans nor native Jeffersonians. Lena Grove is from Alabama. Lucas Burch has been in Alabama and might be from there, but wherever he is from originally, it is not Jefferson. Byron Bunch hails from some unspecified southern elsewhere. Gail Hightower feels tied to Jefferson by nineteenth-century family history but hails from somewhere else and lives apart. Joanna Burden was born there but remains a "stranger" and a "foreigner" because she descends from northerners and abolitionists. And Joe Christmas, orphaned and rootless, comes from some other place and also looks, to Jeffersonian eyes, like a foreigner.

But no one outdoes Mr. and Mrs. Old Doc Hines, who "might have been two muskoxen strayed from the north pole, or two homeless and belated beasts from beyond the glacial period" (342). To say that the Hineses are not indigenous to Jefferson is to drastically undercut the extent of their arctic/southern alienation; they look "as if they belonged to a different race, species" (341). They are nonnative not only in place but also in time: "belated." Faulkner's manner of delivery reinforces these disjunctions by capturing such a gigantic, jarring leap through both space and time in so few words. The Hineses in all their unintentional yet extravagant out-of-placeness point the way toward an understanding of hybrid nonnativeness in *Light in August* that stretches well beyond the novel's most obvious example, Joe Christmas. They are at once human and animal, prehistoric and modern, homeless and homebound. In addition to looking like they might have been muskoxen, the Hineses also look like two bears (368–69), and Mrs. Hines in particular looks "glacierlike, like something made of stone and painted" (369), not just suggestively rocklike but, in a complete refusal of figuration, "exactly like a rock" (402). They look far more foreign than Christmas—so foreign that the narrator largely bypasses more familiar ways of categorizing otherness by way of race, complexion, gender, sexuality, physical capability, or social class.

In the world of *Light in August*, this hyperforeignness extends in other directions, too: for example, many characters are occupationally insecure or ill-suited for the work they do and deeply alienated from it, yet unable to get out from under it. Hightower's career in the pulpit offers one salient example, and he broadcasts additional examples with his hand-painted sign, which advertises various things it is difficult to imagine him actually giving, producing, or doing: "Art Lessons/Hand-painted Xmas & Anniversary Cards/Photographs Developed" (58). Old Doc Hines, who is not a doctor, lives "in filthy poverty" (340) yet works as a janitor. One of the least skillful train passengers in American literary history, his past jobs include work as a brakeman on the railroad. Lena Grove runs away from, among other things, unpaid work as a childcare

Light in August and Werewolves 153

provider, but she is pregnant. The novel is also strewn with objects that seem nonnative because they fuse temporalities or historical periods in confusing ways; for example, a cotton warehouse tank looks "like the torso of a beheaded mastodon" (116). The landscape of Faulkner's South is strewn with Pleistocene and racially marked, racially coded body parts.

My point is that, here and elsewhere in the novel, Faulkner's reach transforms characters and environs in ways that make them less rather than more native. There are many more ways to be nonnative in *Light in August* than to be native. Even the savagery that courses through the book is primarily either nonnative or ecological: the narrator repeatedly describes Mrs. Armstid as a "savage," and, in various places, Joe, Bobbie, tree bark, Mrs. Hines, the "odor of the earth," and Hightower's wife are all called savages or said to be acting savagely, well before the narrative arrives at the "shameless savageness" of the final confrontation among Hightower, Christmas, and Percy Grimm's men. Additionally, the narration posits a wide range of links between characters and animals: characters resemble, variously, sheep, horses, locusts, mules, dogs, eagles, cats, a lioness, a stallion, octopus tentacles, rats, a weasel, two bears, a long snake, a wolf, and various nonspecific beasts, including primordial beasts, an awkward beast, a crouching beast, a full-clawed creature about to spring, "two small, weak beasts," and Byron Bunch's "mind, galloping in yoked and headlong paradox" (401). In *Light in August*, the repertoire of nonnativeness is broad, deep, sometimes dehumanizing, and often strange and estranging.

But the fact remains: there are no Choctaws or Chickasaws in *Light in August*, let alone living, breathing Indigenous characters of any nation. In Choctaw/Chickasaw critic Phillip Carroll Morgan's words, Faulkner "did apparently realize . . . that Indian mythos and centuries of Indian tenure and history were perhaps the most powerful features of northern Mississippi where his family had lived for a scant four generations."[11] And yet, it is as though the world Faulkner gives us in *Light in August* and the world Katherine M. B. Osburn describes in *Choctaw Resurgence in Mississippi*, or the worlds LeAnne Howe (Choctaw) or Louis Owens (Choctaw/Cherokee/Irish) describe in so many of their works, occupy different planets. One point that comes very clear in Osburn's, Howe's, and Owens's work is that Choctaws are *involved*, consistently and significantly and deeply, in state and national politics and in the day-to-day life of Native and non-Native communities in Mississippi.

So where are they in *Light in August*? How might we think about and build on the point that this novel is populated exclusively by non-Natives, and by really, really nonnative non-Natives at that? Can these extraordinarily nonnative figures help us move toward a more grounded,

154   ERIC GARY ANDERSON

more transformative Native southern studies? With *Light in August* as a guiding text, where is the "and" in "Faulkner and the Native South?" How do we even begin to do this "and?" and to go in deep at that?

Werewolves.

To begin, when Faulkner was working on *Light in August* and diving deeply into Joe Christmas and the cultures that create and expel him, he was also joining with a host of other earlier twentieth-century writers and texts whose preoccupations were similar but whose modalities, primarily gothic or horror, were different. As Faulkner composed *Light in August*, Universal Pictures was making movies that proved popular at the time and are now regarded as important, even foundational—*Dracula* (1931), *Frankenstein* (1931), *The Mummy* (1932), and *Island of Lost Souls* (1932), to name but four—all of which cast the monster/s as residually human but primarily undead and/or otherwise liminal. So, too, do two other 1932 releases: *White Zombie*, independently produced but mostly filmed on Universal's lot, and Paramount's *Dr. Jekyll and Mr. Hyde.* Universal's *The Wolf Man* (1941) came later, but *The Werewolf of Paris*, a novel by Faulkner's fellow 1930s Hollywood screenwriter Guy Endore, was published in 1933.[12] And Faulkner's niece Dean Faulkner Wells has transcribed a werewolf story that her uncle himself liked to tell to local children.[13] The story, which likely dates to the early 1940s and as likely borrows from both Endore's novel and the 1941 film, follows a traveler who comes to a remote English country town to visit an aging aunt. Arriving in the deep of a winter night, he takes shelter in a small railroad station and encounters a very large, silent figure who appears to be a disabled woodsman but who turns out to be a werewolf. The traveler is trapped, and the story closes with an efficient, unsettling jump scare. In Faulkner's family, his stories, his Hollywood workplace, and his environs, including a popular culture he wanted to help create, monsters rise up, again and again.

Light in August is replete with monsters and horrors. Its South is remarkably nonnative, as detailed above, and it is also profoundly, disturbingly undead. Perhaps most obviously, it teems with ghosts: phantoms, haunted memories, a living body "like a drowned corpse," "a myriad ghosts of dead sins and delights" (279), a "ghostly embrace" between a man and his chair, romanticized plantation and Civil War ghosts, Burdens and Jeffersonians entangled "in their relationship to one another's ghosts, with between them the phantom of the old spilled blood and the old horror and anger and fear" (47), and more. There are monstrous torsos, such as Hightower's and the beheaded mastodon's, and monstrous faces, such as Joe Christmas's: "His face was gaunt, the flesh a level dead parchment color. Not the skin: the flesh itself, as though the skull had been molded in a still and deadly regularity and then baked in a fierce oven" (34–35). These monsters and monstrosities gang up with ghosts, phantoms, savages, and beastlike people to create the literary equivalent of a horror omnibus, and I would like to build on good work by (among others) Peter Lurie and Aaron Nyerges on the novel's cinematic trappings to argue that particular scenes in *Light in August* have much in common with classic 1930s Universal Pictures monster movies that both capture and provoke melodramatic spectatorial reaction.[14] For example, when Bobbie sees McEachern at the country schoolhouse dance, "upon her face came an expression very like horror" (204), and when McEachern looks at Joe, "it was the face of Satan" he saw (205). After he whales McEachern with a chair, Joe sees Bobbie "writhing and struggling, her hair shaken forward, her white face wrung and ugly beneath the splotches of savage paint, her mouth a small jagged hole filled with shrieking" (205). Then Joe makes a movie monster's exit, "backing toward the door" and "looking steadily and ceaselessly at faces that might have been masks. Then he flung the chair down and whirled and sprang out the door, into soft, dappled moonlight" (206–7). In a similar vein, Joe's entrance into an African American revival meeting while on the run very quickly kindles smoldering associations between horror and racial panic: "Then they saw that his face was not black, and a woman began to shriek, and people in the rear sprang up and began to run toward the door; and another woman on the mourners' bench, already in a semihysterical state, sprang up and whirled and glared at him for an instant with whiterolling eyes and screamed 'It's the devil! It's Satan himself!'" (322). Both scenes take place at night, and in both, Joe acts like a cinematic monster and becomes legible to both other characters and to readers as such. This calls up film critic Robin Wood's point that in "the '30s the monster was almost invariably foreign"[15] (114)—a creature in and of darkness, othered both racially and sexually and often nonnative, whose identity also often hinges on frightening transformations.

But a more pointedly Native southern critical approach allows me to go further: to lycanthropically argue that monsters' transformations are not always or necessarily monstrous. In May 2016, Blackfeet fiction writer Stephen Graham Jones released *Mongrels*, a werewolf novel set in the South. The title alone suggests that Jones shares with Faulkner an interest in denigrated, problematic hybridity and its sometimes-monstrous discontents. But Jones challenges Faulkner's bleak representation of hybridity as an excessively nonnative condition unsatisfactorily illuminated by quick flashes of whiteness (the "whiterolling eyes," Bobbie's "white face"), and hyperbolically in need of quarantining. Jones's novel also challenges readers to rethink Joe Christmas by focusing less on his origins, less on his future prospects, less on his participation in a linear narrative, and more on his processes of transformation throughout *Light in August*. While *Mongrels*, as it unfolds, remains doggedly optimistic about the transformative potential of lycanthropy, *Light in August* depicts a world that allows for a significant amount of discommodious nonnativeness and also allows for characters such as Byron Bunch, whose history is largely unknown and mysterious and whose whiteness is presumed but never confirmed. Yet this world destroys the character most strongly suspected of racial hybridity and miscegenation. Jones's novel helps make visible a further complication in Faulkner's, though: that Joe Christmas goes back and forth, not as a werewolf but like a werewolf; he transforms, he flares up, and he turns back, temporarily debilitated by the change, and along the way he shows himself to be monstrous, yes, but also more than a monster—"hybrid" not just racially but also as the ever-shifting sum total of his "back" and "forth" thoughts and actions. Put another way, he constantly toggles among becoming a monster, being a monster, and noting the presence of a pre-and postmonster humanity.

However, I do not mean to suggest that "hybridity" should be resuscitated and restored to its former prominence as a critical term. Important as it was to late-twentieth-century postcolonial studies in particular, the concept of hybridity has been heavily and convincingly criticized of late by scholars working in various fields, including Native American and Indigenous studies. Cox and Justice succinctly explain, "Criticism in the late 1980s and early 1990s privileged mixed-blood perspectives that understood hybridity and cultural crossing as powerful responses to the limitations of race logics. Often, these inquiries were disconnected from broader political and historical contexts."[16] Perhaps one way of describing this critique is to say that hybridity in an earlier body of critical and theoretical work often served as a possible pathway or relay toward revealing and even resolving complexities and contradictions of individual identity. Transcultural mediation, in this paradigm, often produced either the ability to "be" one thing or the other, or some sort of adaptive, more or less comfortable cultural balancing. But, focusing too intently on a single hybrid protagonist risks missing all the various things that that figure's hybridity does *not* demonstrate about, for example, communities, cultures, histories, contexts, and institutions. As Lisa Brooks (Abenaki) points out,

> One of the central problems with the way hybridity theory has been applied to Native texts is that it does not seem to account for the relationship between community and land. Rather, culture and identity seem to rest within the individual "subject," who seems oddly out of place, displaced, caught between two

> assumed worlds or perspectives that are so intertwined that they no longer
> exist independently of each other. . . . Is this a way to basically say that we are
> all native to this land because European and Native American cultures are so
> intertwined as to melt together into a single multicultural mass?[17]

In other words, the problem with hybridity is that it has too often been used to suggest either an exceptional singularity or a huge overgeneralization; one way or the other, it collapses critical distinctions and complexities in the very act of attempting to make them more visible. Jones does not take on the task of directly solving this theoretical problem. But we can say that his werewolf-human "mongrels" might appear to be "displaced," moving as they do from one southern town, trailer, or junker car to another—except that they travel out of necessity, prefer this serially migratory yet grounded way of life, and identify themselves most strongly not as individuals but as family members and werewolves. As I discuss in more detail below, they articulate and act on desires and preferences they define for themselves even though they are also governed by lycanthropic drives and imperatives.

For Faulkner and his characters, however, hybridity by any name neither illustrates nor encourages truly effective self-determination, let alone self-determination toward new understandings of familial, communal, or regional identity. Indeed, when Joe Christmas elects to identify himself as part black, he suffers as a result. But, as Jay Watson argues, when Christmas does *not* choose to identify himself racially or even as anything at all, the Jefferson community is happy to oblige: "The farther Joe runs, the blacker he will get, the more easily he will be consigned to the black race, whatever truths his body might seem to offer to the contrary."[18] Indeed, "the community will obstinately resolve the crisis [of racialized interpretation and identification] by drawing on received stereotypes about black flight and invoking the racialized metaphor of blood as a momentary stay against category confusion."[19] Joe is damned equally well by both self-determination and self-obfuscation. As Watson suggests, he can run, but he cannot be allowed to hide.

For Stephen Graham Jones, in the early twenty-first century, the werewolves retain their monstrosity but remain resolutely human and largely able to manage their own covert activities. Indeed, in *Mongrels*, the werewolves are the narrator's aunt, uncle, and grandfather: the people he loves, and the people who love him. We are never told whether this werewolf family identifies as Native American, as white, or as some other race or ethnicity; they identify as werewolves, and the narrator wants to be a werewolf because that is what they are. In other words, he recognizes the potentially alien, nonnative monster within his family and possibly within himself as an embodied sign of kinship relations and of home. Jones intently and powerfully emphasizes these generally hopeful negotiations between transformation and recognition as he details the ins and outs and ups and downs of living a werewolf life (and, for the narrator, of living a werewolf life without yet knowing whether he, too, will be a werewolf). Having fully functioning werewolves as blood relatives does not prevent the narrator from telling a monster story that doubles as a coming-of-age story. Robert Spadoni's observation about the 1935 film *Werewolf of London* pertains to *Mongrels* as well; in the film, Spadoni argues, the werewolf's "dawning . . . [is] all the more convulsive because it is a second adolescence, and so this film depicts, simultaneously, a moving forward and a going back, with the latter sense calling to mind the genre's relationship to the repressed and its return."[20] But Jones's youthful narrator also changes the terms of that story; I want to argue that Jones casts werewolves as metaphors for otherness and also as conduits for personal, if not political, self-determination, not just a physical imperative but also an emotional and intellectual alliance—a choice.

Of course, werewolves cannot practice anything like full-fledged self-determination, because few, if any, werewolves choose lycanthropy willingly. But werewolves in *Mongrels* absolutely do have options and act on them. For example, they tell their own stories, and the narrator writes them down—in spite of his Aunt Libby's insistence that he observe werewolf protocol and avoid writing for fear of revealing who and what they are—thereby moving werewolves from a somewhat spotty oral wolflore to a written record of how the narrator remembers and interprets that wolflore. Reading *Light in August* through *Mongrels*, then, clarifies that, while many of the main characters in Faulkner's novel undergo fairly limited transformations of some sort, transformations that stall or remain in the closet or happen only once, Joe Christmas transforms differently. To repeat, he is not a werewolf—but like a werewolf or a shapeshifter, he turns and turns back, frequently and even at times dramatically, and when we attend to these changes, we see more clearly and sharply his ability to recognize and rethink himself. Both *Mongrels* and *Light in August* center on a young male orphan who lives a migratory, outcast life in the South, who believes he is a mongrel, and who expresses fascination about that identity, desire for it, and some significant willingness to understand it as emergent and transformational even as it also renders him feared, scorned, and misunderstood. Both novels examine this character's coming of age and the crimes he commits, and is complicit in, along the way. Importantly, however, both Joe and the young would-be werewolf narrator of *Mongrels* inhabit a story that is ultimately less about who or what or even where he is than about these back-and-forth processes of becoming.

Stephen Graham Jones (Blackfeet) is, as he says on his website, "the author of 22 or 23 books, 250+ stories, and all this stuff here." "Can't seem to stop."[21] Born in 1972, he is originally from west Texas and now lives in Boulder, Colorado, where he teaches at the University of Colorado. Narrated by a teenage orphan who never tells us his name, *Mongrels* opens in Arkansas with the narrator announcing, "My grandfather used to tell me he was a werewolf" (1). This opening chapter closes with, "We're werewolves. This is what we do, this is how we live. If you want to call it that" (27), and by this early point in the novel, the first-person plural pronouns are not the only signal that the narrator very much wants to call it that. We learn early on that his mother died at age fourteen giving birth to him, that no one talks about his father (for reasons that come clear later), and that he has been adopted by his aunt Libby and uncle Darren, who, along with his grandfather, are indeed werewolves. Grandpa, who likes to re-enact his past werewolf attacks on sheep, playing both parts, dies in an awkwardly liminal way before chapter 1 ends: "Grandpa wasn't just half in and half out of the door from the kitchen. He was also halfway between man and wolf" (18). Then, for the rest of the novel, the three living family members travel all over the South, compelled to be transient in part because they cannot afford to become prey: "We know to stay mostly to the south and east. I mean, we're made for snow, you can tell just by looking at us, we're more at home in the snow and the mountains than anywhere, but in snow you leave tracks, and those tracks always lead back to your front door, and that only ever ends with the villagers mobbing up with their pitchforks and torches" (42). Again, the narrator does not yet know whether he's a werewolf in the making—but he says "we" anyway, willingly casts himself as the monster in a Universal horror movie and acknowledges that the South is more an ambivalent recourse than a true home.

Mongrels includes a rich compendium of inside information about werewolf best practices. They brush their teeth and chew mints obsessively because they're paranoid about having dog breath. They have a hard time finding long-term gainful employment. They live in cheap rental houses and trailers. They work odd jobs. They watch a lot of bad television. They subsist. As this all-too-brief capsule summary indicates, there are obvious differences between Faulkner's southern modernist novel and Jones's twenty-first-century Native southern werewolf novel. But, as I have begun to suggest, they share an interest in blood, family, travel, transformations, returns, darkness, and, against all odds, self-determination. As I have also begun to demonstrate, their main characters are also similarly mismatched with their ostensible home places in the South; for both Faulkner and Jones, the South is capable of vastly nonnative modernization and variation without being particularly good at change, let alone the kinds of punctuated transformations that Joe Christmas and the narrator of *Mongrels* desire and experience.

Late at night in *Light in August*, for example, with Joanna Burden's "dark and hidden" house lurking behind him, Joe stands in the darkness and recognizes, "*Something is going to happen to me*" (118). As Heidi Kim perceptively argues, "The racialization of Joe Christmas presages what happens when a foreign presence is not content to remain 'peculiar and barren,' instead nudging its way into the community life and relationships. Christmas breaks the bounds in which the town is content to leave him."[22] Like the werewolf family at the heart of *Mongrels*, Joe questions, wonders about, examines, quietly evades, and at times sharply breaks these bounds more than he seeks to become a member of any given community he passes through or lives in. In this way he stands in sharp if underdiscussed contrast to his less nocturnal counterpart Byron Bunch, whose origins are as mysterious as Joe's but who passes, extraordinarily successfully, as nondescript. Like the werewolves, Joe monitors his own transformations, or lack thereof, and worries about their outcomes.

Joe Christmas, I repeat, is not a werewolf. But as he stands in the midnight air and thinks about his relationship with Joanna Burden, he becomes a werewolf*like* sensorium: "His right hand slid fast and smooth as the knife blade had ever done, up the opening in the garment.... The dark air breathed upon him, breathed smoothly as the garment slipped down his legs, the cool mouth of darkness, the soft cool tongue. Moving again, he could feel the dark air like water; he could feel the dew under his feet as he had never felt dew before" (107). His nakedness presages a transformation that happens more fully later in the novel; it is as if he experiments, here, with presenting himself as a spectacle more than contenting himself with being a spectator. But he still also remains a spectator who, as white people drive by, famously turns his gaze on himself and watches "his body grow white out of the darkness like a Kodak print emerging from the liquid.... It was as though he had merely come there to be present at a finality, and the finality had now occurred and he was free again" (108).

Free from what? A temporal loop, for one thing: "It was as though each turn of dark saw him faced again with the necessity to despoil again that which he had already despoiled—or never had and never would" (234). Depersonalized into a binaristic, repetitive "necessity," with Joanna Burden reduced to a "that which," this nocturnal affair slithers in and out of a horror that they share even as it jumps back and forth from him to, as here, her: "her wild hair, each strand of which would seem to

Light in August and Werewolves 161

come alive like octopus tentacles, and her wild hands and her breathing: 'Negro! Negro! Negro!'" (260). Joe finds himself in deep, "as the fatalist can always be held, by curiosity, pessimism, by sheer inertia. . . . Perhaps he realized that he could not escape. Anyway, he stayed, watching the two creatures that struggled in the one body like two moon-gleamed shapes struggling drowning in alternate throes upon the surface of a black thick pool" (260). He watches the descent of this werewolflike embodiment. The transformations are at once out of control and obsessively under control, becoming more and more self-eradicating and more and more constrictive in their very wildness.

But, as I've suggested, Joe seems more subject to change later, when he is a fugitive. Though, as Watson argues, when he turns fugitive the southern community binds him to a particular racial identity, Joe himself seems to view his fugitive state as both more transient and potentially more transitional—or, perhaps more accurately, more associated with transits of various kinds. "It is as though he desires to see his native earth in all its phases for the first or last time" (338), the narrator tells us late in the narrative, but as elsewhere in Faulkner, an ecologically minded sense of transition also evokes and provokes sensations of horror.[23] Further, according to Alison Peirse, as horror emerges as a genre of sound film and gathers cultural momentum, "the word 'horror' changes from referring to the effect it has on the audience to attaching to a 'type' of film" (8).[24] Joe Christmas undergoes a transition roughly analogous to this: from a spectator who feels horror to a spectacle who embodies it. He transforms from a young man who sees disturbing things and tries to avoid public scrutiny to a man *seen* as a disturbing thing, and a man more inclined than previously to present himself, to the revival meeting as to the people in downtown Mottstown, as a spectacle, or as a spectacle in the making. It's tricky to generalize because, as I mention above, Joe does a fair amount of shifting back and forth throughout the novel: he changes, sometimes regroups, then changes again. Sometimes he does double duty as both spectator and spectacle, of course, from the toothpaste scene right on through to the end. But, by and large, Joe consciously and maybe even willingly transforms from spectator into spectacle, to the extent that he goes to a barbershop in Mottstown and gets a shave and a haircut, as if to tidy up and look presentable in the event of his capture.[25]

"So you run," says the narrator of *Mongrels*. "It's the main thing werewolves are made for. It's what we do best of all" (40). As even Percy Grimm acknowledges, Joe Christmas runs with both stamina and skill. Of course, this running helps us see that many of the characters in both *Light in August* and *Mongrels* appear to be stuck, subject to social, cultural, regional, physiological, and paranormal forces that severely limit their options and prove difficult to run from. Still, as I have suggested, the most complex characters in both novels also show some ability to make choices and even to practice some forms of self-determination. Jones's werewolves and the narrator who identifies as a werewolf even before he knows whether he is one expend much physical, emotional, and intellectual energy thinking about who and what they are, how werewolf identity works, where it comes from, and what its limitations feel like. Without glossing over the violence, the gore, the poverty, or the fashion challenges of day-to-day werewolf life, Jones rehabilitates werewolves and the often-derogatory notion of the mongrel. While the transformations Jones's mongrels undergo are fueled by rage and/or necessity, they also solidify family relationships and act as declarations of love. At one point, the narrator even theorizes that love, not lycanthropy, is "the actual infection in our blood" (221). Within the constraints and confines of systems that put them in boxes they do not want to be put in, that analyze, demonize, infiltrate, poison, and dehumanize their blood against their will, Jones's mongrel werewolves also read and reclaim their own blood in their own ways and for their own purposes. In places, what the narrator says of werewolves is also true of Indians, as here: "Werewolves have always been here. Every variation of us, it has to have happened at some point. Just, it's the remembering that's tricky" (37).

But what about *Light in August?* To circle back to my earlier question, how do we "and" Faulkner and the Native South by way of a Blackfeet writer's novel about werewolves in the South? In her 2007 study *Orphan Narratives*, Valérie Loichot suggests, "By submitting 'magisterial' texts—such as Faulkner's—to a set of theoretical tools developed within the context of the African Diaspora, I propose a political reading, which inverts the trend of interpreting minority literatures through Western theories."[26] A bit more recently, Loichot has written that

> aside from a reference to Joe Christmas's alleged Mexican father, [*Light in August*] does not contain any explicit reference to Latin America or the Caribbean. However . . . the allegedly mixed-race character of Joe Christmas, and the impossibility of naming him in a way other than a constant rebounding between black-and-white categories, is precisely what calls for a Caribbean intervention in reading Faulkner's world.[27]

Like Loichot with "Caribbean," I am thinking about "Native southern" as a critical lens that stands alongside other methodologies. We know how to do feminist readings of works that are not feminist; we can queer

Light in August and Werewolves   163

all manner of texts; we can perform green readings of the most parlor- and ballroom-oriented novels. Why can't we "native southern" a wide range of texts, too?

In the act of raising and beginning to answer this question, this chapter not only accepts Melanie Benson Taylor's challenge (quoted above) that "it is time to do better at assessing the very tangible ways that Indians are deeply embedded in southern terrain" but also sets out to investigate the ways southernness is deeply rooted and dynamically routed on Native ground. I build on my own and others' work in Native southern studies by arguing that native southern is not merely an interest group within southern studies but rather a supple and productive methodology in its own right. A native southern lens helps reveal Faulkner's insistent emphasis on non-Native excesses throughout *Light in August*, which in turn allows me to point out that settler-colonial settlement in Faulkner's South is quite unsettled and in various ways unstable. I've also set aside "Indians in Faulkner," important as that topic is, in favor of reading a Faulkner novel and a native southern novel alongside and through each other. Together, much more powerfully than apart, these novels illuminate the provocative, complicated fragility of both "native" and "southern" orientations. And I've joined with both Jodi Byrd and Taylor in arguing that, as Byrd writes, "the story of the new world is horror, the story of America a crime," and as Taylor puts it, "the crimes committed against American Indians are a nightmare from which we have yet to awake."[28] In this sense, the South's regional particulars do not disappear so much as they fold into a larger nonfictional North American horror narrative.

At the same time, I've also tried to talk back to that horror as Stephen Graham Jones does to werewolves and as Joy Harjo (Mvskoke/Creek) does to fear in her poem "I Give You Back": "I release you, my beautiful and terrible / fear."[29] Werewolves, released, take the shapes of a transformative, and a potentially transformative, anticolonial human/monster hybrid. Indeed, as Stephen Graham Jones makes plain, werewolves cannot make more werewolves. In *Mongrels*, they migrate all over the South and betray little or no interest in settling. Thinking about their travels, their werewolf routes, helps make visible their transformations and recognitions, the ways they turn and turn back.

In turn, this native southern reading helps clarify how and why characters in *Light in August* travel, recognize things, turn, and turn back. In some ways, things are out of the hands of werewolves and Indians and the really, really nonnative characters of *Light in August* alike. In some ways, self-recognition and self-determination are hard pressed to break out of the circle that bedevils some of the last thoughts we hear Joe Christmas thinking:

> It had been a paved street, where going should be fast. It had made a circle and he is still inside of it. Though during the last seven days he has had no paved street, yet he has travelled further than in all the thirty years before. And yet he is still inside the circle. 'And yet I have been further in these seven days than in all the thirty years,' he thinks. 'But I have never got outside that circle. I have never broken out of the ring of what I have already done and cannot ever undo,' he thinks quietly [as] . . . the black tide [creeps] up his legs, moving from his feet upward as death moves. (339)

Joe is right, to some extent, and he is also wrong, to some extent. He's right that he has traveled further than ever before. He's wrong, I am counterintuitively arguing, because when "he thinks quietly," he rethinks himself in a way that again begins to stretch and maybe even open that circle. However briefly, tentatively, and skeptically he transforms before he turns back, these moments of transformative reflection matter. At least he knows that he is in deep.

Near the end of *Mongrels*, Jones offers not a circle but an X. This X marks what is missing in *Light in August* but powerfully present in *Mongrels*: just before he goes on his honeymoon, the narrator's uncle Darren "took his middle finger from his mouth, drew a wet X right on my forehead, told me it marked the spot, and then he was walking up that gangplank. . . . I didn't wipe the X from my forehead until Georgia. No, I mean, that X, it's still there, it's still marking me" (291). With this mark, Darren tells his nephew, "You are one of us (family) even if you are not, or are not yet, one of us (werewolf). As Ojibwe/ Dakota scholar Scott Lyons says, "The x-mark is a contaminated and coerced sign of consent made under conditions that are not of one's making."[30] Darren's "x-mark" on the narrator's forehead acknowledges much of that, whether or not the narrator wiped it off in Georgia. But as Lyons goes on to argue, the "x-mark" can also "symbolize Native assent to things (concepts, policies, technologies, ideas) that, while not necessarily traditional in origin, can sometimes turn out all right and occasionally even good."[31] Darren is a werewolf, but the embodied transformation he offers the narrator is first and foremost a gift not of claws and a long snout but of love. As I bring this exploratory meditation on so many disparate, off-kilter, endangered identities and fragile, tentative transformations to a close, I want to return, one last time, to my opening assertion that the most provocative word in the title of this year's Faulkner and Yoknapatawpha Conference theme is "and." What Joe Christmas, a werewolf named Darren, and a Blackfeet writing about the South have to say to us, when they go in deep together, is that the "and" works like an "x-mark": it speaks unspeakable losses

Light in August and Werewolves 165

and it also signals assent to native southern transformations known and (as yet) unknown, theoretical and yet grounded, past and present and, best of all, future.

NOTES

I'm grateful to Jay Watson and Annette Trefzer for organizing "Faulkner and the Native South" and for inviting me to participate. To everyone who was there, and especially to LeAnne Howe, John Lowe, and Jodi Byrd, thank you! And to Annette, Melanie Benson Taylor, Kirstin Squint, and Gina Caison, so many thanks; this chapter is for you.

1. "Louise Erdrich, The Art of Fiction No. 208," interview by Lisa Halliday, *Paris Review* 195 (Winter 2010), http://www.theparisreview.org/interviews/6055/louise-erdrich-the-art-of-fiction-no-208-louise-erdrich. See also "Louise Erdrich Explores Mysteries and Miracles on the Reservation," interview by Alden Mudge, BookPage (April 2001), https://bookpage.com/interviews/8091-louise-erdrich#.WGQeG5Kw76g. On "Indians and Faulkner," see for example Patricia Galloway, "The Construction of Faulkner's Indians," *Faulkner Journal* 18, nos. 1–2 (Fall 2002–Spring 2003): 9–31.

2. James H. Cox and Daniel Heath Justice, "Introduction: Post-Renaissance Indigenous American Literary Studies," in *The Oxford Handbook of Indigenous American Literature*, ed. Cox and Justice (New York: Oxford University Press, 2014), 1.

3. Melanie Benson Taylor, "In Deep," *South: A Scholarly Journal* 48, no. 1 (Fall 2015): 72.

4. Ibid., 70.

5. William Faulkner, *Light in August*, rev. ed. (1932; repr., New York: Vintage International, 1990): 7. Subsequent references to this text are made parenthetically.

6. See Philip J. Deloria, *Indians in Unexpected Places* (Lawrence: University Press of Kansas, 2004), 3–14.

7. Jodi A. Byrd, *The Transit of Empire: Indigenous Critiques of Colonialism* (Minneapolis: University of Minnesota Press, 2011), xxvii.

8. Leigh Anne Duck, "Peripatetic Modernism, or, Joe Christmas's Father," *Philological Quarterly* 90, nos. 2–3 (2011): 256.

9. Stephen Graham Jones, *Mongrels* (New York: William Morrow, 2016): 249. Subsequent references to this text are made parenthetically.

10. Heidi Kathleen Kim, "The Foreigner in Yoknapatawpha: Rethinking Race in Faulkner's 'Global South,'" *Philological Quarterly* 90, nos. 2–3 (2011): 203.

11. Phillip Carroll Morgan, *Riding Out the Storm: 19th Century Chickasaw Governors, Their Lives and Intellectual Legacy* (Ada, OK: Chickasaw, 2013), 102.

12. Here I would also note that the film believed to be the first werewolf film, *The Werewolf* (1913), features a Navajo shape-shifter who, according to Wikipedia, "transforms into a wolf in order to carry out vengeance against the invading white settlers. Then, 100 years after Watuma's death, she returns from the dead to kill again." See *"The Werewolf* (1913 film)," Wikipedia, https://en.wikipedia.org/wiki/The_Werewolf_(1913_film).

13. William Faulkner, "The Werewolf," in *The Ghosts of Rowan Oak: William Faulkner's Ghost Stories for Children*, recounted by Dean Faulkner Wells (Oxford, MS: Yoknapatawpha, 1980), 39–46.

14. Peter Lurie, *Vision's Immanence: Faulkner, Film, and the Popular Imagination* (Baltimore: Johns Hopkins University Press, 2004), 68–102; Aaron Nyerges, "Immemorial

Cinema: Film, Travel, and Faulkner's Poetics of Space," in *Faulkner and Film: Faulkner and Yoknapatawpha 2010*, ed. Peter Lurie and Ann J. Abadie (Jackson: University Press of Mississippi, 2014), 47–70.

15. Robin Wood, "An Introduction to the American Horror Film," in *Planks of Reason: Essays on the Horror Film*, ed. Barry Keith Grant and Christopher Sharrett, rev. ed. (1990, repr., Lanham, MD: Scarecrow, 2004), 114.

16. Cox and Justice, "Introduction: Post-Renaissance Indigenous American Literary Studies," 8.

17. Lisa Brooks, "At the Gathering Place," in *American Indian Literary Nationalism*, ed. Jace Weaver, Craig S. Womack, and Robert Warrior (Albuquerque: University of New Mexico Press, 2006), 240–41.

18. Jay Watson, *Reading for the Body: The Recalcitrant Materiality of Southern Fiction, 1893–1985* (Athens: University of Georgia Press, 2012), 144.

19. Ibid.

20. Robert Spadoni, "Old Times in *Werewolf of London*," in *The Dread of Difference: Gender and the Horror Film*, ed. Barry Keith Grant (1996; repr., Austin: University of Texas Press, 2015), 404.

21. Stephen Graham Jones, *Stephen Graham Jones*, http://www.demontheory.net/.

22. Kim, "The Foreigner in Yoknapatawpha," 215.

23. See, for example, Eric Gary Anderson, "Environed Blood: Ecology and Violence in *The Sound and the Fury* and *Sanctuary*, in *Faulkner and the Ecology of the South: Faulkner and Yoknapatawpha 2003*, ed. Joseph R. Urgo and Ann J. Abadie (Jackson: University Press of Mississippi, 2005), 30–46.

24. Alison Peirse, *After Dracula: The 1930s Horror Film* (London: I. B. Tauris, 2013), 8.

25. Lena Grove, like Joe, seems to accept her situation in the end, but she is never more than tangentially involved in *Light in August's* horror narrative, and she transforms in the opposite direction, from spectacle into spectator, even tourist.

26. Valérie Loichot, *Orphan Narratives: The Postplantation Literature of Faulkner, Glissant, Morrison, and Saint-John Perse* (Charlottesville: University of Virginia Press, 2007), 4.

27. Valérie Loichot, "William Faulkner's Caribbean Poetics," in *William Faulkner in Context*, ed. John T. Matthews (Cambridge: Cambridge University Press, 2015), 48.

28. Byrd, *The Transit of Empire*, xii. Taylor, "In Deep," 69.

29. Joy Harjo, "I Give You Back," in *How We Became Human: New and Selected Poems, 1975–2001* (New York: W. W. Norton, 2004), 50.

30. Scott Richard Lyons, *X-Marks: Native Signatures of Assent* (Minneapolis: University of Minnesota Press, 2010), 2.

31. Ibid., 3.

From the Mausoleum to a Spider Web

William Faulkner's and Louise Erdrich's
Takes on Hybridity

MELANIE R. ANDERSON

Whenever a new Louise Erdrich novel set in her fictional "postage stamp" of the Great Plains appears, invariably the first comparison in reviews is to William Faulkner's Yoknapatawpha County. In 1988, reviewer Thomas Disch wrote of Erdrich's first three interconnected novels that they "already constitute . . . a North Dakota of the imagination that, like Faulkner's Yoknapatawpha County, unites the archetypal and the arcane, heartland America and borderline schizophrenia."[1] Jace Weaver also comments on the connections between Faulkner and several Native writers: "Acknowledged or unacknowledged, he [Faulkner] has influenced two generations of Indian authors as diverse as Scott Momaday, Louise Erdrich, Leslie Silko, and Geary Hobson, among others." He says specifically of Erdrich that "Faulkner is . . . reportedly one of her favorite authors, and, of all Native writers, she is perhaps the most deliberately, at times even mimetically, Faulknerian."[2] Moreover, in her essay "The Turtle Mountain/Yoknapatawpha Connection," Susan Carr notes several echoes between Faulkner's and Erdrich's oeuvres, including a similar focus on absent central characters such as Caddy Compson in *The Sound and the Fury* and June Kashpaw in *Love Medicine*, a shared openness to experimentation, cyclical uses of time, the primacy of family, and the authors' interest in the connections between lineage and land.[3] Erdrich has noted these connections with Faulkner's work as well. In her essay "Where I Ought to Be: A Writer's Sense of Place," she emphasizes the powerful link between people and place: "The Macondo of Gabriel García Márquez, Faulkner's Yoknapatawpha County, the island house of Jean Rhys in *Wide Sargasso Sea* are as real to me as any place I've actually been."[4] This link that Erdrich, a writer of German, French, and Anishinaabe (Ojibwe) heritage, cites through place and land becomes an ironic tie when we remember that Faulkner's home state, a geographical space full of Choctaw and Chickasaw placenames, takes its name from the Anishinaabe language. Mississippi is "a name," as Weaver notes, "at once still native and yet completely non-autochthonous."[5] The two writers' fiction may share different geographical spaces: for Erdrich, North Dakota and Minnesota, and for Faulkner, Mississippi. Their regions are connected, however, by the Mississippi River, and its history is connected to Erdrich's forebears. As a member of the Turtle Mountain Chippewa band, Erdrich is part of the larger Ojibwe community, which, in turn, is part of the larger language community of the Anishinaabe. Regardless of our current designations of Midwestern or southern writing, prior to European migration and statehood, these locations were embedded in Native space and language.

Another connection between the two authors is their shared penchant for creating epic multigenerational sagas that begin in one novel and spill into other works. Erdrich's novels revolve around the two fictional towns of Argus and Pluto and the nearby Little No Horse reservation in her version of North Dakota and relate stories of numerous families such as, to name a few, the Nanapushes, Pillagers, Kashpaws, Lazarres, Kozkas, and Adares. This emphasis on family history consistently reminds critics of Faulkner's Mississippi county with its own families like the Sutpens, Compsons, McCaslins, and Snopeses. The two writers also have created extensive genealogies in their works, resulting, for Erdrich, in a family tree that is provided in most of her novels to help readers keep track of everyone and, for Faulkner, in the famous maps of Yoknapatawpha to help readers place events and characters within its fictional geographical space. When it comes to the presentation of Native American characters, however, the two differ greatly. Faulkner's Native characters are labeled as full or mixed blood, and these Chickasaws, or Choctaws, depending on the story, usually melt into a dim past time and are doomed for the future. Native genealogies are truncated into a few generations in a handful of stories in the "Wilderness" section of his *Collected Stories* and in *Go Down, Moses*, where they end in the typical fashion of the vanishing Indian myth. By contrast, Erdrich writes about Ojibwe individuals in the Midwest rather than Southeastern Native populations, and according to Louis Owens, "In her published novels . . . Erdrich weaves genealogies and fates as characters appear and reappear in successive, interconnected stories."[6] She focuses on Native survival through characters that extend into numerous novels, such as Nanapush and Fleur who defy the vanishing Indian myth in *Tracks* (1988), and characters with hybrid backgrounds who foster connection and community, like Celestine and Dot in *The Beet Queen* (1986). Throughout her interconnected novels, her unflinching gaze focuses on plagues, termination, dispossession, the Wounded Knee massacre, the colonial horrors of religious conversion, and physical and sexual violence. In the face of this trauma and loss, Erdrich's Native characters, as opposed to Faulkner's, show resilience.

Despite this broad tapestry of Native American experience that Erdrich weaves, Leslie Marmon Silko has taken *The Beet Queen* to task for being too focused on white spaces and characters: Argus is a largely white town next to the Little No Horse reservation, and Native characters are pushed to the edges of the narrative.[7] But, I think this novel uses its focus on marginal characters to emphasize Native American survival and community. As Susan Castillo notes of Silko's and Erdrich's writing, "both describe Native Americans, not as Noble Savage victims or as dying representatives of a lost authenticity, but as tough, compassionate people who use the vital capacity of discourse to shape—and not merely reflect—reality."[8] In *The Beet Queen,* Erdrich uses Fleur, Celestine, and Dot, in particular, as bridges between the spaces of town and reservation and as examples of endurance. Both Faulkner and Erdrich have sprawling family trees in their works, but each writer values the genealogical survival of different families: for Faulkner it is white southerners, and for Erdrich, Ojibwe families. Furthermore, each writer responds to genealogy differently. On the one hand, Faulkner focuses on a limited, patriarchal genealogy that forecloses upon the possibilities of heritage for a character of mixed racial background like Sam Fathers. Erdrich, on the other hand, provides a genealogy for readers of her novels, but her characters do not always have a fixed position in those genealogies, thus she subverts patriarchal codes of descent and allows for the development of alternative forms of family and community. "Hybridity—mixed blood—becomes the space of identity," Carlton Smith writes of Erdrich's novels, "and it is a space that destabilizes notions of origin. It is this temporarily occupied, ephemeral space of becoming that takes primacy over the mythic site of familial and blood origins."[9] I suggest that we can use Erdrich's fiction as a lens for reviewing Faulkner's Native characters, much as Toni Morrison's work has become a lens for discussion of Faulkner's African American characters.[10] Erdrich gives visibility to groups of characters that are elided in Faulkner's fiction.

In her article "The Construction of Faulkner's Indians," Patricia Galloway carefully dissects how "Faulkner assimilated both local and national popular thinking about Indian people," rather than writing in a cultural vacuum, as he often claimed.[11] This leads to two factors that Galloway identifies in Faulkner's portrayal of Native characters. First, the generations leading up to Sam Fathers steadily become an admixture of Indian, European, and African backgrounds, culminating, once Sam Fathers dies without progeny, in a remarkably short family tree. From Ikkemotubbe to Sam Fathers, throughout the core Indian stories, Faulkner adjusted and reduced the genealogy to three generations of variously mixed heritage until Sam Fathers could be a son of Doom and incorporate a mixed racial background. She notes that Faulkner "found a way for a 'doom'-ed Indian race debauched by Europeans to join with the endurance of African women to produce the archetypal figure of Sam Fathers."[12] Second, this dwindling family tree that dies with a childless Sam Fathers reproduces the popular cultural myth of the day that Native Americans were vanishing. Galloway shows how writers and journalists of the time would reference Alexander Pope's verses that begin, "Lo! the poor Indian," by turning the poem into an abbreviation for an anonymous, generalized Indigenous individual called "Mr. Lo."[13] This abbreviation thus became a shorthand gesture toward the disappearance of Indigenous people portrayed as noble, yet superstitious, who were purportedly fading into a bygone time. Unlike Faulkner, whose Native characters end in a doomed hybridity that must give way before a solidifying southern white patriarchy, Erdrich emphasizes survival in her lengthy and complex Indigenous family trees that incorporate hybridity. Whereas Faulkner's Indigenous characters live on the edge and are marginalized, Erdrich's characters often thrive on the edge as a place for possibilities.

Faulkner represents his vanishing Americans, especially Sam Fathers, through the metaphor of ghostliness, which fits quite well in a consideration of how European American writers have represented the Native population in literature. In her book, *The National Uncanny*, Renée L. Bergland explores this phenomenon of spectral Native Americans in the national literature, specifically that of the nineteenth century. According to Bergland, "When European Americans speak of Native Americans, they always use the language of ghostliness. They insist that Indians are . . . ultimately doomed to vanish. Most often they describe Indians as absent or dead."[14] She suggests that this literary treatment was a response to the contemporary push for removal of Native communities from the eastern portion of the United States as the European American population spread westward. She posits that, during the mid-nineteenth century, social position led to spectralization in the national imaginary: "America was haunted by the ghosts of African American slaves and Indians as well as disenfranchised women and struggling workers. The people who were described and imagined as ghosts were those whose existence challenged developing structures of political and economic power. Ghostliness was closely related to oppression and to the hope of denying or repressing the memory of that oppression."[15] In essence, the flipside of American dreams of progressive idealism and equality was the oppression of marginalized groups of people that did not fit the white mainstream cultural, economic, and patriarchal system. This marginalization led to the invisibility of oppressed groups and the concomitant willful forgetting of these populations and the circumstances that oppressed them. This spectralization became important to the creation of a uniquely American identity, and it becomes what Bergland calls "the wish" and "counter-wish" of America. For her, the American subject must "simultaneously acknowledge the American horror and celebrate the American triumph."[16]

Louis Owens also uses such apparitional language to describe Indian characters invented by canonical European-American writers as "phantoms" in his book *Mixedblood Messages*.[17] For him, the vanishing Native figure in American literature has been a "long project of erasure" through "images of otherness and doom."[18] Indeed, he identifies literature wherein characters of mixed racial background seem to vanish as "the 'Chief Doom' school of literature," borrowing Faulkner's Anglicized French name for Chief Ikkemotubbe.[19] He describes these tortured figures (such as, for example, Mark Twain's Injun Joe or Faulkner's Sam Fathers) as "a matrix for the conflicted terrors of Euramerica, the horror of liminality that is the particular trauma of the colonial mind," and he sees these images of the colonized as "mirror[s]" for the colonizer "that give back a self-image with disturbing implications."[20] This distorted reflection of the colonizer and the paradoxical literary absent presence created by ignoring and/or revising the Native past, becomes a theme in much American writing. Writers like Hawthorne develop American themes against the background of a supposedly disappeared Indigenous population, and regardless of the facts, this myth of the vanishing American and the tragic character of mixed background who is doomed to be placeless continues into the twentieth century and is apparent in the work of southern writers. Gene M. Moore notes this distortion of Faulkner's Indian characters, especially in his short stories, in their inability to adapt to changing times and to instead become failed mimics of the corrupt aspects of white society—slavery and commodification. Their hybridity is seen as "exotic" and "grotesque," and their "foreignness . . . raises doubts about their right to claim residence, to be ab-original or 'native,' and thus serves both to justify their expropriation and to reconfirm the white man's sense of national belonging as if it were something natural, even manifestly predestined."[21] This historical dismissal in Faulkner's fiction results from group cultural change and individual racial hybridity. Survival and adaptation are not possible for Faulkner's Native characters.

As noted by Galloway and Owens, Faulkner's fictional Native Americans are vanishing, and they follow Bergland's descriptions pretty closely.

Faulkner's version of an Indigenous past may be romanticized, but it is simultaneously eulogized. Faulkner's Indians pass on their land and their knowledge to white settlers and white mentees, literally, in that they "pass on" out of existence and into the background of the developing South. Faulkner does express, at times, nostalgia for Sam Fathers and a yearning for the kind of relationship he has with Ike McCaslin and for a relationship between mankind and the land that precludes private property and industrial development, but ultimately, the Indigenous characters play a part and then melt into the wilderness to make room for the white southern male characters. In *Disturbing Indians*, Annette Trefzer uses an archaeological metaphor for unearthing layers of Native southern history. Trefzer observes, "In the South, this Native American signifier is often buried under a symbolic creation of the region that minimizes its importance or even negates its presence altogether."[22] In spite of this apparent disappearance, Trefzer illustrates how the discursive portrayal of a buried Native presence is "essential to the southern writers' understanding of region and nation."[23] Native characters, to reiterate Owens, become twisted mirrors for the colonizers in which they view the utility of a constructed "noble" past and the horror of a multicultural future.

Faulkner's Native characters often appear as ghostly anachronisms in his fictional history of Yoknapatawpha. In *Requiem for a Nun* (1951), the original inhabitants of Yoknapatawpha County are a footnote in the historical overview. He imagines them as "obsolete" in "a white man's land."[24] Faulkner also takes up this theme of a vanishing Indigenous population in "The Old People" through his description of Jobaker as a "full-blooded Chickasaw" who is "incredibly lost." He is peripheral and silent save for the "old tongue" he speaks that only Sam Fathers can understand. Ike finds Jobaker inscrutable, and the narrator insists, "Nobody knew his history at all,"[25] thus erasing his presence from a rewritten landscape. Rather than dying, Jobaker merely disappears from Ike's awareness. After Jobaker's death, Sam Fathers moves to the wilderness camp, which isolates him in that primeval space, except during hunting season, and moves him inexorably closer to his fated doom once the bear is killed and Ike does not require his guiding hand.

In Ike's mind, after Jobaker passes away, Sam Fathers is alone and facing obsolescence. In "The Bear," Sam is described as an anachronism, out of place and out of time, and desolately alone: "the wild man not even one generation from the woods, childless, kinless, peopleless" (236). Sam's ancestors are described by their absence as they "who had vanished from it now with all their kind, what of blood they left behind them running now in another race and for a while even in bondage and now drawing toward the end of its alien and irrevocable course, barren, since

Sam Fathers had no children" (159). Sam is presented as a descendant of vanished people, and he is facing his own disappearance. His Chickasaw "blood" is described as "alien," even though Faulkner admits that settlers displaced these Indigenous ancestors. McCaslin Edmonds describes Sam's racial makeup as a "battleground" and a "cage" (161–62). The son of the last chief, Doom, and a slave woman, sold by his father along with his mother to another master, Sam, according to Edmonds, embodies the racial conflicts of the South. And he holds little hope for Sam as an individual rising above this perceived confusion. For Edmonds, Sam has no place in any community. He tells Ike: "Not betrayed by the black blood and not willfully betrayed by his mother, but betrayed by her all the same, who had bequeathed him not only the blood of slaves but even a little of the very blood which had enslaved it; himself his own battle-ground, the scene of his own vanquishment and the mausoleum of his defeat" (162). Images of isolation, disappearance, death, and barrenness surround Jobaker, whom no one understood, and Sam Fathers, whose cultural and racial hybridity leaves him with no clear place in any of the local communities.

In "The Old People," Sam Fathers comes dangerously close to being a ghost before he is dead. He is spiritualized as Ike's wilderness mentor; every stage of Ike's development leads one step further toward Sam Fathers's death. It is difficult for the reader to see future possibilities for Sam Fathers, because his physical body and his interior life are elided as the reader only views him from Ike's perspective. Sam even has access to the mystical side of the wilderness through his detailed knowledge, which verges on the preternatural, of the woods and its fauna. Once Ike has killed his first buck, Sam marks him with the blood, and before the hunting party leaves the wilderness, Sam places Ike within sight of an impressive and seemingly spectral deer that Sam appears to converse with using the old language he used with Jobaker. Ike finds out later from his cousin that while the deer may be a shadow of an older time (like Sam), McCaslin believes Ike saw something because Sam shared it with him too. Sam is not only fulfilling the role of the "vanishing Indian"; he also takes on the stereotypical Indigenous mystical connections to the woods and the animals therein.

Although he is ghostly, mystical, and marginal and has retreated to the wilderness to escape the world of the oncoming train, Faulkner does allow Sam the option of immortality through his transfer of knowledge to Ike, but it requires the complete disappearance of his people and their vestiges from Yoknapatawpha. According to Lewis M. Dabney, Sam is the descendant of nineteenth-century vanishing Indians in the work of Cooper and Melville.[26] Sam, Dabney writes, "accepts [his death, the

Bear's death, and the loss of the wilderness] as the inscrutable Indian of American folk myth, secret, impenetrable, and a fountain head of knowledge."[27] Even though Dabney points out that Ike takes Sam's place and "preserve[s] the ritual," so that "blacks and whites purified by the Indian culture and meeting on this ground [become] Faulkner's romantic melting-pot mythology,"[28] Sam, Jobaker, and the rest of the Native population of Yoknapatawpha have disappeared at this point. As Owens says of the mixed-blood characters in European American literature, Sam Fathers is an anomaly that does not fit—he is the distorted mirror wherein Ike views himself. Sam and Ike may have a close relationship, but it is ultimately one of utility. Sam Fathers accomplishes two purposes: one, his marginalization reinforces his lack of place in the South, echoing Bergland's discursive removal; and two, even though the other characters believe that Sam cannot fit into the twentieth-century South, Ike needs his guidance to become a fully fledged and emplaced American southern white male. Trefzer notes that Sam passes on his Indigenous identity to Ike at a moment when American nationalism is rising in anticipation of US entry into World War II. Furthermore, she posits that it is Sam's disappearance, with the white characters' permission and blessing, that ironically, and tragically, gives him freedom from his isolation and despair, but his "lingering spirit," as she writes, is "essential to the concept of American nationhood."[29] Sam's absence is inevitable, and it haunts Ike and the landscape.

By contrast to Faulkner's abridged Native genealogies ending in quiet obsolescence, Erdrich's second novel, *The Beet Queen*, set in the years from 1932 to 1972, uses hybridity to signify openness, fluidity, and creation. Her hybrid characters do not succumb to the "Doom" of Faulkner's Sam Fathers or obliterate their heritage. Celestine (the daughter of an Ojibwe and French mother and European American immigrant father) and her daughter Dot facilitate connection and build community. Subsequently, Dot becomes the center of a tangled web of marginalized people that represent every part of her background and connect her to family units that sprawl and interact across Erdrich's novels. Smith connects Erdrich's numerous chosen and self-created families in her novels to her predilection for messy and inclusive genealogies. He writes that her "alternate families [are] communities structured not so much by lineage and patriarchy, but rather through the development of a concept of love."[30] Instead of a Faulknerian narrative of "blood" and "vanishings," Erdrich uses images such as the spider web, open windows, and rain when describing Celestine and Dot and their relationships with others. Although Celestine and Dot live in the fictional town of Argus, they cross the boundary between the reservation and Argus quite often, and when

Dot's absentee white father, Karl Adare, asks who her father figures are, she lists Eli and Russell Kashpaw—important Ojibwe characters in *Love Medicine* (1984), *Tracks*, and *The Bingo Palace* (1994)—who live on the nearby reservation, in addition to her godfather, Argus's Wallace Pfef. Celestine and Dot sport the distinctive Pillager grin, and they interact with Celestine's aunt Fleur Pillager, an extremely powerful Ojibwe character who refuses to vanish and leaves her "tracks" throughout several of Erdrich's books on her quest to reclaim her land. Moreover, Dot speaks for her uncle Russell when he is treated by white townspeople as a silent spectacle in the Beet Queen Festival Parade. According to Smith, postmodern ethnic writers revise the frontier from a borderline of violent separation and disappearance to a location of flux and possible creation, "a space of continuously reforged and renegotiated identity."[31] Unlike Sam Fathers, who must retreat to a dwindling wilderness, Erdrich's characters cross the permeable and "slippery" borders between Argus and the reservation. This mobility allows the reader to see both communities and the power relations between them.

One of the central characters in Erdrich's multinovel saga of her North Dakota Ojibwe families is Fleur Pillager, a powerful woman rooted in her community's past and knowledge of shamanistic natural methods of healing and retribution. In *Tracks*, Erdrich's novel about the Dawes Act of 1887 and the federal government's policy of dismantling communal ownership of land through allotment, Fleur survives the final wave of tuberculosis and is one of two remaining members of the powerful Pillager Clan.[32] She is raised by Nanapush, who is the sole survivor of his family and a trickster character. Nanapush is a wily survivor, who is grounded in his community's history and culture and is adept at learning new languages and customs in order to manipulate the system and gain some advantage. Fleur learns some of Nanapush's methods and draws on them when she faces the horrors of dispossession. Fleur, like Sam Fathers, is associated with a bear, except the bear is the source of Fleur's power and the connection to her land near Matchimanito Lake, and, whereas Sam and his bear are doomed to die in a mutual death pact, Fleur lives. At the end of *Tracks* it may appear that she has lost her land to predatory tax laws and lumber interests, but she does not go quietly. She carefully cuts through most of the tree trunks around her cabin, so when the loggers arrive, a strong wind blows the trees down on them. The end of *Tracks* sees her pushing her cart full of her belongings away from her home and the reservation. She may appear to be vanishing like Sam Fathers, but where he ends in hybridity, she begins in it. Erdrich is careful to limn her characters' mixed heritage from the meetings of French fur trappers with the Ojibwe beginning in the 1600s. While her origins are deliberately kept unclear, Fleur's French name hints at this colonial strain of her background, but rather than lacking a place or possibilities, Fleur cleaves to her community and its traditions while adapting to the changing conditions. She repeatedly appears in Erdrich's books, and she does not quit her mission to regain her family land.

For instance, Fleur appears in *The Beet Queen*, even though she is not a main character. Celestine and Dot are Pillager descendants who visit her on the reservation. But Fleur survives off-reservation as well where she rescues the boy Karl (who will become Dot's father and the lover of Celestine and of Wallace Pfef) after he leaps from a moving train. Karl tells the reader what other people think of Fleur: they fear her and think she is a wanderer,[33] but he is saved by her healing touch, and during feverish visions, he sees interconnected images of his family, the land, animals, including a bear, and the train (51). Whereas Sam Fathers, his bear, and the wilderness are threatened by the train symbolizing encroaching modernity in Faulkner's work, Fleur has modified her cart to fit on train tracks, and she uses the tracks for her own purposes. She sells her wares to anyone in town, on the reservation, and in the borderlands of both. This mobility signals her ability to adapt and survive, a skill that she passes on to her descendants.

One of the most powerful scenes in the text illustrating Celestine's and Dot's connections to Argus *and* the reservation takes place in the first section of Part Three, which is narrated by Mary, Karl's sister and Dot's aunt. Here, the previously unseen reservation becomes visible along with Celestine's relatives who inhabit the space. Mary tells us that Celestine goes to visit Fleur, Eli, and Russell, her half-brother, multiple times a year. During the trip out of town toward the reservation, there is a pause when Mary stops at the reservation sign and tells Celestine to take over driving. Whereas Mary is unable to navigate this space and thinks of it as abandoned, Dot thinks of the place as a familiar home and becomes excited when they enter the reservation. Celestine does not drive the truck across the border alone. At the point of transition, Dot wakes up, moves up front, and "helps her mother steer." Dot and Celestine are adaptable and can cross borders. Mary calls Dot "a born traveler, meant to go places" (198). Later, when her father asks Dot about people in her life, she answers, "I go up to Uncle Russell's a lot now. Eli's teaching me to fish" (259).

Dot's relationship with Eli and Russell is evident in another scene during the ill-fated Beet Festival parade. While she watches the attendants unload Russell from the van and strap him on the veterans' float, Dot notes the treatment of Russell: "The guy is bumping him [Russell], dragging him up the side of the float, tipping him so that he sags over once." At this moment, Dot understands that Russell, who is disabled and uncommunicative after a stroke, is thirsty from the heat, and that the attendants will do nothing about it. She immediately begins screaming orders to the attendants to give Russell a drink, and they follow her orders and place him more gently. Although Russell still is riding on a float that portrays a fake battlefield, placed just so among graves and "between the bunkers and crossed rifles" as if he is a stationary part of the scenery, much like his uniform and medals on display in the town museum, Dot becomes his advocate and his voice in this town spectacle (331). Before Dot calls attention to Russell's discomfort and thirst, the white townspeople watching the parade comment that he looks "stuffed." Unlike Faulkner's Jobaker, dismissed as having no history, or Sam Fathers, doomed to the margins, Erdrich's Russell is cared for by Dot, who understands his needs and insists on his individuality and survival in the face of the unresponsive audience.

By the end of the festival, and the novel, an unusual heteroglot community has formed around Dot that is reminiscent of the delicate spider web that formed in her infant hair, a web that Celestine could not bring herself to break. Almost everyone linked to the mother and daughter is present for the crowning of Dot as the Beet Queen, including Mary and Karl, as well as Dot's godfather and uncle. Dot is the celebrated center of this group as she leaves the ground in a plane that prints her name in the sky as the official Beet Queen and seeds the clouds, which results in much needed rain over the community. While she is flying in the airplane high above her multicultural family, she says, "I feel too light, unconnected," and, upon landing, she highlights her happiness to touch the ground (336). As Dot walks toward the grandstand, she sees her mother and says, "In her eyes I see the force of her love" (337). After Celestine and Dot go home, Dot says, "I want to lean into her the way wheat leans into wind, but instead I walk upstairs and lie down in my bed alone." Dot may not lean into her mother as she says she wants to do, but Erdrich ends the novel with a deep feeling of connectedness between mother and daughter. Erdrich writes, from Dot's perspective: "Low at first, ticking faintly against the leaves, then steadier, stronger on the roof, rattling in the gutters, the wind comes. It flows through the screens, slams doors, fills the curtains like sails, floods the dark house with the smell of dirt and water, the smell of rain. I breathe it in, and I think of her lying in the next room, her covers thrown back too, eyes wide open, waiting" (338). Dot's connection to the groups around her is complete when the rain falls from the clouds that she seeded from the airplane over the reservation and Argus. Furthermore, Dot and Celestine are linked in their openness to the outside world—the windows are open and they are uncovered and vulnerable.

As Louis Owens points out, "Like almost every other Indian novelist, Louise Erdrich is a mixed-blood. . . . In her novels, Erdrich draws upon both her mother's Chippewa heritage and her experiences as the daughter of a Euramerican growing up in middle America."[34] Her own intercultural background leads Erdrich to examine and reject mythically doomed characters like Sam Fathers who cannot reconcile his mixed heritage and must retreat from the field of southern history into a dim past. Unlike Faulkner's use of Native characters as ghosts behind the white families in his southern sagas, Erdrich's fiction comes from her lived reality and focuses on resilience and adaptation. Her books explore various facets of Native experience from characters on reservations, to characters in urban environments, and characters who live on the edges of reservation and town in novels such as *The Beet Queen* and *The Master Butchers Singing Club* (2003). "Erdrich's emphasis in all her novels," Owens writes, "is upon those who survive in a difficult world" and their "refusal to acquiesce to static definitions of identity."[35] Celestine and Dot, and Dot in particular, anticipate the struggle for "balance" that becomes a recurrent theme in Erdrich's later novels, and indeed the primary focus of *The Master Butchers Singing Club.* Dot reappears in *Love Medicine* where she is pregnant with Gerry Nanapush's child, thus joining the Pillager and Nanapush families more securely. In the short story "A Wedge of Shade," published in 1989 in the *New Yorker*, Erdrich lets Dot tell the story of how she broke the news to Celestine that she married Gerry. At first, Celestine is worried about Gerry's run-ins with the law because of his activism and his trickster celebrity, but she and Gerry share family ties, and she eventually accepts him as a relative and son-in-law. Celestine and Gerry bond while repairing broken fans to try to bring some relief from the scorching heat. At the end of the story, the three of them sleep together on the floor in front of the fans with the windows open to the night air in a similar tableau to the sleeping characters' openness to the world at the end of *The Beet Queen*, only with the addition of Gerry to the picture.[36]

Toni Morrison has observed that American "culture doesn't encourage dwelling on, let alone coming to terms with, the truth about the past,"[37] and Bergland suggests the practice of "ghosting" groups whose history Americans would rather forget. Faulkner's and Erdrich's stories and novels focus on the past. Faulkner, though, portrays Native cultures as lost forever, while Erdrich emphasizes cultural continuity. Faulkner's work lionizes a character like Sam Fathers but still leaves him lost and obsolete in the contemporary moment. Erdrich's novels stress endurance and the unghosting of the victims of the vanishing American myth. Nancy Peterson calls such work "writing against amnesia," and she includes Erdrich in her study of women writers of color who "imagine interior lives for people who have been rendered invisible or silent in the frames and documents of official history. . . . They outline counterhistories to intervene in the painful amnesia that marks contemporary American culture."[38] Although Erdrich's writing is tied to place and region just as strongly as Faulkner's, she revisits and revises the theme of doomed Native characters in order to privilege cultural survival with characters such as Fleur and Eli, but also Celestine and Dot, who exist on the borders. Throughout Erdrich's continuing expansion of the mosaic of American literature, according to David Stirrup, she explores "the contact zones and deeply intertwined histories of Native and European presence on the plains," and her work "has highlighted the common paths of enmeshed communities at the same time as demonstrating their differences."[39] Rather than having a character like Sam Fathers, who is a living battleground of competing and confusing racial strains resulting in his dissolution "in the mausoleum of his defeat" (162), Erdrich allows Celestine and Dot to build and participate in enmeshed cultural communities. She brings the focus back to the reality of the survival of America's Indigenous individuals as opposed to the sustained effort by white American authors to write them into history.

NOTES

1. Vince Passaro, "Tales from a Literary Marriage," in *Conversations with Louise Erdrich and Michael Dorris*, ed. Allan Chavkin and Nancy Feyl Chavkin (Jackson: University Press of Mississippi, 1994), 163.

2. Jace Weaver, Craig S. Womack, and Robert Warrior, *American Indian Literary Nationalism* (Albuquerque: University of New Mexico Press, 2006), 53–56.

3. Susan Carr, "The Turtle Mountain/Yoknapatawpha Connection," *The Bulletin of the West Virginia Association of College English Teachers* 16 (1994): 18–25.

4. Louise Erdrich, "Where I Ought to Be: A Writer's Sense of Place," in *Louise Erdrich's "Love Medicine": A Casebook*, ed. Hertha D. Sweet Wong (New York: Oxford University Press), 50.

5. Weaver, *American Indian Literary Nationalism*, 62.

6. Louis Owens, "Erdrich and Dorris's Mixed-bloods and Multiple Narratives," in *Louise Erdrich's Love Medicine: A Casebook*, ed. Hertha D. Sweet Wong (New York: Oxford University Press, 1999), 54.

7. See Leslie Marmon Silko, "Here's an Odd Artifact for the Fairy-Tale Shelf," *Studies in American Indian Literature* 10, no. 4 (1986): 177–84.

8. Susan Castillo, "Postmodernism, Native American Literature and the Real: The Silko-Erdrich Controversy," *Massachusetts Review* 32, no. 2 (1991): n.p., accessed October 3, 2016, MasterFILE Premier.

9. Carlton Smith, *Coyote Kills John Wayne: Postmodernism and Contemporary Fictions of the Transcultural Frontier* (Hanover: University Press of New England, 2000), 108.

10. See Carol A. Kolmerten, Stephen M. Ross, and Judith Bryant Wittenberg, eds., *Unflinching Gaze: Morrison and Faulkner Re-envisioned* (Jackson: University Press of Mississippi, 1997).

11. Patricia Galloway, "The Construction of Faulkner's Indians," *Faulkner Journal* 18, nos. 1–2 (2002–03): n.p., accessed August 6, 2016, MLA International Bibliography.

12. Ibid.

13. Ibid.

14. Renée L. Bergland, *The National Uncanny: Indian Ghosts and American Subjects* (Hanover: University Press of New England, 2000), 1.

15. Ibid., 7.

16. Ibid., 16.

17. Louis Owens, *Mixedblood Messages: Literature, Film, Family, and Place* (Norman: University of Oklahoma Press, 1998), 9.

18. Ibid., 25.

19. Ibid., 82.

20. Ibid., 25.

21. Gene M. Moore, "Faulkner's Incorrect 'Indians'?" *Faulkner Journal* 18, nos. 1–2 (2002–03): n.p., accessed October 6, 2016, Humanities Full Text (H. W. Wilson).

22. Annette Trefzer, *Disturbing Indians: The Archaeology of Southern Fiction* (Tuscaloosa: University of Alabama Press, 2007), 5.

23. Ibid.

24. William Faulkner, *Requiem for a Nun* (1951; repr., New York: Vintage, 1975), 34–35.

25. William Faulkner, *Go Down, Moses,* rev. ed. (1942; repr., New York: Vintage International, 1990), 165. Hereafter cited parenthetically in the text.

26. Lewis M. Dabney, *The Indians of Yoknapatawpha* (Baton Rouge: Louisiana State University Press, 1974), 120.

27. Ibid., 147.

28. Ibid., 154.

29. Trefzer, *Disturbing Indians*, 178.

30. Smith, *Coyote Kills John Wayne*, 119.

31. Ibid., 8.

32. Louise Erdrich, *Tracks* (1988; repr., New York: Harper Perennial, 2001).

33. Louise Erdrich, *The Beet Queen* (1986, repr., New York: Harper Perennial, 2001), 50, 52. Hereafter cited parenthetically in the text.

34. Owens, "Erdrich and Dorris's Mixed-bloods and Multiple Narratives," 54.

35. Ibid., 54, 57.

36. Louise Erdrich, "A Wedge of Shade," *New Yorker,* March 6, 1989, http://www.newyorker.com/magazine/1989/03/06/a-wedge-of-shade.

37. Quoted in Nancy J. Peterson, *Against Amnesia: Contemporary Women Writers and the Crises of Historical Memory* (Philadelphia: University of Pennsylvania Press, 2001), 4.

38. Ibid., 16.

39. David Stirrup, *Louise Erdrich* (New York: Manchester University Press, 2010), 158.

Red Laughter

Humor in Faulkner's Native Narratives

JOHN WHARTON LOWE

> The history of American Indian literature reflects not only tribal cultures and the experience of imagination of its authors, but Indian-white relations as well.
>
> —A. LaVonne Brown Ruoff

> I can speak to any audience of any political persuasion because I'm funny, you know. Give me twenty minutes—and I've done it with a conservative crowd. I'll have them laughing at Jesus jokes. And so it's really a passport into other people's cultures. A temporary visa.
>
> —Sherman Alexie

William Faulkner's portraits of Native Americans in his fiction have been hotly debated, and there is no question that his lack of deep knowledge of Mississippi's Native culture forced him to invent rather generously in these tales.[1] To his credit, however, he nevertheless presented multifaceted characters who range from the appalling to the appealing, as they display a full range of human feelings and responses to the environment they inhabit. A little-explored aspect of these tales is their humor. As Faulkner seems to have known, Native cultures in Mississippi employed humor in virtually every aspect of their daily lives. That Faulkner was aware of this is apparent in several ways and is most evident in his story "A Courtship" (1942) but also in "Lo!" (1933); we can even find darker, macabre versions of this humor in the masterful "Red Leaves" (1930) and "A Justice" (1931), but I will only treat the first two stories here, as both tales are overtly comic. Ruoff's observation in the above epigraph runs both ways, as canonical US literature—and especially that of its South—has offered examples of Indian-white relations too.

This chapter outlines Faulkner's uses of humor in these tales and then relates it to actual Native American humor. How do these artificial narrative constructions coincide and conflict with actual practices of comedy in Native communities? How do Faulkner's comic conventions here make his Natives more fully human? Does the comedy work to create intimacy between the characters and the reader? Or, does it caricature and demean the figures in question? I will be particularly interested in the narrator of "A Courtship," who seems to speak in Native-inflected English, but also often code switches into standard English, particularly when quoting non-Native characters. This chapter draws on my previous work on comic Native American writers, such as Alexander Posey, Hanay Geiogamah, Gerald Vizenor, and Thomas King; essays I have written on the humor of the Old Southwest; and my extensive study of southern and ethnic humor in general.[2]

Faulkner's speculations about Native humor in many ways ran counter to popular conceptions of that culture. For much of our history, that stern, unyielding profile of the Indian that used to grace our nickels has dominated the popular imagination; Indians, it was believed, never laughed, despite early testimony to the contrary by Washington Irving. Writing about his 1832 trip to the prairies, he declared Indians to be by "no means the stoics that they are represented. . . . When the Indians are among themselves . . . there cannot be greater gossips. . . . They are great mimics and buffoons, also, and entertain themselves excessively at the expense of the whites . . . reserving all comments until they are alone. Then it is that they give full scope to criticism, satire, mimicry, and mirth."[3] Freud pointed out that humor as a social process requires a social ground, so when we factor in the highly structured tribal communities, it would be surprising if Indians were *not* comically gifted.[4] Yet even today, as Vine Deloria Jr. notes, whites have yet to understand how humor permeates virtually every area of Indian life; indeed, he asserts that nothing in Indian national affairs is possible without it and that people are frequently educated and made militant by biting, activist humor.[5]

Faulkner laces Native humor throughout his story "A Courtship," using it as a "temporary visa," as Alexie puts it, into a culture he knew was alien to most of his readers. At the same time, however, he interbraided the tale with other literary traditions. Yes, the story is about Native American culture, but it is also a variation of traditional pastoral, in that the central theme is the contest of two men—who would be shepherds in tales by Virgil or Theocritus—for the hand of a lady, a shepherdess, if you will. The language, here, however, is quite different, as it proceeds from an unnamed Native narrator, who tells us, "This is how it was in the old days, when old Issetibbeha was still the Man, and Ikkemotubbe, Issetibbeha's nephew, and David Hogganbeck, the white man who told the steamboat where to walk, courted Herman

Basket's sister."[6] Like Benjy of *The Sound and the Fury*, this narrator speaks elliptically, describing things the way an Indian raised in the wilderness might, but with complete understanding. The gap between his formulations and standard English creates comedy. History in this way is rewritten: "The People all lived in the Plantation now. Issetibbeha and General Jackson met and burned sticks and signed a paper, and now a line runs through the woods, although you could not see it. It ran straight as a bee's flight among the woods, with the Plantation on one side of it, where Issetibbeha was the Man, and America on the other side, where General Jackson was the Man" (361). The substitution of the bee's flight for the actually surveyed dividing line cleverly places the Native sense of space and landscape above that of the colonizers.

As Deloria amply demonstrates, Native humor has always deconstructed the white man's version of history through humor. There are countless jokes about Columbus. The classic one has two Indians observing the Spanish ships landing. One turns to the other and says, "There goes the neighborhood." Then there are the myriad riffs on the hapless Custer. One version claims that he showed up well dressed for Little Big Horn, wearing an Arrow shirt.[7] In the story "Lo!" Faulkner's wild reversal of Andrew Jackson's brutal history with Indians constitutes an extended version of this kind of corrective comedy. Moreover, his Natives—at least in these two stories—are concerned with pedestrian, if noble, concerns, such as love, fraternity, land, and skillful dealing. We don't see much Indian stereotyping in "Lo!" and "A Courtship." Indian stereotypes have been the proclaimed target of the contemporary Native writer Sherman Alexie (Spokane-Coeur d'Alene) whose narratives, essays, and interviews are laced with humor, and who is particularly eager to shatter the stereotype of Indian spirituality:

> It's that whole "corn pollen, four directions, Mother Earth, Father Sky" Indian thing where everybody starts speaking slowly, and their vocabulary shrinks down and they sound like Dick and Jane. . . . I just try to write about everyday Indians. . . . You get carpal tunnel syndrome from carrying the burden of your race . . . I'd like to have villains. I'd like to have goofballs.[8]

One could argue that the two protagonists of "A Courtship" are nineteenth-century goofballs, whose courtship of the same woman balloons into a series of comic (and bicultural) competitions. But Faulkner lards his texts with all kinds of humorous representations. The device of comic personification is used to describe Hogganbeck's steamboat: "[Log-in-the-Creek] would stand on the landing to watch the upstairs and the smokestack moving among the trees and hear the puffing of the

184 JOHN WHARTON LOWE

smokestack and its feet walking fast in the water too when it was not cry-
ing" (366). Here, as in the example of the man who makes the steamboat
"walk," the Native narrator employs an "innocent" Native perspective
to describe a machine that evokes wonder among the people, yet his
description is both creative and ironic, and forces the non-Native reader
to think in a new way. Jokes about new, strange, and "unnatural" modes
of travel, Christie Davies tells us, were quite common in the nineteenth
century, and those who master the new technology often like to laugh at
those who haven't.[9] This syndrome continued into the twentieth century.
Zora Neale Hurston, for example, employs this motif in *Jonah's Gourd
Vine* when onlookers laugh at the country bumpkin John Pearson's
amazement before the first locomotive he's seen.

The music of the steamboat's whistle is not the only melody. The lazy
Log-in-the-Creek, a fixture on the heroine's porch, plays a harmonica,
and David performs on his fiddle. It's almost as though we have a set of
dueling musical motifs as well, creating a set of competing dialogics. Of
course, the major kind of oral combat lies in the comic verbal dueling of
the men, whose jibes are a mask for the "bromance" beneath the surface.

Our narrator has a sly wit:

> Then Ikkemotubbe and David Hogganbeck saw Herman Basket's sister. As
> who did not, sooner or later, young men and old men too, bachelors and wid-
> owers too, and some who were not even widowers yet, who for more than one
> reason within the hut had no business looking anywhere else, though who is to
> say what age a man must reach or just how unfortunate he must have been in
> his youthful compliance, when he shall no longer look at the Herman Basket's
> sisters of this world and chew his bitter thumbs too, aihee. Because she walked
> in beauty. Or she sat in it, that is, because she did not walk at all unless she
> had to. (362)

Here the traditional roving eye receives a Native description, capped
off by the image of the "bitter thumbs"—a sexual pun—and a Native
punctuation mark "aihee," which has also been stereotypically ascribed
to Asian American speech.

The narrator also creates comedy by quoting (without knowing it?)
Lord Byron: "She walked in beauty," but immediately undercuts it by
noting her laziness. Here Faulknerians have to be reminded of the hyp-
notic but equally immobile Eula Varner of *The Hamlet*. Laziness, however, was always considered one of the hallmarks of Native peoples.[10]
The comic duel of Hogganbeck and Ikkemotubbe takes many forms:
David out-dances everyone and easily wins eating contests. They also
compete for time with the lady: Hogganbeck and Ikkemotubbe take care

Humor in Faulkner's Native Narratives   185

not to let the other have time alone with her, so they fall into the habit of constant companionship, even sleeping together in the Indian's bed, and, alternately, in Hogganbeck's bed in the steamboat. The story seems to be more interested in the love the men have for each other than in their desire to wed the heroine. We see this from the outset. As their friendship grows, Ikkemotubbe tells Hogganbeck they can't duel with knives because "I do not wish you to be hurt good. . . . On the day of the wedding, I wish you to be present . . . not lying wrapped in a blanket on a platform in the woods, waiting to enter the earth" (370). After a Rabelaisian eating contest concludes, the narrator tells us, "My father said how they loved David Hogganbeck at that moment as they loved Ikkemotubbe. . . . [He] stood before David Hogganbeck with the smile on his face and his right hand flat on David Hogganbeck's chest, because there were men in those days" (373). The contest ultimately devolves into a footrace to a cave one hundred and thirty miles away.[11] The men, naked and greased, are to enter the cave and fire a pistol, and because the cavity is notorious for cave-ins, this risks death. Ikkemotubbe reaches the cave first and fires. The roof collapses but is held up by Hogganbeck, who has just entered. "Hurry," the latter cries, "'Quickly thyself, before it crushes thee. Crawl back.' . . . Ikkemotubbe did, and he remembered David Hogganbeck's buttocks and legs pink in the sunrise and the slab of rock which supported the fallen roof pink in the sunrise too across David Hogganbeck's back" (377). Finding a pole, the Indian props up the roof and tells Hogganbeck, "Quickly, brother. . . . The weight is off thee," and when David can't move, Ikkemotubbe "reached one hand and grasped David Hogganbeck by the meat and jerked him backward out of the hole. . . . [T]he pole . . . snapped and flung him face-down too across David Hogganbeck like two flung sticks" (377–78). Noel Polk used to chortle in conversation with me about this "meat" being pulled and found this passage one of the most comic in what he called "Faulkner's Bawdy."

The white man, injured, vomits blood for two days, causing his "brother" to return home to get a horse to bear his friend back. There they find Herman Basket's sister has wed Log-in-the-Creek. This figure, as noted, is a stereotype of the supposedly "lazy" Indian, as is his lovely but mostly immobile inamorata. However, his name, as was often the case in Native communities, has a special humorous resonance within the group, as names often followed roles played or not played, and could be comic and/or corrective. In other words, he *earned* this name and would have to work to get another. As illustration, in James Welch's Blackfeet novel *Fools Crow*, the main character, White Man's Dog, has a comic name, but it is changed to Fools Crow after his acts of heroism.[12] Faulkner may well, however, see a Freudian joke in Log-in-the-Creek,

186 JOHN WHARTON LOWE

since it is this character, rather than the two protagonists, who "rises" to the occasion in their absence and marries their joint lady love. Faulkner seems to be embroidering, too, on the comic expression "Absence makes the heart grow fonder"—for someone who isn't absent.

This comic tale of dueling courtiers who both lose the girl at the end echoes the basic plot of Zora Neale Hurston and Langston Hughes's 1930 play *Mule Bone*, which similarly employs dialect, folk musicians, and a languorous and ultimately duplicitous heroine. At the play's end, rejecting the demands of their common lady love, the two pals head off together, just as Faulkner's "bromance" partners do here after they discover Herman Basket's sister's marriage.[13] First, however, they trade aphorisms from their respective cultures. Ikkemotubbe recites, "There was a wise man of ours who said once how a woman's fancy is like a butterfly which, hovering from flower to flower, pauses at the last as like as not where a horse has stood"—meaning, of course, where the horse pissed, a reference to Log-in-the-Creek. To this, David replies, "There was a wise man of ours named Solomon who often said something of that nature too. . . . Perhaps there is just one wisdom for all men, no matter who speaks it," to which Ikkemotubbe responds, "Aihee. At least, for all men one same heart-break," as he pulls the crying-rope of the steamboat (380), creating a comic trio of lamentation.

"Lo!" is another story altogether, set as it is in the nation's capital and featuring a comically rendered avatar of Andrew Jackson.[14] The whole story is built on comic inversion, in that Jackson, notorious in actual history for killing and relocating Indians, here is helpless before the persistence of the Native Americans who have invaded the White House, replete with their gnawed bones, live gamecocks, and outlandish combinations of Western and Native dress. Indeed, he doesn't dare confront them directly, but instead gazes at them surreptitiously in a mirror held to a cracked door. Like Jackson, readers listen in on the Natives' conversation: "You don't understand white people. They are like children: you have to handle them careful because you never know what they are going to do next. So if it's the rule for guests to squat all night long in the cold outside this man's door, we'll just have to do it." The speaker also comments on the superiority of this hallway to the frigid tents the government has provided outside. A reply: "You said it. What a climate. What a country. I wouldn't have this town if they gave it to me" (383).

This entire setup revolves around what Freud claimed is the basic element of humor: the forced juxtaposition of opposed elements. It also employs heavy irony because the president, ostensibly all powerful, has been made a prisoner within his own house. Supposedly a fearless Indian fighter, here Jackson tiptoes in his bare feet to escape his guests.

Kimberly Blaeser observes that Native Americans have created various methods for dealing with the "representations and misrepresentations of history." One of these "methods" has certainly been "literary laughter . . . those which, by their humor, work to disarm history, to expose the hidden agendas of historiography and, thereby, remove it from the grasp of the political panderers and return it to the realm of story."[15] Here again, Faulkner seems to be paralleling the literary strategies of Native narrators.

However, in "Lo!" Faulkner shifts gears from the methods he employed in "A Courtship." Rather than employing "Injin' pidgin," the Native visitors at the White House, when speaking among themselves, sound like world-weary tourists in a benighted realm. Indeed, seemingly creating a variation on the dictum "When in Rome, do as the Romans do," one remarks "as long as we are here, we'll have to try to act like these people believe that Indians ought to act. Because you never know until afterward just what you have done to insult or scare them. Like this having to talk white talk all the time" (383). Obviously, their linguistic performance for whites contrasts with the native language they employ among themselves and draws our attention to their ability to code switch, that is, to go back and forth between modes of utterance, a device writers have always used to create comedy. Indeed, the dialect of Faulkner's Natives, like the other varieties from the mouths of his poor whites and African American characters, is often a cloak for profound observations, which are made more palatable for readers. The rustic satirist is less inclined to incur the immediate ire of urbane readers and is often rich, humorous, laden with metaphor, and therefore tactile and appealing.[16] Here Faulkner again gives the apparent weaker characters the upper hand and reverses the usual stereotyped comments that whites usually make about other groups. More importantly, however, this passage underlines the idea of *performing* Indianness, seemingly a necessary ploy in order to get what they want. There are many similarities between the broad humor in Faulkner's Indian tales and those of the Old Southwest humor tradition. We might remember the crafty Simon Suggs's dictum, "It is best to be shifty in a new country." Washington DC is indeed a "new country" for the Natives of "Lo!" and they are appropriately—and effectively—"shifty" in their dealings with the white power brokers. This in many ways also means wearing a comic mask, something that African Americans learned to do early on. As the black poet Paul Lawrence Dunbar memorably intoned, "We wear the mask that grins and lies," a metaphor pointing to the ways in which apparent comic demeanor can cover up darker realities.[17] As Christie Davies notes, "Jokers may deliberately and cleverly misuse language and exploit error. . . . A person who makes a statement with an ambiguous or contradictory meaning may be regarded by his or her listeners as a silly fool who has made a risible mistake or as a subtle wit who has produced a clever joke. . . . In many cases they may well be unsure as to whether the speaker is joking or not. . . . [T]he pretense of error or stupidity can be used as a skillful means of manipulating other people. . . . To succeed in such a game requires a great deal of shrewd understanding and/or a gift for language. Only the clever can play the fool."[18] In Faulkner's tale, the fool seems to be President Jackson. Desperate to get away from his unwelcome guests, he has to sneak down a back staircase with an aide, both carrying their boots in their hands to avoid making a noise.

In many ways too, "Lo!" engages in the humor of the city mouse and the country mouse, but with the country mouse—the Indian—unexpectedly coming out ahead. As Davies notes, "In ethnic jokes about confrontations between country bumpkins and city slickers, it is noticeable that when those who are normally the butts of jokes about stupidity succeed in winning an argument, it is usually a victory of verbal trickery over logic where the 'stupid' one uses language skills to evade the point," and this is exactly what we see in "Lo!"[19]

The Indians, despite the disorientations of Washington, are doing quite well, it seems, as the aforementioned booty they get from the government suggests; moreover, they carry on their traditions, despite strictures. A party of them draw up to the White House on horseback with the bodies of six deer strapped to their steeds, despite Jackson's "strict" orders they not be permitted guns. Like the men in the hallway, the hunters wear beaver hats, frock coats, but clad their legs only in long johns. They are part in, part out of civilization, and their very bodies thus echo the dominant theme of the story, which is shifting boundaries.

The second part of the story is set at the secretary's home, where the president and his aide have fled for counsel. As Gene Moore notes (but without observing the humor of the reversal), rather than depict the traumatic removal of the Indians from their lands, Faulkner shows them dispossessing the president from his home.[20] "Give us some breakfast," the president says to the secretary. "We don't dare go home" (386). Told about the Indians' raid on a farm where they accidentally set fire to a barn, burn a cow, and frighten off a slave, and the owner's demand that all of this be paid for in gold, the president quips, "I suppose the Negro and the cow took them to be ghosts of Hessian soldiers," while a messenger remarks, "I wonder if they thought the cow was a deer" (387).

Comically, Jackson's chief complaint is about the Indians not wearing pants, and we remember that when they invade his bedroom, he isn't wearing them either. He cries to the secretary,

Humor in Faulkner's Native Narratives

Aren't they subject to your Department? I'm just the President. Confound it, it's got to where my wife no longer dares leave her bedroom, let alone receive lady guests. How am I to explain to the French Ambassador, for instance, why his wife no longer dares call upon my wife because the corridors and the very entrance to the House are blocked by half-naked Chickasaw Indians asleep on the floor or gnawing at half-raw ribs of meat?" (388)

Faulkner might have been inspired in his creation of this comic "home invasion" by knowledge of Jackson's well-known penchant for allowing common citizens to tour the white house—here, the intruding Indians take that into an absurd and comic dimension. Then, too, the "underwear" motif creates both a sexual joke, but one with an underlying fear of Native sexuality.

As he often does in his short stories, Faulkner begins things in *media res*, and we remain mystified as to the Indians' motives for some time. The reader might be forgiven for saying "Thank God!" ten pages into the story when what's happening is finally explained by the dressing-gown-clad secretary, who speaks in "cockatoo-crested outrage": "This man, Weddel, Vidal—whatever his name is—he and his family or clan or whatever they are—claim to own the entire part of Mississippi which lies on the west side of this river in question. Oh, the grant is in order: that French father of his from New Orleans saw to that. . . . [F]acing his home or plantation is the only ford in about three hundred miles" (390–91).

It seems that Weddel sold the land adjacent to a white man, who promptly fenced it in and started charging a toll to cross. The Indians bet on a horse race between the toll-taker and the chief's nephew, and when they lose, that night the white man is killed. "'Let us say, died,' the Secretary said primly, 'since it is so phrased in the agent's report. Though he did add in a private communication that the white man's disease seemed to be a split skull. But that is neither here nor there.' 'No,' the President said. 'It's up yonder at the house'" (393). In these exchanges, Faulkner balances the Indians' humor with the comic exchanges and spontaneous witticisms of the beleaguered officials, humor that brings them down from the lofty perches of formal history into the maelstrom of conflicted actual life. Underlying the comedy, however, is the long and tragic history of Indian wars, broken treaties, and the hypocrisy of white's claims of "civilization" and rights to Western lands. Faulkner seems to take on the Native position in this tale and creates a reversal whereby these trickster Indians reveal white chicanery and triumph over it. Such moves, David L. Moore posits, have characterized Native humor for centuries. Indeed, it is "an originary move of Indian humor that reduces the white man from the tragic heroic to the comic human level. He is no longer lord of the realm. His delusion of overcoming and civilizing the wilderness is just that: a delusion."[21]

Ostensibly, the Indians have come to Washington to have the president absolve the nephew of murder, but they obviously have hidden objectives regarding their land rights. The secretary, however, only sees the trivial pretext: "Why should they deny themselves this holiday at the expense of the government? Why should they miss, at the mere price of a fifteen-hundred-mile journey . . . in the dead of winter, the privilege and pleasure of spending a few weeks or months in new beavers and broadcloth coats and under drawers in the home of the beneficent White Father?" (394). Flustered and upset, the president and the secretary hold a mock trial at the latter's home, using dummy papers as, Faulkner tells us, "a clumsy deception." We can read this comic charade as a commentary on the chicanery employed by the federal government for centuries in its dealings with Natives. Weddel leads his nephew in by the hand "like an uncle conducting for the first time a youthful provincial kinsman into a metropolitan museum of wax figures," a sharp jab at the apparently shaken, mystified, and helpless white men. Despite Weddel's feminine appearance and ridiculous garb, the narrator tells us that "there lurked something else: something willful, shrewd, un-predictable and despotic" (395). The shrewdness appears in his mocking pronouncement: "Who performed this murder? . . . That is what we made this long winter's journey to discover. If he did, if this white man really did not fall from that swift horse of his perhaps and strike his head upon a sharp stone, then this nephew of mine should be punished. We do not think that it is right to slay white men like a confounded Cherokee or Creek" (395–96). This self-reflexive humor also reminds the auditors and the readers that all Indians are not alike. As the president signs phony documents that proclaim the nephew's innocence, he asks, "Weddel or Vidal?" "Again the pleasant, inflectionless voice came: 'Weddel or Vidal. What does it matter by what name the White Chief calls us? We are but Indians: remembered yesterday and forgotten tomorrow'" (396). Once again, Faulkner employs a deceptive and subversive self-reflexive humor—always a key element in Native culture—that is more of a commentary on the white men and their ignorance, but also perhaps, a send-up of the myth of the vanishing Indian, which the delegation to Washington mocks.

Weddel demands that the sentence be issued in the House of Representatives, which he calls "the council house beneath the golden eagle" (398). Again, the desperate president and secretary stage a mock trial in the chamber, with the president reading sonnets by Petrarch in a

Humor in Faulkner's Native Narratives 191

solemn tone in Latin. He whispers to the Secretary, "Let us hope that I remember enough law Latin to keep it from sounding like either English or Chickasaw" (399).

The story concludes about nine months later when the president receives a letter from Weddel, stating that another white man bought the ford and was challenged to bet his new concession in a swimming race with the nephew: "Unfortunately our white man failed to emerge from the river until after he was dead" (401). Hysterical at the thought of a second "invasion," Jackson dictates another phony document to the secretary, dispatching it immediately to the Indians to stop their planned trip, deeding them the ford, as long as they don't cross over it into the United States again.

The all-important ford is a signifier for the method of narration as well, as Faulkner ferries the reader back and forth between the harried president and secretary and their Indian guests. I would offer too that the humor, which is common to both groups, also operates like the ferry, crossing boundaries, creating intimacy, and helping both parties get through difficult negotiations, while keeping readers entertained, intrigued, and laughing. As Gene Moore speculates, the story of the ferry is "probably derived from the squiggle for ownership of Colbert's Ferry on the Tennessee River."[22] And indeed, as Elmo Howell points out, the trip to Washington is likely based on the 1831 expedition there of the French/Choctaw Greenwood LeFlore, whose ornate cupola-topped mansion, Patricia Galloway suggests, inspired the gothic steamboat of "A Courtship."[23]

This, too: the Indians in "Lo!" like many tricksters before them, are on the road. Also like tricksters, they are boundary crossers, having come over the line that supposedly fixes them in place and keeps them from crossing the domestic boundary of the president's home and indeed, bedroom. As Lewis Hyde points out, a trickster's role is to cross every boundary and confuse the distinction the line was designed to make: "Trickster is the mythic embodiment of ambiguity and ambivalence, doubleness and duplicity, contradiction and paradox."[24] Times of acculturation like the one featured in this tale create innumerable comic contrasts, as boundaries shift and customs are transformed. The dismay of the white officials in this story often stems from their horror at boundaries being transgressed. Anthropologist Mahadev Apte notes that "the primary objectives of groups in social dynamics may simply be the creation or maintenance of an ethnic boundary, real or imagined. Their focus may be on the ethnic *boundary* that defines the group, because as Fredrik Barth has suggested, 'the cultural features that signal the boundary may change, and the cultural characteristics of the members likewise be transformed.'"[25] Clearly, both the Natives and the Washington officials are on either side of a shifting cultural boundary, which has always been a source, simultaneously, of anxiety and its antidote, humor.

Indeed, skating on this boundary, the trickster Indians of "Lo!" evince a liberating energy, which David Moore, following the lead of Gerald Vizenor, claims "frees native narratives to showcase survivance against American mainstream narratives of manifest destiny, projected tragedy, and stereotypical fatalism, 'the end of the trail.'"[26] And, what has been more representative of all these historical shibboleths than the plight of Native Americans under Jackson's rule?

Moreover, the skillful manipulation of not only the president but also the secretary in charge of Indian Affairs has strong affinity with modern jokes Native Americans tell about the Bureau of Indian Affairs, notorious for its mismanagement and insensitivity, and a longstanding butt of Native jokes. An example: Injun Joe went to the Public Health Service with a headache. The white doctor decided to cut Joe's brain out to take a look at it. When a messenger ran in with news that Joe's house was on fire, Joe headed for the door. "Wait, Joe," cried the doctor, "you forgot your brain!" "That's OK, Doc," said Joe. "After I put the fire out, I'm going to work for the BIA."[27] Jokes like this one enabled Native Americans to deal with infuriating and dangerous issues, especially relations with whites. Keith Basso's *Portraits of the Whiteman* details the myriad and intricate Indian jokes told at the expense of whites, including some choice cartoons by Native artists that offer contemporary examples of the kind of humor Faulkner exploits in his Native tales.

Although Faulkner perhaps didn't know it, there was a venerable tradition of comic criticism of national leaders among Native Americans. In the late nineteenth and early twentieth centuries, Creek journalist Alexander Posey used his newspaper, *The Eufaula Journal*, to needle the "Big Man at Washington" or more directly "President Roosterfeather," a devilish twist on Roosevelt. He employs a Native sage, Fus Fixico, whose letters reflect his dialogues with his sidekick, Hotgun. Fus speaks nonstandard English, mixing tenses and negatives freely, as in "I didn't had not time to write. My cotton was bust open. . . . I had to pick it out like everything."[28] This form of dialect writing is also employed by Faulkner. The use of dialect illustrates Mary Douglas's formulation of a joke as a play upon form, bringing disparate elements into configuration, in that "one accepted pattern is challenged by the appearance of another which in some way was hidden in the first" and "a successful subversion of one form by another completes or ends the joke for it changes the balance of power,"[29] exactly what Faulkner attempts to portray in "Lo!" Here's an example of how Posey pulls this off: "Well, so Big Man at Washington . . . say this time the

Injin was had to change his name just like if the marshal was had a writ for him. So, if the Injin's name is Wolf Warrior he was had to call himself John Smith or maybe so Bill Jones. . . . [B]ig man say Injin name like Sitting Bull or Tecumseh was hard to remember and don't sound civilized like General Cussed Her or old Gran Pa Harry's Son."[30] We recall here how the white men in "Lo!" can't handle Indian names either. Posey's comic observations work on two levels. First, the opposition of Sitting Bull and Tecumseh to General George Armstrong Custer and General William Henry Harrison is a reminder of both Indian wars, the Battle of Tippecanoe in 1811 and the Lakota Sioux victory at the Battle of Little Big Horn in 1874. Second, the phonetic rendering of the white officers' names into comic significations explodes their sainted images. Fus Fixico often talks to Hotgun about Indian delegations to Washington too: "Well, reckon so them Injin delegates was all in Washington looking at lots a things to talk 'bout and was drink lots good whiskey instead old sour sofky like at home. One Snake Injin says he was stay at Washington put near six months maybe and had good times."[31] Vine Deloria points to the fact that Native humor like that isn't always pacifying: "Often people are awakened and brought to a militant edge through funny remarks."[32]

It is likely as well that Faulkner was creating his Indian tricksters out of his knowledge of sharpsters depicted in Old Southwest humor, such as Sut Lovingood and Simon Suggs, whose antics he had echoed in many of his own stories and novels, especially in *The Hamlet*. Still, his transposition of Southwest humor to Native American characters here comes close to the way trickster functions in Native oral narratives. Apte claims that the trickster's activities, which flout social norms, appeal to individuals' suppressed desires and provide vicarious pleasure. Tricksters "appear to be disorderly, chaotic personalities . . . [and] manifest extremely inappropriate and socially deviant behaviors and actions. Their acts . . . [make] tricksters misfits in human societies because of their refusal to abide by the established sociocultural norms."[33] This is exactly the way the Indians seem to Jackson and his aides in "Lo!" a story consonant with the Native American tradition of the trickster, usually a small animal like a rabbit, a coyote, or a raven, that is able to outsmart larger animals and take on, quite often, human form. This protean nature seemingly is shared by Weddel, who is half French and obviously much more aware of the white man and his ways than the president suspects. He tricks the federal government into hosting him and his minions, giving them food and new clothes, and absolving them of not one, but two murders of white men that they have bamboozled by the pretended sale of the invaluable ford. Paula Gunn Allen remarks that the trickster Coyote is a metaphor for "continuance": [He] "survives and a large part of his bag of survival tricks is his irreverence. Because of this irreverence for everything—sex, family bonding, sacred things, even life itself—Coyote survives. . . . [H]e has . . . such great creative prowess."[34]

Faulkner abundantly demonstrates that Native Americans have what Apte claims is a dominant cultural value: "People in all walks of life are either encouraged to acquire a sense of humor or are praised for having it. . . . Societal consensus in America seems to be that a personality with a sense of humor is more sociable, easier to get along and to work with, innovative, and capable of facing adversities and overcoming them, and is therefore more desirable than one without."[35] Faulkner would seem to agree with this assessment. He once stated, "We have one priceless universal trait, we Americans. That trait is our humor. What a pity it is that it is not more prevalent in our art. This characteristic alone, being national and indigenous, could, by concentrating our emotional forces inward upon themselves, do for us what England's insularity did for English art during the reign of Elizabeth. One trouble with us American artists is that we take our art and ourselves too seriously. And perhaps seeing ourselves in the eyes of our fellow artists will enable those who have strayed to establish anew a sound contact with the fountainhead of our American life."[36] Faulkner's characters in these Indian stories are only a few of his shifty operators, who never cease to amuse. Far from being stoic—and therefore silent—these Natives are conniving, crafty, and in "Lo!" quite vocal about the trickster maneuvers they are playing in Washington. As Faulkner understood, Trickster's ways increasingly fit in with our American image of ourselves, whether we are Native or non-Native: we may, as a people, be hedonistic, secular, or existential, but we are always evolving, changing, and maybe, like Coyote in his old age, ready to put down roots. Trickster's laughter brings us together, relaxes tensions, and clears the ground for compromise and understanding. So maybe Faulkner understood his Native American characters better than we thought. He would no doubt agree with Abenaki writer Joseph Bruchac's assertion that a deflating humor and a trickster approach to storytelling can often make a point better than straightforward realism.[37]

As I suggested earlier, we find elements of these comic conventions today in the work of contemporary Native writers like Vizenor, Welch, Geigomah, and Erdrich.[38] In his foreword to LeAnne Howe's recent *Chocktalking and Other Realities*, Dean Rader remarks that "moments of misunderstanding, of painful racial ignorance, elicit not anger, not reproach, but humor. . . . She trades easy antagonism for a kind of wry bemusement. . . . The voice does not cry or scream. It laughs, or chuckles, or sighs. Much of the humor [in Howe's] pieces arises out of the gaps between what people imagine about Indians, what popular culture tells them Indians are, and what they do when confronted with LeAnne."[39] Rader concludes by observing that Howe's opting for comedy is appropriate, since "Tragedy has a partial basis in fear, while comedy is partially based on hope. I don't know that laughter is always the best medicine; it can be a brutal weapon. But I do think that humor highlights commonalities rather than spotlights transgressions" (vi). He closes by reminding us of N. Scott Momaday's observation that "humor is really where the language lives. . . . It's very close to the center and very important" (vii). Clearly, Faulkner and Howe are on the same frequency here, whether or not the Mississippi maestro knew anything at all about Native humor.

A final note: Faulkner three times in his career assembled existing short stories he had written, added one or two more, and proclaimed them to be novels. Two of them, *The Unvanquished* and *Go Down, Moses*, have a curious structure; both begin in comedy and end in tragedy. The former introduces us to the tragic days of the Civil War with an incongruously comic take, "Ambuscade," but later builds to the decline and fall (and death) of first Granny and then her son-in-law, John Sartoris. *Go Down, Moses* similarly creates guffaws out of the story of a runaway slave in "Was," but then moves to increasingly dark narratives that end with an execution and mourning. We know that "Red Leaves," Faulkner's most tragic Native tale, was written in 1930, while the comic "A Courtship" was composed more than a decade later, in 1942. It is possible that Faulkner was once again contemplating a series of stories he could meld into a novel, and that "A Courtship" would begin a linkage of existing tales and ones perhaps he intended to write, a sequence that would end tragically, as in the other two novels mentioned. In all three sets of stories, however, the creation of both comically and tragically linked narratives is suggestive of Faulkner's lifelong determination to examine issues and problems from multiple perspectives and his conviction that comic takes could sometimes be as illuminating as more somber ones. Native Americans have always employed humor in a similar way, understanding that tales can be instructive, and valuable, when comic hooks capture—and captivate—a listening audience.

NOTES

The first epigraph is found in A. LaVonne Brown Ruoff, *American Indian Literatures* (New York: Modern Language Association of America, 1990), 2.

The second epigraph is found in Sherman Alexie, interview by Joshua B. Nelson, "Humor Is My Calling Card: A Conversation with Sherman Alexie," *World Literature Today*, July 2010, www.worldliteraturetoday.org/humor-my-green-card-conversation-sherman -alexie-joshua-b-nelson.

1. See, for instance, Annette Trefzer, *Disturbing Indians: The Archeology of Southern Fiction* (Tuscaloosa: University of Alabama Press, 2007); Melanie Benson Taylor, *Reconstructing the Native South: American Indian Literature and the Lost Cause* (Athens: University of Georgia Press, 2011); and Robert Dale Parker, "Red Slippers and Cottonmouth Moccasins: White Anxieties in Faulkner's Indian Stories." *Faulkner Journal* 18, nos. 1–2 (2002–2003): 81–99.

2. John Lowe, "Coyote's Jokebook: Humor in Native American Literature and Culture," *Dictionary of Native American Literature*, ed. Andrew Wiget (New York: Garland, 1994), 193–205; John Lowe, "Theories of Ethnic Humor: How to Enter, Laughing," *American Quarterly* 38 (1986): 439–60.

3. Washington Irving cited in Keith Basso, *Portraits of the White Man: Linguistic Play and Cultural Symbols among the Western Apache* (New York: Cambridge University Press, 1979), x.

4. Sigmund Freud, *Jokes and Their Relation to the Unconscious*, trans. James Strachey (1905; repr., New York: Norton, 1963), 179.

5. Vine Deloria Jr., *Custer Died for Your Sins: An Indian Manifesto* (London and New York: Macmillan, 1969), 147.

6. William Faulkner, "A Courtship," in *Collected Stories of William Faulkner* (1950; repr., New York: Vintage International, 1995), 361. Hereafter cited parenthetically.

7. Deloria, *Custer Died for Your Sins*, 148–49.

8. Sherman Alexie, in David L. Moore, *That Dream Shall Have a Name: Native Americans Rewriting America* (Lincoln: University of Nebraska Press, 2013), 305. Moore's chapter "The Last Laugh: Humor and Humanity in Native American Pluralism" offers a rich meditation on Native comic forms and purposes. See also Eva Gruber, *Humor in Contemporary Native North American Literature: Reimagining Nativeness* (Rochester, NY: Camden House, 2008).

9. Christie Davies, *Ethnic Humor around the World: A Comparative Analysis* (Bloomington: Indiana University Press, 1990), 24.

10. See Christie Davies's presentation of the frequent use in ethnic jokes of people as either stupid or canny/stingy. In the United States, southerners, Poles, and African Americans have often been portrayed as stupid in jokes, while Jews, Scots, and New England Yankees are pictured as canny/stingy. And stupidity is often coupled with the ascription of laziness, as in William Byrd's famous assessment of early North Carolinians: "Surely there is no place in the World where the Inhabitants live with less Labor than in N Carolina. . . . The Men, for their Parts, just like the Indians, impose all the Work upon the poor Women . . . 'tis an Aversion to Labor that makes People file off to N Carolina, where Plenty and a Warm Sun confirm them in their Disposition to Laziness for their whole Lives." See William Byrd, II, "From *The History of the Dividing Line*," in *Southern Writing, 1585–1920*, ed. Richard Beale Davis, C. Hugh Holman, and Louis D. Rubin Jr. (New York: Odyssey, 1970), 99.

11. Faulkner could be criticized for having his characters run such a long race to the cave, but Don Doyle tells us that Chickasaws were remarkable "for being able to run incredible distances of one and two hundred miles through the forest." See Don Doyle, *Faulkner's County: The Historical Roots of Yoknapatawpha* (Chapel Hill: University of North Carolina Press, 2001), 39.

12. James Welch, *Fools Crow* (New York: Viking, 1986).

13. Langston Hughes and Zora Neale Hurston, *Mule Bone: A Comedy of Negro Life* (New York: HarperCollins, 1991).

14. William Faulkner, "Lo!" in Faulkner, *Collected Stories of William Faulkner* (381–403), 383. Hereafter cited parenthetically.

Humor in Faulkner's Native Narratives

15. Kimberly Blaeser, "The New 'Frontier' of Native American Literature: Disarming History with Tribal Humor," in *Native American Perspectives on Literature and History*, ed. Alan R. Velie (Norman: University of Oklahoma Press, 1994), 38–39.

16. This ingenious use of dialect was quite widespread among ethnic Americans who were struggling with stereotypes in the nineteenth century, but the practice has extended into our own era. For a full discussion of the creative use of dialect by ethnic citizens, see Gavin Jones, *Strange Talk: The Politics of Dialect Literature in Gilded Age America* (Berkeley: University of California Press, 1999).

17. Paul Laurence Dunbar, "We Wear the Mask," in *The Collected Poems of Paul Laurence Dunbar*, ed. Joanne M. Braxton (Charlottesville: University Press of Virginia, 1993), 71.

18. Davies, *Ethnic Humor Around the World*, 147.

19. Ibid., 19.

20. Gene Moore, "Chronological Problems in Faulkner's 'Wilderness,'" *Faulkner Journal* 18, nos. 1–2 (2002–2003): 65.

21. David L. Moore, *That Dream Shall Have a Name*, 323.

22. Gene Moore, "Chronological Problems in Faulkner's 'Wilderness,'" 62.

23. Elmo Howell, "President Jackson and William Faulkner's Choctaws," *Chronicles of Oklahoma* 45, no. 4 (1967): 252–58; see also Patricia Galloway, "The Construction of Faulkner's Indians," *Faulkner Journal* 18, nos. 1–2 (2002–2003): 24.

24. Lewis Hyde, *Trickster Makes This World: Mischief, Myth, and Art* (New York: North Point, 1998), 7. The foundational study of the trickster figures is Paul Radin, The *Trickster: A Study in American Indian Mythology* (New York: Schocken Books, 1972).

25. Mahadev Apte, *Humor and Laughter: An Anthropological Approach* (Ithaca, NY: Cornell University Press, 1985), 113.

26. David L. Moore, *That Dream Shall Have a Name*, 314.

27. Deloria, *Custer Died for Your Sins*, 161.

28. Alexander Posey, *The Fus Fixico Letters*, ed. Daniel F. Littlefield and Carol A. Petty Hunter (Lincoln: University of Nebraska Press, 1993), 55.

29. Mary Douglas, "The Social Control of Cognition: Some Factors in Joke Perception," *Man* 3, no. 3 (1968), 361–76.

30. Posey, *The Fus Fixico Letters*, 87.

31. Ibid., 60.

32. Deloria, *Custer Died for Your Sins*, 147.

33. Apte, *Humor and Laughter*, 230.

34. Paula Gunn Allen, *The Sacred Hoop: Recovering the Feminine in American Indian Traditions* (Boston, MA: Beacon, 1986), 158.

35. Mahadev Apte, "Ethnic Humor Versus 'A Sense of Humor,'" *American Behavioral Scientist* 30, no. 3 (1987), 29.

36. William Faulkner, foreword to *Sherwood Anderson and Other Famous Creoles*, in *Essays, Speeches, and Public Letters by William Faulkner*, ed. James B. Meriwether (London: Chatto and Windus, 1967), n.p.

37. Meredith Ricker, "A *MELUS* Interview: Joseph Bruchac," *MELUS* 21.3 (1996): 175.

38. For examinations of contemporary Native American literature including the writers mentioned, see David L. Moore, *That Dream Shall Have a Name*, and Joseph L. Coulombe, Reading Native American Literature (New York: Routledge, 2011).

39. Dean Rader, foreword to *Chocktalking on Other Realities*, by LeAnne Howe (San Francisco: Aunt Lute Books, 2013), i–vii. Hereafter cited parenthetically.

Contributors

Eric Gary Anderson is associate professor of English at George Mason University, where he coordinates the Native American and Indigenous studies minor and was the recipient of a University Teaching Excellence award in 2014. Author of *American Indian Literature and the Southwest: Contexts and Dispositions* (1999) and essays in such distinguished scholarly journals as *PMLA*, *American Literary History*, *American Literature*, and *ESQ*, he has also coedited *Undead Souths: The Gothic and Beyond in Southern Literature and Culture* (2015) and "Southern Roots and Routes: Origins, Migrations, Transformations," a special issue of *Mississippi Quarterly*.

Melanie R. Anderson is an assistant professor of English at Glenville State College (West Virginia). She is the author of *Spectrality in the Novels of Toni Morrison* (2013) and coeditor of the collections *The Ghostly and the Ghosted in Literature and Film: Spectral Identities* (2013) and *Shirley Jackson, Influences and Confluences* (2016).

Jodi A. Byrd is a citizen of the Chickasaw Nation and associate professor of English and gender and women's studies at the University of Illinois at Urbana–Champaign, where she is also a faculty affiliate in the National Center for Supercomputing Applications. She is the author of *The Transit of Empire: Indigenous Critiques of Colonialism* (2011). Her articles have appeared in *American Indian Quarterly*, *Cultural Studies Review*, *Interventions*, *J19*, *College Literatures*, *Settler Colonial Studies*, and *American Quarterly*. Her current project, "Indigenomicon: American Indians, Videogames, and Structures of Genre," interrogates how the structures of digital code intersect with issues of sovereignty, militarism, and colonialism.

Gina Caison is an assistant professor of English at Georgia State University. Currently, she is completing a book manuscript titled "Red States: Indigeneity, Settler Colonialism, and Southern Studies." She is also coproducer of the documentary film *Uneasy Remains*, which

CONTRIBUTORS

examines the history of the collection and study of Indigenous human remains within the University of California system.

Robbie Ethridge is professor of anthropology at the University of Mississippi, where she joined the faculty in 1997. Author of *Creek Country: The Creek Indians and Their World* (2003) and *From Chicaza to Chickasaw: The European Invasion and the Transformation of the Mississippian World, 1540–1715*, she has also coedited three scholarly collections on the ethnohistory of Southeastern Indians and is founding editor of the journal *Native South.*

Patricia Galloway is professor of archival enterprise in the School of Information at the University of Texas. A former editor and projects officer at the Mississippi Department of Archives and History, she is the author of *Choctaw Genesis 1500–1700* (1995) and *Practicing Ethnohistory: Mining Archives, Hearing Testimony, Constructing Narrative* (2006), and the editor of *The Hernando de Soto Expedition: History, Historiography, and "Discovery" in the Southeast* (2005). Her essay "The Construction of Faulkner's Indians" appeared in "Faulkner's Indians," the 2002–03 special issue of the *Faulkner Journal.*

LeAnne Howe, an enrolled citizen of the Choctaw Nation of Oklahoma, is Eidson Distinguished Professor in the Department of English at the University of Georgia. Her many books include two novels, *Shell Shaker* (2001) and *Miko Kings: An Indian Baseball Story* (2007); *Evidence of Red: Poems and Prose* (2005); a nonfiction collection, *Choctalking on Other Realities* (2013); and a coedited essay collection, *Seeing Red, Pixeled Skins: American Indians and Film* (2013). Founder and director of the WagonBurner Theatre Troop, she is also a playwright and filmmaker, and in 2006–07 she was the John and Renée Grisham Visiting Writer in Residence at the University of Mississippi.

John Wharton Lowe is Barbara Methvin Professor of English and Latin American and Caribbean Studies at the University of Georgia. He is the author or editor of seven books, including *Calypso Magnolia: The Crosscurrents of Caribbean and Southern Literature* (2016). He is currently completing *Faulkner's Fraternal Fury: Sibling Rivalry, Racial Kinship, and Democracy* (under contract, Louisiana State University Press) and is researching the authorized biography of Ernest J. Gaines.

Katherine M. B. Osburn is associate professor of history at Arizona State University, where she has taught since 2011. Her publications include *Southern Ute Women: Autonomy and Assimilation on the Reservation, 1885–1934* (1998, 2nd ed. 2008); *Choctaw Resurgence in Mississippi: Race, Class, and Nation Building in the Jim Crow South, 1830–1977* (2014); and numerous essays in Native American history. She was the recipient of an NEH research fellowship in 2008.

Melanie Benson Taylor is associate professor and chair of Native American studies at Dartmouth College. She is the author of two books, *Disturbing Calculations: The Economics of Identity in Postcolonial Southern Literature, 1912–2002* (2008) and *Reconstructing the Native South: American Indian Literature and the Lost Cause* (2012), and her essays have appeared in numerous journals and collections, including *The Cambridge Companion to William Faulkner* and *American Cinema and the Southern Imaginary.* Professor Taylor's current work in progress includes two book projects with a direct bearing on this year's conference theme: "Indian Killers," an exploration of violence in contemporary American literature by and about Native peoples, and "Faulkner's Doom," a study of Faulkner's Indian characters as refractions of economic anxiety in the modern South. She is also editing a *Cambridge History of Native American Literature*, forthcoming from Cambridge University Press in 2018.

Annette Trefzer is associate professor of English at the University of Mississippi, where she is a member of the interdisciplinary faculty working group on Indigenous studies. Author of *Disturbing Indians: The Archaeology of Southern Fiction* (2007), Trefzer is also coeditor of the essay collection *Reclaiming Native American Cultures* (1998), a special issue of *American Literature* on "Global Contexts, Local Literatures: The New Southern Studies," and four volumes in the Faulkner and Yoknapatawpha Series for the University Press of Mississippi.

Jay Watson is Howry Professor of Faulkner Studies at the University of Mississippi and the director of the Faulkner and Yoknapatawpha Conference. He is the author of *Forensic Fictions: The Lawyer Figure in Faulkner* and *Reading for the Body: The Recalcitrant Materiality of Southern Fiction, 1893–1985*, which received Honorable Mention for the 2013 C. Hugh Holman Award sponsored by the Society for the Study of Southern Literature. He is also the editor of *Faulkner and Whiteness* and *Conversations with Larry Brown* and coeditor of five volumes of the Faulkner and Yoknapatawpha Conference proceedings.

Index

Page numbers in *italics* refer to illustrations.

1927 flood, xxvii, 51, 53

Abenaki, 156, 194
Absalom, Absalom! (Faulkner), xx–xxvi, xxvii, 20, 27–28, 40, 67
Adare, Karl, 175
Aeronautics Branch of the United States Department of Commerce, 111
African Americans, vii, ix, xi, xviii, xxvi xxxiii, 15–16, 18–20, 23–31, 33, 39–42, 46, 54, 68, 70, 74–75, 77–78, 89, 93–94, 96, 104–6, 108, 112, 128, 138–39, 155, 157, 161–62, 164, 169–70, 173–74, 187–88
African Diaspora, 162
Africans, xvii, 68
afropessimism, 27
Ah-Keah-Boat, Kim, 85
Aikers, Donna, 123
Al WiFaq Street, 12
Alexie, Sherman, 181–83
Algonquian Indians, 93–94
alhamdulillah, 13
Allah, 12
Allen, Elizabeth "Betsy" Love, 23, 26, 106–9
Allen, John, 106, 107, 109
Allen, Paula Gunn, 111, 193
Altimira, 143

Amazon, 143
"Ambuscade" (Faulkner), 195
American Board of Commissioners for Foreign Missions, 78
American Indian literary studies, 25
American Indian studies, 15, 56
Amerindians, 24
Amman, 12–13
Anderson, Eric Gary, ix, xii, xxx–xxxi, xliv, 6, 18
Anglophilia, 17
Anishinaabe, 167–68
Annales school, 117, 129n2
Anthropocene, 31, 53, 57, 62
Arab Revolt, 11
Arab Spring, 11
Arabian Desert, 12
Arabs, 84
Archeology and Indians, 96
Arizona: Scottsdale, 10; Window Rock, 10
Arkansas, vii, 16, 159
Armstrong Academy, 9
As I Lay Dying (Faulkner), xix, xxvii, 40
Asian Americans, 184
Assiniboin, 89
Atchafalaya, 4; basin 51
Austen, Jane, 17
Australia, 19
āyōtōchtli, 60

201

INDEX

Baptist Mission Society of Kentucky, 104

Baptists, 78

Barker, Deborah, 106, 112, 114

Barr, Caroline, 112

Barth, Fredrik, 191

Basso, Keith, 192

Battle of Little Big Horn, 183, 193

Bayou people, 59

"Bear, The" (Faulkner), xv, xxviii, xxx, xxxvin41, 17, 70, *71*, 75, 77, 95, 137–44, *138*, 172, 175

"Bear Hunt, A" (Faulkner), 45, 95

Beet Queen, The (Erdrich), 168–69, 174–78

Bergland, Renée L., 170–71, 174, 178

Bienville, Jean Baptiste, xxv, 7–8, 11

Bilaad Ash Sham, 11, 13

Bilbo, Theodore, 96, 121, 123

Bingo Palace, The (Erdrich), 175

BioShock Infinite, 16

Black Belt, 69

Black Slaves, Indian Masters (Krauthamer), 28

Blackfeet, xxvii, xxxi, 148, 159, 162, 164, 185

Blaeser, Kimberly, 187

Bloch, Marc, 117

Bone, Martyn, 58

Bonnifield, Paul, 118

Brooks, Lisa, xvii, 61, 156

Bruchac, Joseph, 194

Bruno, Reverend Father, 8

Bull, Sitting, 45, 193

Bumpers, Fuller L., 24, 32

Bureau of Indian Affairs (BIA), 97–98, 192

"Buzzards of Coincidence: Cyrus Harris and William Faulkner's Yoknapatawpha County" (Morgan), 5

Byrd, Commodore William, III, 24

Byrd, Jodi A., xviii, xxvi, xliv, 6, 51, 112, 150, 163, 165

Byrd, John 22–24

Byrd, Michael, 24

Byrd, Roy Neal, 22

Byrd, William Leander, ix, 23–24

Byrd, William, II, 24,

Byron, Lord, 184

Caddo Public Schools, 9

Canada, 19, 22

Canadian Methodist Conference, 77

Canard, Roly, 10

Caribbean, 24, 151, 162, 166

Carr, Susan, 167

Carter, George, 111

Cartwright, Keith, 63

Cass Lake, Minnesota, 10

Castillo, Susan, 169

Catholics, 126

Catlin, George, 86–89

Center for the Study of Southern Culture, xlv

Cesaire, Aime, 24; *A Tempest*, 24

Chambers, Moreau, 126

Chicago, Illinois, 97

Chickasaws, vii, viii, x, xvi, xviii–xxix, xxxi–xxxii, xliv, 3, 5–6, 8–11, 15–20, 22–26, 28, 31, 35–38, 44, 46, 66–70, 72–75, 77–78, 83–84, 89, 93–94, 99–111, 120, 124, 137, 139–40, 144, 149–50, 153, 168, 172–73, 189, 191

China, 151

Chinese, 151

Chippewa Tribe, vii, xxxi, 10, 93, 168, 178

Chisholm, John, 100

Chitto, Joe, 121–23

Chocktalking and Other Realities (Howe), 194

INDEX

Choctaws, viii, x–xi, xvi, xx, xxv, xxix–
xxxi, xliv, 3–11, 15, 19, 23, 25, 28,
31, 36, 44, 60, 66, 68–70, 72, 74,
77–79, 83, 86–88, 93–97, 100–102,
104, 107–8, 110–11, 116–17,
119–29, 149–50, 153, 168, 191
Christian Advocate, 82
Chtulucene, 31
Chukchu Imoshi, 4
cingulata, 60
Civil War, 11, 44, 69, 72, 74, 154, 195
Cleopatra, 12
Cobb, Samuel, 122
Coca-Cola, 46
Colbert, George, 24
Colbert, Sally, 24, 26, 108–9
Colbert's Ferry, xxi, xxiii, xxxviiin65,
191
Cold War, xiv, 34, 97–98, 103
*Collected Stories of William Faulkner,
The* (Faulkner), xxii, 168
Collier, John, 98, 121, 122, 123
colonialism, xvii–xviii, xxvi, xxix, xxxiii,
xliv, 15, 17, 19–20, 22, 26–29, 57,
117, 122, 128, 151
Columbia University, 9
Comanche, 33, 91n27, 91n28, 115n63
Confederates/Confederacy, 23, 35,
44, 55–59, 74, 103
Congressional Record, 125
Cook-Lynn, Elizabeth, 25
Cooper, James Fenimore, ix, xiv, xv,
94, 173
Coulthard, Glen, 25
"Courthouse, The" (Faulkner), 71
"Courtship, A" (Faulkner), xxxii, 70, 71,
72, 77, 100, 181–83, 187, 191, 195
Cowley, Malcolm, xiii, xx–xxii, 47, 76,
93, 119
Cox, James H., 148, 156
Coyote (trickster), 193–94

Craig, John, 100
Creek, vii–x, xxxii, 10, 82, 142, 144,
163, 190, 192
Cronon, William, 118
Custer, General George Armstrong,
183, 193
Cutthroat, 3

d'Iberville, Pierre Le Moyne, 7
Dabney, Lewis M., xvi, xx, 173–74
Dakota, 25, 164
Davies, Christie, 184, 187, 196n10
Dawes Rolls, 36, 47n8
de Vitry, Chevalier Soeur Blonde,
70, 72
decolonization, 20, 118
Deloria, Vine, Jr., 12, 134n63, 141,
182, 183, 193
"Delta Autumn" (Faulkner), 89,
90n8, 138
Dene, 25
Derrida, Jacques, 117
Dickens, Charles, 17
Digital Yoknapatawpha project, xliv
Dimock, Wai Chee, 50
Disch, Thomas, 167
Disturbing Indians (Trefzer), 172
Doaksville (Choctaw Nation), 23
Doctor Who, 16
Donaldson, Susan, 105
double threading, 50, 63
Douglas, Mary, 192
Doyebi, 85
Doyle, Don H., 47n8, 100, 119–20,
196n11
Dr. Jekyll and Mr. Hyde (film), 154
Dracula (film), 154
Duck, Leigh Anne, 98, 151
Dust Bowl, 118
*Dust Bowl: The Southern Plains in
the 1930s* (Worster), 118

204 INDEX

Dwight, Ben, xxv, 9–11
Dwight, Simon Timothy, 9

"Ecological Indians," xxvii–xxviii, xxx, 62, 135–45
Egypt, 12
Eisenhower administration, 98
Endore, Guy, 154
England, xxiv, 67, 72, 107, 150, 194; English art, 194; English colonists, xxiii, xxxixn74; English common law, 107, 154, 182–83, 191–92; English language, 114n41; English trade with Chickasaws, 90n6
environmental studies, 56, 135
Erdrich, Louise, xxxi, xxxii, xliv, 148, 167–79, 194
Erotic Life of Racism, The (Holland), 27
Ethridge, George H., 124
Ethridge, Robbie, 3, 6
Eufaula, 80
Eufaula Journal, The, 192
Euramerica, 171, 178
Eurocentrism, 51, 104, 118
"Evangeline" (Faulkner), 39, 40

fabussa, 126
Falkner family: 68–69, 108; John Wesley Thompson, 69; Murry, 69; William Clark, 69, 90n9
fani miko, 9
Faulkner and Yoknapatawpha Conference, xliii–xlv, 3, 66, 112, 164, 200
Faulkner Journal, xliii, 18, 127, 135
Faulkner's Country: The Historical Roots of Yoknapatawpha (Doyle), 119
feminism, 31, 107, 162
Fisher, John, 107
Fisher v. Allen, 107
First Nations Indians, 77, 81

Fixico, Donald, 97
Flags in the Dust (Faulkner), xix, 43
Folsom, David, 104
Folsom, Sophie, 86
Fools Crow (Blackfeet), 185
Forrest, Nathan Bedford, 69
Foucault, Michel, 117
Francisco, Edgar Wiggin, 35
Frankenstein (film), 154
Franklin, Benjamin, 23
Freud, Sigmund, 182, 185, 186
"Fus Fixico Letters" (Posey), xxxii, 192–93

Gaia, 31
Galloway, Charles Betts, 66–69, 77, 80–83, 85
Galloway, Ethelbert, 69
Galloway, George, 69
Galloway, Patricia, xvi, xviii, xxix, xxx, xliv, 6, 18, 99, 112, 131n25, 135, 145n2, 169–71, 191
Geiogamah, Hanay, 182
genocide, 5, 40, 98
Georgia, vii, 142, 164
Glancy, Diane, 110
Glissant, Édouard, xvii, 29
Global South, xxx, 24
Go Down, Moses (Faulkner), xiii, 34, 36, 66, 71, 95, 127, 136–38, 168, 195
God, 7, 12, 18, 189
Goodstoney, James (Stoney), 77, 81
Great Father Aba, 126
Great Spirit, 122
Gregorian calendar, 52, 54
Gribben, Alan, 129
Gulf South, 60–61
Guyana, 24

Hamlet, The (Faulkner), 184, 193
Hammer, Joshua, 11

INDEX

Haraway, Donna, 31
Harjo, Joy, x, 163
Harris, Cyrus, 25, 108
Harris, Leslie, 7, 14
Harris, Wilson, 24
Harrison, General William Henry, 193
Harrison, Pat, 126
Hartman, Saidiya, 26
Harvey's Scouts, 69
Hassan, Beni, 13
Heart of Darkness (Conrad), 24
Hemingway, Ernest, 94
Hiroshima, 98
History of the Dividing Line betwixt Virginia and North Carolina, The (Byrd), 24
Hobson, Geary, x, 167
Hogan, Linda, x, 110
Hoka, 100, 101, 102
Holland, Sharon, 27
Hollywood, xxxi, 33, 43, 154
Honey Grove Texas High School, 9
Hong, Sharon Linezo, 58–59
Houma, xxvii, 51, 59, 60, 61, 62
House Made of Dawn (Momaday), xvi, 97
Howe, LeAnne, xii, xxv, xliii, 15, 22, 110–11, 112, 153, 165, 194–95
Howell, Elmo, xvi, 191
Hughes, Langston, 186
Hummingbird, Jimmy, 85
Hunt, Sarah, 21
Hunter, Mary Jane, 9
Hurricane Katrina, xxvii, 7, 51, 53, 59–60, 62
Hurston, Zora Neale, 184, 186
Hyde, Lewis, 191

"I Give You Back" (Harjo), 163
"Idyll in the Desert" (Faulkner), 44
In-cun-no-mar, 26

Indian Mission Conference, 80
Indian mounds, xxvii, 42, 45, 51–52, 54–55, 57, 125–26
Indian Reorganization Act (IRA), 121–22
indigeneity, xiv, xviii, xix, xx, xxi, xxii, xxvi, xxvii, xxxviii, xliv, 11, 15, 17, 19, 21, 22, 23, 25, 27, 28, 29, 30, 31, 46, 50, 51, 94, 95, 127, 129, 146, 198
Indigenous studies, xxxii, 17, 20, 26–27, 29, 35, 150, 156
Ingomar Mounds, 25, 26
International Indian Council, 80
Iraq, 12
Island of Lost Souls (film), 154

Jackson, Andrew, xxii–xxiii, xxxii, 37, 39, 72–73, 75–77, 80, 83, 89, 104, 109, 124, 183, 186, 188–89, 191–93
Jackson Daily News, 124
"Jail, The" (Faulkner), *71*
Jane Eyre (Brontë), 24
Jicarilla Apaches, 46
Jim Crow, 59, 200
Jonah's Gourd Vine (Hurston), 184
Jones, Stephen Graham, xxxi, 148, 151, 155–59, 162–64
Jones Academy, 9
Jordan, 11–13
"Justice, A" (Faulkner), xx, xxviii, 70, *71*, 72, 75–76, 89n2, 95, 181
Justice, Daniel Heath, ix, x, 51, 149

Kayapo Indians, 143–44
Kelman, Ari, 7
Kerr, Robert S., 9–10
Kim, Heidi, 151, 160
King, Thomas, 182
King Talal Street, 12
Kiowa, 82–83, 85
Kozkas, 168

206 INDEX

Krasnoff, Mark, 60–62
Krauthamer, Barbara, 28
Krech, Shepard, xxx, 135, 136, 146n4
Kubrick, Stanley, 46
Kwakwaka'wkaw First Nations, 21

Ladd, Barbara, 98
LaDuke, Winona, 142, 144
Lagash, 11
Lakota cowboys, 22, 26
Lakota Rosebud Indian Reservation, 22
Lakota Sioux, 193
Lamar, L. Q. C., 69
"Land That Is Open," 3, 5
"Land That Spreads Out," 3, 5, 13
Latin America, 162, 199
Laverne, 111
Lazarres, 168
Ledgers of History, The (Wolff), 35
LeFlore, Greenwood, 79, 104, 124, 191
Light in August (Faulkner), xiii, xxxi, 148–65, 166n25
Littlefield, Daniel F., x, xi, 24
"Lo!" (Faulkner), xxii–xxv, xxviii, xx, xxxii, 70, *71*, 75, 76–77, 83, 89, 91n22, 95, 109, 124, 131n18, 132n38, 181, 183, 186–88, 191–94
Loichot, Valerie, 162
Lose Your Mother (Hartman), 26
Lost Cause, xi, xxviii, 53, 55–58, 61, 94, 200
Louvre, 11
Love, Thomas, 24, 108, 198
Love Medicine (Erdrich), 167, 175, 178
Love's Travel Stop, 17
Lowe, John Wharton, xxxii, xliv, 6, 112, 165
Lower Mississippi Valley, 7, 9, 11

Luke, Munch, 126
Lurie, Peter, 155
Lyons, Scott Richard, xxix, 101, 164

Mahadev, Apte, 191
Malmaison, 91n22
Manifest Destiny, 94, 192
Marlow, Oklahoma, 111
Martin, John, 100
Mason, Bertha, 24
Master Butchers Singing Club, The (Erdrich), 178
Matchimanito Lake, 175
McCarroll, John Ramsey, 35, 48
McDonald, James, 9
McDougall, Reverend John Chantler, *81*
McHaney, Thomas, 54
Mean Spirit (Hogan), 110
Mecca, 126
Medusa, 31
Memoir of a Choctaw in the Arab Revolts (Howe), 11
Memphis, Tennessee, xxi, 16, 42, 84
Memphis Commercial Appeal, 124
Mentz, Steve, 52, 55, 58, 60
Merchant and Farmer's Bank, 44
Methodist Episcopal Church South, 66
Methvin, J. J., *84*
Mexico, 6
Middle East, 11, 67
Milky Way, 12
Mink, Louis O., 117
Mississippi: vii, xi, xv, xvii, xix, xx, xxi–xxx, xliii–xlv, 6–7, 15–20, 23–25, 28, 33, 35, 39, 54, 67–68, 70, 78–79, 83–86, 89, 93–97, 99–102, 104, 106–12, 116, 120–28, 149–50, 153, 168, 181, 189, 195; Biloxi, 7; Canton, 69; Chickasaw County, xxvii, 37; Delta, xliv, 50, 58, 66, 74,

90n8; Desoto County, 17; Grenada, 104; Hernando, 17; Holly Springs, 24, 35–36; Kosciusco, 69; Lafayette County, xliv, 69; Marshal County, 17, 23; *Mississippi Guide*, 96; Mississippi River, 53, 79, 81, 168; Monroe County, 107; Neshoba County, 95; Natchez, xvi, 8, 93–94, 105; New Albany, 108; Oxford, xliv, 3, 15, 95, 100; Pascagoula, 93; Philadelphia, 95, 121; Pocahontas, 149–50; Pontotoc, xix, xxxi, 83, 109, 123, 150; Ripley, 69; Tunica, 8; University of Mississippi, xliii, 3, 37, 69; Winston County, 125–26

Mississippi Choctaw Indian Federation (MCIF), 121–23, 125

Mississippi Choctaw Welfare Association (MCWA), 121, 124–25

Mixedblood Messages (Owens), 171

Mohawk, 25

Momaday, N. Scott, 141–42, 167, 195

mongrels, 157, 162

Mongrels (Jones), 148, 155–61, 163–64

Moore, David L., 189

Moore, Delilah Love, xxvii, 23–24, 26, 36

Moore, Gene M., x, xvi, 127, 171, 188, 191

Moore, Mary, 23

Moreton–Robinson, Aileen, 19, 21, 29

Morgan, Philip Carroll, xix, xxvi, 5, 25–26, 104, 106, 108, 153

Mother Earth, 183

Mother Mound, 125–26

"Mountain Victory" (Faulkner), xxviii, 70, 71, 74, 91n22, 95, 131n18

Muckenfuss, Margaret Galloway, 69

Muckenfuss, Ralph, 69

Mule Bone (Hughes), 186

Mummy, The, 154

Muskogee District, 80

Muslims, 126

Mvskoke, 163

My Louisiana Love (Verdin), xxvii, 50–63

Nabataeans, 12

Naga, 31

Nahuatl, 60

Nanapush, 168, 175, 178

Nanapush, Gerry, 168, 175, 178

Nanih Waiya, 125–27

Naqub Desert, 12

National Uncanny, The (Bergland), 170

Native American sovereignty, xii, xvii, xviii, xxi, xxv, xxvi, xxviii, xxix, xxxii, 19, 20, 23, 26, 29, 30, 35, 56, 62, 93–112, 142–44, 149

Native American studies, viii, xi, 50–51, 56, 150, 156

Native southern studies, ix, xii, xxii, xxx, xxxii, xxxiii, 148, 154, 163

Native Studies, xviii, xx, xxiv, xxv, xxvii, xxxiii, 20, 55–58, 63

Nebraska, 22, 85

Neshoba County Democrat, 124

Neshoba County Fair, 97

Neshoba Indians, 95

New England, 73

New Orleans, xx, 7–8, 70, 72–73, 105, 189

"'New' Social History in the Context of American Historical Writing, The" (Veysey), 117, 129n3

new southern studies, ix

New World, xvi, xxiii, xxxi, 26–27, 46, 163

New World genocide, 98

New York Times, 98
New Yorker, The, 178
New Zealand, 19
NewSouth Books, 129
Nobel Prize, 34, 47, 93
noble savages mythology, ix, 33
North America, xxiii, xxxii, xxxiii, 21, 27, 30, 143, 163
North Carolina, vii, 6, 24, 69
North Dakota, xxxi, 167–68, 175
Nyerges, Aaron, 155, 165n14

O'Beirne, H. F., 25
Office of Indian Affairs, 121, 124, 126
Oglala Pine Ridge Indian Reservation, 22
Ojibwe, 167–69, 174–75
Oklahoma: x–xi, xxxviiin71, 10, 13, 14, 29, 35, 37–39, 66–68, 81–85, 87, 91n27, 92n30, 95, 99, 109, 111; Allen, 11; Marlow, 111; Tahlequah, 6; West Ada, 12
Old Ben, xxx, 137, 139–41
"Old Man" (Faulkner), xxvii, 42, 51–63
"Old People, The" (Faulkner), 70, 71, 72, 75, 77, 100, 137, 172, 173
Old Mexico, 46
Oregon State University, 11
orphan narratives, 162
Ortiz, Simon, 105
Osburn, Katherine M. B., xxix, xxx, xliv, 89, 96, 112, 153
Oskison, John Milton, xxxii, 110
Overlook Hotel, 46
Owens, Louis, 153, 168, 171–72, 174, 178
Oxford Convention and Visitors Bureau, xlv
Oxford Handbook of Indigenous American Literature, The, 148

Paige, Amanda L., 24
Palace of the Peacock (Harris), 24
Parker, Judy Goforth, 106
Parrish, Susan Scott, 53
Payakan, 143–44
Pekinese, 46
Peppler, Randy, 10
Peterson, Nancy, 178
Petrarch, xxiv, 190
Pfef, Wallace, 175–76
Philip, Kenneth, 98
Pickwickian England, 75–76
Pima–Maricopa Council, 10
Pitchlynn, John, 86, *86*
Pitchlynn, Peter, 9, *86*, 87, *86–88*
PMLA (*Publications of the Modern Language Association of America*), 63
Pocahontas, xxxi, 30, 149–50
Polk, Noel, 96, 185
Poor Buffalo, 82, 91n27
Pope, Alexander, xxiv, 170
Portable Faulkner, The (Faulkner), xx–xxi, *71*, 76, 93
Portraits of the Whiteman (Basso), 192
Posey, Alexander, 182, 192, 193
postcolonial studies, xvii, xviii, 156
Posthumous Papers of the Pickwick Club, The (Dickens), 76, 78
Postsouthern Sense of Place in Contemporary Fiction, The (Bone), 58
Povinelli, Elizabeth, 30
Powhatan, 150
Presley, Elvis, 40
Pullback Party, 23
Pumphrey, Popeye, 42
Pylon (Faulkner), 111

Qualla Boundary, 6
Queen Elizabeth, 194

INDEX

Racial Integrity Act, 30
Rader, Dean, 194–95
"Red Leaves" (Faulkner), xix, xx, xxxviii, xxxviiin58, 38, 47n7, 70, *71*, 76–77, 95, 100, 181, 195
Regency Hotel, 12
Removal Treaty of Dancing Rabbit Creek, 95, 121, 124
Requiem for a Nun (Faulkner), xiii, xxvii, xxviii, xxxviiin65, 34, 36, 39, 44, 70, *71*, 73, 76–77, 93–112, 172
Reynolds, Benjamin, 100
Rhys, Jean, 24, 167
Riding Out the Storm (Morgan), 5
"Rose for Emily, A" (Faulkner), 17
Ruoff, A. LaVonne Brown, 181

Sacred Hoop, The (Allen), 111
Samson (Cree chief), *81*
Sanctuary (Faulkner), xiii, xxvii, 33, 42, 45
Sandhills, 22
Sartoris (Faulkner), xiii
Satan, 155
Saturday clothes, 77, 83
Scots-Irish, 37
Scott, Pearl Carter, 111
Scottsdale, Arizona, 10
Searching for Sequoyah (Howe and Fortier), 6
Seenum, James (Pakan), *81*
Senate Subcommittee on Indian Affairs, 124
Sentinel, 123
settler colonial studies, 20, 28
Sexton, Jared, xxxiii, 20–21, 26
Shell Shaker (Howe), 110
Shining, The (Kubrick), 46
Silko, Leslie Marmon, 97, 167, 169
Simms, William Gilmore, ix, 94

Simpson, Audra, 25
Sitt, 12
Sivils, Matthew Wynn, 54
Smith, John, xxxi, ix, 150, 193
Smith, Paul Chaat, 33–34
Smithsonian Institution, 125, 126
Smithsonian Magazine, 11
Snyder, Christina, 108
Sound and the Fury, The (Faulkner), xiii, xxi, xxvii, 39, 116, 167, 183
Southeastern Ceremonial Complex, 16
southern studies, ix, xxxi, 52, 56, 58–59, 63, 148, 163
Spadoni, Robert, 158
Spider Woman, 31
Square Books, xlv
Squint, Kirstin, xliv, 6, 112, 165
Star Trek, 16
starvation, 5
Stegner, Wallace, 25
Steinhauer, Reverend R. R., *81*
Stirrup, David, 179
Student Pilot's Permit, 111
Sunday clothes, 71, 73, 76–77, 83–84
Syria, 11, 13

Talley, Alexander, 79
Tattooed Serpent, 8
Tecumseh, 193
termination, 94, 97, 98, 100, 169
Theda Perdue, viii, 47, 101, 114n41
Theocritus, 182
Tobah, Frank, *85*
Town, The (Faulkner) 46, 99
Tracks (Erdrich), 168, 175
Trail of Tears, 110
Trans-Mississippi and International Exposition (1898), *85*
Treaty of Pontotoc, 99
Trefzer, Annette, xvii, xxviii–xxix, 3, 6, 116, 119, 125, 128, 165, 172, 174

INDEX

Tribal Business Committee (TBC), 121
trickster, xxxii, 37, 175, 178, 189, 191–94
"Turtle Mountain/Yoknapatawpha Connection, The" (Carr), 167
Twain, Mark, xv, 129, 171

Umma, 11
United States Indian Congress (1898), 85
Universal Pictures, 154–55
University of Illinois, 15
University of Jordan, 13
University of Michigan, 9
University of Nebraska Press, viii
University of Strasburg, 117
Unvanquished, The (Faulkner), 195

Valentine, Nebraska, 22
Vatican, 126
Verdin, Monique, xxvii, 50–63
Virgil, 182
Virginia, xxxi, 30, 74, 150; Richmond, 24
Vizenor, Gerald, 110, 182, 192, 194

Warrior, Robert, ix, x, 56, 58
Washington Post, 98
Wassi Town, 39
Watson, Jay, 3, 56, 58, 98, 112, 114n29, 114n39, 116, 157, 161, 165
Weddel, Saucier, 74–76
"Wedge of Shade, A" (Erdrich), 178
Welch, James, 185, 194
Wells, Dean Faulkner, 154, 165
Werewolf of Paris, The (Endore), 154
West Ada, Oklahoma, 12
"Where I Ought to Be: A Writer's Sense of Place" (Erdrich), 167
White, Hayden, 117, 129n4

white supremacy, xi, 15, 103, 105
White Zombie, 154
whiteness studies, 29
Wichita Mountains, 6
Wide Sargasso Sea (Rhys), 24, 167
Wi-jún-jon, 88, 89
Wild Palms, The (Faulkner), 42, 51
"wild tribes," 80, 83
Willis, E. B., 69
Winans, William, 79
Wishart, Davis, 61
Wolf Man, The (film), 154
Wolf, Aaron, 11
Wolfe, Patrick, 28–29
Wolff, Sally, 35–36
Womack, Craig, ix–x, 51
Wood, Robin, 155
World War II, 97
Wounded Knee, 169
Works Progress Administration (WPA), 126, 132, 133

Xingu Dam, 143

Yakni Patafah, 3, 5, 13
Yalobusha River, 104
Yoknapatawpha (as word), xix, 36, 48n15
Yoknapatawpha chronicle, xiii, xvii, xix, xx, xxvi, xxvii, xxxviii, 34, 101
Yoknapatawpha Connection, 167
Yoknapatawpha County xv, xviii, xxi, xxi–xxii, xxvii, xxxviii, xxxvn30, xxxviiin65, xxxviiin71, 5, 18, 34, 46, 50, 63, 66, 68, 70, 76, 78, 93, 94, 99, 101, 103, 108, 119, *138*, 141, 146, 151, 167, 168, 172, 173, 174
Yokni Patafa, 26

Printed in the United States
by Baker & Taylor Publisher Services